Electronic Communication
Across the Curriculum

Electronic Communication Across the Curriculum

Edited by

Donna Reiss
Tidewater Community College–Virginia Beach

Dickie Selfe
Michigan Technological University

Art Young
Clemson University

National Council of Teachers of English
1111 W. Kenyon Road, Urbana, Illinois 61801-1096

Staff Editor: Kurt Austin

Interior Design: Tom Kovacs for TGK Design

Cover Design: Marjoram Productions

Glossary: Patricia Webb

NCTE Stock Number: 13087-3050

Library of Congress Cataloging-in-Publication Data

Electronic communication across the curriculum/edited by Donna Reiss, Dickie Selfe,
   Art Young.
         p.   cm.
      Includes bibliographical references and index.
      ISBN 0-8141-1308-7
      1. English language—Rhetoric—Study and teaching—Data processing.
   2. Written communication—Study and teaching (Higher)—Data processing.
   3. Interdisciplinary approach in education—Data processing. 4. Academic
   writing—Study and teaching—Data processing. 5. Electronic mail systems in
   education. 6. Electronic discussion groups. I. Reiss, Donna, 1944–   . II. Selfe,
   Dickie, 1951–   . III. Young, Art, 1943–   .
   PE1404.E437   1998
   808'.042'0285—dc21   97-47688
                                                                  CIP

Contents

Foreword   ix
    Cynthia L. Selfe

Introduction: The Promise of ECAC   xv
    Donna Reiss, Dickie Selfe, and Art Young

**I Programs: From Writing Across the Curriculum to Electronic
Communication Across the Curriculum**   **1**

1. Using Computers to Expand the Role of Writing Centers   3
    Muriel Harris

2. Writing Across the Curriculum Encounters Asynchronous
Learning Networks   17
    Gail E. Hawisher and Michael A. Pemberton

3. Building a Writing-Intensive Multimedia Curriculum   40
    Mary E. Hocks and Daniele Bascelli

4. Communication Across the Curriculum and Institutional
Culture   57
    Mike Palmquist, Kate Kiefer, and Donald E. Zimmerman

5. Creating a Community of Teachers and Tutors   73
    Joe Essid and Dona J. Hickey

6. From Case to Virtual Case: A Journey in Experiential
Learning   86
    Peter M. Saunders

7. Composing Human-Computer Interfaces Across the
Curriculum in Engineering Schools   102
    Stuart A. Selber and Bill Karis

8. InterQuest: Designing a Communication-Intensive Web-Based
Course   117
    Scott A. Chadwick and Jon Dorbolo

9. Teacher Training: A Blueprint for Action Using the World
    Wide Web   129
    Todd Taylor

II Partnerships: Creating Interdisciplinary Communities   **137**

10. Accommodation and Resistance on (the Color) Line:
    Black Writers Meet White Artists on the Internet   139
    Teresa M. Redd

11. International E-mail Debate   151
    Linda K. Shamoon

12. E-mail in an Interdisciplinary Context   162
    Dennis A. Lynch

13. Creativity, Collaboration, and Computers   170
    Margaret Portillo and Gail Summerskill Cummins

14. COllaboratory: MOOs, Museums, and Mentors   180
    Margit Misangyi Watts and Michael Bertsch

15. Weaving Guilford's Web   190
    Michael B. Strickland and Robert M. Whitnell

III Classrooms: Electronic Communication Within the
       Disciplines   **205**

16. Pig Tales: Literature Inside the Pen of Electronic Writing   207
    Katherine M. Fischer

17. E-Journals: Writing to Learn in the Literature Classroom   221
    Paula Gillespie

18. E-mailing Biology: Facing the Biochallenge   231
    Deborah M. Langsam and Kathleen Blake Yancey

19. Computer-Supported Collaboration in an Accounting Class   242
    Carol F. Venable and Gretchen N. Vik

20. Electronic Tools to Redesign a Marketing Course   255
    Randall S. Hansen

21. Network Discussions for Teaching Western Civilization   263
    Maryanne Felter and Daniel F. Schultz

22. Math Learning through Electronic Journaling   273
        Robert Wolffe

23. Electronic Communities in Philosophy Classrooms   282
        Gary L. Hardcastle and Valerie Gray Hardcastle

24. Electronic Conferencing in an Interdisciplinary
        Humanities Course   296
        MaryAnn Krajnik Crawford, Kathleen Geissler,
        M. Rini Hughes, and Jeffrey Miller

Glossary   305

Index   309

Editors   317

Contributors   319

Foreword

Cynthia L. Selfe
Michigan Technological University

This book stands as a testimony to change and to the role of teachers in making change. It attests to the productive agency that teachers, students, and program administrators can exert at the intersection of two powerful and complex educational movements—when writing-across-the-curriculum (WAC) classes begin to take advantage of innovative computer-supported communication environments and become what the editors of this book have termed *Electronic Communication Across the Curriculum* (ECAC). The important ECAC case studies that the editors and authors have provided here add to our profession's cumulative knowledge about the educational projects in which we are all involved: they reveal more about the complex nature of communicative texts and the robust ways in which such texts are changing in our increasingly technological culture; more about how good teaching and learning about written communication can be supported and encouraged within academic settings; more about how authentic written communication tasks can take advantage of a wider range of audiences outside the academy; more about the formation, function, and operation of groups and individuals who choose to collaborate in communicative activities; and more about the kinds of social agency that writers, readers, and teachers can exert in their lives as literate citizens.

To understand these contributions, however, it is necessary to recapture a bit of history. Before we can claim some understanding of how we have come to this important current point of intersection—and where we want to go from here—we need the context and perspective gained only by looking at those efforts that have preceded our own.

Twenty years ago, as college faculty were just beginning to use computers to support instruction in writing and as a group of individuals at Michigan Tech were just developing one of the first WAC programs, faculty across the country were generally skeptical about—and often openly resistant to—recognizing the value of both technologies: WAC as a technology of teaching that could support disciplinary learning and computers as a technology of communication that could support the teaching of writing.

Pioneers like Art Young, who during the late '70s and early '80s was helping colleagues implement WAC programs in a variety of departments and on a number of college campuses across the country, faced faculty in mathematics, biological sciences, forestry, engineering, and physics who considered writing the purview of lower-division English courses. These faculty frequently understood writing as a set of skills to be mastered by students in the first few years of college so that they could then progress to the study of much more difficult content matter. Few faculty during that period connected the writing that they were asking students to do on essay tests, in lab reports, and in final design projects with the specialized processes of analysis and problem solving that constituted professional knowledge within their own discipline. Rather, most teachers understood writing as a way for students to display information learned in class or through the reading of a textbook, generally for purposes of direct evaluation by a teacher.

And while some of these same faculty were using computers—primarily mainframes—in their teaching in the late '70s, these expensive and relatively fragile machines were generally devoted to the manipulation of numbers, data, and complex algorithms.[1] Computers, which grew out of the military culture during the period between World Wars I and II, were kept in air-conditioned rooms out of sight and reach of both faculty and students. To make use of these machines, users laboriously punched representations of data onto cards, fed them into a card reader, and sometime later received a printout of their job. The computers were tended by a class of technology specialists trained in the relatively new science of computer use. The idea of using such machines as environments for writing or composing was less than realistic for several reasons. First, time on such machines was shared as a precious commodity—the computers were relatively slow in comparison with today's technology. Jobs were, thus, ordered and run by technicians, often on a twenty-four-hour schedule, and few people had the kind of extended and direct access to a mainframe that would make electronic composing possible in any realistic way. Second, although some limited kinds of text composition were possible on these machines, the line editors and formatters that made such input possible were so primitive that they resisted any natural rendition of composing processes. Finally, given the expense of mainframes and the lack of status accorded to the teaching of writing at most institutions, the concept of allocating valuable computer resources to individuals in support of their personal composing efforts was generally unfathomable and seldom attempted.

Changes in both situations, however, were not long in coming. By the early '80s, WAC was well established at Michigan Tech, at Beaver College, and at a number of other schools around the country. Given the consistent efforts of early WAC pioneers, faculty in a variety of disciplines represented at these schools were experimenting with writing not simply as a method for communicating student knowledge to teachers for purposes of evaluation, but also as a medium for disciplinary learning and a technology that supported intellectually challenging problem solving. By 1982, at least two books on WAC had been published— *Writing in the Arts and Sciences* (1981) by Elaine Maimon et al., which described writing-across-the-curriculum practices at Beaver College, and *Language Connections* (1982) by Toby Fulwiler and Art Young, which detailed WAC curricular efforts at Michigan Tech—and a number of articles[2] were available for faculty who wanted ideas about how to integrate writing into their classrooms. Several of these articles, moreover, had been published in the professional journals of disciplines outside of English[3], indicating the growing interest that faculty in other disciplines had in the notion of writing as a way of learning content matter and as a means of practicing problem solving. Increasing emphasis, in all of these pieces, was placed on the processes of composing, the value of writing as a medium for thinking, the effectiveness of writing as a medium that supported and encouraged learning. These changes were hastened, as well, by a number of factors that exerted tendential force in the larger culture of education: among them a series of perceived crises in education caused by what some educators saw as a pattern of declining literacy demonstrated by falling standardized test scores; related concerns about increasingly diverse college populations introduced, in part, by open admissions and, in part, by the baby boom; the recognition that academics needed to address increasingly complex and globally defined problems that denied narrow disciplinary solutions.

Important changes also characterized the use of computers in support of writing efforts. Supported by a computer industry that benefited from both military and space program advances in electronics, the first fully assembled microcomputers came out on the market in 1977–78, and, shortly thereafter, found their way into writing classrooms. The low cost of such machines, which quickly became known as personal computers, their ease of use, and the availability of inexpensive and effective word-processing software that was invented specifically to support the act of writing made these machines valuable from the very beginning as communication environments. The subsequent invention and growth of networking hardware and software, which eventually allowed both the local and global linking of individual machines and, thus, the exchange of written information among individuals, magnified this effect. Computer-supported writing and communication environments supported a process-based approach to composition through the production of multiple drafts; cut-and-paste revisions; and invention, outlining, and spell-checking packages. Networks would eventually support peer-group exchanges of drafts, online discussions of rhetorical decision making, and Web-based research, among many other WAC-related approaches.

In the early '80s, therefore, the convergence of the two technologies—that of WAC as a technology supporting teaching and learning of content matter in a variety of disciplines and that of computers as a technology supporting the teaching of writing in a variety of contexts—was not difficult to understand or predict. But it also did not come about without a series of pedagogical challenges. What surprised some teachers of writing, especially those who had already fought the early battles associated with writing across the curriculum, was the strange version of professional amnesia that often seemed to accompany the use of computers as writing environments during the early 1980s. Even experienced faculty who had already come to terms with some of the important premises of WAC—the value of writing as a medium for thinking and learning, and the recognition that the processes involved in writing were as valuable in many cases as the end product, for instance—seemed prone, in those early years, to want to use computers to address surface-level correctness rather than to encourage writing as a way of thinking.

During this period, many teachers and departments invested a great deal of money on drill-and-practice tutorials designed to eliminate such perennial problems as agreement errors, dangling modifiers, and comma splices; on the grammar-checking software, which often exhibited a 20 percent error rate and which never provided rhetorically specific advice for writers; and on paper-grading and response packages which allowed teachers to incorporate canned commentary on surface-level mechanical problems on students' papers. And although these packages sold well in the early '80s and were prominently featured in many computer-supported writing facilities across the country well into the '90s, they failed to produce consistent results in terms of student writing. There was no consistent evidence that they functioned to improve the quality of student writing over time, and teachers in a range of disciplines ultimately came to recognize this fact.

Ultimately, the same lessons about writing that had provided the intellectual foundations for WAC—the focus on writing as a process of thinking and learning that was refined over time and through multiple drafts, on the wide range of skills and strategies required of writers, on the socially-constructed nature of writing as a medium of both thinking and communication—also came to inform faculty members' understanding that computers had much greater and wider-ranging potential as open-ended and flexible writing environments than they did as mechanical tutorial devices.

It was thus that the stage was set for a series of important sea changes in computer-supported writing pedagogies—and these began to be felt in the early '90s. Teachers who continued to work with computers gradually realized that technology was useful not as a mechanical tutor, but, instead, as a broadly based support system and medium for the writing and learning that students in all disciplines were doing. Pre-packaged tutorials and focused modules of computer-assisted instruction grew dusty on shelves, while students and teachers gravitated toward the more open and flexible composing environments represented by e-mail, listservs, and, eventually, the Internet and the World Wide Web. Using such environments, WAC faculty in a range of disciplines began to experiment with writing-intensive learning activities: online problem solving in art and publications classes; computer-supported collaboration on business and finance reports; online journaling for math and computer-science students; the exchange of problem-solving approaches and insights across traditional curricular boundaries.

Characterizing each of these innovative applications and each of the chapters that have been included in this important collection is the fact that technology recedes into the background—providing a fertile and flexible environment for writing, thinking, and exchange—while writers, writing processes, and the exchange of information remain in the foreground. The way we think of writing has changed from a set of simple discrete skills that can be accumulated in one or two lower-division English courses to a complex suite of strategies for thinking and learning, strategies that are employed over the full course of students' time in college and in a wide variety of workplace settings. Computers have changed from a technology that supports only the manipulation of numbers to a technology that also supports robust and flexible communication and language environments within which students learn to navigate, associate, create, solve problems, analyze, and identify sources of information.

Another change is also evident. Far from being skeptical about writing as a way of thinking and learning, or about computers as robust and flexible environments for such efforts, faculty in many disciplines are hungry for ideas that will help them exploit the intersection of these two promising technologies. If there is a consistent question I am asked when visiting other institutions to share ideas with faculty about WAC efforts, it is, "How are other teachers using computers to support writing across the curriculum?" How, in other words, can we take advantage of *electronic* communication across the curriculum (ECAC). This book provides a series of case studies that offer responses to this query. And these responses are tested in the crucible of real classroom constraints, by teachers who worry about both the intended and the unintended effects of their instruction; who have too little time and too much disciplinary-specific content to convey to students; and who are responsible for the learning that goes on in math and accounting, in art and marketing, in Western civilization and biology.

Finally, one more word about change. The ECAC contributions described in this volume remind me that change does not stand still—although many of the precepts of good teaching remain more constant. The specific computer applications described in these chapters, you will notice, are for the most part, allocated to the status of end notes—they really matter very little because they are simply time-bound instantiations of a computer world that experiences a new technological generation every eighteen months. Indeed, most of the pedagogical approaches and activities described in this volume could be accomplished using several different kinds of programs, applications, or tools—or even, in some fashion, without resort to computer-based writing environments. What is important about each of the chapters in this book, then, is not the technology of computers but the ways in which the technology of writing is used to encourage thinking and learning in ECAC environments. For this lesson, and for the many outstanding examples of great teaching that are so generously presented in these pages, I commend this book to the attention of colleagues.

Notes

1. During this period, it should be noted, a few pioneering linguists and literature scholars were also experimenting with the use of mainframe computers to construct such things as concordances, dictionaries, collocations, and indexes, as well as to do machine translations for morphological and syntactic linguistic analyses. For descriptions of such projects, see Susan Hockey's book, *A Guide to Computer Applications in the Humanities* (1980).

2. See, for example, Randall Freisinger's "Cross-Disciplinary Writing Workshops: Theory and Practice" in *College English* 42.2 (1980): 154–66; Toby Fulwiler's "Showing, Not Telling at a Faculty Workshop" in *College English* 43.1 (1981): 55–63; and Randall Freisinger and Bruce Petersen's "Writing Across the Curriculum: A Theoretical Background" in *fForum* 2 (1981): 65–67.

3. See, for example, Cynthia Selfe and Freydoon Arbabi's "Writing to Learn: Engineering Student Journals" (1983) in *Engineering Education* 74.2: 86–90, and R. H. Merritt's "Liberal Studies in Civil Engineering" (1981) in *Civil Engineering* 51.11: 71–73; and D. Stine and D. Karzensk's "Priorities for the Business Communication Classroom" (1979) in the *Journal of Business Communication* 16: 15–30.

Introduction: The Promise of ECAC

Donna Reiss
Tidewater Community College–Virginia Beach

Dickie Selfe
Michigan Technological University

Art Young
Clemson University

This book began with a heat wave. Sitting under a tree to escape a sweltering July afternoon in Houghton, where Michigan Tech had twenty years before nurtured some of the earliest initiatives in writing across the curriculum (WAC) and a decade before had published the first issues of *Computers and Composition* (C&C), a group of summer scholars chatted about ways to extend to our colleagues across the curriculum what we were learning about computer-supported writing. Among us were WAC and writing center program directors and staff as well as writing teachers.

This place, these people, and the time were right for *Electronic Communication Across the Curriculum*. Here, in 1977, eighteen people from fifteen disciplines at Michigan Tech, where Art Young chaired the Humanities Department, had met at the Keweenaw Mountain Lodge for WAC sessions conducted by Toby Fulwiler and Robert Jones. In the summer of 1980, Cindy and Dickie Selfe arrived at Michigan Tech from Texas and by 1983 were putting together small clusters of computers to support writing. Fascinated by the student-centered dynamics, they subsequently established two computer labs. In these labs, every summer for the past decade, teachers from around the United States and from several other countries have gathered for two weeks for the workshop directed by Cindy Selfe, familiarly known as "computer camp" and more formally as Michigan Technological University's Computers in Writing-Intensive Classrooms. At this workshop, where the discussions include both writing instruction and writing that supports instruction, many of the teachers who attend are active in writing centers, technical communication, distance learning, and other programs where they work with colleagues to design instruction that uses WAC theory and practice with electronic communication as the medium. Fortunate coincidence had brought to Michigan Technological University that summer of 1995 three teachers from dissimilar institutions whose ideas about the future of WAC and C&C were remarkably alike and whose enthusiasm for that conjunction would become *Electronic Communication Across the Curriculum*: Art Young of Clemson University, one of the founders and principal theorists and practitioners of the writing-across-the-curriculum movement; Dickie Selfe of Michigan Technological University, manager of one of the nation's early computer-supported writing facilities and an instructor/rhetorician interested in the practical aspects of teaching with technology as well as issues of access and authority in electronic environments; and Donna Reiss of Tidewater Community College, a Virginia writer-editor and composition-literature teacher who also conducts faculty workshops in computer-supported communication in English and across the curriculum.

The three of us conceived *Electronic Communication Across the Curriculum* as a response to a transformation in our culture that has significant implications for teaching and learning in higher education. As our communities and our schools at every level move online, educators are looking for ways that new technologies can help students learn biology, history, management, math, accounting, art, engineering, philosophy, and English, some of the disciplines represented in this volume. At the same time, educators are looking for applications that encourage students to communicate, think critically, and collaborate— to become literate, lifelong learners. Recognizing that resources in education vary widely, this collection emphasizes ways to use and to share the most widely available, most accessible, and most affordable electronic tools and also presents some of the technically complex, expensive forms of information technology that support instruction in any discipline and across disciplinary boundaries. Included are word processors; electronic mail; newsgroups; MOOs, MUDs, and other synchronous conferencing systems; multimedia development systems; and World Wide Web (WWW)-related applications. Classroom teachers; teachers in training; program directors for writing, technical communication, professional development, and communication across the curriculum; deans; librarians; and directors and support staff for instructional technology will find in these chapters practical models for institutional and departmental programs and for assignments within and across disciplines. Before we review these models, some initial observations about WAC history and recent explorations of electronic communication systems will help illustrate how we have reached this educational moment.

WAC-Computer Connections

Writing across the curriculum, with its goals of improved learning and communication, began on college campuses in the 1970s as a response to the belief that college students, working professionals, and all citizens need sophisticated writing abilities in order to succeed in the "information age" with its increased emphasis on knowledge, communication, and human services. While some people might have predicted that reading and writing would be less important in the age of videos and computers, just the opposite has proved to be true. In many ways, personal and professional success in the electronic age demands more rather than fewer sophisticated literacy skills. For most professionals, computer literacy has come to be defined not as the ability to read specialized codes, operate sophisticated equipment, or write computer languages but rather as facility with computers to aid thinking, communicating, remembering, organizing, number crunching, predicting, and problem solving. College administrators and instructors in all disciplines express doubt that college students are developing the reading and writing skills necessary to participate in a rapidly expanding knowledge industry as they proceed through upper level and graduate level courses; employers express concern that the communication abilities of recent college graduates are not what they should be in order to establish and build successful careers in business, science, public service, and other areas.

In the 1980s the concept that was implicit in WAC from its very beginnings— that all language abilities were interrelated and vitally important—was explicitly recognized. Writing across the curriculum (WAC) became communication across the curriculum (CAC) at many colleges and universities, as in Clemson University's Communication Across the Curriculum program and Radford University's Oral Communication Across the Curriculum program, a complement to Radford's longstanding successful WAC program. While continuing to envision writing as central to the academic enterprise, such CAC programs emphasize speaking, visual communication, reading, critical thinking, advocacy, social negotiation, and problem solving across the curriculum. Thus in the 1990s, with increased access to e-mail, the World Wide Web, and other forms of electronic communication, the evolution of WAC into CAC continues in the area of electronic communication across the curriculum (ECAC).

The conceptual bases for WAC, CAC, and ECAC have common origins: the use of written, oral, and visual language in ways that support learning as well as communication and the use of interactive pedagogy that promotes active learning. Most early WAC programs followed the pioneering work in England of James Britton, Tony Burgess, Nancy Martin, Alex McLeod, and Harold Rosen, who sought to establish programs on two of the primary functions of written language: (1) writing to learn, in which the main goal of the writing is to help writers learn what they are studying, and (2) writing to communicate, sometimes referred to as "learning to write," in which the main goal of the writing is to help students learn to communicate to others what they are learning and what they have learned. In theory and in practice, of course, these two functions often overlap in important ways depending upon the purpose, audience, and context for writing, especially with electronic writing, as you will discover in reading about specific practices in this volume.

Perhaps because postsecondary schools have been assimilating CAC concepts into their curricular design, educators everywhere are incorporating writing to learn and assigning writing in their disciplines whether or not they've ever participated in or even heard of WAC or CAC programs. But the technologies themselves also seem to be facilitating this process. The most basic applications of the Internet involve writing, and every student who uses these tools is participating in an activity that might be characterized as communication in or across the curriculum. Those educators interested in interactive distance education, in contrast to pedagogy that relies primarily on taped or live broadcasts of lecture presentations, have been in the forefront of electronic communication across the curriculum, for "in on-line curricula there's no escaping writing and no teacher thinks of it as an 'extra responsibility,'" says Chris Thaiss, coordinator of the National Network of Writing Across the Curriculum Programs (1996, 8). Indeed, the technology seems tailor-made for implementing CAC learning strategies: "What is e-mail but the epistolary pedagogy so often used by WAC advocates? Now students use writing-to-learn letter exchanges not only across classes and campuses but across the world. What are newsgroups and chat rooms but tools for the kinds of collaborative conversation and composition WAC has modeled?" (Reiss 1996, 722). It's not surprising, then, that many CAC directors and computer-supported writing teachers have become interdisciplinary instructional technology leaders at their institutions. The conjunction of CAC and C&C is further evident in the agenda of the 1997 national conference on writing across the curriculum, where for the first time a hands-on computer workshop, *WAC and the Electronic Classroom: A Multidisciplinary Workshop on Computer-Supported Writing to Learn,* was offered by teachers from several disciplines in secondary and postsecondary education (Chavez et al.). The 1999 conference also will feature at least one similar session.

But the influence of technologies has not changed the basic tenets of CAC. Indeed, we expect these technologies to extend our ability to institute CAC concepts like writing to learn and collaborative learning. Electronic media also can extend our ability to expose students to a variety of purposes and audiences as well as to spread students' involvement in complex communication projects across the curriculum and across their tenure at our institutions. These CAC tenets should guide our use of communications technologies that allow groups of people to "speak" at the same time, synchronously, or to contribute to an ongoing conversation at times that best suit their schedules, asynchronously. However, as this volume illustrates, the technologies themselves may well change the scope and nature of our CAC efforts. As Trent Batson, one of the early developers of computer-supported collaborative writing and current Director of Academic Technology at Gallaudet University and director of the Epiphany

Project for professional development, and Randy Bass, Director of the Center for Electronic Projects in American Culture Studies, remind us, "Although the technology may not have been necessary for a focus on [the learning] process or collaboration (or an appreciation of views of the social construction of knowledge), it may be necessary for the realization of those efforts" (1996, 43). After all, when engineering and technical communication students design a multimedia teaching environment, they are learning the content as they communicate with text, sound, and images (see Selber, this volume). When students in Rhode Island debate issues in international business with their counterparts at universities in Turkey and Germany, they are writing to learn as well as to communicate with a specialized audience of students whose own language is not English; in turn, their debate partners sharpen their critical skills and practice their English with an authentic audience (see Shamoon, this volume). And of course, business courses throughout the United States now simulate the business world's project-based teams with online activities (see Saunders, and Venable and Vik, this volume).

One national initiative that recognizes this conjunction of CAC and C&C is Steve Gilbert's Teaching, Learning, Technology Roundtable (TLTR) project through the American Association of Higher Education (AAHE). In its publication *Change*, the AAHE promotes institutional efforts toward a collaborative learner-centered curriculum, and technology is one of the linchpins of such efforts. In the March/April 1996 issue, Gilbert reflects on changes taking place on campuses, including the collaborative learning fostered by conferencing software familiar to writing teachers, "an unusually felicitous convergence of pedagogy and technology" (17). And at his seminars and workshops, Gilbert credits the decade of computer-supported collaborative writing in English studies for developing instructional applications of information technology that can be applied across the curriculum. As a further tribute to this convergence of Communication Across the Curriculum with Computers and Composition, Cynthia Selfe of Michigan Technological University, one of the pioneers of computers and composition, received the 1996 Educom Medal Award for faculty whose contributions to educational technology improve access for students and teachers and improve the quality of instruction—the first woman and the first English faculty member to be so recognized. *Electronic Communication Across the Curriculum* demonstrates this broad base of instructional technology with programs, cross-disciplinary partnerships, and individual disciplinary projects.

A Changing World

Our interest in the technological manifestations of CAC does not come from the academic community alone. We recognize that computers, and the networks that connect them, will continue to have a substantial impact on every aspect of our culture. Already, almost every issue of education-related publications foresees massive change in higher education concurrent with cultural changes brought on by information technologies. In his 1995 survey of computers in higher education, for example, Kenneth C. Green reports a dramatic expansion, more than double since 1994, in the use of electronic mail (1996b). His 1996 survey shows that 25 percent of courses at responding campuses used electronic mail (1996a). Popular publications like *Newsweek* and *USA Today* and the *Chronicle of Higher Education* have regular features and sections on information technology that routinely provide e-mail addresses and World Wide Web addresses. It's no longer surprising, therefore, that newspapers and computer magazines have gone online, that one of our country's first magazines, the one-hundred-plus-year-old *Atlantic*, has a Web edition, or that both plain text and hypertext scholarly journals are proliferating online, some of the e-journals refereed as rigorously as their print counterparts.

Responding to such transitions in information media, *Electronic Communication Across the Curriculum* offers models of instructional applications of information technology for institutions entering or expanding the ever-changing environment of technology initiatives and CAC programs. The projects in this collection will help individuals, programs, and even entire institutions revitalize their programs or initiate alliances between CAC practitioners and technology specialists. Along with CAC pioneer Barbara Walvoord, we believe that these initiatives are possible because with new technological tools "lines blur between writing and other forms of communication and between classrooms and other learning spaces" (1996). This volume recognizes and responds to that dissipation of genre and disciplinary boundaries with practical, adaptable classroom, college-wide, and intercollegiate practices.

A Difficult Medium

As we encourage colleagues, departments, and students to invest time, money, and expertise in electronic, cross-curricular endeavors, we are as keenly aware of the risks involved as we are of their educational potential. Our response is, we hope, proactive. For instance, because we come from such differing institutions—a large, comprehensive, four-year university; a medium size, technological university; and a multicampus community college—we understand the disparity of access to technology in higher education among institutions and among departments within institutions. Nonetheless, we find reassurance in the alliances forming as teachers and technicians share information and ideas. Many of the educators represented here have confronted inequalities. They have developed creative ways of dealing with them and have become advocates for wider student and faculty access through interdisciplinary computer labs and free or inexpensive student Internet accounts.

Teachers themselves face dilemmas as they embark on ECAC projects. These authors are collaborating on technology-intensive interdisciplinary projects that are not easily accounted for in tenure and promotion guidelines across our campuses, though we hope recent efforts by organizations like the Modern Language Association and the National Council of Teachers of English will help committees see how important it is to begin revising those guidelines (Schwartz et al. 1995; Katz, Walker, and Cross 1997). In a survey of fifty-five institutions of higher education on the logistics of using and maintaining technology-rich labs and centers, teachers suggested that they often had little or no prep time or release time for innovative, technology-rich courses which they almost universally considered more work than typical courses. Those same teachers often found themselves primarily responsible for the technical support of students and often responsible for the systems that the teachers themselves were using (D. Selfe 1996). Our hope is that books such as this will lend educational momentum to these efforts and that by taking risks with new technologies, we can smooth the way for more substantial technical support along with curriculum development, scholarship, and computer-assisted instruction.

At an institutional level, integrating electronic communication activities and projects across the curriculum often involves competing sets of motivations between teachers and administrators. In an analysis of the impact of communication technologies on higher education, Kenneth C. Green and Steven Gilbert ask a pertinent question and provide their own answer:

> Will information technology (IT) lead to the kinds of productivity gains and associated cost savings touted by its most ardent advocates? Alas, not soon, and certainly not soon enough for those both in and out of academe understandably eager to control instructional costs or for the evangelists who promise that information technology will enhance faculty productivity. (1995, 2)

They conclude that content, curriculum, and communications—rather than productivity or economic savings—are the appropriate focus of and rationale for campus investments in information technology (21). Because we concur, we have tried to produce a book where concerns with content, curriculum, and communication are foregrounded, where projects and programs are contextualized, and where authors were encouraged to be forthright about the challenges they observed. The excitement and commitment they felt will be obvious as you read. It is their intention and ours to take advantage of new electronic media, confronting its challenges as we go.

Made in the Shade: Unique Features of ECAC

By the time we three came together to seek shade from the unseasonable afternoon sun in Houghton in June 1995, the use of computers for communication across the curriculum was becoming more widespread and influential on college campuses, propelled into the cultural mainstream by increased access to and lowered prices for personal computers as well as by aggressive technological initiatives from many institutions. *Computers and Composition (C&C)* had evolved from a collection of short pieces on grammar checkers and word processors to an international print and World Wide Web journal that includes provocative articles on research, learning theory, and cultural literacy. Clearly, the time was right for CAC to connect with C&C.

What we soon realized and what the response to our call for proposals—a call publicized entirely online—reinforced was a wealth of work already in progress. A biology teacher had joined an English teacher to develop electronic science journals; an art class in one state had collaborated with a writing class in another state to produce a print publication on racism; online engineering and business projects had expanded into curricular models for entire departments and institutions; debates were taking place across countries and continents; philosophy students were philosophizing for each other as well as their teachers; and students were taking responsibility for public relations by developing World Wide Web sites for their college. Because the impact of computers on writing instruction has been well documented elsewhere, we have not included chapters strictly on writing courses. And while we appreciate the merits of discipline-specific software like anatomy and physiology modeling packages, physics simulations, or multimedia history programs, our inclination toward shared resources and collaboration drew us and the contributors to those more widely available communications platforms that schools, colleges, and (more and more frequently) homes are using.

Just as computer-communication tools have generated new ways of writing, the teachers who have used these platforms have chosen a variety of formats and voices for their contributions here. Some resemble the professional writings typical of their own disciplines; others have the more casual tone and diction of a magazine article or after-dinner speech; still others attempt to reproduce the multivocal nature of electronic mail and conferencing with chapters that contain dialogue more like a drama or a transcript than like a traditional book chapter. The voices of students as well as teachers are represented throughout the collection in a variety of contexts. Featured in many chapters is electronic mail. Neither postal mail nor spoken conversation, though it shares some characteristics of both, e-mail has already influenced the typography of a traditional composition studies print journal, *CCC*, in an article that is groundbreaking both for its dialectical nature and for its efforts to simulate a variety of media: In "Postings on a Genre of Email," Michael Spooner and Kathleen Yancey use interlaced columns to visually represent the conversational nature of their discussion and cite snippets of e-postings. Whether or not e-mail is a new genre, our students using this platform as an instructional tool achieve one of the central objectives of CAC: "The medium allows us to claim what is ours—as it makes the audience real" (1966, 265). If we could have done so, we would have made the audience of this book "real" by incorporating a World Wide Web discussion forum into our text; instead, we have a companion Web site. The Web is a format that didn't exist five years ago but that now links readers of this book and of the book's Web site to many of the resources recommended by the chapter authors.

Information technology has great potential, of course, but it has also complicated the publishing process. Some of the projects described in this book used the Web as a delivery method or as a class publication. As this book was being prepared for publication, postings on the electronic discussion list WEBRIGHTS-L dealt with issues of the relationship between traditional book publishers and their cyberwriters and included Michael Greer, our editor at NCTE, an advocate for Web publication as a companion to print publication. One of the contributors to this collection, Gail Hawisher, received permission from NCTE to publish her chapter as part of an online journal before the print book went to press. These variations on the boundaries of form and genre are characteristic of much of the writing and learning in computer-supported communication just as they have been in communication-across-the-curriculum pedagogies.

Reading ECAC

Because our readers are likely to be varied, we have developed a number of strategies for approaching ECAC. We have anticipated some of your interests by clustering chapters into three sections. In the initial section, "Programs: From Writing Across the Curriculum to Electronic Communication Across the Curriculum," we illustrate how ECAC can influence entire programs and how ECAC principles might be applied across institutions. We follow this section with "Partnerships: Creating Interdisciplinary Communities," a series of ECAC projects that reach across borders of various types: classrooms, disciplines, regions, and even countries. Part Three, "Classrooms: Electronic Communication Within the Disciplines," focuses on individual and team-taught disciplinary projects. And the Foreword by Cynthia L. Selfe, well-known theorist and practitioner of both C&C and CAC, places this volume in perspective, anchoring the book with important insights and historical background that will help both educators who have substantial ECAC experiences and those novice swimmers in this educational ocean of potential and peril.

Part One—Programs: From Writing Across the Curriculum to Electronic Communication Across the Curriculum

The interdisciplinary programs featured in this initial section promote effective uses of interactive pedagogies that envision students as developing language users and active inquirers. Such programs are often, but not always, housed in writing centers, WAC programs, technology-rich facilities, or campuswide teaching/learning centers. They seek to build bridges across disciplines and have discovered that electronic technology may enable them to build virtual bridges that will convey more commerce and communication between and among disciplines than ever before. These programs have discovered also that the technology may be not just the means for travel and exploration, but also a motivating presence in itself, creating attractive opportunities for adventuresome students and faculty alike to innovate, collaborate, and improve education. Readers involved with established programs will find in Part One a variety of ways to integrate ECAC into—and thereby strengthen—their programs; and readers developing such a program for the first time will find here a variety of models they can adapt or combine to fit their particular contexts.

Of course, designing and implementing an effective ECAC project such as an e-mail exchange with another class does not require a campuswide program. Many of the chapters in Parts Two and Three demonstrate this quite clearly. However, when we consider the broader institutional issues involved in our teaching, often it is advantageous for either an informal or a formally recognized group of colleagues to join together to define issues and to promote changes across disciplinary boundaries and thus affect the entire campus culture. This has been the role for many WAC programs—to support curricular changes such as writing-intensive courses and to support faculty development projects such as WAC workshops or summer grants to encourage innovation in teaching. The emergence of ECAC has created new challenges: providing access to technology, defining the educational purposes of technology, developing budget alternatives, and evaluating faculty performance, among other institutional matters. Therefore, ECAC programs, which we define loosely because they take vastly different forms as they emerge on college campuses, perform the familiar WAC programmatic goal of spreading the word across disciplines about new and useful pedagogies, even as their responsibilities grow with the addition of important technology issues. Part One introduces readers to a variety of models for such programs.

We begin this section with Muriel Harris, a pioneer in the development of university-wide writing centers, describing the multifunctional OWL (online writing lab) at Purdue University. She argues convincingly that the use of electronic tools creates new and important dimensions of learning not possible within traditional tutorial-based writing centers. Electronic tools such as the World Wide Web, e-mail, and synchronous conferencing are integrated into the writing center's particular mission to benefit students, tutors, and teachers. Harris concludes with a frank discussion of the obstacles as well as the possibilities for building an OWL.

The next chapter describes innovative ways that ECAC has influenced the WAC program and its writing-intensive courses at the University of Illinois at

Urbana-Champaign. Gail E. Hawisher and Michael A. Pemberton, faculty members in the Center for Writing Studies, analyze the potential and the problems of introducing asynchronous learning networks into courses in English and electrical engineering. They present teacher expectations and then quote from students' electronic texts in order to inquire about what makes electronic conferences meaningful and educationally useful. From their classroom-based research, Hawisher and Pemberton are able to provide some broad-based suggestions for integrating electronic networks into courses across the curriculum.

On the surface, Mary E. Hocks and Daniele Bascelli of Spelman College have taken the most technical approach to ECAC: establishing a multimedia teaching facility and an impressive ECAC program. Their emphasis, however, is sound, innovative student-centered CAC pedagogy made possible and supplemented by sophisticated technologies. As a result, they have been able to encourage faculty from a wide array of communication-intensive liberal arts courses to incorporate multimedia and World Wide Web development for themselves and for their students.

Mike Palmquist, Kate Kiefer, and Donald E. Zimmerman of Colorado State University reflect on their efforts to expand ECAC by appealing to both students and faculty, by locating the program in the campus Writing Center, and by developing computer-supported communication, hypermedia, and World Wide Web-based instructional software. In particular, they view networked communication as one method of tackling the difficult problem of attracting faculty who are less than enthusiastic about assigning writing, as a traditional WAC program would recommend. Thus, they have developed an Online Writing Center that directly supports student writers and generates faculty support because of the enthusiasm the students share with their teachers.

Joe Essid and Dona J. Hickey of the University of Richmond demonstrate how ECAC has become an integral part of their training of Writing Fellows, who in turn provide support for their university's writing-intensive core courses as well as courses in the major. Writing Fellows are undergraduate students from all majors who learn theories and practices of composition and the uses of electronic tools and then assist faculty in the disciplines with assignment design and the writing process.

Peter M. Saunders proposes a distinctly different approach to ECAC. He describes the development of a "learning platform" that provides business students with virtual case studies that are information-rich and use several media. The Professional Writing Center at Lehigh University, which Saunders directs, is a component of their writing-across-the-business-disciplines program. The center seeks to initiate change by helping learners experience communication "as fundamental to all social interaction within a real or simulated business context outside the classroom." ECAC has provided this WAC program with another option: rather than attempting to initiate pedagogical changes within the fifty-minute class period, they promote similar changes through virtual cases.

The next chapter illustrates how technical communication and engineering departments can collaborate effectively on interface design issues. At the same time such collaborations help the university accomplish its goals and objectives concerning undergraduate education and technological expertise. Stuart A. Selber of Texas Tech University and Bill Karis of Clarkson University demonstrate how the technical knowledge of an increasing number of English faculty in designing World Wide Web pages and hypertext projects can promote interdisciplinary collaborations that benefit all students.

Scott A. Chadwick of Iowa State University and Jon Dorbolo of Oregon State University describe how theoretically sound, student-centered, writing-intensive, World Wide Web-based courses can change the nature of typical distance learning programs. They developed an introductory philosophy course, InterQuest, that became the programmatic model for other courses with similar principles, including CalcQuest.

Part One concludes with a speculative piece by Todd Taylor of the University of North Carolina–Chapel Hill. Taylor calls for changes in CAC based on a grass-roots approach in developing Web sites. For Taylor, the power of the Web works in ways that should not be overlooked simply because they seem obvious. While the Web connects local interests to national and international ones, it also is an ideal architecture for connecting local interests to one another, thereby creating on every campus the "community of scholars" that has been a central goal of WAC programs from the very beginning.

Part Two—Partnerships: Creating Interdisciplinary Communities

The chapters in the second section of this volume highlight two of the most attractive features of electronic communication: its support for collaboration and for integration of text with other media, particularly with graphics and sound. We emphasize electronic collaborative learning both because it has been one of the theoretical and practical bases for WAC and CAC since their inceptions and also because it has become more dynamic and multifaceted through well-designed virtual learning communities like those described here. Writing to and with their partners, online students actively discover and construct meaning, negotiate conflict, and produce both informal and formal publications for authentic audiences, even when they never meet physically. In this section, students in a variety of disciplines and at different locations collaborate on projects using e-mail, conferencing software, MOOs, and the World Wide Web.

The section starts with Teresa M. Redd's fascinating collaboration between an all-black composition class at Howard University and a predominantly white class of graphic artists at Montana State University. Students who never met were able to confront racism in their personal lives and in their communities and to use the tensions of that examination to produce a print publication in which the art students illustrated the texts of their composition partners and created their own texts as well.

An e-mail debate that fosters global awareness and critical thinking is the focus of Linda K. Shamoon's chapter. Students at the University of Rhode Island corresponded with students at the University of Bilkent, Turkey, and at Technical University, Braunschweig, Germany, as part of their coursework in management information systems and business management using a model that can be applied in any discipline.

In a collaboration between biology students and humanities-oriented first-year composition classes at Michigan Technological University, Dennis A. Lynch reports on what he considers a "failed" use of e-mail discussion lists to integrate "two worlds of activity: two ways of teaching and learning." Students themselves were involved in assessment of the list discussions, and that process of reflectiveness and student control led Lynch to understand his misconceptions about the media and instructors' roles in such discussions.

Margaret Portillo and Gail Summerskill Cummins from the University of Kentucky use the straightforward and powerful heuristics of e-mail discussions between students in interior design and composition to explore creativity, a concept that could be emulated by any number of disciplines: "music, kinesiology, architecture, or communications." Students developed their own texts in order to examine visual and verbal communication as well as aesthetics.

COllaboratory is an online learning community supporting a series of courses in the Rainbow Advantage Program at the University of Hawaii. Program director Margit Misangyi Watts and Michael Bertsch describe the various ways their students serve their own local community by using MOOs and e-mail to make connections with writers a continent away.

Michael B. Strickland and Robert M. Whitnell use the tradition of student empowerment at their small, liberal arts institution to involve students in the development of an interdisciplinary World Wide Web presence for Guilford College. They explore the potential for sustained student involvement in the educational and administrative dynamics of postsecondary institutions.

Part Three—Classrooms: Electronic Communication Within the Disciplines

The third section gives insight into the potential and challenges of using ECAC within disciplinary contexts. Readers will find a wide range of projects designed and carried out by individuals or small teams of teachers who use an array of technologies to encourage written and visual communication experiences valuable in many disciplines. They offer models general and practical enough to use as we continue exploring applications of networked communication systems in all areas of education, and they do this by attending, as do all good teachers, first to the intellectual, emotional, and curricular needs of students. Here, perhaps more than anywhere else in this volume, the reader will become aware of disciplinary concerns as authors examine the essence of their individual approaches. Although these chapters describe courses in particular disciplines, we are confident that the techniques, theory, and practices from every chapter in this final section can be an inspiration to any dedicated teacher who would like to take advantage of ECAC pedagogies.

Shifting from traditional journal writing notebooks to electronic journal groups gave the students in Katherine M. Fischer's honors section of a class in approaches to literature at Clarke College a new understanding of and excitement about their readings. Writing to each other instead of to the teacher fostered an awareness of language and audience that helped them understand and appreciate the literary process.

Electronic approaches to writing for learning transformed the engineering students in Paula Gillespie's literature classes at Marquette University, enhancing their awareness of alternative readings of a literary text and stimulating the use of supporting explanations and citations in their messages to classmates. The idea for class e-mail came to Gillespie from a math colleague; the result was a collaborative presentation that encouraged teachers in other disciplines to try electronic journals.

Deborah M. Langsam and Kathleen Blake Yancey wanted to encourage students to think and talk about the role of science in their own lives in a biology class with two hundred non-major students. Using a model developed with Yancey, her colleague at the University of North Carolina-Charlotte, Langsam gave students a forum for asking questions and receiving direct assistance, and her "biochallenges" provided students with issues that allowed them to make the connections between scientific processes and their own experiences.

Recognizing the importance of communication skills and teamwork for the accounting profession, Carol Venable and Gretchen Vik of San Diego State University developed an interactive team-taught model of instruction to inculcate both interpersonal and workplace skills. Collaborative conferencing and Internet research are central components of their class on reporting for accountants.

Randall Hansen of Stetson University, hearing the call from industry for highly communicative graduates who synthesize information readily, redesigned an introductory, writing-intensive marketing course. In that design he included Internet listservs, electronic journal writing, online class materials, WWW research strategies, and electronic publishing.

Maryanne Felter and Daniel F. Schultz designed a challenging "Western Civ" course for community college students based on the concepts of collaborative learning and writing-to-learn and using several technologies: local, on-site network discussion sessions; e-mail; and Internet access. They discuss the problems of their first effort and make suggestions for the future.

Robert Wolffe uses e-mail journals to mediate the math anxiety and uncertainty of elementary and early childhood teachers. Discussions included content summaries, learning processes, frustrations, and successes, and encouraged specific cognitive and affective growth in students while providing a great deal of in-process feedback to the teacher.

Because large lecture classes seemed counter to the intellectual and dialectical nature of philosophy classes, Valerie Hardcastle and Gary Hardcastle incorporated electronic communication into their teaching at Virginia Tech. An informal discussion area personalized the class and fostered active participation from students who might never have spoken in class.

MaryAnn Krajnik Crawford, Kathleen Geissler, M. Rini Hughes, and Jeffrey Miller present a four-way conversation about their experience with students at Michigan State University in a team-taught, writing intensive, interdisciplinary humanities course entitled "The U.S. and the World," where they require writing-to-learn activities through e-mail list discussions. Their conversation is an informal and collaborative analysis of the students' e-mail discourse. The e-mail transcripts enabled these teachers to reflect critically on their pedagogical theories and practices and to gain a better understanding of how students use the conversational language of e-mail to serve both personal and academic purposes.

As you peruse these chapter summaries and our table of contents, we encourage you to explore the models from other disciplines as well as your own, for neither the technological platforms nor the pedagogies are discipline-specific—and the potential for variation is everywhere. Although individual chapters highlight uses of communications technology in specific fields or as collaborations among disciplines, each one is adaptable to a wide range of other learning environments. The biology students using e-mail in Deborah Langsam's class, for example, could have responded to biochallenges with the running commentary that is central to Valerie Hardcastle's and Gary Hardcastle's philosophy classes. Paula Gillespie's electronic journals for literature would work for Randall Hansen's marketing students, and his business models of online research and interaction could be adapted for engineering courses or technical writing classes. The World Wide Web development project at Guilford College could be adapted at the class or department level by any college interested in involving students in campus life while they learn about the Internet. The MOO at the University of Hawaii and the international e-mail debate at the University of Rhode Island offer replicable models that cross oceans.

Electronic Communication Across the Curriculum provides postsecondary teachers and program administrators with contextualized maps of exciting, challenging professional terrain. Teachers new to ECAC activities will find models to emulate. For more experienced teachers, these chapters will inspire new project ideas, variants they can use for their own classes.

Although this book offers opportunities for sampling activities in a range of disciplines, we realize that many academics will come to this reading task with specific objectives in mind and a number of intellectual and institutional forces compelling them to investigate ECAC. For that reason we present here some suggestions for selective reading.

Technology Focus

Distance Learning: Although most communication technologies can and probably should be considered as media in which distance learning programs can be conducted or enriched, these authors specifically mention distance learning programs: 4/Palmquist-Kiefer-Zimmerman, 8/Chadwick-Dorbolo, 11/Shamoon, 14/Watts-Bertsch

Electronic Mail and Other Text-Based Communication Platforms: 1/Harris, 3/Hocks-Bascelli, 4/Palmquist-Kiefer-Zimmerman, 5/Essid-Hickey, 8/Chadwick-Dorbolo, 10/Redd, 12/Lynch, 13/Portillo-Cummins, 14/Watts-Bertsch, 16/Fischer, 17/Gillespie, 19/Venable-Vik, 21/Felter-Schultz, 22/Wolffe, 23/Hardcastle-Hardcastle, 24/Crawford-Geissler-Hughes-Miller

Multimedia: 3/Hocks-Bascelli, 4/Palmquist-Kiefer-Zimmerman, 7/Selber-Karis, 20/Hansen, 21/Felter-Schultz

World Wide Web: 1/Harris, 3/Hocks-Bascelli, 4/Palmquist-Kiefer-Zimmerman, 7/Selber-Karis, 8/Chadwick-Dorbolo, 9/Taylor, 15/Strickland/Whitnell, 19/Venable-Vik, 20/Hansen, 23/Hardcastle-Hardcastle

Disciplinary Focus

Cross-Disciplinary Programs and Partnerships: 1/Harris, 3/Hocks-Bascelli, 4/Palmquist-Kiefer-Zimmerman, 5/Essid-Hickey, 9/Taylor, 10/Redd, 11/Shamoon, 12/Lynch, 13/Portillo-Cummins, 14/Watts-Bertsch, 15/Strickland-Whitnell

Business: 6/Saunders, 11/Shamoon, 19/Venable-Vik, 20/Hansen

Education: 9/Taylor, 22/Wolffe

Engineering: 2/Hawisher-Pemberton, 7/Selber-Karis

Humanities: 2/Hawisher-Pemberton, 3/Hocks-Bascelli, 8/Chadwick-Dorbolo, 10/Redd, 12/Lynch, 13/Portillo-Cummins, 14/Watts-Bertsch, 16/Fischer, 17/Gillespie, 21/Felter-Schultz, 23/Hardcastle-Hardcastle, 24/Crawford-Geissler-Hughes-Miller

Math-Life Sciences: 12/Lynch, 18/Langsam-Yancey, 22/Wolffe

The educational goals and interactivity described in *Electronic Communication Across the Curriculum* inspire creativity in both teachers and students, and the media themselves encourage ongoing collaboration. Increasingly, professional conferences and publications devote space to computer-supported instruction, expanding the forums for educators to discuss theories and technologies and offering hands-on computer workshops to model interactive learning. We invite you to participate in these ECAC conversations: e-mail the authors or editors, join listserv discussions such as WAC-L and CCAC-L, and contribute your own ideas through the ECAC World Wide Web site (http://www.ncte.org/ecac).

Works Cited

Batson, Trent, and Randy Bass. 1996. "Primacy of Process: Teaching and Learning in the Computer Age." *Change* 28.2: 42–47.

Britton, James, Tony Burgess, Nancy Martin, Alex McLeod, and Harold Rosen. 1975. *The Development of Writing Abilities (11–18)*. London: Macmillan Education.

Chavez, Carmen, Ralph Lelli, Donna Reiss, Carol Venable, Gretchen Vik, and Robert Wolffe. 1997. "WAC and the Electronic Classroom: A Multidisciplinary Workshop on Computer-supported Writing to Learn." Workshop at the Writing Across the Curriculum Third National Conference. College of Charleston, South Carolina. February 6–8.

Cooper, Marilyn M., and Cynthia L. Selfe. 1990. "Computer Conferences and Learning: Authority, Resistance, and Internally Persuasive Discourse." *College English* 52.8: 847–69.

Gilbert, Steven W. 1996. "Making the Most of a Slow Revolution." *Change* 28.6: 10–23.

Green, Kenneth C. 1996a. "Campus Computer Use Is Increasing, but Not as Fast as in Previous Year." *The Chronicle of Higher Education* 21(November): A21–22.

Green, Kenneth C. 1996b. "The Coming Ubiquity of Information Technology." *Change* 28.2: 24–28.

Green, Kenneth C., and Steven W. Gilbert. 1995. "Great Expectations: Content, Communications, Productivity, and the Role of Information Technology in Higher Education." *Change* 27.2: 8–18.

Haas, Christina. 1996. *Writing Technology: Studies on the Materiality of Literacy*. Mahwah, NJ: Erlbaum.

Katz, Seth, Janice Walker, and Janet Cross. 1997. "Tenure and Technology: New Values, New Guidelines." *Kairos* 2.1. [http://english.ttu.edu/kairos/2.1/index_f.html]. 7 May 1997.

Reiss, Donna. 1996. "A Comment on 'The Future of WAC.'" *College English* 58.6: 722–23.

Schwartz, Helen, et al., eds. June 1995. "Evaluating Computer-Related Work in the Modern Languages: Draft Guidelines Prepared by the MLA Committee on Computers and Emerging Technologies in Teaching and Research." [http://jefferson.village.virginia.edu/mla.guidelines.html]. 29 November 1996.

Selfe, Cynthia L., and Richard J. Selfe. 1994. "The Politics of the Interface: Power and Its Exercise in Electronic Contact Zones." *College Composition and Communication* 45.4: 480–504.

Selfe, Dickie. 1996. "Our Necessary Ambivalence toward Computers and Composition: Support for Technologies, Technology Users, and Innovative Teaching." Paper presented at the annual meeting of the Conference on College Composition and Communication. Milwaukee, Wisconsin. March 28.

Spooner, Michael, and Kathleen Yancey. 1996. "Postings on a Genre of Email." *College Composition and Communication* 47.2: 252–78.

Thaiss, Chris. 1996. "When WAC Becomes AWE." *Composition Chronicle* 9.6: 8–9.

Walvoord, Barbara. 1996. "The Future of WAC." *College English* 58.1: 58–79.

I Programs: From Writing Across the Curriculum to Electronic Communication Across the Curriculum

1 Using Computers to Expand the Role of Writing Centers

Muriel Harris
Purdue University

As writing centers integrate into communication across the curriculum (CAC), electronic communication tools are reshaping and expanding tutorial instruction, adding dimensions of learning not possible in the traditional tutor and student collaboration. Consider the differences as well as the instructional value of these two very different scenarios for writing center tutorials:

Tutorial A: In a writing center with no online connection available
A student in an economics course comes in to talk about a possible topic for a paper, and the tutor tries to help her see that the topic, the future of Hong Kong when it reverts to Chinese rule, is too broad. They discuss possibilities for narrowing and, after some brainstorming, create a list of topics to consider. The student then leaves and the next day tries the library. She comes up with a few sources but wonders if she is on track. Two days later, she meets again with the tutor, who suspects that her search strategies are weak. They discuss methods for searching for information, and again, the student leaves to try out what she has just learned. The tutor watches her walk out, not entirely sure that the student now has more sophisticated searching methods at her fingertips, but hoping that she has acquired some sense of how to plunge in.

Tutorial B: In a writing center with an OWL
A student in an economics course comes in to talk about a possible topic for a paper, and the tutor tries to help her see that the topic, the future of Hong Kong when it reverts to Chinese rule, is too broad. Using their Online Writing Lab's (OWL) World Wide Web site, the tutor and student sit together at a computer and link to the OWL's collection of online search engines—gathered together for easy access—choose one of the popular search tools, and enter her topic. The search engine reports 612 items found, and as the tutor and student browse through some of the entries, the student sees how vast her net is and why she must refine her topic. The tutor explains how to narrow a search by means of the Boolean operators that can be used in a key word search, modeling for the student what it means to choose terms linked by "and" or "not," and so on. They try out some terms to limit her search, and when she is confused and seems to be losing sight of her goal, they return to the assignment sheet distributed in class, talk for a bit about what the student might want to write about, and

return to some online searching, this time in the university's online catalog. The student finds some entries on the exodus of business people from
Hong Kong, and this connects in her mind to a topic in her textbook about
models for currency movement across international borders. After some
tutorial talk, she's beginning to define her focus, and then with some clicks
of the mouse, they go back to a search engine for material. This time the
tutor sits back, watching how the student conducts the search, offering
some advice as the student demonstrates what she is learning about how to
search for information. After the student copies a source, she and the tutor
link to one of the online handouts in OWL about how to integrate sources
and spend a few minutes discussing how the student will incorporate sources
in her writing.

As we can see from these scenarios for tutorials, OWLs can enhance tutorial
collaboration by permitting the tutor to accompany the writer through writing
processes to which tutors previously had no access. Electronic communication
tools such as Web sites fit easily into the educational mission and pedagogy of
writing centers because they encourage the kinds of collaboration that are integral to writing center theory and practice. The key terms for such theory and
practice are collaboration, interaction, and individualization, for tutors meeting
with writers interact in one-to-one settings as writers develop their texts. Tutorials provide a non-evaluative, low-risk space for writers to collaborate with a
knowledgeable peer—to become, through questioning and discussion, an active participant in their own learning. Meeting writers during the writing process means that tutors can discuss composing strategies and can accompany
writers as they move through various stages of drafting. Moving all of this to an
online environment creates new opportunities and modes of instruction, some
of which are not available otherwise, as well as new sets of problems to contend
with. To provide an overview of this and other aspects of how an OWL can
enhance CAC, I offer first a discussion of the various ways that electronic communication can be adapted to writing center collaboration, both within the center in face-to-face tutorials and also beyond the walls of the center to distance
collaboration by means of e-mail and synchronous tutoring. Then, a discussion
of how writing centers can also offer resources for writers and for teachers
suggests other uses of electronic communication in supporting campus-wide
interest in writing-intensive courses in all disciplines. Included also is a close
look at our OWL at Purdue University, to illustrate concerns of funding and
staffing an OWL. Finally, I offer some thoughts on both the obstacles and opportunities that arise when building OWLs to accompany campus involvement
in CAC.

OWLs in Tutorial Collaboration

As evident in the scenarios offered above, incorporating an OWL into a tutorial
means that a tutor can help a student learn to access and retrieve online materials, and tutor and student can then move smoothly into discussing the resources

they are finding. Helping students look more closely at the site and discussing the credibility and/or credentials of the source can easily be part of—and appropriate to—tutorial conversation. Irene Clark (1995) makes a compelling case for this role of the writing center in assisting students to acquire what she terms "information literacy," defining it as "the ability to access, retrieve, evaluate, and integrate information from a variety of electronically generated resources" (203). As Clark reminds us, "the current process students engage in when they conduct research presumes linearity and solitude, rather than process, recursiveness and collaboration" (203), and writing centers are uniquely well situated to work with students to acquire this type of communication literacy in any major or discipline. The tutorial conversation that accompanies online work allows tutors both to help students acquire electronic literacy skills and also to assist students in seeing how to synthesize information they find in the resources they are locating. Online resources unfortunately invite (even facilitate) a kind of cut-and-paste writing no different from the result of stringing together quotations from hard copy texts, but a tutor's questioning can model for students the questions they need to ask themselves as they build their arguments. "How will you use this piece of information?" "Why is it useful?" "What does that information do to further your point?" Such questions asked during the tutorial as the tutor watches the student locate online resources can help the student see why synthesis is needed. The conversation that is an integral part of any tutorial will help the student to articulate her thoughts more fully as she responds to the tutor.

Really useful tutorial talk helps the student begin to see how she will construct her argument and which of her sources will be relevant. Moreover, after some time spent on all this, the tutor can invite the student to do some drafting onscreen at the computer where they are sitting together. When the tutor returns later to see how the student is progressing, the tutor can see whether more tutorial talk is needed or whether the student is ready to continue on her own. The tutorial agenda, as usual, stays flexible in order to move to whatever writing process assistance the student needs. Unlike tutorial A, where the collaborative environment doesn't facilitate help with the many stages of online information seeking, a tutorial in a writing lab with an OWL allows the tutor to be present at a point of need, to assist the student in learning how to move through complex composing processes.

Distance Collaboration

Because the educational mission of writing centers involves reaching out to students in a variety of ways to meet a variety of needs, distance learning beyond the walls of the center is a natural extension of writing center services. Many writing centers have grammar hotlines which allow interaction by phone, some centers have established satellite centers in various departments on campus, and others have sent tutors to residence halls and library study rooms. Moving to an online environment is yet one more form of outreach. While some distance communication programs have proved problematic and not entirely successful, others offer great potential and have generated widespread use and interest.

E-mail

Initially, writing centers offered e-mail tutoring, meeting students through text on screen. The assumption was that this provided students at far ends of the campus or living off-campus a way to make use of a writing center without having to be there physically. The SUNY-Albany writing center found some students willing to interact in this way (Coogan 1995), and at the State University of New York at Plattsburgh College, students taking nursing courses at remote sites are using e-mail and fax to interact with the campus writing center, though faxing may become too cumbersome as the service grows (Dossin 1996). The e-mail OWL at Clarke College's writing center is used primarily by adult students in night classes and by other students whose courses in computer science, business management, and so on are taught at their worksite. The use of e-mail from their worksite became a way for them to access the writing center (Fischer 1996).

While e-mail interaction with students meets a need, it has not generally been a runaway success. Even when a writing center component was carefully built into a writing-across-the-curriculum program emphasizing distance learning at the University of Illinois, student participation was minimal (Pemberton 1996). Similarly, at the University of Wyoming, where commuting distances are great and there is a strong emphasis on providing distance learning to off-campus students, the OWL e-mail service has had limited use, despite the large number of courses offered through distance learning (Nelson 1996). At the University of Missouri—Columbia, the writing center for students in writing-intensive courses offers online tutoring, but Andrew White, the director, reports that they average only about two to four requests per week for online help. White (1996) concludes that although he recommends that students try online tutorials, he finds "a tremendous amount of energy gets expended for the relatively small results/response/interest." The major use of Purdue's e-mail service has been the instant availability of dozens of instructional handouts that can be requested by e-mail commands to the automatic server. Questions sent by e-mail are primarily from Internet users around the world. Even then, the majority of our e-mail contacts rarely move beyond a single question-and-response interaction, despite our attempts to engage writers in discussion.

There has been no study that offers insights as to why students are not frequent users of e-mail for online interaction with tutors, but a number of factors suggest that e-mail tutoring will not gain widespread popularity—though it may continue to be useful in places where distance learners have no other options. As any tutor knows, many students have difficulty articulating their questions or verbalizing what they want to work on with a tutor. Part of tutor training is learning to listen and to engage in the kind of conversation that will help the student make such concerns explicit. Thus, since e-mail requires the writer to have some facility in question-asking, it may be an intimidating way for writers to initiate conversations with unknown, unseen tutors, especially for students at some distance from the campus who have not established a personal connection with the writing center. For students who do have access to the center, there is a definite preference for one-to-one meetings with tutors. In writing center evaluations, students frequently rate their experience highly because they appreciate, even welcome, the human interaction. E-mail, despite its convenience, may seem too cold, too demanding for those students who know that they can walk over to their writing centers, almost all of which are staffed by people who have worked with great intensity and fervor to create warm, inviting environments with coffee pots steaming away, candy dishes at the reception desk, and plants and posters to advertise their student-friendly attitude. E-mail is also constrained by its lack of real-time interaction and the lack of shared space in which to look at a paper with the tutor. If the student wants to engage in an informal conversation or has a number of questions or has a messy working draft or a minimal outline (as many students do when they walk in), e-mail is too limiting. E-mail usually results in a nonsynchronous interaction and delays in getting a response, and it requires that the student submit an entire paper if there are larger questions about the whole text. Tutors will also miss the phatic cues that enrich tutorial interaction. Thus, a number of factors work against the instructional effectiveness of e-mail tutoring; moreover, writing centers are exploring other forms of distance interaction with more success.

Synchronous Conferencing

Developing new writing center approaches online has invited explorations of interesting new instructional spaces. One response to the need for real-time interaction has been the development of a Multi-user dimension, Object Oriented environment (referred to as a MOO) as an online means for tutor and student to write back and forth (Jordan-Henley and Maid 1995). MOO tutoring creates a way for student and tutor to meet online and exchange written comments. Jordan-Henley and Maid set up their MOO project so that tutors at Maid's institution, the University of Arkansas at Little Rock, could tutor students at Jordan-Henley's institution, Roane State Community College, in Tennessee. Though the tutors used their prose exchanges with their students to suggest informal tutoring environments, the search continues for technology and/or software that will permit a number of features of collaboration that are important and integral to the nature of tutorial conferencing. When communication is limited to text interaction, much of the visual and auditory interaction that tutors depend on in face-to-face collaboration is lost (Harris and Pemberton 1995).

Another feature needed for successful collaboration is shared space, space designed to support the *relationship* of the collaborators and to provide means for the collaborators to interact with or manipulate the text the writer is creating (Schrage 1995, 94–95). A writing center with tutor and student sitting side-by-side at a table, viewing a text together and talking about it in real time, provides most of the essential elements of collaboration as described by Schrage, but lacks a means for manipulating the text together. With a computer handy and the text onscreen, student and tutor can view the results of cutting and pasting, insertions, and so on. Video-conferencing across distances, with some way to view the writer's text and to work with it, perhaps even to be able to see each other as tutor and student engage in real-time conversation and hear each other speak, has the potential to be a means for very effective online collaboration. As better (and cheaper) hardware and software are developed for this, video-conferencing may prove to be very successful, or better solutions may be just around the corner.

Resources for Writers

More successful than text-based interaction online have been writing center initiatives in the World Wide Web environment. Here OWLs have soared and are finding a variety of ways to provide educational assistance that both continue to meet the central missions of writing centers and also provide previously unavailable opportunities to work with writers and faculty. By doing so, writing centers are finding ways to view the Internet as a tool for writing instruction, both at the tutorial table and outside the walls of the writing center.

When our OWL at Purdue expanded from its initial incarnation as an e-mail service to become both a Gopher and a World Wide Web site, we added our online e-mail collection of dozens of handouts on writing skills to our Gopher and World Wide Web sites. These online materials, created originally in hard copy to accompany tutorials in our Writing Lab, are a great attraction, serving as a magnet for teachers on campus who become aware of free and easily accessible materials that will be useful for their disciplines. In adding to our existing collection, as we respond to requests for additional materials from various faculty, we are beginning to build partnerships with teachers we might not have met otherwise. Because all of these materials are available on the Internet, we are also providing writing assistance to a worldwide community so diverse that we can only begin to guess where links to our pages exist or to track the many thousands of "hits" our site gets each week. As William Plater (1995) reminds us, "an evolving global economy is restructuring the formal educational systems of countries worldwide" (7), and as companies and government agencies educate their employees, they are using electronic means to provide information for personnel spread out over the globe. Thus, it should not surprise us when we get messages that our materials are being used for online training of personnel in government agencies such as the United Nations or NASA, in businesses such as auto manufacturers in Sweden or engineering firms in Belgium, in high schools in British Columbia and New England, and in universities on other continents. Our site has become a link on a great variety of Web pages. An anthropology teacher in New England created a link to our OWL on a Web page for his class as easily as a computer science faculty member here on our campus made OWL the writing tool on the Web page for his course.

As our OWL links to an expanding group of other OWLs also putting their instructional handouts online, there is now a growing pool of readily accessible materials available anywhere writers have access to a World Wide Web browser. While writing centers do not focus on or emphasize their role in dispensing resources, this aspect of an OWL is an expansion of a service most centers have offered—providing print resources on writing. Moreover, the availability of resources attracts some faculty to our Web site and makes them aware of materials and services that might help their students. For example, a faculty member in a department on our campus—who heard his colleague talk about the OWL link she had added to her class page—called to talk about how the Writing Lab might help with writing assignments in his class. Having never thought about providing his students with writing assistance for the papers he assigns, he was dipping a toe in a universe he had never much thought about before. Our future plans are to keep adding materials on writing that faculty in various disciplines tell us are relevant to the writing their students do (for example, online materials on report formats for engineering students and more on audience concerns for courses where we've worked with faculty now more aware of having their students write for specific audiences).

Additional resources for writers on our OWL are links to the most useful World Wide Web search engines as well as links to sites with useful information. The goal here is to assist writers searching for information needed for their writing assignments, to assist them not only with an immediate writing need but to help them acquire online information-seeking literacy as well. Because the Internet is a bewildering array of thousands of sites and has no map or index, students who have had little guidance in foraging on the Internet need a user-friendly beginning, a place where they don't initially have to remember the alphabet soup of URLs, those complex Internet addresses that will get them to sources they may want. OWL eases writers' entry onto the Internet, and as interest in OWL expands, we are meeting with teachers in various disciplines who don't have their own sites but for whom we can add starting places, that is, useful links to accompany their writing assignments. For Art and Design students writing reports on contemporary art, we have links to the Louvre and

other museums; for students in journalism classes we have links to other student publications online. Our OWL is also the focus for teacher and student
workshops. When invited, our staff members visit computer classrooms or meet
with teachers interested in incorporating the Internet into their classes. For teachers, we are finding that the most difficult step is to envision how the Internet
might be woven into their syllabi and into their writing assignments. OWLs can
also be sites for instructional programs as, for example, at Colorado State University, where the Online Writing Center includes modules and hypertext tutorials on writing skills in general and writing skills for specific courses such as
technical journalism, speech, and electrical engineering (Leydens 1996;
Palmquist, Kiefer, and Zimmerman 1998).

Resources for Teachers

OWLs in Online Discussion Groups

Online discussion groups about writing for teachers in other disciplines, like
student e-mail services, have had mixed reviews. Disappointing reports of minimal use by teachers are common (Blalock 1996). At Purdue, following a lively
two weeks of intense writing-to-learn workshop discussion with liberal arts
faculty interested in adding writing to their courses, we tried to continue the
conversation about writing by means of a listserv. A graduate student whose
task was to provide consulting support for this group during the next semester
describes the low use of that electronic discussion group he set up as follows:

> The response . . . was certainly minimal, although they may have responded
> better if I had prompted them more often. Obviously, they were all consci-
> entious teachers, and seemed to respond best when a question was posed
> which asked for practical advice. They seemed much less inclined to theo-
> rize about situations and more willing to offer suggestions or examples
> from their own classes and experience. (Nagelhout 1996)

At Stephen F. Austin State University, the results were similar:

> We have a local list called COMPTALK, intended to generate conversa-
> tion about writing here, a campus without a WAC program at the moment.
> We currently have about 50 subscribers, most of whom are silent. The list
> is sporadic, but it is only in its second semester. But faculty who are sub-
> scribed have said that they like the idea and the possibility for further/
> future interaction. (Blalock 1996)

Similarly, the writing center director at the University of Texas at Austin notes
that their listserv has "a fairly long list of subscribers who are faculty teaching
what we call substantial writing component courses. . . . Only a few faculty
contribute to discussions, and mostly they don't initiate discussion" (Kimball
1996a).

Teacher Resources

At the University of Wyoming, plans for their OWL include World Wide Web pages for faculty to access information about writing across the curriculum. Included will be examples of scoring guides that people use across campus since there is high interest in how to evaluate writing (Nelson 1996). As part of the online services being built by the Writing Center at the University of Texas at Austin, there will be a Web page designed to serve as a resource for faculty teaching writing-intensive courses with links to online resources for writing in various disciplines, an online manual for faculty teaching writing-intensive courses, and short, informal essays by faculty members on designing writing assignments and other topics for the writing-intensive classroom (Kimball 1996b). The teacher resource section of our OWL at Purdue presently has materials teachers can use with their students and links to useful sites for their fields of study, and our plans for expansion of this section of our OWL include adding materials designed to help teachers respond to student writing, especially writing done by English-as-a-second-language students. An OWL with a rich teachers' resource section will be a continuation of this traditional role for writing centers in providing suggestions for style sheets, writing assignments, and so on, and an OWL can add to all that an online space for teachers around campus to talk with each other about writing. When all this is prominent on a university's Web site, it emphasizes the university's commitment to enhancing literacy skills, to promoting the sharing of information, and to building a sense of a university community committed to common goals.

Funding and Staffing an OWL

While OWLs can enhance the work of their institutions as well as the institution's CAC program, OWLs are not easily or quickly hatched and require close tending as they develop. Securing funding initially is a challenge because administrators need help in thinking about a new kind of instructional space, about why it is needed, and about how an OWL is integral to the institution's mission. In our case at Purdue, I found that beginning modestly and presenting a growing OWL helped university administrators see why it should be supported. It took several years to secure funding not only for the necessary upgrades in equipment (see the Technical Endnote for a description of current hardware and software) and even more years to acquire adequate technical support. Now, some years after our OWL project was initially launched on a limited basis, we have two graduate students, each with an assistantship equivalent to teaching one course per semester. One, a doctoral student in our Rhetoric and Composition program, coordinates the instructional aspect of the OWL, helping with staff training, conducting workshops with teachers, overseeing content development and computer use in the Writing Lab, and working with me to set future goals. The other graduate assistant, an engineering student, is our technical coordinator, working on maintenance, routine data collection, new equipment needs, programming that is required as we add to the OWL, and other hardware and software concerns. My experience has been that while university administrators eventually understand the need for hardware and software, they need much more coaxing before committing recurring funds to solve the critically important need for personnel.

The staffing for our OWL is our Writing Lab's tutors, and while some are initially selected to join the staff because of their interest in and knowledge of online communication, all are trained by our OWL content coordinator. Because our Writing Lab is housed within an English department which funds these tutors as part of their graduate student teaching assistantships, all are graduate students in English. As director of the Writing Lab and senior coordinator of the OWL project, I have found my own training on the Web and online environments to be a course in self-education as I constantly seek information from any source that helps to define directions for growth that are consistent with our Writing Lab's goals in terms of effective writing center theory and practice and that fit our institution—its students, its teachers, and its mission.

Obstacles and Possibilities When Building an OWL

While there is significant potential for OWLs to contribute to communication across the curriculum, OWLs are not—as I have suggested—easily hatched or casually nurtured into further growth. My experience at Purdue confirms what I have heard from others. The planning and fund-raising to initiate and then to continue to coordinate the growth of an OWL take far longer than anticipated (and can dominate a director's work schedule), and developing the OWL is a study in frustration. It is hard to identify sources of money, difficult to convince an administration that recurring funds for personnel are needed, and confusing to learn how to do battle with all the logistical difficulties in getting systems up and running. Campus politics intrude, faculty don't want to be bothered, systems break down, and planning is usually impossible because the Internet is such a dynamic, rapidly changing environment that today's plans are out-of-date by next semester and the hardware that finally arrives may soon be outdated. And there is often a computing center to cope with which is, at best, reluctant and more likely to be hostile or unhelpful. But the rewards can be great. At Colorado State University, the Writing Center's online services were a way to offer writing assistance to a faculty where there was some resistance to a writing across the curriculum program (Palmquist and Leydens 1995–96). At other institutions, students unable to come to the writing center as part of their distance learning courses now have tutorial assistance with writing skills integrated into their courses. Moreover, that student in Tutorial B will surely write a better paper. She will also acquire information literacy strategies as she learns how to search the Internet for information, and she can certainly look forward to using these strategies in the workplace she will enter.

An OWL has other possibilities as well, for its Internet access will help the institution achieve global prominence far beyond the campus. Purdue's OWL, as mentioned, has many thousands of users in schools, colleges and universities, industries, government agencies and laboratories, and private users in North America, Europe, the Middle East, Asia, and South America (about 300,000 requests during our spring 1996 semester were from off-campus users of our Web site). The widespread use of our materials by high schools surely assists in student recruitment as well, for as one high school teacher in California wrote us, when he downloaded our materials and distributed them in classes, his students no longer think of Purdue as just a place with the Boilermakers football team. Such examples are added advantages, confirmation of the successes of OWLs to reach out and serve society at large. On campus, the immediate importance of an OWL is its ability to enhance the educational experience of the students who use it. With careful thought given to purposes and goals, an OWL becomes an integral part of a writing center's interaction with a communication across the curriculum program, and together they offer their campus learning environments for enhancing literacy skills not previously available. Students can have tutorial assistance as they move through complex writing processes for assignments in any discipline, and they need not even journey to the writing center to do so. Reaching out to students and faculty across campus and at distant sites is a writing center mission that reinforces and enables institutional missions for global education. Moreover, the writing center working with its communication across the curriculum program becomes an integral part of the university's ability to carry out its vital mission of preparing students for the literacies they will need to function effectively in society. Given the rapidly growing workplace emphasis on the importance of computer literacy and online information gathering, a college education must incorporate the acquisition of such skills. A writing center's OWL integrated with programs in communication across the curriculum are powerful tools for institutions to achieve such goals.

Notes

The Purdue University Online Writing Lab (OWL) can be accessed as follows:
    World Wide Web site: http://owl.english.purdue.edu
    E-mail: owl@cc.purdue.edu
    Gopher site: owl.english.purdue.edu

See Figure 1.1 for the homepage of the Purdue University OWL's Web site and Figure 1.2 for the page (*Writing-Related Resources*) that is the top link from the "Resources for Writers" button on the homepage.

Technical equipment: The Purdue University OWL is connected to the Internet through the campus computing system, but we have our own server, an Apple Macintosh PowerPC 7250/120 Workgroup Server, powered by WebStar. For further information, use the link *About Our OWL* on the OWL homepage.

Figure 1.1. Purdue University's OWL Web site homepage.

Resources for Writers

Writing-Related Resources

We've tried to collect a variety of resources (both our our own handouts and links to other writing-related sites) to help you meet a variety of writing demands. Please let us know if you find other relevant resources!

Our Own Handouts on Writing Skills

We have over 100 documents available for you and offer three different ways to look for handouts:

- Our index of handouts lets you search all our documents by category.
- If you're unfamiliar with those general categories, you can read summaries of each.

On-line Resources for Writers

•In addition to the annotated lists below,• check out our extensive collection of Writing Labs on the Internet and our pointers to search tools and directories.

Our pointers to resources include

- Indexes for Writers
- Online Reference Resources
- Guides to Style and Editing
- Business and Technical Writing
- Children and Writing
- Professional Organizations
- ESL-Related Sites [UPDATED]
- Academic Writing Concerns
- Listserv Groups

eXciteseeing TOURS We're an ExciteSeeing Tourstop!

Indexes for Writers

In addition to the resources listed at Search Tools and Directories, you might want to check out the following sites, which are related more directly to writing.

- Inkspot: Writer's Resources on the Web lists resources for all kinds of writing endeavors, including fiction, journalism, business and technology. Another source for all kinds of writing activities is John Hewitt's Writing Resource Center.

Figure 1.2. Writing-Related Resources page (top link from "Resources for Writers" button on the Purdue OWL homepage).

Works Cited

Blalock, Glenn. 1996. "Re: Local Listservs." WAC-L@postoffice.cso.uiuc.edu. 15 February 1996.

Clark, Irene. 1995. "Information Literacy and the Writing Center." *Computers and Composition* 12.2: 203–9.

Coogan, David. 1995. "E-Mail Tutoring, a New Way to Do New Work." *Computers and Composition* 12.2: 171–81.

Dossin, Mary. 1996. "Re: Your OWL." Personal e-mail. 19 April 1996.

Fischer, Katherine. 1996. "Re: OWLs 'n WAC." Personal e-mail. 19 April 1996.

Harris, Muriel, and Michael Pemberton. 1995. "Online Writing Labs (OWLS): A Taxonomy of Options and Issues." *Computers and Composition* 12.2: 145–59.

Jordan-Henley, Jennifer, and Barry Maid. 1995. "MOOving along the Information Superhighway: Writing Centers in Cyberspace." *Writing Lab Newsletter* 19.5: 1–6.

Kimball, Sara E. 1996a. "Re: local listservs." WAC-L@postoffice.cso.uiuc.edu. 15 February 1996.

———. 1996b. "The Undergraduate Writing Center at UT Austin Goes On Line." *The ACE Newsletter* 9.4: 7–8.

Leydens, Jon. 1996. "Re: OWLs 'n WAC." Personal e-mail. 19 April 1996.

Nagelhout, Edwin. 1996. "Re: Question about WAC Workshop." Personal e-mail. 18 February 1996.

Nelson, Jane. 1996. "Re: Your OWL and WAC." Personal e-mail. 16 April 1996.

Palmquist, Mike, and Jon Leydens. 1996. "The Campus Writing Center as the Focus for a Network Supported Writing Across the Curriculum Program." *The ACE Newsletter* 9.4: 15–17.

Palmquist, Mike, Kate Kiefer, and Donald E. Zimmerman. 1998. "Communication Across the Curriculum and Institutional Culture." In *Electronic Communication Across the Curriculum,* edited by Donna Reiss, Dickie Selfe, and Art Young, 57–72. Urbana, IL: NCTE.

Pemberton, Michael. 1996. "Border Wars on the Electronic Frontier: The Online Writing Center and WAC at the University of Illinois." Paper presented at the annual meeting of the Conference on College Composition and Communication. Milwaukee, Wisconsin. March 28.

Plater, William M. 1995. "In Search of the Electronic Classroom." In *The Electronic Classroom: A Handbook for Education in the Electronic Environment,* edited by Erwin Boschmann, 3–13. Medford, NJ: Learned Information.

Schrage, Michael. 1995. *No More Teams! Mastering the Dynamics of Creative Collaboration.* New York: Currency Doubleday.

White, Andrew. 1996. "Your OWL Inquiry." Personal e-mail. 29 April 1996.

2 Writing Across the Curriculum Encounters Asynchronous Learning Networks

Gail E. Hawisher
University of Illinois at Urbana-Champaign

Michael A. Pemberton
University of Illinois at Urbana-Champaign

The writing-across-the-curriculum (WAC) movement has been a powerful force for change in American higher education. In the twenty years since Barbara Walvoord first established a WAC program at Central College in Pella, Iowa (Russell 1991), and Art Young and Toby Fulwiler introduced such a program at Michigan Technological University (Young and Fulwiler 1986), the movement has made its mark on the country's institutions of higher learning. At colleges and universities where there are WAC programs, faculty often assign more writing, are likely to become more involved in their students' learning, and often change their pedagogical approaches to more interactive and participatory modes with students writing frequently in response to their instructors and classmates. WAC instructors, moreover, often assign different kinds of writing—assignments which are shorter but completed more frequently, assignments targeted at audiences other than the instructor, and assignments which have the explicit aim of helping students learn the subject matter of the course. In such writing-to-learn WAC classes, faculty also tend to lecture less and to encourage students to participate more, often viewing the classroom as a space where teachers and students come together to engage in exciting intellectual activity.

But if the spread of WAC throughout the nation's colleges and universities has been significant, and we think it has, the increased use of computer-mediated communication or what our campus calls asynchronous learning networks (ALN) has been extraordinary. In ten short years, the use of computer networks in the service of learning has become commonplace (Hawisher, LeBlanc, Moran, and Selfe 1996), and one need only glance at the weekly *Chronicle of Higher Education* to note the plethora of articles that promote ALN.[1] Those of us who have worked with computer networks recognize their promise, but we also realize that computer networks can be used to support teaching approaches every bit as ill-considered as those found in old correspondence courses where instructors send out course materials to students who are then expected to absorb the material and send back answers to prescribed questions, sometimes illustrating all too vividly Freire's banking model of education (Freire 1986). What is often lacking in these computer-supported network approaches are the critical interactions between the instructor and students or among the students themselves—the kinds of reciprocal exchanges found frequently in many WAC classes where teachers and students become learners-in-progress, collaborating and interacting in such a way that they form new communities of learning. In our minds, the twenty-year-old WAC movement has much to teach those of us who use computer networks for teaching, those of us, if you will, who use ALN. We use the term ALN to distinguish it from everyday networked discourse or from the computer-mediated communication that we engage in through e-mail or professional listservs. ALN, in other words, denotes online class activities that have the explicit function of promoting learning and thus corresponds more closely to the profession's notion of WAC contexts. Both WAC and ALN are capable of reshaping the social contexts of classes if we bring to them the necessary kinds of critical thinking and pedagogical values that successful educational innovations require.

In this chapter, then, we would like to offer our experiences as a basis for what we can and cannot expect when WAC and ALN come together. We first describe the beginnings of an online WAC program at the University of Illinois and describe how teachers used ALN in their classes. In describing our own experiences, we set forth several pedagogical principles which emerged from our work and which apply to our own teaching in online conferences. Following our discussion of online WAC contexts, we then turn to a description of how we experimented with ALN in the Writers' Workshop, the university's tutorial facility, and of how we were unable to attract sufficient student participation to allow us to experiment more fruitfully with online consultations. We end with a few broad-based suggestions that have come to guide our own use of electronic networks in writing-intensive courses.

Background

As way of background, we need to explain that the Sloan Foundation awarded the University of Illinois a sizable grant in early 1995 to experiment with ALN. Not unlike today, there were at this time a great many articles in the popular press touting the promise of the Internet as a provider of "distance learning," and there was much talk about the possibility of American universities offering degrees earned primarily in virtual contexts (e.g., Honan 1995, Blumenstyk 1996). From the start, however, the Sloan grant at the University was conceived of as what the Sloan Foundation calls "on or near-campus" learning. In awarding the grant, Frank Mayadas of the Sloan Foundation stated,

It is most natural to associate the ALN concept with distributed classes of off-campus learners. However, it is also worthwhile to explore benefits and outcomes from such networks implemented for traditional on-campus students. While most of the communication on campus is face-to-face, the special benefits of asynchronous problem-solving collaboration, assistance from teaching assistants and faculty, and other kinds of networked access need to be explored, and are of interest to us.

Thus, in 1995, the Center for Writing Studies began extending its earlier experiments with ALN into classes that were part of its writing-across-the-curriculum program. At the University of Illinois, WAC is one of the three programs which comprise the Center for Writing Studies. The Center was established in 1990 to improve undergraduate education through WAC and the drop-in tutorial facility which was also created at this time and which we subsequently named the Writers' Workshop. Undergirding the two undergraduate emphases is a cross-disciplinary graduate program which we argued would provide a committed faculty and intellectually engaged teaching assistants to work in the Center programs. Part of the mission of the WAC program was to support a second writing course, Composition II, but from the start we construed our mission as encompassing more than the support of a second writing requirement. We argued that if WAC practices are introduced to all faculty who are interested and who attend the four-day WAC seminars for which they receive a stipend, the WAC culture will begin to change the way teaching is carried out across the university. Because the university is one of the nation's largest research universities, this was no small challenge, but over the years more than 250 faculty members have attended our seminars and have also come back to the yearly seminar to demonstrate for their colleagues their own WAC practices. In the time in which we have worked to establish the Center and its programs, we have been gratified to see evidence of small, incremental changes in teaching practices at the university which we believe are making a difference in the way students learn (see Prior, Hawisher, Gruber and MacLaughlin for a more complete description of the program). ALN became yet another way in which we could work with faculty members and teaching assistants to improve pedagogy across the university.

Thus, in the proposal to Sloan, we had written that ALN would be incorporated into selected classes participating in the University's WAC programs, all taught by several faculty we recruited from five years of WAC seminars. Using the commercial packages of PacerForum and FirstClass (see Figures 2.1 and 2.2), faculty teaching courses in art education, classics, comparative literature, economics, electrical and computer engineering, English, film, and urban planning adopted ALN in one or more or their classes and experimented with different kinds of assignments, all using the online environment as a supplement to face-to-face discussions. In addition to setting up discussions for students, we also created a space where faculty could discuss with one another their experiences using WAC and ALN, an e-space which functioned similarly to the international listservs of WAC-L and Donna Reiss's CCAC-L but which included only faculty teaching in the program. (See Figure 2.3 for an example of a faculty exchange.)

The Center also hired two additional teaching assistants, one from engineering and the other from communications, both of whom were funded through Sloan and primarily worked with the Writers' Workshop. (In Figure 2.4 Pemberton introduces the engineering TA, Bevan Das, and the Writers' Workshop to any student in the WAC classes who has signed onto PacerForum.) In what follows, we focus on our own experiences in using learning networks, along with those of one of our engineering colleagues, Burks Oakley. We try to examine more closely the reasons for our successes and failures in online teaching, all of which reflect the kinds of thinking that we also encountered in discussions with other WAC faculty. Our experiences—and conclusions—resonate closely with theirs.

ALN and WAC

We knew in advance that ALN was not likely to be effective without careful planning and sensitivity to the dynamics of online interaction in an academic environment. One of the authors of this chapter, Gail Hawisher, had team-taught

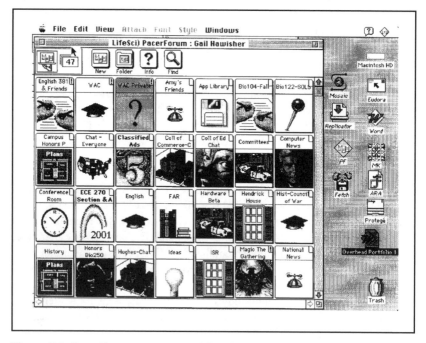

Figure 2.1. PacerForum, a commercial ALN package.

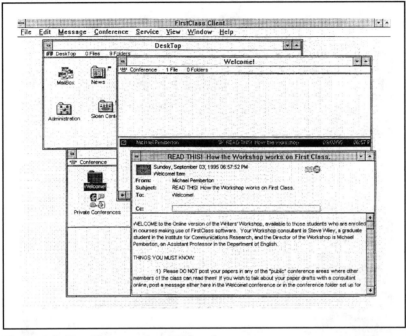

Figure 2.2. FirstClass, another ALN package.

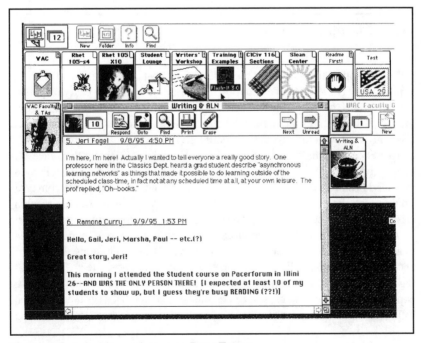

Figure 2.3. A faculty exchange on PacerForum.

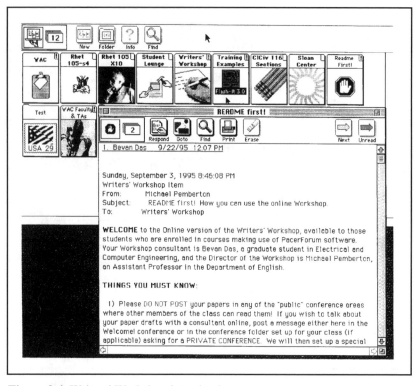

Figure 2.4. Writers' Workshop introduction.

a class several years before in which she and her co-teacher had asked students
to post on the class's e-mail discussion list summaries of their weekly responses
to the readings. Although the two instructors envisioned lively discussions growing out of the postings, predictably such discussions didn't occur. In retrospect,
it is a mystery why the instructors should ever have expected animated online
conversation over the readings when we consider the assignment they gave. All
they had required of students were the postings of summaries of their more
extended print responses, an activity that understandably led to little conversation. In fact, the posting and subsequent reading of seventeen weekly summaries became an exceedingly tedious activity for instructors and students alike.

An examination of the instructors' goals and assumptions seems to reveal
that the two teachers expected from the e-mail class discussions the sorts of
encounters common to lists where one hundred or more people are participating (and not posting summaries, we might add). The teachers automatically
expected the characteristics, say, of personal e-mail and listservs to take hold in
a class discussion of some seventeen students. What we learned from this expe-

rience was that even when postings were not graded per se, the tendency for students was to see their work as occurring in an educational context and therefore subject to evaluation. Regardless of how informal and supportive teachers expected these spaces to be, students still saw (and continue to see) their participation as required and graded.

Over the years Hawisher and her colleagues have tried to develop different online assignment strategies which they shared with the WAC instructors. Some of the strategies turned out to be more successful than others, with the effectiveness of the assignment depending ultimately on a particular instructor's goals for the online interaction. A few instructors tried to involve students by responding conscientiously to each of their postings, while others wanted the e-spaces to be exciting intellectual centers inhabited primarily by students (Hawisher and Selfe 1991).

ALN in English 381

The second author of this chapter, Michael Pemberton, used FirstClass in his course on the Theory and Practice of Written Composition throughout the Spring 1995 semester. The course is primarily aimed at students majoring in the teaching of English and is largely made up of students in their junior year with a few sophomores, seniors, and graduate students in the course as well. In an effort to address some of the problems faced by other WAC instructors who had used ALN in their courses, Pemberton worked to meet three specific goals as he introduced the FirstClass software to the students in the class. First, he made sure that students were well trained to use the software and felt comfortable with it early in the term. One full class session was devoted to hands-on training in a campus computer lab, and he made sure that students were able to log on successfully and perform all of the essential posting procedures that were important for assignments that would come later in the course. Additional time was spent with individual students on a case-by-case basis if they needed more detailed explanations than could be given in a large-class setting. Second, he made students accountable for posting on a regular basis, requiring them at first to post messages twice a week on two separate days, then modifying that requirement to a minimum of two postings a week on whatever day or days they chose. The experiences of other instructors—and his own earlier unsuccessful use of class newsgroups—had demonstrated rather convincingly that teacher encouragement alone would not ensure regular student participation in ALN discussion groups (Eldred 1991). In his course, therefore, students were told that their postings would be tallied each week and that their contributions on FirstClass would play a heavy role in the 15 percent of their final grade that depended upon "participation." Though students at first resented the twice-a-week rule, most of them slipped quickly into a routine that enabled them to meet this requirement with little difficulty. Third, Pemberton tried to integrate

ALN into the course in ways that seemed natural to ALN, the FirstClass software package, and the goals of the course. When he violated this general guideline for one of the course assignments, the result was spectacularly underwhelming (as will be explained below).

For his course, ALN was used, first of all, to provide a forum to discuss issues central to the focus of the course but which could not be covered in the fullest measure in regular one-hour class meetings. A special "discussion area" was created with a wide assortment of possible topics related to writing instruction that students could contribute to. These topics included "Dealing with Dialect," "What About Grammar?" "Personal Stories," "History," "Writing Theory," "Multiculturalism," "Computers and Writing," and "School Administrations." Some of the online discussions became quite active, averaging eight to ten posts a day at some points, and some students frequently posted half a dozen messages or so each time they sat down at a computer, depending on how strongly they felt about the issues classmates were confronting. Two women who rarely said much during in-class discussions were among the most "vocal," contributing close to a hundred messages apiece during the course of the semester. Some of the topics provoked quite animated discussions, notably on the issues of multiculturalism and teacher responses to writing. The following two unedited posts by students in the course were typical of such discussions:

> *Michelle*[2]: I believe we do not have the right to say on the student's paper (I don't care how bigoted it is) "what about the bill of rights?" We can, however, say "Have you considered how to answer people who would argue that your opinions do not stand up against the bill of rights?" You see, the first tactic implies that the teacher is ARGUING with the student's POSITION while she is EVALUATING the student's work. Let me repeat—this is unethical! And, students will develop an unhealthy fear of stating their opinions in their papers for fear of retribution from you, the teacher. . . . As teachers, we must evaluate the student's work apart from our own biases. Then we can, if we want, discuss opinions in class or on a separate peace of paper. If I could simply grade students depending upon how close they come to my opinions when they write then hey, I could flunk anyone in the class that doesn't agree with me. Then what have you got? You've got a group of students who aren't really learning to think and argue for themselves. Rather, they are learning only to spout back the opinions that you give them. . . .
>
> Let me clarify something—I did not agree with the student's opinions in the paper we read today. But, I did make a serious effort to dissociate my evaluation of the piece from my personal views on the issues discussed. I was alarmed at many other people who didn't seem as willing to do so. Forgive me if my language is harsh here, but I simply cannot stand by when I think some are going to make as grave an error as I am seeing them make. Folks, no matter how bigoted or ludicrous the opinion, you cannot punish a student for thinking differently. It's a fact of life. So let's get over the "oh I disagree with you so I can't think of anything nice to say" attitude. We're all supposed to be professionals. Let's act like it. (4/1/96)

Teresa: What I meant to say (sorry if I was unclear) is this: I am not going to look the student in the eye and tell him "You're wrong." I'm not even going to think it. He has every right to think whatever he will. What he MUST do in my classroom is support his beliefs. Yeah, I wrote "Bill of Rights?" in the margin, and you might remember how Tim was saying that the student needs to anticipate the arguments that his audience may have, well, that's why I wrote "Bill of Rights?" If the student decides to THINK about opposing viewpoints, if he CARES ENOUGH to look into how others may think, or if he even bothers to logically think through his opinions, he may find things that could surprise him. Asking a student to think about opposing viewpoints, and especially to justify his OWN opinions is NOT telling him he is wrong. If he can logically explain his viewpoints, knowing what the arguments against him will be, he will strengthen his own opinions. (Something I see as good). Asking a student to anticipate other's questioning, and asking him to make some sense of his own opinions logically is in NO WAY "shoving my opinion down his throat."

You called me irresponsible. Well, sorry, but I think it is entirely irresponsible of ANY teacher, regardless of the subject matter, to not try to expand their student's minds. I REFUSE to pass on any student from my class who hasn't had exposure to something new. I DON'T mean saying "here is what you should think." I mean plopping all the possible opportunities down in front of the students and saying, "find yourself, find your place in the world, find out what you really think. If you only learn one new thing outside the subject matter, fine, that's one thing more you didn't know before."

Remember: "The hottest fires of hell are reserved for those, who, in times of moral crisis, retain their neutrality." (4/3/96)

One of the characteristics of these two postings that impressed us was the students' total engagement with their own interchange. We would argue that classes dealing with response to student texts seldom engage in so nuanced or extended a discussion in off-line contexts. Note that Michelle is saying that it's not enough to avoid disagreeing with students' points of view by responding with questions to students' arguments—writing teachers, she argues, must also refrain from conveying their disapproval by crafting their questions carefully and tactfully. This is the sort of sophisticated thinking that we often seek from students but seldom encounter. We hasten to add that such conversations do not accrue automatically to online environments any more than they do to off-line environments. Pemberton's care in structuring the class—the training provided and the participation required—contributed to the students' feeling comfortable enough with the medium and with one another to dispute others' viewpoints with reasoned arguments. Later we will show some excerpts where this sort of engagement was more difficult to achieve.

Another of Pemberton's goals was to use ALN as a space where members of collaborative groups could stay in contact with one another, make arrangements for face-to-face meetings, and share information on their collaborative projects. Each group had a separate "space" on FirstClass with the option of making their conference area completely private or accessible to other members of the class. Though some groups made infrequent use of these conference areas, most groups used them not at all. Other, simpler technologies—such as the telephone— seemed more natural for keeping in touch and arranging meetings, while the regular three-times-a-week meetings in class provided ample opportunities for group members to exchange drafts and other reference materials. In this regard, then, ALN attempted to provide a service that was more easily provided else- where. The small-group conference areas became a "path of most resistance" with too many logistical hurdles to overcome for relatively minor benefits. As a consequence, they were largely ignored.

Finally, a special conference area was created for collaborative groups to post their completed projects—a detailed teaching plan for an instructional unit in English at the high school level. Groups were required to post these lesson plans two days before they were scheduled to present them in class, thereby giving other class members the opportunity (ideally) to look them over, think about them in advance, and ask pertinent questions after the presentations. Even though it seemed apparent that few other students in the class examined the lesson plans in advance (one of the features of FirstClass is that it can provide a list of the subscribers who have read a particular posting), quite a few more read and saved the posted plans in the days that followed. One of the things that was stressed often in the days leading up to in-class presentations was how valuable such lesson plans had proved to be to future teachers in the course who would soon, presumably, be teaching in state high schools. A number of students took this advice to heart and "stocked up" on the instructional units other groups created and wrote about.

In essence, then, two of the ways in which ALN was used in the Theory and Practice of Written Composition course were productive: out-of-class online discussions and central clearinghouses for useful information tied to course assignments. The third way ALN was used—as a contact site for members of collaborative groups—was remarkably unsuccessful because it violated the "natural" ease-of-use principles Pemberton had established initially for its imple- mentation in the course.

ALN in Electrical and Computing Engineering 270

When we turn to an electrical and computing engineering course on circuit analysis, we are struck by how seamlessly the ALN component of the course fits with its professor's goals. Ostensibly Professor Burks Oakley set up the ALN component as a way of having students receive help in working out the weekly assignments for this introductory course. ECE 270 is essentially a sopho- more engineering course; in this particular semester 350 students enrolled. The students completed network-based homework and quizzes over the weekly material and also posted any questions they had about the homework problems to the PacerForum conferencing system. Undergraduate teaching assistants, who had already taken the course, were available to help students with their questions until 11:00 p.m., and other students often helped each other with problems as well. In addition, we found that there were few times when Oakley himself wasn't available to answer questions and encourage his students. His immediate goal for the ALN-based course was to improve student learning through the use of immediate feedback and online help. At the end of the course, he also awarded students extra credit for independent projects they worked on and posted on PacerForum. Here is a sampling of the engineering course's postings:

> *Ian* (1:09 AM): I was wondering if you could give me some help with finding the phase angle in active filter problems in general. The attached picture is just one example of a problem which has given me some trouble. Since I am getting the parameters right to meet the specification I am pretty sure that I have the mathematical relationship down. What is the best approach to finding the phase angle in when you have a negative sign. It seems when I try a way that makes sense I am wrong. In this problem for example why can't you find the angle by summing the angle from the RfC1s terms on top, which should be +90, and the angle from the R1C1s +1 term on the bottom, which should be -45 degree with taking the - sign into consideration?
>
> *Burks Oakley* (4:15 AM): Ian—Sorry for taking so long to respond. For this circuit, the basic configuration is that of an inverting amplifier, so there must be a minus sign (-180_ phase shift) in the transfer function. At high frequencies (in the "passband" of this high-pass filter), the jw term in the numerator and the jw term in the denominator cancel (note that 1+jw is approximately jw at high frequencies), so the high frequency phase is -180_. At low frequencies, way below the critical frequency, the term in the denominator is approximately 1, but you still have the jw in the numerator (+90_) and the MINUS sign (-180_), so the low frequency phase is -90_. At the critical frequency, the 1/(1+j1) term contributes an angle of -45_, so the transfer function has an angle of -135_ at the critical frequency.
>
> Hope this helps.

From the dialogue included here, it becomes apparent that Oakley attributed much of the learning that took place in his course to the timeliness of his or the teaching assistants' responses. His tongue-in-cheek "sorry for taking so long to respond" reflects the satisfaction he derives from answering students' queries on a timely basis. Note also that in the above dialogue Ian posts the message well into the early hours of the morning and that Oakley, not so much a night owl as an early riser, responds barely three hours after the posting. And we hasten to note that in daytime hours the response time in Oakley's classes can usually be measured in minutes rather than hours. As we review the engineering class's postings, however, we are also struck by the thinking "aloud" that goes on and by the teamwork that also takes place as the circuit analysis solutions are reached. In other words, in good WAC fashion the students often come upon the answers to the problems they pose after they have been able to articulate the problem and after they write (or talk) it through with classmates. Consider, for example, the following exchange:

> *Jason* (11:02 AM): I am having trouble trying to figure out how the current splits to go through the two capacitors C1 and the 80uF one. I do not know if we went over this in class but I do not think so. I know that the voltage across those two cap. should be equal, but that is as far as I can get.

> *Ernest* (12:41 PM): I am having the same problem. I don't recall being taught how to do this??

> *Chris* (12:49 PM): I'm thinking that if you know the voltage across the pair in parallel, There's no reason why you can't combine them into one capacitor, solve the problem just as you did for C2, and you've got your answer. . . Anyone feel free to shoot me down if I've made a wrong assumption!

> *Dave* (1:53 PM): Following Chris's advice, and checking signs VERY closely, I did somehow get the right answer. Play around with the numbers you get and test them. Then try to figure out why.

> *Jason* (2:54 PM): I figured out that you can find the equivalent cap. and find the voltage across that equivalent cap. Chris was right though, you have to pay attention to the signs. Hope that helps.

It's also interesting to look at the differences in the kinds of discourse that characterize the postings of the humanities classes when compared to the engineering classes. Oakley especially was struck by how discursive the humanities students postings tended to be—how what he would consider "efficiency of prose" was often neglected in the humanities students' attempt to explain fully a particular point of view. The length of Pemberton's students' messages were several paragraphs, and Hawisher omitted paragraphs her students wrote in order for the chapter to conform to the length expectations of the editors. We also found that not unlike our WAC experiences with faculty in other disciplines, the ALN experiments led us to compare our classes with those of our colleagues and to reflect on our own goals for discipline-specific classes. Sharing our teaching experiences across campus also had the unexpected result of encouraging dialogue among the various faculty as to what constituted appropriate ALN writing in the various classes.

Crafting Online Assignments

As we mentioned earlier, faculty from a variety of disciplines incorporated learning networks into their writing-intensive classes, and one of the problems that especially the faculty in the humanities courses faced related to how we might structure online assignments so that they elicited the kinds of thoughtful responses Michelle and Teresa demonstrate in Pemberton's classes. Clearly, students need to perceive the subject matter as meaningful, though the "meaning" it has for them can be constructed along any one of a variety of dimensions—personal, intellectual, academic, or professional, to name just a few. But even more importantly, students sometimes need to be encouraged explicitly— given "permission" as it were—to use forms of discourse that go beyond the relatively narrow and confining conventions of academic prose when responding to specific assignments online. As we alluded earlier, students are strongly aware that their online interactions take place in an academic, and therefore evaluative, context. The pressure to produce online texts which mimic the standard forms of academic essays can, accordingly, be difficult to overcome.

One example of this phenomenon, an eventually successful assignment that grew out of our online experiences and which Hawisher posted for the students in her Writing and Technology class, involved the use of the print magazine *Wired*. The Writing and Technology class, English 382, is primarily a junior level class again aimed at students who are majoring in the teaching of English. Because of the technology component, however, several students signed up for the course who were not English majors but who nevertheless were planning to enter the teaching profession. For this reason, Hawisher tried to construct assignments which focused on teaching but not necessarily on English teaching. As stipulated below, for the assignment, she wanted the students to work on their response while she was attending the 1995 convention of the Conference on College Composition and Communication. Specifically, the assignment asked students to analyze the usefulness of *Wired* magazine for their teaching, but it was part of a larger general goal for the course which required students to think critically about the kinds of resources—online and print—that they would find appropriate for their teaching.

> *Gail Hawisher:* Today, in class, I'm going to give each of you a recent copy of WIRED Magazine. I'd like you to look it over, read some of the articles, and decide for whom the magazine seems intended and whether it has value for you . . . and/or for your teaching.
>
> I'd then like you to decide how—if at all—you could use it in your classes for teaching. If you think you can, post here a teaching plan to be used in conjunction with an article, series of articles, pictures, advertisements, or some other aspect of the magazine. If you can't, please post an extended argument against its pedagogical utility, giving examples from the issue you have.
>
> With a little bit of luck, I'll try to read some of your postings from my hotel room in Washington, D.C. If at all possible, post your assignment here on or before next Monday, the 27th. Thanks!
>
> *Mark:* To begin, I recently had an argument with a friend about the issue of presentation vs content. I argued that in today's technology driven world

that presentation was as important as content. I said that a piece of writing could not rely solely on either aspect in order to be taken seriously. He contended that a paper should be judged on content alone.

The creators of WIRED would seem to take my side of the argument. Although at first it seemed that they focused more on layout and that almost turned me off in itself. But on a closer inspection the articles were well written and very informative to even a computer novice such as myself. (two more paragraphs follow)

Robert: First of all, this magazine impressed me. It impressed me in terms of both the aspects that I assume hold constant across issues (format, type of articles) and the specific issues that this one issue brings up.

The one single thing that struck me most about this magazine was the prevalence and omnipresence of advertisements. I assume that this is a characteristic not unique to this issue. This is accentuated by the fact that a lot of the ads are hard to distinguish from the actual stories and articles. I think this is by design in a way. The magazine's designers seem to have a similar mindset in designing their magazine that advertisers do in designing ads. Catching the reader's eye, displaying something provocative, and getting readers to look twice are important goals. In a more conventional news magazine like Time or Newsweek, having catchy-looking stories is not a prime goal in designing. (four paragraphs follow)

This is getting way too long. So, in short, my teaching suggestion is to use the whole magazine, including the advertisements, if it is to be used at all. I would be uncomfortable copying an article and giving it to students, since it comes from a context that is so imbedded in corporate interests. I would encourage students to make connections among the stories, the format, and the advertisements.

Gary: The most efficient (and therefore perhaps the best) pedagogical classroom use I envision for this "Wired" magazine edition is found in its advertisements. (The articles are to some extent interesting. However, it would seem that one for the most part needs to wade too far past the quasi-ridiculous and "inefficiently" speculative, at least for class purposes.) As a result, I, again, see a much greater value (and more efficient use) in its advertisements. (two paragraphs follow)

Carl: Gary . . . although I have no idea what you mean by quasi-ridiculous and inefficiently speculative, I would disagree that the articles are useless for classes. In fact, my issue contains several that I would consider using, such as "The Man Who Stole Michael Jackson's Face" about a guy who manipulated Michael's face onto a nude female body and got sued for stealing his image, which could lead into issues of intellectual property; "The Last Human Chess Master" which is about when computers are able to fully reproduce human activity. . .what then will distinguish between humans and computers? There are some others.

I thought I'd discuss the gender issues thing—it just so happens that my issue contains a letter critiquing WIRED for its white-maleness. It goes like this:

Time to Walk the Walk:

I am becoming increasingly impatient with the decidedly boogie-white-male, "liberal" slant with which Wired approaches certain issues concerning information technology. Wired seems knee-deep in a kind of "white-male"-ness that is more of a consciousness than a statistical state of being determined by skin color of genitalia. In other words, I am not as concerned with the number of "actual" white males who occur in the mag either as writers or subjects, as I am with the specific nature of the content. (three paragraphs omitted)

Anyway, does this issue touch of in anyone else's mag?

What we find interesting in these postings is that despite the instructor's intent to engage students in discussion while she's out of town, the assignment initially elicits almost the same type of postings that the earlier "summary" assignment elicited. Although the students don't write summaries, they seem to be posting in a vacuum with little sense of an audience other than the instructor, reproducing (somewhat more informally) the kinds of paper assignments they have traditionally completed over the years. And they do this in spite of the fact that they had been carrying on engaged online discussions throughout the semester. This was the first time, however, that the instructor gave them a specific assignment to respond to. Up until this assignment, they had been responding to in-class presentations and discussing online different kinds of computer applications with which they were experimenting in class along with discussing the various readings assigned for the course.

Hawisher read these responses rather dishearteningly from Washington, D.C., and lamented having given the assignment until she encountered the fourth response. Here Carl responds, "Gary . . . although I have no idea what you mean by quasi-ridiculous and inefficiently speculative, I would disagree that the articles are useless for classes." Carl names the person he's addressing and begins to question Gary's assessment of *Wired*'s pedagogical utility. From this point on, the students seemed at least to be talking to one another and often commented on another posting before setting forth their own evaluations.

> *Joan:* Did anyone else attend Andrew Ross' lecture on Friday (he's the head of the American Studies dept. at NYU)? (three paragraphs omitted)
>
> What struck me most about [*WIRED*] is its "maleness" for lack of a better term. By that I mean its ads and articles and fillers seem to be geared toward an audience that is cynical and irreverent about "traditional" values (career, marriage, family, the house in the suburbs). Kind of like Rolling Stone meets the Sharper Image catalog.
>
> *Carl:* Many (myself included) have criticized WIRED for its consistent "white male-ness"—especially the advertisements. However, advertisers gear ads, obviously, towards their consumers. . .and I'd wager that they know exactly what the readership of WIRED is (majority male? Probably. Majority white? Probably.) and they gear their ads to that group of people. Are the advertisements in EBONY a problem because they target African-American readers? What do you think? How about Rolling Stone's ads that appeal to, generally, younger music listeners. At what point are the magazines biased and at what point are they just representative?

Brian: After reading through several issues of "Wired", I have to agree with Carl and Joan that the magazine unquestionably targets white males. I would have to say, however, that it targets teenage white males. I think that part of the reason for the flashy ads is to display many of the new capabilities of desk top publishing. Where better to display cutting edge graphics then in a magazine that deals with cutting edge technology. I think part of there image also stems from their desire to target a younger audience. For those who have been raised on MTV and video games, this medium is not all that unfamiliar. Likewise, with the attention span of Americans dramatically declining due to the "clicker," a product almost needs flashy advertisements to ensure that their product will be seen. (three paragraphs follow)

Gail Hawisher: Great observations here! And thanks for the joke, Barbara :)) Let me add something I took off of Edupage, and we can use it to start our in-class discussion Monday.

> *The Wired Revolution*
> While saluting *Wired* magazine's worthy premise as a publication that addresses the social and cultural effects of digital technologies, the director of the 21st Century Project at the University of Texas blasts *Wired* for its "fevered, adolescent consumerism, its proud display of empty thoughts from a parade of smoke-shoveling celebrity pundits, its smug disengagement from the thorny problems facing postindustrial societies, and most annoyingly, its over-the-top narcissism. If this is the revolution, do we really want to be part of it?" (*New Republic* 1/9-16/95 p.19)

What do you think? In many ways, I'm rather taken with *Wired* for the sheer energy displayed. I did, however, have to laugh at Joan's observation that it seems to be a cross between the Sharper Image catalogue and Rolling Stone magazine. I wonder if it could be transformed into a magazine that suits more of us more of the time. . . .(two paragraphs follow)

Although Hawisher came to regard the assignment as effective (i.e., students not only made insightful observations about *Wired* but also responded to one another's posts), it's interesting that she never stipulated in the opening assignment that students should respond to one another and comment on one another's ideas. For her, with over ten years experience online, this sort of behavior was a given. We would like to think that the modeling of what she considered appropriate online response (e.g., the use of writers' names, a little bit of praise, a little bit of commentary, an idea offered, some questions) was a strategy to which students responded well and which they too tried to incorporate into their own online repertoire. Our tentative conclusion, however, is that students interpret online assignments as being not very different from the customary paper assignments they receive—especially when they have little experience with online writing. As we all learn in WAC workshops, good teaching involves letting students in on our expectations for them: we need to discuss with them beforehand what they—students and instructor—would regard as the successful completion of an assignment. This should not be new to any of us who work with WAC.

Indeed, the more successful online assignments seemed to have much in common with the classroom practices that we frequently advocate in WAC seminars. Those faculty who emerged from their ALN experiences most satisfied with the results generally followed the "classroom practices" Toby Fulwiler recommended many years ago for writing assignments grounded in WAC theory. Among his recommendations, for example, those to which the faculty adhered most closely included the following:

- Prepare a context for each assignment. When students are asked to write about something related to the subject in your class, it's often possible to plant fertile ideas in advance that will help generate more comprehensive writing.

- Ask students to write about what they know, not what you already know. Where possible, make your assignments approximate real communication situations, where the writer/speaker communicates something to a reader/listener who wants to learn more about it.

- Use peer(s) . . . to motivate and educate each other.

- Integrate writing into the daily activity of your classroom. Effecting this generalized advice can actually have a profound effect on all the formal writing you require of your students. (1986, 27–29)

When instructors neglected to use these precepts as guidelines, invariably their and their students' online experiences were less satisfying than they would have liked. Not only was a great deal of advanced preparation necessary for the classes but, like all pedagogical innovations, ALN needed to be attended to on a daily basis with students needing subtle and not-so-subtle reminders from the instructor that the online context was every bit as important to learning as the class's face-to-face encounters.

ALN and WOW (The Writers' Online Workshop)

Partially as a result of our largely successful implementation of ALN into WAC classes, we also decided to extend to the WAC classes the services of the Writers' Workshop, the drop-in and now online writing lab of the Center for Writing Studies. Because ALN was being used extensively by courses that were designated writing-intensive, it seemed fitting that the Writers' Workshop provide some significant support to the students in Sloan courses via ALN. As mentioned earlier, the Sloan Center gave us funding for two TAs in the Writers' Workshop who were specifically intended to provide online writing help to Sloan courses, with one TA assigned to courses using FirstClass and the other to courses using PacerForum.

From the beginning, there were important obstacles to confront and negotiate with the instructors of the online WAC courses. The first was the issue of permission. Not all WAC instructors wanted Workshop TAs to have access to their course discussion areas, and not all instructors wanted the Workshop conference folder to appear on their students' desktops. Several crucial weeks when writing assistance could have been provided to students were lost while administrative issues of this sort were being resolved.

The second obstacle to confront was one of icon placement. Where, exactly, should the conference icon for the Writers' Workshop appear? This was not a trivial question, as it turned out, and we discovered that the decisions we made about placement —or those that were forced upon us for political and practical reasons—were often the single most significant factor that determined the degree to which students availed themselves of online Workshop resources.

Both PacerForum and FirstClass (and many other online conferencing software packages) have hierarchical structures. That is, when users log in, they are presented with an opening "desktop" containing an assortment of icons that will each open new windows or discussion threads. When these new windows are opened, they generally overlay the desktop and obscure the icons beneath them, effectively removing the icons from immediate perception and easy access. Though it made sense initially to put the Workshop icon at the highest level where it could be seen whenever students logged in, what we subsequently found was that the icon was quickly covered by message windows early in each session and students soon forgot that the Workshop was available as an online resource for their writing. (See Figure 2.4.) We suspect that had the Workshop icon been placed at a level where it would be constantly visible—inside the course discussion area, for example—then students might have been more likely to make use of the Workshop online. The issue of visibility, then, emerged as an important one for us, as we would counsel other instructors to consider it as well when constructing their own ALN networks.

The third obstacle to address was what our policies of use should be. Because there were, when all administrative and permissions issues were resolved, approximately seven hundred students who would have access to the Writers' Workshop area via ALN, we felt it was important to set some relatively clear and somewhat restrictive policies for use that would explain to students what sorts of help they could expect via ALN and that would keep the two TAs assigned to monitor the Workshop's online areas from being overwhelmed with work. The policies we decided upon were similar to those which held in the walk-in Writers' Workshop: consultants would look at and provide feedback on drafts, but they would not be proofreaders or graders. Our preference was that students submit drafts with specific questions that they wanted to have answered, and in this way we hoped to head off the potential result that students would routinely send consultants their drafts without engaging in any sort of dialogue.

We wanted students to reflect on their writing before submitting it and to provide some guidance for the TAs' responses. Our hope was that the consultants could engage in the same sort of dialogic interaction online that characterized their interactions with students in face-to-face conferences. However, our policies at the start may have inadvertently discouraged students from accessing the Workshop. In retrospect it might have been a more effective policy to encourage all students in WAC classes to turn to us for help and then negotiate the terms under which we would advise them.

The Writers' Workshop's presence online was largely ignored by students, for reasons already alluded to, for reasons that should have been obvious in retrospect, and for reasons which were embodied in the very structure of the ALN course-specific discussion areas. Over the course of an entire semester, the Workshop TAs had only a handful of interactions with students, and most of those interactions consisted of only a single inquiry and response.

The placement issue, as mentioned earlier, presented a significant difficulty for students. Most of their online work took place in the course discussion folders, and these folders, when opened, obscured the folders that lay underneath. Since the Writers' Workshop folder did not appear in the discussion folder devoted to the specific course the students were working in, students tended to forget about the Workshop as an online resource. Further, since most students logged into their ALN accounts to participate in class discussions or to get pertinent information from the course instructor (syllabi, assignments, or class notes), and since most of them used public sites on campus to log in rather than doing so remotely from their home computers, they were generally not likely to have their written work with them on disk to send to the TAs in the Workshop.

A more obvious reason for the lack of student interaction with the Workshop online was the comparative ease with which the students could see Workshop TAs in the campus writing center. Most students at the University of Illinois live either on campus or close to it. Getting to the writing center poses few problems, and getting an appointment to talk with a Workshop TA is only a matter of making a simple phone call. Students knew that if they printed out a copy of their draft and brought it into Workshop they could get a full hour of detailed, tightly focused, and fully interactive feedback on what they had written. They didn't need to save their drafts to a disk, carry their disks to an on-campus computing site, log in to their ALN accounts, open the Workshop folder, arrange for a private conference space in the Workshop discussion area (if they didn't want their drafts to be seen by other students), open their document, cut and paste it to an ALN message, send it to the Workshop, and then wait a day or so for a reply. Making a visit to the Writers' Workshop was not only easier than sending a document online, but also more worthwhile in terms of the amount of time and effort invested. Given the resident student population at the University of Illinois, this phenomenon seems obvious in retrospect, though it was our hope that more students would have taken advantage of the Workshop's online presence while they were otherwise connected to ALN.

A third and more telling source of interference with the Workshop's ability to provide online assistance was the ease with which students could communicate with instructors and course TAs who were also regularly available on FirstClass and PacerForum. Students generally saw little value in asking Workshop TAs to review their paper drafts when the instructors and departmental TAs—those who would eventually be assigning grades to the papers—were also available for the same type of review. One of the reasons why writing centers tend to be so often used by students is their routine availability; writing centers are generally open for many more hours than instructors are generally accessible during their office hours. ALN, however, tends to equalize this disparity. Now instructors can be reached and consulted at the students' convenience, while the Workshop TAs are—just the reverse—restricted in the speed with which they can respond to student writing.

Concluding Comments

In its efforts to use asynchronous learning environments effectively, the teaching profession faces many challenges. We have listed three recommendations here, all of them aimed at helping instructors reconsider their goals and approaches—rethinking what it means to teach and learn while developing critical perspectives on the ways the new technologies can and cannot abet learning. The recommendations we make are few in number, but they may help guide our thinking about ways in which WAC can inform higher education's use of ALN over the next several years.

- ALN should be integrated fully into the course and integrated in ways that students and instructors perceive as useful. That integration should not, by the same token, attempt to supplant modes of instruction that are already useful and effective.

- Students need to be made accountable for their participation in ALN. Mere instructor encouragement and good will are generally not enough to overcome the initial inertia most students experience when they take on what appears to be an extra burden.

- We need to be sure that networked classes make use of the best and most current knowledge of writing across the curriculum pedagogy and of the knowledge we have gained about the use of computers and writing in theory and practice.

Finally, we think it important to note that these recommendations have grown out of our own experiences at a large research university with plentiful computer resources but also with difficult logistics to overcome in providing computer training for students and faculty members. At other smaller campuses, the problems encountered in instituting online teaching may be fewer—or greater. At the very least, they will be different. But we are heartened by our experiences with WAC and learning networks over the past few years and will continue to refine our approaches for the online component of the Writers' Workshop (e.g., Harris and Pemberton 1995). Indeed, we believe that the bringing together of WAC and ALN, in the hands of good teachers and with an adequate technological infrastructure in place, can contribute to an improved culture of teaching on college campuses. If we use electronic contexts wisely—if we recognize that they are not likely to reduce the amount of work or teaching on the part of instructors but that they can improve the quantity and perhaps quality of students and instructors' interactions—we may well be able to use learning networks to extend and improve upon what more than two decades of WAC has taught us.

Notes

1. Frank Mayadas of the Sloan Foundation coined the term Asynchronous Learning Networks (ALN) to denote educational contexts in which learning is made possible through current, affordable technology. According to Mayadas,

> Remote resources in this context can mean other people: students learn from their peers and also from experts such as tutors or faculty. Remote resources can also include more static resources such as library or software-generated simulations, access to laboratories at a distance or access to the work product of several remote collaborators, such as a jointly-created database, or a report. Asynchronous means that access to any remote resource is at the student's convenience, "on demand," so to speak. Asynchronous access is made possible mainly by advances in computer and communications technologies. A student, for example, can contact a colleague or a teacher through e-mail, or engage in discussion with a group through a conferencing system or bulletin board; he/she may participate interactively in a team project with other students that requires problem analysis, discussion, spreadsheet analysis or report-preparation through a modern commercial groupware package. See http://www.sloan.org/education/aln.new.html.

2. Students' names used throughout the chapter are pseudonyms.

Resources

The following URLs may be consulted in conjunction with this chapter:

ALN: http://w3.scale.uiuc.edu/scale/

Center for Writing Studies: http://www.english.uiuc.edu/cws/index.html

Writers' Workshop: http://www.english.uiuc.edu/cws/wworkshop/writer.html

The following listservs may also be consulted:

WAC-L: To join the writing-across-the-curriculum list, send the following one-line message to listserv@postoffice.cso.uiuc.edu: subscribe WAC-L firstname lastname

CCAC-L: To join the computer-supported communication-across-the- curriculum list, send the following one-line message to listserv@VCCSCENT.bitnet: subscribe CCAC-L firstname lastname

Hardware and Software:

Students accessed Macintoshes and IBMs at the University of Illinois's Computing and Communications Services Office sites. PacerForum works primarily with Macintoshes, but a Windows version of the program is currently being beta-tested. FirstClass works on both Macintosh and Windows platforms.

FirstClass. SoftArc Incorporated, 1036 Union Road #325, West Seneca, NY 14224; http://www.softarc.com

PacerForum. AGE Logic, 12651 High Bluff Drive, San Diego, CA 92130.

Works Cited

Blumenstyk, Goldie. 1996. "Western States Continue to Plan 'Virtual' College." *Chronicle of Higher Education* (14 June): A30–31.

Eldred, Janet. 1991. "Pedagogy in the Computer-Networked Classroom." *Computers and Composition* 8: 47–61.

Freire, Paulo. 1986. *Pedagogy of the Oppressed.* Translated by Myra Bergman Ramos. New York: Continuum.

Fulwiler, Toby. 1986. "The Argument for Writing Across the Curriculum." In *Writing Across the Disciplines: Research Into Practice,* edited by Art Young and Toby Fulwiler, 21–32. Upper Montclair, NJ: Boynton/Cook.

Harris, Muriel, and Michael Pemberton. 1995. "Online Writing Labs (OWLS): A Taxonomy of Options and Issues." *Computers and Composition.* 12.2: 145–60.

Hawisher, Gail E., and Cynthia L. Selfe. 1991. "The Rhetoric of Technology and the Electronic Writing Class." *College Composition and Communication* 42(February): 55–65.

Hawisher, Gail E., and Cynthia L. Selfe. 1992. "Voices in College Classrooms: The Dynamics of Electronic Discussion." The Quarterly. 143.3 (Summer): 24–28, 32.

Hawisher, Gail E., Paul J. LeBlanc, Charles Moran, and Cynthia L. Selfe. 1996. *Computers and the Teaching of Writing in American Higher Education, 1979–1994: A History.* Norwood: Ablex.

Honan, William H. 1995. "Professors Battling Television Technology." *New York Times* (April 4): Sec. A, 8.

Mayadas, Frank. 1995. "Sloan Center for Asynchronous Learning Environments." http://w3.scale.uiuc.edu/scale/.

Prior, Paul, Gail E. Hawisher, Sibylle Gruber, and Nicole MacLaughlin. Forthcoming. "Research and WAC Evaluation: An In-Progress Reflection." In *WAC and Program Assessment: Diverse Methods of Evaluating Writing Across the Curriculum Programs,* edited by Kathleen Yancey and Brian Huot. Norwood, NJ: Ablex.

Russell, David. 1991. *Writing in the Academic Disciplines, 1870–1990: A Curricular History.* Carbondale: Southern Illinois University Press.

Young, Art, and Toby Fulwiler, eds. 1986. *Writing Across the Disciplines: Research Into Practice.* Upper Montclair, NJ: Boynton/Cook.

3 Building a Writing-Intensive Multimedia Curriculum

Mary E. Hocks
Spelman College

Daniele Bascelli
Spelman College

The Mellon Multimedia Curriculum Development Project

Spelman College's Writing Program is currently engaged in a three-year curriculum development project on teaching communicative skills with technology. In January of 1996, Spelman, a historically black college for women, received a generous Mellon Foundation Grant of $400,000 to develop fifteen new courses in three phases. The grant, entitled Using Technology to Teach Writing and Communication Across the Curriculum, targets faculty who teach writing-intensive courses in the arts, humanities, and social sciences. This project uses writing-across-the-curriculum (WAC) collaborative efforts as a basis for creating communication-intensive courses taught in the computer classroom. The curriculum development efforts are housed in the Writing Center and have the support of the Writing Program director, assistant director, multimedia project coordinator, and five student assistants.[1] We focus on intensive faculty training with multimedia software and hardware, including Web authoring software, with the end goal of delivering the newly acquired expertise to students in a particular course. This focus on multimedia and Web authoring was a result of a very simple observation. In the past Spelman's communication efforts in WAC courses were largely text based. However, professional writing in most fields has become a combination of image and word, and publishing, increasingly, includes online delivery of the final product on CD or over the World Wide Web (Lanham 1993). Because multimedia combines verbal, visual, and auditory forms of communication, these projects teach complex writing and planning skills while reinforcing skills of visual literacy. Traditional disciplines have expanded their scholarly interests and delivery mechanisms to include many new media forms: still images, sound, video, and animation to name a few. As a result we built into the grant support for extensive training for five faculty members each year, release time for course development, and five multimedia development workstations. Although we are still in the beginning stages, we believe our project is already helping teachers help students perform meaningful communicative, writing, and design work in the multimedia computer classroom.

This program builds directly upon our Comprehensive Writing Program (CWP), which has enjoyed great success at Spelman since 1979.[2] A key part of our program is working regularly with faculty to develop writing intensive courses in all major departments. The electronic writing classroom, supported by the Writing Center and our campus computing department, has traditionally been a resource for some English and writing-intensive courses on campus. The Mellon Grant is now allowing us to bring more of those courses into the computer classroom in sophisticated ways. Faculty bring us their expertise in what is already an innovative and diverse liberal arts curriculum. We begin with a traditional syllabus from the disciplines, but in the course revision, the instructor collaborates with the CWP staff to develop writing-to-learn assignments and projects that incorporate electronic communication and multimedia technology. Our first multimedia courses include Latin American Art; Oral Narratives; and Race, Class, and Gender in Brazil. Each instructor begins the project with a plan to integrate frequent writing and electronic communication, as well as educational multimedia and Web-based academic research, into their courses. These faculty are, in most cases, novices with both the new writing technologies and the multimedia technologies, though most have some experience with browsers for the World Wide Web. We thus face dual challenges: the normal challenges involved in WAC, which require ongoing training, consultation and course revision within multiple learning contexts, and the added challenge of mastering new technology and communicative learning activities made possible by the computer classroom. Not surprisingly, our colleagues are meeting these challenges with enthusiasm and success as they teach their courses in what is a completely new learning environment. As Arturo Lindsay remarks about his Latin American Art course: "This has been the most challenging and the most rewarding teaching experience I've had in a long time. I can see the potential of continuing to teach in this classroom. I know I'm getting much better work out of my students." Their immersion in new communications technologies and new media helps teachers imagine better ways to foster collaborative learning and ongoing electronic writing and communication activities in their courses.

At the same time, we recognized early on the difficulty and discomfort of delivering courses in a high-tech classroom for the first time. Few of our faculty had experience with the Macintosh operating system, or with protocols for teaching in a networked computer classroom. The training itself took much longer than we expected: we had to offer additional workshops and one-to-one instruction to help faculty master very complex software programs. While the grant described a one-year cycle for course development, in reality faculty members needed up to twice as long to develop and deliver their multimedia course. We also found that the teachers required a great deal of support while teaching their classes. In effect, each course required co-teaching, constant technical support, and an extensive time commitment from the CWP staff. The teachers themselves had to commit much more time and effort than they anticipated, and, sometimes, this commitment was impossible to combine with a three-course teaching load and other college demands. Students also expressed a need for more documentation, examples, and demonstration of computer techniques and software. These problems forced us to reevaluate our faculty training, redesign our support procedures for these classes, and develop more materials for the students.

In the first phase of the Mellon Project we had to consider the following challenges:

1. How do we effectively engage veteran teachers in pedagogies for an electronic writing classroom?
2. What faculty training paradigm works best?
3. How does a teacher best incorporate electronic communications into writing intensive classes?
4. Which classroom techniques and assignments work best for the students?

Engaging the Faculty

The grant itself offers many incentives to engage faculty in intensive technical training and course revision. We provide stipends for summer workshops, release time from teaching one course, and funds for educational multimedia titles suitable to the course being offered. The grant provides faculty travel money to attend an educational technology seminar or conference, or to conduct a research trip related to the course. Faculty use a high-end multimedia development computer and peripherals through the term of their "mini-grant," and have access to our other Writing Center and Computer Classroom resources, such as a file server and Web server.[3] Most important, the staff, faculty, consultants, and student assistants associated with the grant are all available for ongoing support and training. This support infrastructure was anticipated in advance and put into place by the Writing Center the year before the Mellon project began. Our Office of Computing and Information Technology (CIT) provided the groundwork, the ongoing technical support, and the funding for student assistants in the Writing Center's computer facilities. In collaboration with CIT, we are building a network of on-campus support personnel that includes academic computing staff, students, and veterans of our project.

Before beginning the faculty training, we needed to raise the awareness of the potentials for teaching which the networked multimedia computer classroom has made available. The first step was to hold seminars and workshops where educators who have already successfully used computers in teaching could share their insights and techniques with a wide and self-selected audience of Spelman faculty. We found that the strongest response came from faculty already interested in WAC and other Writing Program initiatives. Faculty who had already explored cross-disciplinary writing shared our idea that using computers for communications-intensive courses was a logical enhancement of WAC techniques. In many ways, this self-selection of project candidates facilitated the first phase of the project since we shared learning experiences in the past and had common points of reference in the WAC workshops.

The next important step was to solicit from faculty their ideas of how best to incorporate electronic writing into their traditional course curriculum. This was, in fact, a major part of the selection criteria for the first group of faculty brought into the project. The concept was that faculty should posit ways in which the use of the networked multimedia computer classroom could ideally function as a teaching and learning enhancement vehicle for their respective courses. The faculty submitted course proposals that included specific strategies for increasing students' technological savvy and communication skills while interacting with a number of computer resources for research, writing, oral and electronic communications, and professional development. The successful proposals included development plans in which students worked toward a final project which incorporated specific electronic and multimedia communications activities that resulted in a tangible, educational project. From the various submissions, the Writing Program Committee selected the most promising course ideas based on the given criteria.[4] These proposals were then revised into syllabi during the training and helped us to select workshop topics and the consultants we would hire to deliver some of the seminars.[5] Successful proposals were chosen from the arts, humanities, and social sciences.

Thus, at this juncture we were able to begin to resolve what directions our training should take and how our faculty were going to use the available resources. Significantly, our early interaction with faculty dealt more with their concerns about integrating computer classroom teaching with their traditional curriculum into a pedagogically effective whole than it did with issues of technical skill. This meant that we attempted to weight the training workshops in favor of the development of teaching modalities best suited to the computer classroom rather than specific computer skills. Instead of setting off into totally new pedagogical models, we found that our faculty conceived of the actual classroom use of electronic communications along the lines of familiar writing-intensive paradigms. Some recurring motifs included the use of microthemes to generate longer presentations, sequencing of assignments toward a long research project, and creating assignments that foster discipline-specific research skills.

These conceptions about how to best integrate the use of new technology and traditional classroom techniques allowed us the freedom to select specific points during each course in which to teach the necessary software and hardware skills to the students. We (the CWP staff and faculty, and student peer assistants) delivered short lessons in technology with the course professor and allowed for immediate hands-on practice by students. We usually took a different student through each procedure while explaining the techniques and allowed the others to watch that student's steps on an overhead projector. Staff and student assistants provided further support during open lab hours so that all students could get substantial practice in the new computer skills. These student assistants were trained by our staff in the same techniques, and with the same programs being taught to the faculty. Some students developed technical proficiency more quickly and helped others with class projects.

Faculty Workshop Paradigms

Our workshop paradigm was selected from two possible models. The first model is based directly on professional multimedia and Internet courses offered by the Georgia Institute of Technology's School of Literature, Communication and Culture and by its Center for NewMedia Education.[6] Their model includes an intensive and condensed project-oriented training program given in multiple-day or quarter-long courses. Its primary goal is to instruct professionals in the use of specific software and hardware, as well as theory and techniques for graphic and multimedia design.[7] The Multimedia Production Workshop offered by the Center then brings all these skills together in the form of a coherent project.[8]

The other model is based on spaced and incremental workshops which can be delivered over the entire school year before and while teachers are actually offering their new courses. This model allows for a flexible integration of classroom experience with the technology skills being learned, and allows for a more gradual process of learning the technology. Because skills are introduced gradually, students and the teacher can provide feedback while the classroom's technology lessons are implemented. This interactive process allows for a more pedagogically aware workshop environment than does the former model. We chose this latter model during the first phase of our project in large part because of the intrusion of the Atlanta Olympics on our summer schedule, but specifically because we thought it meshed better with the skills of the particular faculty members and gave them a longer period of time to collaborate with us on pedagogical modalities suited to the networked multimedia computer classroom. We had to plan six months in advance to design and deliver this extended series of workshops.

We held workshops for faculty development over the entire academic year, usually meeting every two weeks. We hoped that this would fit best into busy faculty schedules and yet provide a stable platform for faculty to acquire an in-depth knowledge of the new technology. This decision allowed us the freedom to schedule workshops in the semester before and during the teaching of the computer classroom courses. It also facilitated our ability to intervene in the individual classes at select moments and assist the faculty with technical issues in scanning, presentation software, Web page design, and so on.

For many workshops, specifically for the multimedia tools workshops, we hired outside consultants as expert seminar leaders. For our consultants, we collaborated directly with Georgia Tech's Information, Design and Technology Program by identifying their MA students with technical expertise and offering them a valuable teaching experience. We also hired several course teachers from their NewMedia Education program to consult on our project, to deliver work-shops, and to demonstrate their own multimedia applications. These consult-ants led many of the hands-on workshop sessions while we aided in the delivery and gave individual instruction during workshop sessions. Workshops gave fac-ulty an overview of multimedia development and then offered hands-on prac-tice with software tools and peripherals. Workshop topics were broken down into specific process or tools segments, and we gave two workshops on each topic. Each workshop lasted no more than three hours and was offered when all the selected faculty could attend. The workshops always emphasized how the technology could be used in specific courses for teaching and for student par-ticipation in communicative processes. Our workshop topics included the fol-lowing:

> Protocols for file-sharing and completing assignments in the networked computer classroom
>
> Introduction to multimedia hardware and software, emphasizing educa-tional applications
>
> How to conduct Web research and to use the Georgia On-line Library Learning tools
>
> Using multimedia software to enhance oral presentations
>
> Capturing and working with digital image resources
>
> Capturing and working with digital audio resources
>
> Introduction to digital video editing
>
> Web design tools and principles

These workshops added a considerable workload to the project faculty. How-ever, we were pleased with the skills the teachers acquired and could pass on to their students. The workshops were small, with no more than six faculty learners who worked with an expert leader and two floating assistants, usually ourselves and a student assistant who had at least intermediate knowledge of the software and peripheral devices. The floaters could circulate around the room and intervene whenever a learner became stalled, could encourage individual exploration, or could relate how certain multimedia or communications software might be used in specific classroom situations. The small group dynamics made possible by this concentration of learners and leaders contributed greatly to a successful workshop.

The normal introductory workshop in each topic area consisted of an expert presentation on the topic, followed by hands-on exercises. The subsequent workshop was entirely hands-on and encouraged individual exploration and discussions about potential pedagogical uses for the technology. The project faculty always inquired as to the best classroom communications or research uses for each topic, so we and our consultants presented them with research and demonstrations of pedagogical uses for each topic. We often collaborated about the pedagogical issues for each course or discipline during these workshops and focused on follow-up that would allow students to complete a particular assignment using the software tool. For example, our digital imaging workshops allowed Arturo Lindsay to design a class assignment in which his students selected works to support their interpretive thesis about particular Latino/Latina artists. They then scanned in artwork, used graphic software to enhance or select significant detail, and finally incorporated their work into a slide presentation. Rarely was a workshop purely a technical learning exercise.

Unfortunately, scheduling workshops that all the project faculty could attend was sometimes impossible during the school year. Often project faculty had to be absent for conferences, colloquia, personal emergencies, and so on. Therefore, some people were occasionally left behind and had to meet with us individually to catch up with the rest of the group. Fortunately, we had staff available for direct support of the project faculty. In these instances, individual mentoring became essential to achieve a common skill level while addressing different learning curves. These sessions ended up being effective for implementing computer communications pedagogy into the classroom because issues of specific course content could be examined in detail. Since we had often observed the classes in progress, team taught certain electronic communications skills with the course professors, and provided support to students outside of class, we became collaborators on course design. As we got to know the course content and teaching styles of the faculty, we were able to suggest ways to combine course content with new technology. This process also allowed for very productive interactions on classroom activities between faculty and students.

We found that mentoring allowed the advantages of being direct and pointed toward issues of immediate curricular concern. It was effective for solving individual teachers' needs and suiting their styles, and could be applied immediately and enthusiastically with strong and favorable student reactions. Unfortunately, because we found solutions for each teacher's needs on a one-to-one basis, these ideas were not always effectively communicated to other teachers with similar problems. As we queried the entire group, we found that they needed a better forum for sharing successful strategies. We anticipate including a regular face-to-face forum to discuss ongoing classroom issues. One person suggested that some of the workshops given during the semester become even more pedagogically oriented and less technically oriented than now. Another, complementary, suggestion would allow for an electronic discussion space to explore classroom issues before and as they arise in teaching situations.

In retrospect, we have concluded that in our second phase, the next group of faculty should have both workshop paradigms in order to more completely develop their skills. The intensive project-oriented model is best for imparting and practicing computer skills, while the incremental workshops and mentoring are best for developing and refining computer classroom teaching modalities. The project-oriented model allows intensive hands-on experience with the end project as motivation for using the various software; it is best delivered during summer training sessions and can draw upon the skills of outside experts to build an understanding of what can be done in a multimedia environment. Subsequent workshops during the semester can be directed more towards implementation, i.e., how to teach using computer classroom techniques and how to teach students to use multimedia authoring in their own projects. Moreover, faculty can incorporate the techniques learned during actual in-class exercises and ideas generated during mentoring sessions, thereby overcoming the unevenness of the learning process.

Incorporating Electronic Communications into the Classroom

The courses that feature multimedia for our Mellon grant are typically writing- and research-intensive junior and senior level courses. They incorporate, for the first time, complete immersion into the networked computer environment of all assignments and student work, with an emphasis on Web research. These courses all center on the electronic teaching environment of our computer writing classroom. Starting from the traditional lecture-discussion teaching modes, we encourage interactive and collaborative pedagogies as a basis for all classroom activity. Faculty transpose traditional lecture notes and discussion materials into interactive activities or graphical multimedia presentations that can serve as models for their students' presentations. We also train teachers to use synchronous communication programs, electronic conferencing, and networked file-sharing to form the basis of their assignments, collaborations, and written exchanges between students.

Perhaps the most elementary problem when incorporating inherently inter-active technology into the classroom is to overcome the instinct veteran faculty have to lecture. The layout of our classroom helps to subdue this instinct be-cause it is physically de-centered. Our networked classroom consists of seven carrels each with three computer stations that face into each other. We limit the course size to twenty-one students, one per workstation, but many upper level classes are smaller. There is a "teacher's" station at one end of the room, but it has been rarely used during teaching sessions. Projection is usually done from a computer in the center of the room. All our teachers seem to be drawn into closer proximity with the students by this classroom design, and usually take a seat at one of the carrels. There is no obvious focal point in our classroom, except when the portable projector shines images or lessons onto a portable screen, so the teacher tends to become a participant rather than a dominant figure on a podium. The de-centered classroom forced our instructors to change their classroom delivery and personae. While several teachers embraced this new style, others resisted the de-centering of their role as instructor.

The teachers all responded to this classroom with different modifications of their styles of teaching. Rick Langhorst, teaching Spanish Composition 307, found that he tended to circulate more and that students tended to initiate Span-ish conversations with each other and engage in spontaneous collaboration dur-ing writing exercises. Steven Knadler, a veteran in the computer classroom who teaches several English composition courses, used synchronous collaboration software to generate oral and electronic discussions on network-delivered exer-cises. Some faculty, notably Dalila DeSousa, teaching Senior Seminar in His-tory for the first time in a computer classroom, and Geneva Baxter, who is a veteran computer classroom English composition instructor, decided to split their class time between the traditional lecture/discussion mode in a "standard" classroom and the computer classroom. They used the computers for specific in-class activities such as Web research, synchronous conferencing, and multi-media presentations.

The art history course taught by Arturo Lindsay was so well suited to the visual presentation capabilities of the computer classroom that it simply high-lighted the interactive possibilities of a lecture-discussion course. Many classes centered around images and slide shows on a large screen or from shared files on students' computer desktops. Arturo used the network to set up an electronic bulletin board where he posted his lecture notes, critical essays, and informa-tion of interest such as art show notices. Arturo's students also posted their questions and observations on this bulletin board. During class discussions and in-class writing assignments, the class often connected to the bulletin board to compare notes, to develop further ideas, or to begin inventing their own analy-ses of course topics. The success of this bulletin board has encouraged Arturo to make it a hypertext database that incorporates an index and clickable hotlinks to additional references.

One important pedagogical adjustment was universal to the computer classroom courses, however, and that was the need to deliver discrete instructional modules on the use of computer tools and techniques during class time. These are given as short, partial class presentations that usually combine a course assignment with a new software tool. While different faculty chose to focus on different electronic vehicles for the major student projects, there was a shared need to instruct students in basics such as the networked computer classroom protocols, cross-platform compatibility issues, digital capture of images and sound, and Web Page authoring programs. For these skills we developed an in-class workshop model very similar to the tool-specific incremental faculty workshops. Initially, teachers scheduled very little class time for technical instruction. This approach to integrating computer lessons into the course content inspired the teachers to allot more time to instruct students on multimedia and communications in the computer classroom.

We always try to incorporate the specific computer tools or skills we are teaching into an ongoing class assignment. For instance, an early Web research session will have the students search for specific course-related topics. We provide students with a set of Web bookmarks and some URLs for them to begin their research. From there they are encouraged to follow hyperlinks to other sites and to save their own bookmarks to a network file for other students to look at later. They are later shown how to save images, text, and sound so that they can begin to develop Web pages and/or multimedia projects of their own. They are also asked to define technical terms which are common to the software they are using, thus gaining confidence in their competence in a world of abstruse computer jargon and advanced technology. All of these early skills contribute to multimedia projects and Web sites that are completed later in the semester.

The popularity and effectiveness of their students' computer learning motivated the teachers as well to become more independent in teaching the technology because it related directly to class assignments and learning. During the first class meetings, computer classroom teachers did little or none of the technical teaching. As the semester wore on, they no longer saw computer pedagogy as something that belonged to the "expert" staff, but as a set of skills that they themselves increasingly possessed. They occasionally gave technical instruction and developed a considerable amount of autonomy in the computer classroom. Teachers mastered certain routine collaborative writing activities over the electronic network. The more complex goals of multimedia development, however, still relied upon our expert intervention. We expected the teachers to develop these skills much earlier in the semester, and found that they persisted in needing significant support both in and out of the classroom.

To address these needs, we often incorporated the same samples and documentation in the faculty training and classroom teaching environments. This crossover gambit made faculty familiar and comfortable with the tools and teaching techniques. Because they had been through the same training, they could anticipate their students' interests and difficulties. Teachers also found that they could use their own class time to explore and develop their skills. In general, we believe short, frequent instruction facilitated the incremental learning of computer tools and techniques because we could focus on what worked well and what could be improved. Instead of having details buried in the expanse of a long lecture, the details became one subject of the class itself—problems to be discussed and resolved, with the solutions incorporated into future lessons.

As students participated in these sessions, they looked forward to learning more about the world of computing itself and were proud to author their own multimedia projects. Since there was no delay between the acquisition of software tools and the production of student work, they got to work immediately and enthusiastically. Students rarely missed sessions they knew were going to include a computer lesson, perhaps because they quickly learned the difficulty of catching up. We also believe that the high attendance rates occurred because students enjoyed these sessions and felt increased confidence in their expertise. Students not only had the opportunity to engage in electronic collaboration with the newest technologies, but, for the first time at Spelman, they became involved in the development of multimedia and Web resources that reflect their ideas and research in a particular area of study. It fostered a sense of themselves as intellectuals and as professional communicators who are looking toward the future, whatever their career goals may be.[9]

Most students have also tended to become less intimidated by the more daunting technical aspects of multimedia and electronic communications as their familiarity increased. The collaborative work and synchronous communications software, as well as their ability to record images and sound of their own choosing, were immediately and overwhelmingly popular with students. They loved the ability to instantly communicate with each other, not only in electronically mediated words, but over distances and with pictures and sounds they can edit and manipulate. Students from "regular classes" often come in with a computer classroom student to learn how to use the tools our students have begun to master. "Our" students have become electronic communications mentors across the campus.

Multimedia Course Projects

Each course was designed to feature a culminating multimedia project that would allow students to practice and apply the technical skills developed over the semester. These multimedia projects were developed over the semester as specific writing assignments that were then translated into multimedia projects. For example, in the Spanish Composition course, students explored research questions throughout the semester on six Spanish-speaking women artists: Isabel

Allende, Rigoberta Menchu, Gabriela Mistral, Nancy Morejon, Celia Cruz, and Eva Peron. Early in the semester the students wrote numerous microthemes in Spanish based upon research questions that they were then expected to explore via the Web.[10] Conducting primary research using a World Wide Web browser led them to numerous university and library sources, including Spanish-language Web sites.[11] This experiment gave students essential practice and skills in electronic academic research, while also exposing them to numerous possibilities for Web site design and organization. Finally, they broke into groups in the final third of the semester and combined their research to create Web pages on each woman artist. Students developed these multimedia projects within the specific learning and communicative context of advanced Spanish composition.

Multimedia presentations can also be a continual part of the class assignments, but take different formats at different stages, building into a final project. In the Latin American Art History course, students used multimedia presentation tools, scanners, and slide shows on an overhead LCD projector to give numerous talks to the class about their ongoing research on one particular artist. They began with a slide show talk about a particular country using maps and demographic material found on the Web and CD-ROM resources. The goal of this assignment was to show the diversity of Latin American and Latino/Latina cultures. Students then created interactive slide presentations that presented a thesis for research, an outline of the argument, and several key works by the artist. This kind of exploratory multimedia presentation, where the audience views a kind of performance, can be described as a communicative event between a writer and an audience that is specifically designed to provoke dialogue and collaboration (Balsamo and Hocks).[12] During these performances, the entire class evaluated the research plan in context of the assignment, analyzed the images on screen, and collaborated on research resources during these presentations. These students combined their presentations with text into a long multimedia research essay that included images, text, slides, and a Web site on Latin American Art.[13]

We are currently in the first stage of implementing students' projects in these new courses, in which students are authoring multimedia presentations for the classroom and the World Wide Web. In the next stage, students will be working in small groups to create interactive video and Web-based projects. Students are now beginning course projects in which they create short videos with sound using sophisticated tools for digital video and sound editing. These projects are designed either as stand-alone interactive presentations or interactive Web sites. We teach the teachers and the students writing and design processes that involve intensive collaboration in the group projects. Modeling processes that are widely used in multimedia design companies, students assume the roles of project director, navigation expert, graphics expert, and content expert. The project director runs the initial planning meetings, fields ideas and obtains a consensus about what project to undertake. The group then co-authors a project description and presents it to the instructor for commentary. The navigation person leads the group in storyboard development, in which they draw each screen on paper and describe what elements will be included. These storyboards are submitted to the instructor for feedback and approval. The group then begins to develop a prototype of the project using a multimedia authoring tool. The content person conducts research and writes scripts, while the graphics person develops media and collects visual elements. The project director works on editing the video and sound resources while the navigation person creates the screen's interactive elements (links or buttons) in the design software tool. By the end, of course, different group members all help one another to complete this mini version. The assignment ends with an oral presentation of the finished project to the class and a critique of each other's projects.

Because of increasing interest and publicity among the students, many projects using this model are being planned outside of the classroom as well. One group of students from the Latin American Art course will edit interviews of local and visiting artists. Another group of students, under the mentorship of faculty participant Kimberly-Wallace Sanders in Women's Studies, plans to research our Spelman archives and interview Spelman alumnae. Our Bambara Writers group plans to publish the student-edited and authored Women's Center Newsletter on a Web site.[14] Another group of seniors plans to edit and publish a student journal of research essays in math and science. With these efforts, our Web site will move beyond the courses to showcase student work broadly and bring more opportunity for dialogue and exchange between Spelman and other campuses.

Recommendations

Based on the experiences of our first year to develop an interdisciplinary curriculum for electronic communications, we can recommend paths to follow and pitfalls to avoid.

The most important recommendation we can offer is to organize your effort well in advance. A year of planning is a good yardstick, especially if you need to procure hardware and software to get your computer classroom into operation. The budget needs to be ample and carefully managed to account for equipment, software licenses, staff salaries, consultant fees, training materials, and repairs. Housing the curriculum project in an established academic center or department offers additional stability and support for your efforts. Building upon other faculty development programs works very well. Workshops need to be planned well in advance and specific goals set for each workshop series. Remember that knowledge of the tools is wasted without an equal knowledge of the pedagogical modalities which this technology makes possible.

To be successful, innovative computer communications course development should also have a well-publicized outreach program across the campus. Advertise technology and pedagogical seminars across the campus to get as much input as you can before and during your development initiatives. By raising the profile of your initiative, you will be able to get wider support than you expect. These seminars also provide a good showcase for evaluating the potential long-term consultants you may be considering for your program of faculty development workshops. In one case, we brought in a potential consultant, Adam Arrowood from the Georgia Tech Office of Information Technology, and had him deliver a seminar to all interested faculty on Web page design. His seminar gave examples and explanations of how to use Web pages in conjunction with a convening class and looked forward to the technical innovations that would make the Internet an ever more powerful and diverse medium of communications. Themes from his seminar figured prominently in course proposals we received later, and therefore also in our workshop planning and material. Several faculty members asked if he could be available as a consultant in the future. We immediately recognized that he was to be a valuable long-term consultant, and have subsequently received much support and training from him and contacts to other good consultants. This example shows us that the strengths of our experts will play a large role in the total worth of our curriculum development project.

Besides careful selection of your consultants, you need to arrange for direct support on campus. Keep in mind, when organizing a curriculum and skills development program, that you cannot leave the equipment to take care of itself. It is imperative that the physical infrastructure be fully operative and tested before you start the formal project. It often takes many months to get a networked multimedia classroom up and running, so plan for an extended break-in time. Buy all of the software and peripherals in advance so that you won't have to learn as you go. Most of all, have some alternate plans to fall back on should key technology not work as you expect.

All of this takes a robust budget to initiate and creative planning to accomplish. Identify an appropriate educational technology grant to jump-start your program and provide seed money for future development. Your basic start-up requirements include: project leadership and staff, up-to-date equipment, consultants, and a great deal of ongoing technical support. It is best to have somebody on campus who can be dedicated to supporting the technical needs of your project quickly and reliably. If possible, this support should come under the direct supervision of your group.

Once the grant period ends, you will have to creatively restructure your program. You will need to establish, with the campus administration, an ample operating budget for repairs, supplies, and educational resources. Collaborative efforts with campus computing, established writing or technology centers, and key departments will help build a sustainable project and permanent budget. To maintain an ongoing, trained staff you can set up formal internships for undergraduate and graduate students, offer academic credit for classroom assistants, and set up exchanges with other schools that have complementary resources. Veterans of the original project can provide expertise and advice to future faculty and students.

A final recommendation is to avoid inflated expectations, especially early in your program. It takes time to get the physical infrastructure to work well and it takes time to work out the training and pedagogical paradigms that will work best in your particular circumstances. We highly recommend a phased program such as ours because it gives you room to grow, evaluate, and improve. A phased-in implementation of your program, lasting over a period of years, makes it easier to anticipate and implement changes to your original proposals. The preliminary phase should consist of campus outreach and profile building for your program while you recruit faculty, select consultant experts, and build up your infrastructure. Begin your project as an exploration into the uses of multiple educational and communications media while you and your faculty develop the pedagogical modalities best suited to this environment. Accept that in the first phase you are going to make mistakes. Sometimes faculty will feel overwhelmed by the technology and the program staff will need to take a greater mentoring role than expected, even in the course delivery. Sometimes an entire class will not develop multimedia projects as sophisticated or as complete as expected. For those directing the project, these are signposts which indicate to you ways in which you can refine your training and redefine your goals throughout the project. It is important that such events are not perceived as failures, but valuable learning experiences for students and faculty alike.

Notes

1. For an example of electronic communications activities that build upon a WAC program and are housed in the Writing Center, see Palmquist et al. 1995.

2. See Royster 1992 for a description of the history and success of Spelman's Comprehensive Writing Program.

3. HARDWARE: The faculty workstations consisted of five Apple Macintosh 8500/ 120 computers with 60 megs of RAM and Applevision 1710 AV monitors. Five Zip drives are used for portable storage. The classroom computers are twenty-two Macintosh Performa 6214 PCs with 24 megs of RAM each. Everything is connected via a 10 base T Ethernet network with a Macintosh Server 8150/110 with 80 megs of RAM and a 4 gig external hard drive. We have a separate Macintosh 8150/110 Web Server. Peripheral equipment includes two Apple Color OneScanners, a Marantz PMD 222 cassette recorder for professional sound capture, and a QuickCam digital camera. We have an Apple Color LaserWriter 12/600 PS and three Apple LaserWriter 16/600 PS printers. A 8500/120 computer is used as our digital video capture station and has an APS 4 gig

Raid array connected by a Qlogic fast and wide scsi card for fast playthrough. The VHS video editor is a Panasonic Ag-1980. An Epson ELP 3000 portable projector is used for instruction and multimedia presentations.

SOFTWARE: The most widely used software included Claris Works 4.0, Microsoft Office 4.2a (Word 6, Excel 5, and PowerPoint), Adobe Photoshop 3.0.5, Adobe Pagemaker 6.0, Adobe Premiere 4.0.1, Adobe Illustrator 6.0, Adobe PageMill 2.0, Macromedia Freehand 5.5, Macromedia SoundEdit 16, Daedalus 1.3.6, and Aspects 1.5.2.

4. This ongoing advisory committee acts as an interdisciplinary body that steers and advises the Writing Program. It includes Jann Primus, Biology; Fred Bowers, Mathematics; Freddye Hill, Academic Dean; Rick Langhorst, Foreign Languages; Arturo Lindsay, Art; Madeline Picciotto, English; Dalila DeSousa Sheppard, History; Bruce Wade, Sociology; Newtona Johnson, Writing Center; and Mary Hocks, English.

5. All revised multimedia course syllabi are available on our Web site: http://www.wcenter.spelman.edu.

6. See the Web site for the School of Literature, Communication and Culture: http://www.lcc.gatech.edu.

7. For more information on the theory and practice of graphic and multimedia design, see Kojima 1996; Kristof and Satran 1995; Lopuck 1996; Miller and Zaucha 1995; Mok 1996; Nielsen 1995; Siegel 1996; Weinman 1996; and Weinman 1997. For an excellent bibliography, see Terry Harpold's "Resources for Multimedia Designers" Web site at http://www.lcc.gatech.edu/faculty/harpold/resources/mm.html.

8. See the Web site for the Center for NewMedia Education: http://www.newmedia-coned.gatech.edu.

9. We have systematic evaluations and case studies of our courses planned to test these assumptions.

10. We teach the use of microthemes (short, highly focused essays that reinforce several cognitive strategies) and sequenced assignments in our Faculty Seminars. See Bean et al. 1982 for the classic model of microthemes.

11. Web sites for research included the following: Directorio Global Net en Espanol <http://www.dirglobal.net/>; Latin American and Iberian Studies <http://www.library.ucbs.edu/subj/lais.html>; Latin American Network Information Center <http://lanic.utexas.edu/>; Web Museum of Latin America <http://museos.web.com.mx/>; Latin American Library <http://www.tulane.edu/~latinlib/lalhome.html>; World Wide Art Resources <http://wwar.world-arts-resources.com/index.html>.

12. See also Joyce's description (1988) of "exploratory hypertexts" as a performance to an audience.

13. The class Web sites and selected student projects, with their permission, can be viewed on our Writing Center Web site throughout our project. Our address is http://www.wcenter.spelman.edu/.

14. The Bambara Writers Group is a student group for aspiring writer/scholars that sponsors eminent visiting writers, usually women of African descent.

Works Cited

Balsamo, Anne, and Mary E. Hocks. Forthcoming. "Designing Feminist Multimedia." In *Re-Visioning Technology and Design: Feminist Perspectives,* edited by Joan Rothchild. New York: Bay Press.

Bean, John C., Dean Drenk, and F. D. Lee. 1982. "Microtheme Strategies for Developing Cognitive Skills." In *Teaching Writing in All Disciplines,* edited by C. Williams Griffin, 18–27. Washington: Jossey-Bass.

Joyce, Michael. 1988. "Siren Shapes: Exploratory and Constructive Hypertexts." *Academic Computing* (November), 10–42.

Kojima, Hisaka. 1996. *Digital Image Creation.* Berkeley, CA: Peachpit Press.

Kristof, Ray, and Amy Satran. 1995. *Interactivity by Design: Creating and Communicating with New Media.* Mountain View, CA: Adobe Press.

Lopuck, Lisa. 1996. *Designing Multimedia: A Visual Guide to Multimedia and Online Graphic Design.* Berkeley, CA: Peachpit Press.

Miller, Marc D., and Randy Zaucha. 1995. *The Color Mac: Production Techniques.* 2nd ed. Indianapolis, IN: Hayden Books.

Mok, Clement. 1996. *Designing Business: Multiple Media, Multiple Disciplines.* Mountain View, CA: Adobe Press.

Nielsen, Jakob. 1995. *Multimedia and Hypertext: The Internet and Beyond.* Boston: AP Professional.

Palmquist, Mike, Dawn Rodrigues, Kate Kiefer, and Donald E. Zimmerman. 1995. "Network Support for Writing Across the Curriculum: Developing an Online Writing Center." *Computers and Composition* 12.3, 335–53.

Royster, Jacqueline Jones. 1992. "From Practice to Theory: Writing Across the Disciplines at Spelman College." In *Writing, Teaching, and Learning in the Disciplines,* edited by Anne Herrington and Charles Moran, 119–131. New York: Modern Language Association of America.

Siegel, David. 1996. *Creating Killer Web Sites: The Art of Third-Generation Site Design.* Indianapolis, IN: Hayden Books.

Weinman, Lynda. 1996. *Deconstructing Web Graphics.* Indianapolis, IN: New Riders Publishing.

Weinman, Lynda. 1997. *Designing Web Graphics 2: How to Prepare Images and Media for the Web.* Indianapolis, IN: New Riders Publishing.

4 Communication Across the Curriculum and Institutional Culture

Mike Palmquist
Colorado State University

Kate Kiefer
Colorado State University

Donald E. Zimmerman
Colorado State University

WAC challenges deeply held institutional attitudes toward writing, learning, and teaching: attitudes that are reinforced by the differentiated structure of knowledge and education.

> — David Russell, *Writing in the Academic Disciplines, 1870–1990: A Curricular History*

Over the years that we've worked to establish writing—and, more broadly, communication—across the curriculum at our university, we have bumped up against every "deeply held institutional attitude" that Russell lays out in his analysis of WAC. Because of a unique combination of circumstances at Colorado State University, our approach to Communication Across the Curriculum (CAC) is succeeding because we embrace two other instrumentalities that also challenge deeply held attitudes about writing, learning, and teaching—computers and community.[1]

Our approach differs in three ways from typical approaches to CAC in American colleges and universities. First, unlike more traditionally conceptualized CAC programs, in which faculty are the primary audience for CAC training and support, we have expanded our CAC outreach efforts to include direct support for students. Second, we have relied heavily on computer technologies to support CAC across our campus. Third, building on an existing community of writers and teachers on our campus, we have located our CAC program in our campus writing center.

Elsewhere, we discuss in greater detail the rationale for adopting our approach to CAC (Palmquist et al. 1995). Briefly, however, our decision was shaped by a series of studies that we conducted in the first year of funded work on our CAC development project. (For reports of these studies, see Thomas 1994; Vest et al. 1995, 1996; Zimmerman and Palmquist 1993; Zimmerman et al. 1994). Our studies suggested, among other things, that the faculty we hoped to work with in our CAC program were unenthusiastic about using communication activities in their courses in ways typically advocated in CAC programs.

Resistance from faculty is often cited as a primary obstacle to the long-term success of CAC programs (Couch 1989; Holladay 1987; Kaufer and Young 1993; McLeod 1989; Soven 1992; Strenski 1988; Swanson-Owens 1986). We found, as is typically the case at other institutions, that much of the resistance stemmed from the challenge of teaching large classes and time constraints imposed by demanding research agendas. We also learned, however, that our faculty were concerned about the difficulties of providing thorough grounding in both disciplinary content and communication skills without exceeding a state-mandated limit on required course credits. We concluded, as a result, that a traditionally conceptualized CAC program was unlikely to meet the same level of success on our campus that it has met at other institutions (Russell 1991; Walvoord 1992; A. Young and Fulwiler 1986; R. Young 1991).

In the face of faculty reluctance to take on a major role in supporting CAC in their classrooms, we decided to expand our CAC outreach efforts to include direct support for students. This decision was based on our recognition that we could use our campus network to support students in two primary ways: (1) by helping students obtain feedback on communication assignments from their instructors, their classmates, and writing tutors (e.g., tutors in the campus Writing Center and in the Oral Communication Center); and (2) by providing access to instructional programs that addressed communication issues. Essentially, we realized that we could build on the then-emerging notion of an Online Writing Center to provide support for communication instruction across the university. (For discussions of online writing centers, see Child 1994; Ericsson 1994; Harris 1994; Palmquist 1994; see also Rodrigues and Kiefer's 1993 discussion of the Electronic Writing Center.)

Our decision to directly support students has not meant abandoning traditional CAC outreach to faculty. We continue to offer CAC workshops and to consult with faculty. We have also created instructional software that addresses faculty concerns about designing, evaluating, and responding to communication assignments. Rather than shifting our focus away from faculty, we have expanded it to include both faculty and students. In a sense, we have combined an approach to CAC that views faculty, to use Richard Young's (1991) phrasing, as "agents of change" with Tori Haring-Smith's (1987) "bottom-up" approach to CAC, which views students as the primary audience for CAC efforts.

Focusing our CAC efforts on students as well as faculty led us to the final decision that has shaped our CAC program: locating the program within our campus Writing Center. The Writing Center is highly visible on our campus, offering both formal tutoring for underprepared students and walk-in support for undergraduate students, graduate students, and faculty. The decision to locate our CAC program in our campus Writing Center is one we share with a minority of CAC designers (Harris 1992; Holladay 1987; Russell 1991). Yet it is one that has a number of advantages, among them ease of access to experienced tutors and a general awareness among students and faculty about the benefits of seeking advice from tutors.

Our decision to expand the audience for CAC on our campus by directly supporting students and our related decisions to use computer technologies and the campus Writing Center to create campus-wide support for CAC have attracted support for CAC across the university. As we were completing work on this chapter, our university made a long-term commitment to support our CAC program, agreeing to fund a new tenure-track position to direct the program, to support a graduate assistant for the director, and to fund a writer/programmer for Web site development. Even more important for the long-term success of CAC on our campus, our efforts have helped us form a community of collaborators across disciplines who share our concern about students' writing and speaking abilities. This community includes faculty in communication disciplines—business communication, composition, journalism, speech communication, and technical communication—that share common interests in communication but who, because of departmental boundaries, have often worked in isolation on our campus. It also includes faculty in non-communication disciplines who have begun to work with us on communication instruction in their classrooms.

Below, we discuss the network communication tools and instructional software supporting CAC on our campus, and then we explore the communities created by the need to share expertise about writing, learning, teaching, and disciplinary knowledge. We conclude the chapter by reflecting on the long-term outlook for our CAC program.

Network Communication Tools and Instructional Software for CAC

For the past three years, we've worked to develop software to support students as they write and speak for course activities and to support faculty using writing and speaking activities in their courses. To help students access support materials easily, we have made them available through our Online Writing Center, the focus for CAC activities on our campus. We use the phrase "Online Writing Center" to refer both to the place where faculty and students can turn for support with communication activities and to the collection of software that can be used to support those activities. The Online Writing Center can be reached via electronic mail (by mailing to tutor@vines.colostate.edu) and via the World Wide Web (see Figure 4.1).[2]

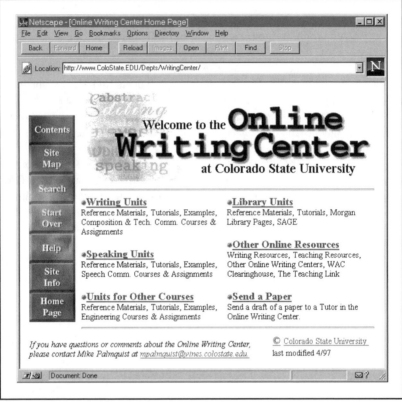

Figure 4.1. The Online Writing Center homepage.

Support for Students

The Online Writing Center supports students through four kinds of instructional units, direct communication with tutors in the Online Writing Center, and the Online Writing Center's "Other Online Resources" pages. We will consider the instructional units and communication options shortly. The "Other Online Resources" pages help students locate resources at other sites on the World Wide Web, ranging from other Online Writing Centers to specific resources such as style and citation guides, dictionaries and glossaries, thesauri, grammar guides, and sites that explore concerns related to English as a second language.

Instructional Materials

Reference Materials provide explanations and commentary about communication genres, processes, or issues, such as writing a summary, writing an argu-

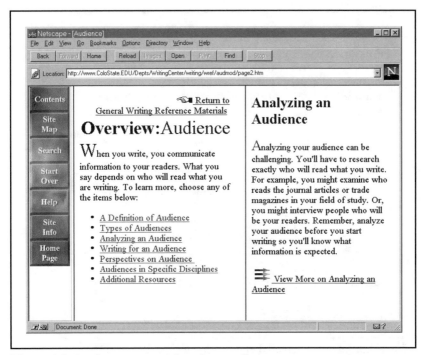

Figure 4.2. A reference materials unit on audience.

ment, or giving an informative speech (see Figure 4.2). Reference Materials look much like online textbooks: hierarchical hypertexts that use an overview (or home) page and a frame-based layout for multiple screens of text and graphics to be presented on the same "page." Sections of a particular Reference Materials unit appear as separate pages linked to the overview page. Each section can have multiple subsections, and so on. Reference Materials are designed to help readers locate information quickly. We provide tables of contents for each Reference Materials unit, as well as for the overall Web site. Students can also use a search program to look for specific kinds of information. Reference Materials also link to related Annotated Example Texts and Speeches and to Interactive Tutorials.

Annotated Example Texts and Speeches present readers with model texts and speeches (the latter provided via video clips) annotated by teachers and experienced writers or speakers (see Figure 4.3). Readers select sections of a text or speech by clicking on a list on the left side of the screen. The text is displayed in the center of the screen. Readers view annotations, displayed in the right-hand frame, by clicking on blue "comment" icons within the text or next to a video clip. While reading comments about specific aspects of the text

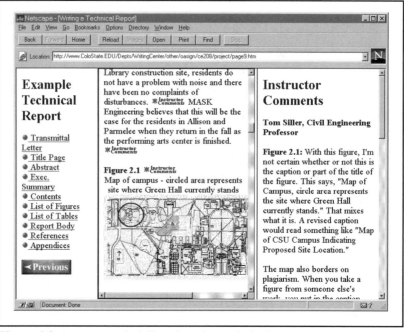

Figure 4.3. An annotated civil engineering technical report.

or speech, students can jump from annotations to relevant Reference Materials, Interactive Tutorials, and Web sites.

Interactive Tutorials present interactive exercises to support specific composing processes, such as generating ideas, revising a paper, or developing pro and con arguments on a particular topic (see Figure 4.4). Tutorials are brief—typically no more than twenty screens. Students using the Tutorials write throughout the exercise so that they finish with notes or a draft to refer to later in their composing process: at the end of a Tutorial, student responses are collated in a form that can be edited, saved, printed, or e-mailed. In contrast with Reference Materials, Tutorials are linear. Readers can move back and forth through the Tutorial, but they cannot jump ahead. However, Tutorials are displayed in a separate window that floats above or alongside the browser, thus allowing students to switch between the Tutorial and Assignments, Reference Units, or Annotated Examples.

Online Assignments provide information about communication assignments in a particular class (see Figure 4.5). Assignment units attempt to replicate the process of discussing assignments during class. In a typical class, teachers hand out a formal assignment sheet and then discuss it in detail with their students. Following this initial discussion, students usually ask questions such as, "What

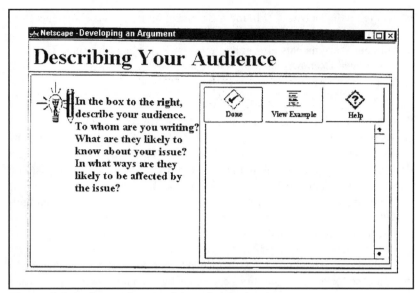

Figure 4.4. An interactive tutorial on developing an argument.

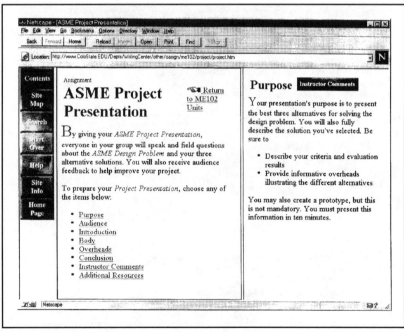

Figure 4.5. An assignment in mechanical engineering.

do you really mean by . . .?" In the Assignment units, we use comments from instructors to present this information. In addition to detailed discussions of an assignment, Assignments also link to relevant Reference Materials, Tutorials, and Annotated Examples, as well as to related Web pages.

Communication Tools

Students can also use the Online Writing Center to contact tutors or their instructors through electronic mail, chat, or Web forums. Students can use a forms-based e-mail program, which we call "Send a Paper," to simplify sending a draft of a communication assignment to a tutor (see Figure 4.6) or, using a "mailto:" address on our Web Site, they can use the standard e-mail programs built into most browsers. Our assessment studies indicate that students unfamiliar with e-mail find the "Send a Paper" program easier to use than standard e-mail software. In addition, the "Send a Paper" program allows students to elicit specific feedback about their drafts because it prompts them to write briefly about their understanding of the assignment, their goals as writers, their audience, and so forth. These questions can be customized for specific courses and the program can be accessed from within particular Online Assignments.

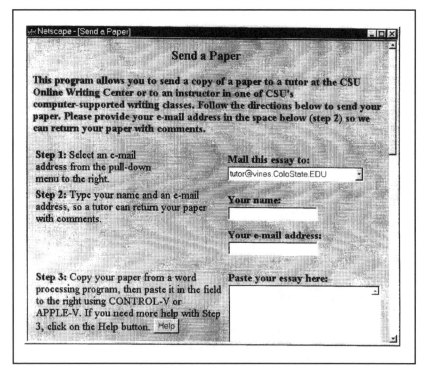

Figure 4.6. The "Send a Paper" program.

Support for Teachers

Despite focusing primarily on students, the Online Writing Center also provides support for faculty. We are currently developing software to support faculty who have not before assigned writing in their courses, but in the meantime faculty can click on Additional Online Resources. This page accesses a Reference Materials unit on designing communication assignments, responding to communication assignments, and using writing to support student learning. The Additional Online Resources page also links to teaching resources and Web sites on writing and speaking instruction. Finally, faculty can also access the Writing Across the Curriculum Clearinghouse (http://www.colostate.edu/depts/WAC). The Clearinghouse provides information on teaching practices, program design, and research studies. It also provides a comprehensive list of WAC and CAC programs, a list of individuals who can provide various kinds of support for starting and maintaining WAC and CAC programs, and a Web forum on WAC and CAC issues.[3]

Instructional Uses of the Online Writing Center

The Online Writing Center challenges the attitudes and sites that "differentiate structures and knowledge" on our campus. Teachers initiate student use of the Online Writing Center with both in-class and out-of-class assignments. For example, in computer-supported writing classes, Online Writing Center materials accessed during class support lessons designed by individual teachers. A teacher can begin a class by asking students to generate ideas using one of the prewriting Tutorials, or a teacher could ask students to review a Reference Materials unit on library research after introducing an assignment that draws on outside sources.

Students also initiate use of the Online Writing Center to meet a variety of learning goals. Students in a writing class can use the "Send a Paper" program to exchange papers with their classmates or to ask for feedback on their drafts from their teacher or a Writing Center tutor. Students can also access the class page on the Online Writing Center and use a Web Forum, which supports threaded discussions just like a newsgroup.

In the campus Writing Center, a tutor might ask a student to use Online Writing Center materials to generate ideas, revise a paper, or review the conventions of a particular genre. A student might work through materials prior to a tutoring session—perhaps via electronic mail after the student has sent a paper to a tutor—or during or immediately after a tutoring session, using a computer in the campus Writing Center.

Online Writing Center materials also supplement communication and disciplinary classes taught in traditional classrooms. Students in a writing or speech class, for instance, might use materials on the Online Writing Center as homework. Similarly, students in a disciplinary class might review an Online Assignment or a Reference Materials unit before making formal presentations or turning in a lab report. If an Online Assignment is used, it is likely that the instructor for the course consulted with CAC faculty prior to making the assignment; the faculty member may also have helped develop the content of the Reference Materials unit. When used in disciplinary courses, the Online Writing Center supplements rather than replaces information provided by the instructor on the specific communication assignment.

Even in courses in which the instructor is not specifically working with CAC faculty or advising students to use resources available through the Online Writing Center, students can use those resources as they work on communication assignments. Similarly, students in such courses can seek feedback on their drafts via electronic mail or by visiting the campus Writing Center in person. Students learn of these services through other courses they've taken or simply by noticing the Online Writing Center while browsing the university's Web site.

As work continues on the development of the Online Writing Center, we are assessing the use of the instructional software and the network-communication tools in classrooms, in the campus Writing Center, and in our usability testing lab. We are now expanding the use of the Online Writing Center to students enrolled in all sections of our required, all-university composition course; in speech communication courses; in technical communication courses; and in a range of disciplinary courses.

The Impact of the Program on Students and Faculty

We turn now to the second of the features that strengthen our CAC efforts—the communities created by the need to share expertise about writing, learning, teaching, and disciplinary knowledge. We anticipated that using computer network tools would allow us to reach a greater number of students than we would have through a traditional WAC approach, and students have indeed begun to use the Online Writing Center inside and outside of the classroom. Access to the Online Writing Center—and through it to Writing Center tutors, communication faculty, disciplinary faculty, and classmates—has allowed students and faculty to use communication programs and instructional software both on and off campus. Even more important, awareness among students and faculty of the existence of the Online Writing Center continues to grow, resulting in greater use of its resources and greater support for communication assignments. But it takes time to build a community, and our work in the past few years is only now beginning to show the importance of involving as many members of the university community as possible in the development and implementation of such an multifaceted project.

Initial reactions to the Online Writing Center were decidedly mixed. A number of faculty expressed concerns that the materials might replace instruction—and, indeed, instructors. The design of the Online Writing Center, however, combined with efforts to inform colleagues about the educational philosophy underlying the programs have helped us eliminate these concerns. That philosophy—to supplement rather than to replace communication instruction and to expand the repertoire for interaction among faculty and students rather than to replace face-to-face interaction with computer-mediated communication—has strongly informed the design of our instructional software and our use of network-based communication.

That philosophy has also shaped the roles we have asked tutors in the campus Writing Center to adopt when they interact with students over the network. During our assessment of their reactions to the programs in the first semester in which the Online Writing Center was implemented, we found that our tutors resisted using the "Send a Paper" program in particular and network-based communication in general. Their responses to our questions indicated that their resistance emerged from their training as tutors and from their concern that network-based interactions would replace, rather than supplement, face-to-face interaction. The tutors told us that their training and experience in the Writing Center clearly showed the value of extended discussions with students about the context for a writing assignment. Electronic mail—and even real-time chat—did not support these extended discussions. More important, because the students who sent drafts over the network seldom came into the Writing Center, tutors felt that the "Send a Paper" program reduced interactions with students.

In turn, we asked tutors if walk-in visits to the Writing Center had dropped off. When they said no, we discussed the benefits of sending papers across the network. First, we explained that many of the students who were sending papers found it a convenient way to get feedback on their writing. Students who might not have—or want to make—the time to visit the Writing Center might send a paper to a tutor for feedback. As a result, the "Send a Paper" program was increasing the number of students with whom tutors could work. Second, we explored ways that the "Send a Paper" program brings more students into the Writing Center. By responding to students with substantive feedback and then asking them to set up an appointment to visit a tutor, tutors invite face-to-face work with students. Finally, we told them that—even in cases where students were reluctant or unable to meet with a tutor—tutors could suggest activities or identify instructional software that might help particular students improve as writers. For instance, a student having difficulty with a fairly straightforward convention such as attributing quotations might benefit from using the "Working with Quotations" Reference unit. Or a student having difficulty considering opposing arguments might find the "Arguments Against Your Position" Tutorial useful.

Fortunately, students and instructors in our writing classrooms reacted positively from the start to the Online Writing Center. Several instructors encouraged their students to use the "Send a Paper" program to get additional feedback on assignments, several used the tutorials and hypermedia programs during class, and still others encouraged students to use the programs outside of class. Our classroom observations, interviews with students, and usability testing sessions showed that students found the programs easy to use. However, students also indicated (as is the case with the early drafts of many textbooks) that the programs would benefit from additional revision. As we complete work on this chapter, we have hired a full-time writer to work on new hypermedia documents and tutorials. We have also budgeted time for additional editing of our existing software.

Reaction from disciplinary faculty was also mixed. Our first attempts to develop software for an electrical engineering course failed when the instructor, who was teaching the course for the first time, was unwilling to spend the time needed to explore how communication activities might fit into her course. Despite the active support of the chair of her department, she strongly resisted working with us—largely, she said, because it was her first time teaching the course and she was uncertain about how it would play out over the semester. In response, we shifted our focus to a course taught by a more experienced teacher who wanted to work with us. This collaboration was much more positive and produced a comprehensive Reference Materials unit that aids students as they work on an eight- to ten-page scientific report.

Our initial partnership with the electrical engineering faculty on our campus has led to partnerships with faculty in our other engineering disciplines and, more recently, has expanded to include faculty in the humanities, social sciences, and sciences. In each case, these partnerships have grown from a recognition that the Online Writing Center could support curricular innovation in a specific course or departmental curriculum. A faculty member in civil engineering contacted us after reading of our work in *Engineering Education*. He is revising the undergraduate curriculum in civil engineering to emphasize more group work, critical thinking, and communication. We are now collaborating on several instructional packages to support the new curriculum. Similarly, a faculty member in mechanical engineering revising the second-year undergraduate sequence has enlisted our help in developing tailored instructional materials that support oral presentations and final project reports.

Most recently, we have begun working with faculty in our own college to develop computer-based support for speaking and writing activities in humanities courses. As with our other partnerships, the impetus for collaboration came when faculty found that our approach to CAC would benefit their efforts to revise their curricula.

Perhaps the most gratifying outcome of our efforts to create a network-sup-ported CAC program has been the strong sense of community that has emerged among the communication faculty and graduate students who have worked on the project. The number of master's theses and projects focused on CAC has exploded in just the last two years, and graduate students are more and more often inviting members of different departments to contribute multidisciplinary perspectives on their communication projects. Before faculty began working together to develop our CAC program, faculty in composition, business com-munication, journalism, speech, and technical communication had relatively little interaction. Now, we're clearly benefiting from the different perspectives and experiences that we bring to CAC projects. Those differences have not always resulted in harmonious interactions, but we've found that focusing on a shared goal has allowed us to work around our disagreements. In many ways, the communication faculty involved in the Online Writing Center have formed an ad hoc department: we sometimes find that we have more in common with colleagues from another of these departments than we do with other faculty in our own.

Institutional Changes and the Long-Term Success of CAC

Our CAC program has emerged from a collaborative effort among faculty from several departments. Thus far, it has been tied most closely to a research project funded through the Center for Research on Writing and Communication Tech-nologies, an interdisciplinary research center housed in the College of Liberal Arts. While we continue to seek funding to continue the project, we recognize that a crucial element in securing the long-term success of our CAC program is to shift its ownership and development from the Research Center to the Writing Center. As a result, for the past year we have worked to secure long-term insti-tutional funding for the program.

In addition to designing our CAC program, then, we gave ourselves the task of creating the institutional support structure within which it can continue its mission. The structure we believe is likely to be most effective on our campus is one in which the program remains in the Writing Center and is administered through the university composition program (which, in turn, is housed in our English department). We recognize that strong arguments exist on both sides of the question of whether to tie a CAC program to a particular department. How-ever, we are persuaded that the institutional context in which we work favors this arrangement. During the week prior to completing this article, working within the English Department's and the College of Liberal Arts' long-term funding plans, we obtained approval to hire a full-time, tenure-track director of the campus Writing Center (currently a nine-month, non-tenure track appointment), a full-time writer/programmer, and a graduate teaching assistant who will assist with the administration of the campus Writing Center.

Success in securing institutional grounding for our CAC program emerged from our success at expanding the community of scholars that resulted from our previous development efforts. Success in ensuring the long-term success of the program as an educational enterprise can only come, we believe, if we can continue to attract more faculty to that community. We are confident, given the success we have enjoyed so far, that our program is likely to be successful over the long term. But we recognize that we must continue our efforts to build communities of shared concerns about writing, speaking, thinking, and learning, communities that bind students and teachers into shared allegiances rather than differentiated structures.

Notes

1. The research reported in this article was supported with funding from Colorado State University and the Colorado Commission on Higher Education. The authors gratefully acknowledge the contributions made by the other members of the project team: Thad Anderson, Luann Barnes, Marla Cowell, Greg Boiarsky, Cathy Crim, Karen Criswell, Douglas Flahive, Jake Hartvigsen, Steve Hill, Dawn Kowalski, Donna LeCourt, Jon Leydens, Marilee Long, Michel Muraski, Kathy Northcut, Amy Polisso, Ron Tajchman, Greg Thayer, Laura Thomas, Martha Tipton, and David Vest. We also thank Dawn Rodrigues for her role in early discussions about the design of our CAC program.

2. Initial development of the Online Writing Center was conducted using Asymetrix Multimedia Toolbook, which runs under Windows. We chose to use Toolbook because, at the time we began developing the Online Writing Center, it offered significant advantages over similar development programs. It also provided us with a relatively straightforward way to develop interactive software. At that time, the capabilities offered by the World Wide Web were extremely limited. In September 1996, however, we shifted development from Toolbook to the Web. We made this decision for three reasons: (1) Toolbook is a Windows-based program, which restricted our ability to run our software on other platforms; (2) to run our software, we needed to install a "run-time" version of Toolbook on individual computers, a labor-intensive task that was often plagued by hardware and software incompatibilities; and (3) the capability of the World Wide Web to support graphics, audio, video, and other forms of interaction with users had increased significantly since we began our development project. Although the shift to the Web required extensive work translating our software into HTML files, we were able to transfer much that we had learned about interface and document design from our work using Toolbook.

3. As we were completing work on this chapter, the WAC Clearinghouse was being designed by a group of faculty from several institutions.

Works Cited

Child, Bob. 1994. "Politics: Conflicts between Humanists and Technologists and How Tensions Affect the Development of Online Writing Environments." Paper presented at the annual meeting of the Conference on College Composition and Communication. Nashville, Tennessee. March 17.

Couch, Ruth. 1989. "Dealing with Objections to Writing Across the Curriculum." *Teaching English in the Two-Year College* 16.3: 193–96.

Ericsson, P. 1994. "WAC Learns to Fly: The Birth of an Owl." Paper presented at the tenth annual Computers and Writing Conference. Columbia, Missouri. May 20–23.

Haring-Smith, Tori. 1987. *A Guide to Writing Programs: Writing Centers, Peer Tutoring Programs, and Writing Across the Curriculum.* Glenview, IL: Scott-Foresman.

Harris, Muriel. 1992. "The Writing Center and Tutoring in WAC Programs." In *Writing Across the Curriculum: A Guide to Developing Programs,* edited by S. H. McLeod and M. Soven, 154–75. Newbury Park, CA: Sage Publications.

Harris, Muriel. 1994. "Trade-Offs: What Is Gained and What Is Lost When Writers and Tutors Interact via Machines?" Paper presented at the annual meeting of the Conference on College Composition and Communication. Nashville, Tennessee. March 17.

Holladay, John. 1987. "Institutional Project Grant: A Report on Research into Writing-Across-the-Curriculum Projects." Abstract from ERIC: ED298995.

Kaufer, D., and Richard Young. 1993. "Writing in the Content Areas: Some Theoretical Complexities." In *Theory and Practice in the Teaching of Writing: Rethinking the Discipline,* edited by Lee Odell. Carbondale: Southern Illinois University Press.

McLeod, Susan H. 1989. "Writing Across the Curriculum: The Second Stage, and Beyond." *College Composition and Communication* 40.3: 337–43.

Palmquist, Michael. 1994. "Computer Support for Writing Across the Curriculum: Theoretical Perspectives." Paper presented at the annual meeting of the Conference on College Composition and Communication. Nashville, Tennessee. March 18.

Palmquist, Michael, Dawn Rodrigues, Kathleen Kiefer, and Donald Zimmerman. 1995. "Enhancing the Audience for Writing Across the Curriculum: Housing WAC in a Network-supported Writing Center." *Computers and Composition* 12: 335–53.

Rodrigues, Dawn, and Kathleen Kiefer. 1993. "Moving toward an Electronic Writing Center at Colorado State University." In *Writing Centers in Context: Twelve Case Studies,* edited by J. A. Kinkead and J. G. Harris, 216–26. Urbana, IL: National Council of Teachers of English.

Russell, David R. 1991. *Writing in the Academic Disciplines, 1870–1990: A Curricular History.* Carbondale: Southern Illinois University Press.

Soven, Margot. 1992. "Conclusion: Sustaining Writing Across the Curriculum Programs." In *Writing Across the Curriculum: A Guide to Developing Programs,* edited by Susan H. McLeod and Margot Soven, 189–97. Newbury Park, CA: Sage Publications.

Strenski, Ellen. 1988. "Writing Across the Curriculum at Research Universities." In *Strengthening Programs for Writing Across the Curriculum,* edited by Susan H. McLeod, 31–41. New Directions for Teaching and Learning, No. 36. San Francisco: Jossey-Bass.

Swanson-Owens, Deborah. 1986. "Identifying Natural Sources of Resistance: A Case Study of Implementing Writing Across the Curriculum." *Research in the Teaching of English* 20.1: 69–97.

Thomas, L. 1994. "Educating Electrical Engineers for Workplace Communication: A Qualitative Study." Master's thesis, Colorado State University.

Vest, David, Marilee Long, and Thad Anderson. 1996. "Electrical Engineers' Perceptions of Communication Training and Their Recommendations for Curricular Change: Results of a National Survey." *IEEE Transactions on Professional Communication* 39. 1: 38–42.

Vest, David, Marilee Long, Laura Thomas, and Michael E. Palmquist. 1995. "Relating Communication Training to Workplace Requirements: The Perspective of New Engineers." *IEEE Transactions on Professional Communication* 38.1: 11–17.

Walvoord, Barbara E. 1992. "Getting Started." In *Writing Across the Curriculum: A Guide to Developing Programs,* edited by Susan H. McLeod and Margot Soven. Newbury Park, CA: Sage Publications.

Young, Art, and Toby Fulwiler. 1986. *Writing Across the Disciplines: Research Into Practice.* Upper Montclair, NJ: Boynton/Cook.

Young, Richard E. 1991. "Designing for Change in a Writing-Across-the-Curriculum Program." In *Balancing Acts: Essays on the Teaching of Writing in Honor of William F. Irmscher,* edited by Virginia A. Chappell, Mary Louise Buley-Meissner, and Chris Anderson, 141–58. Carbondale: Southern Illinois University Press.

Zimmerman, Donald E., and Michael Palmquist. 1993. "Enhancing Electrical Engineering Students' Communication Skills." In *Proceedings of the IEEE International Professional Communication Conference,* Philadelphia, October 5–8: 428–31.

Zimmerman, Donald E., Michael Palmquist, Kate Kiefer, Marilee Long, David Vest, Martha Tipton, and Laura Thomas. 1994. "Enhancing Electrical Engineering Students' Communication Skills—the Baseline Findings." In *Proceedings of the IEEE International Professional Communication Conference,* Banff, Canada, September 28–October 1: 412–17.

5 Creating a Community of Teachers and Tutors

Joe Essid
University of Richmond

Dona J. Hickey
University of Richmond

Administrators of WAC programs and writing centers tend to believe in social constructivist theories of knowledge. Hence, they often ask themselves questions about authority: the roles writers play as both teachers and students. How can teachers give up their authority, their centrality in the classroom, without giving up their expertise? How can they model collaboration for student writers and for tutors so that students learn from each other? How can technology support the exploration of these questions and the implementation of collaborative pedagogies?

Consider, for example, the focus on authority in the following transcript of a synchronous electronic conference. Here, four tutors-in-training use the software to discuss a typical problem—how to assist a writer who has received harsh criticism on a paper:

Tutor 1:
During the conference, I would try to point out the positive points of the paper along with the things that could use improvement. I would also try to phrase criticism in the form of a question in order to avoid sounding too authoritarian. Finally, I would remind the writers that my commentary is only a collection of suggestions, and they could choose what to change and what not to change.

Tutor 2:
I think Tutor 1's point about criticism is important. We don't want to seem as though we're a "mean professor" or too authoritarian. [I would ask the writer] Where is the first place you would start with improving this paper?

Tutor 3:
As tutors we should not take the side of the teacher or the student, but simply move away from this topic and begin focusing on the actual writing . . . by getting the student to focus on a goal.

Tutor 4:
I agree with Tutor 1. I think it's important to not seem authoritative. One

way of conveying your equality to the tutees is by making the conference
very conversational. By doing so, you can discuss both the positive and
negative aspects of the paper without seeming too superior.

Tutor 2:
So we all agree that we should not be too authoritative and remain neutral.
Additionally, we should focus on both the positive and negative points of
the paper. But where do we head from there?

As this electronic conversation reveals, tutors arrive at an issue that informs
much of their work: the nature of the tutor/writer relationship. It is important
that the tutors-in-training arrived at this question and their consensus about
neutrality in an online synchronous conference in our composition theory class,
rather than face-to-face or at the writing center. Through the visual record of
such conferencing across the semester, students can see knowledge as a process
of continually negotiated conversation.

Our course, "Composition Theory and Pedagogy," which prepares peer tutors for our writing center and "Writing Fellows" for our WAC Program, includes several uses of technology, including role-playing exercises in which
tutors plan strategies for tutorials with resistant or hesitant writers. We also use
a class newsgroup, electronic mail, and the World Wide Web, technologies that
seem to minimize face-to-face dialogue at a small, private university that offers
a high teacher-student ratio. So that readers might see how our story compares
to their own, we'd like to offer here some information about the University of
Richmond before we describe more specifically how and why we combine tradition and technology in our approach to tutor-training.

The University of Richmond is an independent, privately endowed institution that provides a comprehensive academic program for more than three thousand men and women. It offers degree programs in the liberal arts and sciences
and in business, as well as graduate and professional programs in law, business,
leadership studies, and selected areas of the arts and sciences.

In assisting students to select and prepare for careers and for graduate and
professional study, the university is committed to improving student literacies—
cultural, textual, and technological. In service of this goal, WAC and an enhanced writing center were proposed on our campus in 1990 to integrate writing
instruction into the core curriculum and across levels of study and disciplines.
These proposals and the plan to create a networked English lab were in keeping
with the university's objectives and strategic plan. Creating "electronic classrooms" is part of the university's commitment to "substantial and continuing
investments in technology" for the purpose of "enriching and intensifying the
intellectual life on campus" (*Engagement in Learning* 1994).

A networked English lab seemed ideal for the acquisition of literacies in a
collaborative setting. When we piloted the three-credit training course in the
fall of 1992, we wanted students to learn social constructivist theory and apply

it in the Writing Center, as part of a weekly practicum. Although we anticipated the potential for that mode of learning in the intensely collaborative environment of networked computing, we underestimated the degree to which technology would enrich teacher-student dialogue and help students become more active learners.

Writing Across the Curriculum at Richmond: Faculty Involvement

The WAC program, based on the models at Brown University and Swarthmore, is voluntary. Participating faculty from across disciplines agree to attend two orientation meetings and to require at least two substantive writing assignments in the course for which they have requested WAC assistance. One of those assignments must be due in the first half of the semester. Faculty also agree to require mandatory conferences between students and Writing Fellows so that peer tutoring can be collaborative—a dialogue between students, both of whom have something to contribute at the session. We want to avoid a hierarchy in which the writer turns in a draft and the Writing Fellow tells how to fix it. We also want faculty to recognize the value of such collaboration and perhaps change their perceptions and practices in order to foster learning communities in their classrooms.

As yearly assessments show (see specific data on page 82), faculty involved in WAC have begun to make changes of their own initiative. They have assigned write-to-learn activities, have increased attention to the writing process (more detailed guidelines, more pre-writing, more re-writing), and have changed the way they respond to papers, echoing Writing Fellow commentary. Even after the program's first year, for example, faculty began to focus more on content and global structure than on mechanics. These changes come about slowly, naturally, and thus more meaningfully than they would if faculty were required, at the outset, to change their teaching practice to accommodate WAC.

To be sure, all faculty want students to write better and are committed to do what they can to facilitate that learning. Commitment varies according to the time and energy faculty can expend in a given course and according to previous training and experience in the teaching of writing. Some, understandably, given their own history as students, see writing as testing, not learning. Unsure about their own ability to motivate, or respond to student writing, faculty welcome the assistance of Writing Fellows and regularly recommend as potential Writing Fellows undergraduates who demonstrate strong communication abilities in their courses. Often those same students return to the faculty member's course as Writing Fellows.

Since participating faculty recommend students to the program, most Writing Fellows and peer tutors are not English majors. Like their professors, they represent different disciplines: biology, leadership, psychology, sociology, international studies, math, theater, and political science. Many students who complete the course are offered paid positions as Writing Fellows, Writing Center tutors, or administrative assistants. Often students assume all of these roles, gaining experience in both programs.

What Writing Fellows Do

A Writing Fellow is assigned to a particular faculty member's course where he or she is responsible for the following:

- reading and writing response to no more than fifteen drafts for two or more assignments (how many depends on the nature of the writing tasks);
- meeting with each student in conference to discuss revision strategies (usually, the writer brings knowledge of the subject matter; the Writing Fellow brings knowledge of rhetoric. Sometimes each brings both);
- and meeting with the professor as needed to discuss expectations and student progress.

Currently, over forty faculty members participate in WAC, rotating in and out of the program, according to their teaching schedules. Now four years old, the program includes, in any given semester, fifteen to twenty faculty and thirty-five to forty Writing Fellows. With such a diverse group of students and faculty, many of whom have little experience with collaborative learning, we find it daunting to have only one semester in which to provide Writing Fellows and tutors experience with collaborative work and a variety of tutorial strategies and writing heuristics. As part of this accelerated program, we want them to become independent of any one approach to tutoring. As in the scenario at the beginning of this chapter, tutors and Fellows must be able to conform their practice to the learning needs and temperament of the peer with whom they are working. Collaborative theory matters greatly for undergraduate tutors who might be tempted to imitate traditional professors by evaluating a draft rather than motivate revision through engaging in dialogue with a writer. In a one-semester course, we need an effective and quick means to teach the relationship between collaborative theory and practice. That need has been met by instructional technology because programs like synchronous and asynchronous conferencing provide visible evidence of the process toward consensus and the construction of knowledge.

Disorienting and Reorienting Prospective Fellows

The training of Writing Fellows emphasizes how computer-assisted environments support contemporary rhetoric and composition theory. Early in the semester, instructors and students discuss the theory of the collaborative class-room, including Bruffee's (1984) contention that "knowledge is a social con-struct generated by a community of knowledgeable peers" and Hawisher's and Selfe's (1993) assertion that new methods of instruction are mandatory for a "prefigurative" society whose educators and elders cannot adequately predict the direction or scope of social or technological change. Fellows-in-training also hear a chorus of scholarly voices calling for change in writing instruction, such as Bartholomae's (1980) proposal that we adopt a more sophisticated no-tion of "error" and Sommer's (1982) critique of how professors' commentary discourages meaningful revision.

On a campus in the midst of implementing large-scale curricular change, the advice of these and other writers has helped us integrate technology and WAC. In the networked lab, students practice theories of collaborative learning and peer-tutoring that they will need when assigned to the WAC program or writing center. For example, e-mail exchanges with scholars such as Mick Doherty and Dickie Selfe help students learn how to engage in the ongoing conversation in the field. The value is twofold: they recognize that knowledge is transactional, not static, and they can learn how to question their peers' knowledge by engag-ing them in dialogue about writing. Not every student who enters the training class is successful in these dialogues, and without that skill they do not make good Writing Fellows and tutors. That quickly becomes apparent as the class uses technology. Each semester a few students cling to a teacher-centered model of learning, one antithetical to both the nature of the Fellows program and to the networked computer classroom. Often these students have been recommended for the WAC program on the basis of their strong editing skills, and are sur-prised to find that in the training class we actively discourage their "correcting" other writers' work or ideas. We encourage "facilitative," rather than "direc-tive," commentary in which readers respond not as authorities, but as peer in-quirers, motivators, and collaborators. In other words, we are teaching ways to offer guidance without exerting control over the writer's choices (Straub 1996).

In newsgroup discussions of contrasting theories of composition, many of the same students who assume control over other writers' texts tend to want more direction themselves in selecting "the right approach" to a particular prob-lem. They want us to assume control of their own choices. Finally, with a politi-cally conservative student body, it should be no surprise that in every class one or two prospective Fellows find collaborative learning "touchy-feely," associat-ing it with left-leaning politics. As the writer of one anonymous evaluation de-spaired, the instructor "has a Ph.D. and knows this stuff backwards and forwards. It would be more effective if he would communicate this to his students rather than allowing them to flounder on their own."

These examples are not news to anyone who has ever trained peer tutors, but the problem of resistance and a sense of floundering are compounded by the nature of the WAC program. In our writing center, the director reviews reports, talks to student supervisors, and sees writers on a regular basis. In our less centralized WAC program, once a Fellow is placed in a class, the director of WAC may not hear about a problem with a Fellow until a tutee or faculty member complains. And yet the answer is not WAC police wearing little blue shirts and packing red pencils in their pocket holsters.

So we shake up prospective Fellows on the first day in class. The disorientation begins when the students walk into our lab and find that they may be sitting with their backs to the teacher. In designing the training class for Writing Fellows, the authors had the luxury of tailoring the design of our classroom to the pedagogy of our classes. When the English Writing Lab, the site for the training class, was designed, space for a seminar table was eliminated in order to fit more labs into the floor plan. With the approval of the chair of English and the director of University Computing, we abandoned the original configuration of our lab, typical of what has been derided as a "proscenium classroom" dominated by the teacher's personality and agenda (Barker and Kemp 1990). In fact, in our other campus labs, rows of immovable work stations face the teacher, an arrangement making the optimal use of floor space but working against active, collaborative learning. In the English Lab, however, we dispensed with the teacher's podium and moved the lab furniture into clusters of three or four work stations. We were also open to students' suggestions for additional refinements, and one Writing Fellow's clever idea has changed all of the classes taught in the room: during seminar discussion, students roll their chairs into about 200 square feet of unused space between the teacher's work station and the white boards, and away from the distractions of the computers.

The Class Newsgroup

Most discussions of readings and tutorial problems begin before class, with exchanges using a class newsgroup. We see debates, even arguments, about tutoring begin online and then continue face-to-face. The student-led discussions can be lively, even heated, about matters such as the influence of technology, social background, and gender on writers' practice and senses of revision. Consider this reply to a post in which a student claimed that it was natural for some poor students to be left behind educationally, since "that is life and you have to accept it." This reply, with the subject "A Post/Tirade," quickly appeared:

> That people can sit back and defensively offer a knee-jerk reaction like "life's not fair" or lets "give them (meaning those living in poverty) jobs before we worry about computers" is without serious consideration and is, to me, offensive. Students in a fourth-grade classroom . . . are NOT responsible for the inequalities in their education. These children are not learning on the job, they are struggling to learn in their classrooms.

This discussion led to the issue of how access to educational technology might affect students' writing ability. Each semester the level of debate varies, with the "hot button" issues of one semester eliciting only polite discussion or even yawns the next. Surveys of Fellows reveal that those who most enjoy posting responses to the class newsgroup claim that it offers more time for reflection and provides less distraction than either synchronous conferencing or face-to-face discussion about their reading and tutoring practice.

Are such electronic exchanges, often noteworthy for the instructors' lack of intervention, productive to the students' training as Fellows? The Fellows' work, done without direct supervision of the program director, demands maturity and careful judgment. A lack of these qualities often becomes apparent early in online work. So after we have modeled and practiced productive conversation with students, we intervene less and less as the semester passes. At the same time, we carefully observe students' participation. Hard experience with our first few classes of Fellows revealed that the online work provides an indicator of future success in the WAC program. Specifically, students who fail to post responses to the newsgroup, or who habitually post mediocre responses not related to an ongoing discussion, tend to forget deadlines, appointments, and other commitments once they become Fellows. We find that in most cases the newsgroup posts and subsequent discussions serve the benign purpose of testing how well the Fellows can think for themselves, while working within a community of peers, and base their strategies upon theory, experience, and educated guesses: the tools of the peer-tutor's trade.

WAC and Core

Our interdisciplinary Core course, required of all first-year students, draws faculty from all the disciplines on campus. Instructional technology, especially newsgroups and the Web, plays an increasing role in the classes staffed by Writing Fellows. Because the Core course makes up at least one third of our WAC offerings in any semester, and because it offers Writing Fellows a specific set of challenges, we create a mini-Core practicum in the training course. A participating faculty member volunteers to work with us in the following way:

1. The faculty member visits class to discuss a writing assignment.
2. Each prospective Fellow reads and provides written commentary for a student's draft in the class, then meets with the student to discuss revision strategies.
3. The faculty member returns to our class to discuss how well we met student and faculty expectations.
4. We repeat this process one more time.

"Core" has been required for all first-year students since the 1994–95 academic year, and its goals include developing students' "ability to read, think, speak, and write"; engaging students in serious discussion "of the problem of giving meaning to life"; establishing "a foundation for University-wide conversation about serious questions" (Core Course Committee 1995). Faculty from most departments teach the class, and each instructor may conduct the course freely as long as she assigns papers, gives two exams, and adopts a standard syllabus. Guidelines for Core instructors encourage collaborative learning; most professors use seminar discussion as their teaching model, although a few still shift the balance to lecture.

Teaching Commentary—Synchronous Conferences

All prospective Writing Fellows have completed Core, and although they share common readings, pedagogy can vary widely, as suggested above. To assist students with diverse classroom experiences, Fellows often use synchronous conferencing to recreate and solve common problems: unclear assignments; disgruntled, lost, or resistant students; grammar-focused faculty; papers returned with scant, overwhelming, or confusing commentary.

We have asked ESL students, biology majors, and Core students to contribute drafts of revised essays for the conferencing exercises previously described. With the writers' permission, Fellows then go online to prepare commentary and plan for hypothetical tutorials that would begin in half an hour. Later, using the class newsgroup, the Fellows critique their work in the synchronous conferences or compare it to actual experience as apprentices in the writing center or with a section of Core. Using transcripts in this manner has been judged effective in a number of different sorts of classrooms (Kolko 1993; Reiss 1995). Consider this analysis, completed after the student had reviewed a semester's worth of conference transcripts:

> Looking at our posts, one notes the frequency with which we use one another's names—think about what that suggests. Were we, in fact, writing to someone, writing for an audience? . . . In some ways this might be more valuable than writing papers—because in papers, audience is seldom, if ever, so clear.

In making the conferences as realistic as possible, we wanted the technology to be as transparent as possible. The chaos that Moran (1991) claims can attend large-group conferences would not serve our purpose, so we had students work in small groups and return to analyze what was "said" online. Responses such as the one quoted were typical; students avoided the anomie they might feel in an unstructured online environment where an exercise is completed and then forgotten. After two years of working with synchronous conferencing, we find that the follow-up evaluation of the conference is often the most important part of the entire exercise, since Fellows can see where they might not have effectively prepared for an actual conference with a writer. Evaluations of the exercises note that tutoring success depends more on common sense or the application of an appropriate tutoring method than upon flashes of genius. Most respondents also note that the synchronous exercises and subsequent study of transcripts increase their knowledge of course materials through sharing ideas with a large group and having the discussion available for further study.

Program Assessment and Goals

We have conducted assessment surveys of the program since spring 1993. Participating faculty, students enrolled in their classes, and Writing Fellows complete surveys in either the spring or fall semester of the year. Assessment results show the following areas of strength and weakness.

Strengths

- Overall, participants are pleased with how the program is working.
- The training course does a very good job of preparing Writing Fellows to handle their responsibilities.
- Responses from recently graduated Writing Fellows indicate that the training courses also prepare them for graduate school and careers beyond the schoolhouse gate. Several Writing Fellows/tutors have found teaching/ writing center assistantships. One was hired as a technical writer by Princeton's Particle Physics Lab, another by a publisher to establish Internet-based writing training for employees.
- Respondents are fairly satisfied with the logistics of the program.
- There is growing evidence that WAC is fulfilling its function of placing the teaching and learning of writing at the level of individual courses across disciplines and at all levels of study; WAC is also fulfilling its corollary function of using writing to enhance the thinking and learning process.

Although faculty do not attend special seminars in the teaching of writing, as they do in other WAC programs based on the Writing-Intensive model, they nonetheless make noticeable changes as described earlier. The most important, we believe, is the addition of write-to-learn activities, which demonstrate to faculty and to students how writing can be used other than as a means of testing. We explain some of these changes in the nature of assignments and in teacher-response through a "trickle up" theory: Writing Fellows' written response to students and conferences with faculty often guide faculty to change their own practice. Thus, the relationship between Writing Fellow and faculty is itself collaborative. As evidence for the "trickle up" theory, here are some specific data from 1995's assessment that reflect previous assessments:

- 8 of 11 faculty required some other writing besides the number of papers required in the WAC program. Most of this other writing was in the form of write-to-learn activities. 75 percent of student respondents described the same activities. 65 percent indicated that this other writing enhanced their learning.

- 7 of 11 faculty changed the way they responded to papers. They described more concern with content; and some faculty described "echoing" writing fellow commentary.

In a moderately sized program of a young age, these results are encouraging. We are pleased with the successes thus far, yet we are also mindful of problems that we are working to resolve.

Weaknesses

- Students need to keep appointments and submit better quality drafts to Writing Fellows.
- Faculty and Writing Fellows need to communicate better and more often.
- Similarly, there needs to be increased and better communication between Writing Fellows and students in a WAC course, and between writers and tutors in the writing center.
- Faculty members need to stress to students that the benefit of WAC is directly proportional to the amount of effort/thought that they put into their drafts.

What We're Doing to Improve

A successful WAC program depends on clear communication of expectations among professors, Fellows, and students. That is what influences the quality of assignments, the quality of drafts, attendance at conferences, and Teacher-Fellow consistency in written response to student writing. Improving the quality of communication is what WAC is about, after all, and it is what influences continual change in the way we train Writing Fellows and tutors. Incorporating contemporary learning theory within the training course has helped potential tutors and Fellows make more informed decisions about their practice in addressing the various learning needs of individual writers. Incorporating instructional technology has helped us create a community of learners so that tutors and Fellows have both a model and the experience of collaboration as they apply theory to practice in the Writing Center and WAC program. Additionally, conferencing software, as well as newsgroups and e-mail, helps tutors practice interpersonal skills in tutoring dialogues. Face-to-face discussions in role-playing sessions help them see how body language and tone of voice can work against collaboration. In training undergraduate tutors, however, it's not always easy to strike the right balance between emphasizing knowledge of composition/rhetoric theory and emphasizing interpersonal skills. Both are crucial to the success of WAC and writing centers, and we need to be mindful of it each semester that we face a new group of students.

In the fall of 1996, prospective Fellows began work on an electronic tool that will assist us in improving communication between Fellows, faculty, and students. The Fellows' Handbook reinforces the practice of collaborative learning with computers. The Handbook takes the form of a Web site created by Fellows in the training class. The collaborative project features small teams of Fellows who

- complete projects about writing in the academic disciplines assisted by the WAC program (most recently, working with ESL students, writing in biology and chemistry, and writing with technology)
- critique and revise other teams' entries, forge links to national and local resources
- develop a set of tutoring guidelines and "quick tips" for working with different types of writers and assignments
- and submit documents for peer review and scrutiny by scholars who visit the site.

The project will grow with each class of Fellows, and we hope, when the site is relatively complete, to use it in training faculty for the WAC program.

New Challenges

While we have a working model for bringing other teachers into the WAC program, we face a very different challenge as the university admits an ever larger number of students who speak English as a second language. Currently, the university plans to offer a summer transition program for some incoming ESL students, and Writing Fellows will be assigned to assist instructors in classes. The Fellows' training class will soon include more TESOL readings and a unit taught by a faculty member who teaches in the summer program. The exchange of information will flow both ways; the English classes for the ESL students will make heavy use of technology, especially newsgroups and electronic mail, familiar to the Fellows assisting the TESOL faculty in the summer program. We expect that, as with paper commentary, Fellows will "teach the teachers" how to integrate technology into their curriculum with success.

Our WAC program does not aim to spread technology across the curriculum, but we hope to link WAC to other programs that do. Our Faculty Technology Fellows project, which designates a "technology guru" in each department, spun off a Student Technology Fellows initiative. These students originally were hired to help peers use the campus network in dormitories. The program has evolved rapidly, and Student Technology Fellows now lead workshops for faculty and assist them in one-on-one tutorials. We hope to enhance this program by selecting several Writing Fellows to assist WAC faculty as they create class Web sites, use newsgroups, electronic mail, MOOs, or synchronous conferencing. Meanwhile, the university plans to begin a Teaching and Learning with Technology Roundtable, and this would further increase the awareness of good uses of instructional technology across the curriculum.

Collaborative learning has always included the teacher, but the focus has usually been on how students create knowledge. In the possible link between WAC and instructional technology, however, teachers would become co-learners with their students. Our Writing Fellows and tutors have the skills needed for the new millennium. Will teachers make the shift to learn from Writing Fellows who can provide a student's perspective on working with students from Ghana or Guatemala, how the Core class is changing their peers' perception of Islam, and "What's Cool" this week on the Web? It's our hope that teachers will make this much-needed paradigm shift. The WAC program, with its use of technology in the service of collaborative learning, provides one model for doing so.

Note

Our English Writing Lab consists of eighteen custom-built multimedia Pentium machines and a teacher's station. The machines are connected using a Novell LAN that provides access to software for Windows 95. The room has a Hewlett-Packard 3si laser printer and a high-resolution multimedia projector. For synchronous conferencing, students used the Daedalus Group's Daedalus/DOS and, most recently, W. W. Norton's Connect 1.0 for Windows. Newsgroups are handled by a remote VAX server, and all other software is stored on a UNIX server. Most files that students exchange are ASCII text. The Web browser for our syllabus is Netscape (version 3.0 as of the writing of this article). Most HTML files for class are written and saved in Rich Text Format, converted to HTML using the Macintosh program RTF-HTML Converter or PageMill, and embellished using Photoshop for Macintosh or MacDraw Pro.

Works Cited

Barker, T. T., and F. O. Kemp. 1990. "Network Theory: A Postmodern Pedagogy for the Writing Classroom." In *Computers and Community,* edited by Carolyn Handa, 1–27. Portsmouth, NH: Boynton/Cook.

Bartholomae, David. 1980. "The Study of Error." *College Composition and Communication* 31.3: 253–69.

Bruffee, Kenneth. 1984. "Peer Tutoring: A Conceptual Background." Paper presented at Brown University Conference on Peer Tutoring. Providence, Rhode Island. November.

Core Course Committee. 1995. "Core 101-102: Exploring Human Experience." Syllabus, 1995–96.

Hawisher, Gail E., and Cynthia Selfe. 1993. "Tradition and Change in Computer-Supported Writing Environments: A Call to Action." In *Theoretical and Critical Perspectives on Teacher Change,* edited by Phyllis Kahaney, L. A. M. Perry, and Joseph Janangelo. Norwood, NJ: Ablex.

Kolko, Beth. 1993. "Using Interchange Transcripts Recursively in the Writing Classroom." *Wings* 1.1: 4.

Moran, Charles. 1991. "We Write, but Do We Read?" *Computers and Composition* 8.3: 51–61.

Reiss, Donna. 1995. "Professional Development Across Disciplines with DIWE." *Wings* 3.2: 6–8.

Sommers, Nancy. 1982. "Responding to Student Writing." *College Composition and Communication* 33.2: 148–56.

Straub, Richard. 1996. "The Concept of Control in Teacher Response: Defining the Varieties of 'Directive' and 'Facilitative' Commentary." *College Composition and Communication* 47.2: 223–251.

University of Richmond. 1988. Faculty handbook. Richmond, VA: Author.

University of Richmond. 1994. *Engagement in Learning*. Richmond, VA: Author.

Resources

University of Richmond. "Writing-Across-the-Curriculum." http://www.richmond.edu/~wac

University of Richmond. "Writing Center." http://www.richmond.edu/~writing

6 From Case to Virtual Case: A Journey in Experiential Learning

Peter M. Saunders
Lehigh University

Experiential Learning: Bridging Management and Business Communication

Experiential learning in management education has had a long and productive history beginning with Harvard Business School's attempts in 1909 to bring realistic business situations into the classroom with the case method. Later, cases were supplemented with computer simulations and games (Chiesl 1990). Games and simulations, like cases, have been used in business education to provide learners with a broader picture of business forces, and to teach them how to maintain congruence between environmental constraints and organizational needs (Elgood 1984, 9). In 1993 it was estimated that 95 percent of business schools used business games in policy and marketing courses (Wolfe and Chanin 1993, 38).

As an instructor of business communication at a university teaching business graduates and undergraduates, I was determined to bridge the gap between management and communications pedagogies. A literature search uncovered a substantial body of literature in my discipline documenting the pedagogical value of using cases and simulations to teach business communication (Couture and Goldstein 1985; DiGaetani 1989; Gale 1993; Hartman 1992; Hugenberg 1992; Jameson 1993; Orth and Brown 1984; Rozumalski and Graves 1995). However, while a number of Harvard cases under the heading "management communication" were available, none dealt directly with the nature of language and social construction as processes of communication. Cases included in business communication textbooks were generally short (no more than a couple of paragraphs) and failed to provide enough context to capture the complexity of the problem-solving environment, and only a few required learners to work with primary materials.

I was also aware of recent movements in professional writing, organizational and compositional studies toward experiential learning, but could discern a fundamental philosophical difference between the emphasis given by man-

86

agement and by these latter disciplines to the role of language and interpretation in determining meaning. The "writing to learn" movement, for instance, with its emphasis on knowing as the activity and process of the mind making meaning from experience (Britton 1983; Emig 1981; Zinsser 1988), and shifts in composition theory (process theory, the social context of writing) placed greater emphasis on social context and individual cognitive processes shaped by and shaping cultural contexts (Berkenkotter and Huckin 1995; Catron 1984; Fisher 1971; Knoblauch 1989; Rozumalski and Graves 1995; Scharton 1989; Tedlock 1981). This interpretative perspective sees all communication and all organizations as transactions, and it sees organizations and communication as symbolically constructed and changed entities.

In contrast, the functionalist's perspective, implicit in most business cases, games, and simulations, views communication as an interaction between managers, organizations, and an environment. Such a perspective supports the systems approach which positions organizations as external, concrete entities in need of integration and control. Managers are, therefore, trained to be decision-makers, analyzers, and controllers of contingencies, and organizations are affected by their decisions, policies, procedures, structures, and processes. While social constructionists do not deny the physical nature of business organizations, they emphasize the fact that organizational structure is not a static thing but an ongoing process which continues to take new shape as individuals making up the organization transact meaning through communicative events (Pepper 1995, 11). Comparing the functionalist to the interpretative paradigm, Linda Smircich notes that in the latter, a manager is "a framer of contexts, a maker and shaper of interpretive schemes . . ." (1983, 227) and organized actions occur "through the achievement of shared meanings" (226). It seemed logical that this split would make an interesting subject for a business communication case.

Developing a Communication Case to Bridge the Gap

Because of the paucity of available communication cases addressing the interpretative/functional perspectives, I developed a communication case entitled "The Case of the Unhappy Client." The challenge, as I saw it, was to embrace experiential learning by using the case method and at the same time demonstrate the interpretative/functional perspectives at work in a real-world situation. Using the telecommunication industry for this case, learners were asked to trace a series of misunderstandings which developed between a general manager, a technical services coordinator, his assistant, and a client. To create the "feel" of the actual communication process, I provided all correspondence between the principal people involved as well as background information on the telecommunication industry. Whereas most paper cases are tied to a narrative structure, "The Case of the Unhappy Client" uses the "in basket" technique, thus permitting learners to experience the flow of communication across distinct discourse communities. The intent was not only to have learners read about miscommunication, but also to expose them to the same linguistic and cognitive processes which contributed to the breakdown in communication, processes such as inferencing, attribution, and coordinated management of meaning. While carrying out a "functionalist task" of problem solving, it was hoped that learners would discover the impact the interpretative powers play. The case required that students discover the causes for these miscommunications and, using writing strategies taught in the course, create effective bad news and persuasive documents.

"The Case of the Unhappy Client" was used in hard copy format in an introductory business communication course open to sophomores and juniors from all disciplines. Because the case required knowledge of rhetorical strategies for handling negative news and persuasion, the case was introduced to students, who worked in teams, immediately after these subjects were discussed. Student response to the case exercise was positive, as indicated by the following comments:

- I liked the fact that it provided a realistic context in which to apply the tools acquired in this course. I also enjoyed the process of searching through past documents to solve a set of questions.

- Being a detective was the best part of the unhappy client.

- It reflects a real situation; communication obstacles and misinterpretations happen all the time; it was interesting to experience/observe/read about the events and functions that structure a company; the company itself was sophisticated and produced a life-like example. "No Mickey Mouse Stuff!"

- It felt as if it was real life. That part was a bit interesting.

- I found it very challenging and enjoyed being assigned to such a task. It made me feel a part of the whole situation, as if it were real.

At the heart of all experiential learning theory lies the fundamental idea that active involvement with concrete experience produces learning. Student references to "real life" when commenting on their experiences working with "The Case of the Unhappy Client" were gratifying and motivated me to seek ways to make this case even more concrete, more experiential. While the paper case and in-basket methodology seemed somewhat effective, these formats, nevertheless, presented certain limitations. The paper case removed learners from *experiencing* the socially constructed, contextual aspects of business, aspects which figure largely in the interpretative/functional perspectives and the problem-solving process. The split created by printed texts seemed to rob learners of any sense of immediacy which electronic texts could create. Hard copy also did not provide learners an opportunity to use information technology as a tool. Most employees today would have to rely on information technology to search and retrieve information regarding clients, sales data, product descriptions, etc. More important, printed texts gave them little sense of the role information technology played in creating and sustaining the sense of community within a firm or industry.

There were other drawbacks to the use of the hard copy case format. Arts-and-science students unfamiliar with business concepts and processes and the case method felt they were at a greater disadvantage than business students. Furthermore, most students, regardless of their majors, were unfamiliar with the telecommunication industry and commented that more introductory material on this industry should have been provided. (Logistically, it was simply not feasible to offer such information in the lecture schedule.) Finally, students for whom English was their second language also found the language difficult and performed poorly on the written assignments. The case method clearly was a step in the right direction, but it appeared that a more experiential method might overcome these limitations. Since the movement in business and communication education was toward greater reality and experiential learning, it seemed logical that I might be able to combine both the case method and the use of a computer simulation to achieve these goals. One other development influenced my decision to move beyond the use of the traditional case format to a computer simulation.

WAC, Business Communication, and the Development of a Learning Platform

Besides teaching a business communication course, I also served as the director of a professional writing center. Part of my responsibilities included supporting the university's writing-across-the-curriculum (WAC) effort. Although the university had an active writing clinic, an elective business communication course, and a funded professional writing center, our efforts to integrate writing into the business curriculum met with little success. In the spring of 1986 the College's faculty voted to introduce a writing requirement into its curriculum. There was evidence that business and industry were finding graduate competencies wanting in writing and communication (Addams 1981; Halpern 1981; Stine and Skarzenski 1979; Swindle 1982) and that faculty in a number of business subject areas were getting good results with the introduction of writing as a tool for learning (Crowe and Youga 1986; DeLespinasse 1985; Dickerson 1978; Drenk 1982; Field et al. 1985). While Lehigh faculty agreed that composition courses taken in the first year were important, there was a general feeling that writing skills were being allowed to erode. Faculty agreed that writing was a vehicle for both communication and learning. The economics department in particular was influenced by Zinsser's *Writing to Learn*. In essence the College of Business and Economics accepted and agreed to try to implement the idea of "writing across the curriculum."

As Fulwiler and Young (1990) have noted, while some WAC programs have made real changes in undergraduate and graduate education, others have floundered even with sufficient funding. At my institution, although faculty wanted to support the WAC cause, most felt that their course content would be compromised if their course concentrated on writing. Most faculty were willing to have someone from the writing clinic deliver a fifteen- to twenty-minute "lecture" on how to improve one's writing. Scheduling such visits proved difficult. Reflecting their functionalist perspective, faculty looked upon communication issues as "training" and writing and speaking as tools. Many faculty felt that a quick review of the rules of punctuation would be sufficient. Language and its ability to construct and deconstruct the reality of business was not a familiar concept, nor one easily accepted. Although our Center offered these "motivational" lectures each semester, because they lacked any instructional component, student writing performance remained unchanged.

My immediate concern was to find some way of integrating writing and communication issues into our business courses and somehow avoid many of the obstacles which WAC administrators have been encountering ever since WAC began in the mid-1970s. A few points were clear: first, trying to win faculty approval would take too long; second, because integration was not possible in many courses, our successes would be partial at best; third, students and some faculty would continue to view communication issues and skills as irrelevant as long as the curriculum continued to exclude, demote, and, therefore, divorce communication from the study of organizations and management theory.

Ironically, because of rigid disciplinary barriers, I soon became convinced that I was looking in the wrong direction for a solution. Like so many WAC directors, I was attempting to initiate change within the forty- or fifty-minute class period; but what if the changes we wanted could take place outside the class in the computer lab in a simulated environment? My study of communication, organization, and composition theory had convinced me that communication instruction and its key issues stood a better chance of succeeding if communication could be experienced by learners as fundamental to all social interaction within a real or simulated business context outside the classroom. Could a solution to the problem of integrating business communication and writing across the curriculum lie in the direction of experiential learning?

From Case to Learning Platform

In 1993 I began developing a simulation of the electronic network of the telecommunication firm I had used in my paper case. My goal was to create a traditional simulation which would model some system or process, such as the grapevine or rich communication, allowing learners to explore key variables and how they interact and affect performance (Teach 1990, 94). Writing help would be integrated into the simulation so students could access this information as the need arose. Learners would role-play company employees and would be given data and information about internal and external communication constraints, critical decisions which must be made, and tasks to be completed. As in most simulations, mine would require that multiple decisions be made along the way as learners work within the framework of the system under investigation. Learners would play not against other players, but rather against the system. And because language and interpretation would be crucial to the case, I preferred to have all learner correspondence sent via e-mail to my office. Once received, I would then send back a response or a series of responses. By this method I was able to monitor the progress learners were making.

Figure 6.1 ("The Office") illustrates the opening screen to the simulation, which represents the learner's office where all work is carried out. The options menu located at the top of the screen provided access to e-mail, training, company databases (including customer, personnel, supplier files, product information, and financial data), summaries of meetings, and selected utilities such as the address and appointment files. Students who selected the "training" option could access a file entitled "Instructor's Comments" which offered some sug-

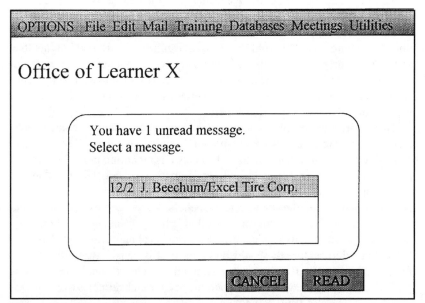

Figure 6.1. "The Office."

gestions about how the problems presented in the case might be approached. Students were also encouraged to look at the Quicktime video "lecture" on how to handle bad news. By selecting the "file" option, learners could access a word processor, create a response and "mail" it to their fictional manager. When students first log on, they discover that a message from their boss, R. Medley, is waiting for them. By having each student's name appear on the screen, I tried to strengthen the illusion that each learner was intimately tied to the context of the events which were to occur on the screen. The first action learners take is opening and reading this document.

Essentially, this document informs learners that their boss, R. Medley, faces a complaint from an irate client, Janet Beechum. The message provides a few sketchy details and then asks that the learner search through the correspondence and e-mail folders and decide "what went wrong." Learners are then to e-mail a summary of their findings to Medley and to draft a letter for Medley's signature setting the client straight and retaining her goodwill. These documents were sent directly to the instructor via the college's e-mail system.

In a usability test, four students were asked to "work the case"; their reactions were essentially the same as those students who had worked with the paper case, which was encouraging. In transferring hard-copy documents to the electronic medium, I was able to achieve a greater sense of realism by having students complete all their work on the computer and by creating the illusion that their manager had actually given them a problem to solve and was counting on their problem-solving skills. One student commented, "It is realistic; it possesses a challenge of not only having to write but to investigate and to come up with a solution (enjoyable). Role playing—responsibility to resolve the situation. Interesting once the problem surfaces. Definitely more good points than bad." On the negative side, testers continued to complain about their unfamiliarity with the telecommunication industry, the lack of language support for second language learners, and their uncertainty about how the case method worked and what was expected of them.

There were other problems not mentioned by these students that needed correcting. Unlike in other business games and simulations such as *The Executive Game*—which require learners to make decisions regarding price, investment, production volume, and research and development which are then acted on by a mathematical model—in this simulation I wanted to explore socially constructed processes and the realities they create— beliefs, values, genres, and communication practices—variables normally excluded from business simulations. Unfortunately, I could see that my computerized version of the "Case of the Unhappy Client" failed to capture these added dimensions. Because my simulation was to be an organizational/social-process simulation, a closed simulation focusing primarily on data management of economic or financial variables over a period of time, while valid from a functionalist's point of view, imposed too many restrictions on the processes I wanted students to explore. As Linda Putnam (1983) points out, "functionalists assume a unitary view of organizations; that is, organizations are treated as cooperative systems in pursuit of common interests and goals" (36); whereas "interpretivists are more likely . . . to adopt a pluralistic perspective by treating the organization as an array of factionalized groups with diverse purposes and goals" (37). With these points in mind, work began on a learning platform which would permit students to work on their case problem and support their learning needs at the same time.

Figure 6.2 ("The Map") reproduces the "learning platform" screen which appears after students first log on to the system. Moving across the screen from top left to right, I added a computer icon linking learners to their offices where individual cases were worked on. To add greater realism and to help students get the feel of what a telecommunication firm is all about, I provided more context on my simulated telecommunication company which I called the Corporation of the Future (CoF). Using multimedia and information technology to mirror the world my students would work in, I added information which conveyed the multiple dimensions of community (social, linguistic, political) by

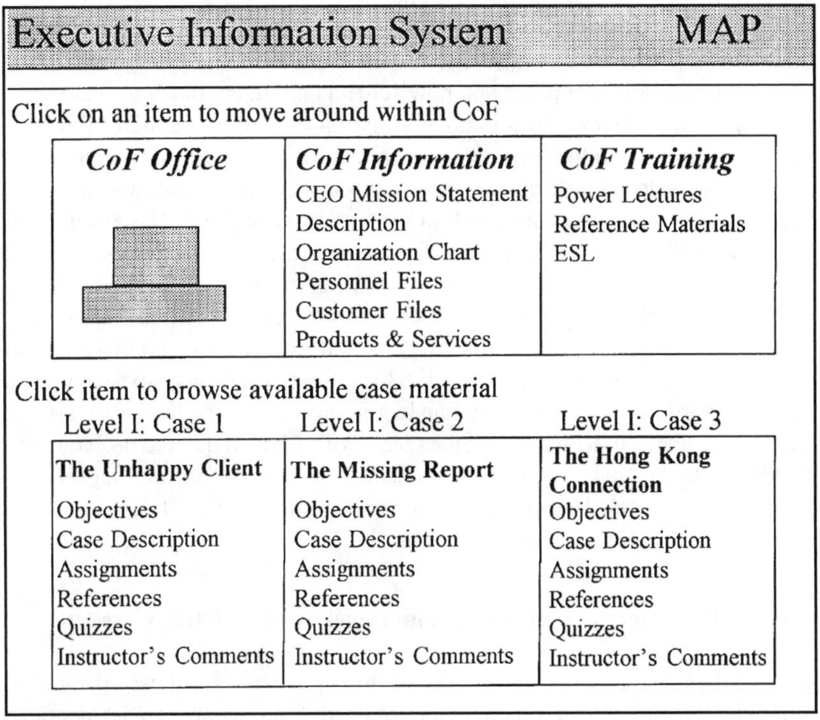

Executive Information System		MAP
Click on an item to move around within CoF		
CoF Office	**CoF Information**	**CoF Training**
	CEO Mission Statement	Power Lectures
	Description	Reference Materials
	Organization Chart	ESL
	Personnel Files	
	Customer Files	
	Products & Services	
Click item to browse available case material		
Level I: Case 1	Level I: Case 2	Level I: Case 3
The Unhappy Client	**The Missing Report**	**The Hong Kong Connection**
Objectives	Objectives	Objectives
Case Description	Case Description	Case Description
Assignments	Assignments	Assignments
References	References	References
Quizzes	Quizzes	Quizzes
Instructor's Comments	Instructor's Comments	Instructor's Comments

Figure 6.2. "The Map."

adding the following items under the heading "CoF Information": a company mission statement narrated by the CEO of the firm and delivered via Quicktime movie, a description of what a telecommunication firm does, an organization chart, financial statements, more explicit details about each employee including photographs, and a short Powerpoint presentation on the products and services offered by the firm. Such additions meant that I could retain the possibility of using CoF as a tactical-decision simulation, but I could now provide learners with enough information to give them the feel of what a telecommunication firm is all about and a look at the people who work there.

Because I wanted to integrate writing and communication instruction into the fabric of the platform and to support ESL learners, I expanded the concept of training to include lectures on how to handle bad news and on how to work with cases, and shorter lectures on inferencing, the interpretative perspective, and information technology as communication content and process. Reference materials and an ESL help button were added. For selected documents, the ESL help button would appear at the top of the screen. When students clicked on this button, difficult idioms, verb forms, and jargon would be highlighted. When students clicked on a highlighted expression or word, a box would appear offering information on the meaning of the item.

The bottom half of the screen provided case-specific information such as course objectives, case description, details on assignments due, references, quizzes, and instructor's comments on how students might approach the case.

Like many of today's corporations, CoF required extensive use of information technology to collect, process, transmit, and disseminate information. And while most students, influenced by the functionalist perspective, would see the technology as transparent and look to the "information," the "Case of the Unhappy Client" required that they learn about the interpretative perspective and how the very technologies they were using, like the cognitive processes they were using, were keys to solving the case problem. As Christina Haas (1996) has noted, "a technology is not an object, but rather a vital system that is bound to the world of time and space; that is, a technology is always inextricably tied both to a particular moment in human history and to the practical action of the human life world in which it is embedded" (xii). I hoped that the problem embedded in the "virtual case" would raise questions about when information technology should be used to solve communication problems and when face-to-face communication should be used.

Student Performance and Perception: Paper versus Virtual Case

Students' grades were not significantly different in classes that used the virtual simulation versus the ones using paper; indeed, both classes' grades declined when students were faced with "negative news" assignments. Perhaps students had difficulty with the case study per se for a couple of reasons. First, they simply did not have the opportunity to practice the rhetorical skills or develop the knowledge of human psychology required by this type of case study. Performance with paper and virtual cases may decline if learners have not first mastered the specific strategies required by case problems.

Second, it was also clear from the post-questionnaire comments that a number of students still found the technical concepts (telecommunication) and language associated with satellite transmission intimidating despite a glossary of terms available to them. In most cases in the real world, of course, employees have months and sometimes years to learn the discourse of their place of employment or industry. Students also require immersion in the linguistic landscapes of the workplace reflected in the cases they are to work on *before* they attempt to work these cases. Indeed, instructors may have to make linguistic tradeoffs when creating paper and virtual cases.

Students were also asked to indicate their preferences for the following teaching methods: the case method, reading a textbook, attending a lecture, other methods. Students consistently chose attending a lecture over the case method, but when asked specifically about "The Case of the Unhappy Client," separate from the case method as a general method of learning, a significant number of students from both groups indicated they preferred the paper and virtual case over other methods! More of them rated this specific case as interesting and challenging and said they would like assignments like it. The experiential nature of the case method appears to have universal appeal, even to first-time case and computer users. Indeed, the computer and the use of information technology offer case writers an opportunity to increase this realism, as the following student comments indicate:

- I liked the "detective work" that was involved. I found it very realistic having to dig for the information. (Use of the computer made this necessary. All the information was there but we had to navigate through the system to get at it.) The case itself reflected the political nature of organizational problems and had many people and departments involved.

- I liked it because I found it relevant to life. In university courses it is rare (at least in my program) to encounter practical learning tools. I was very impressed overall with the assignment and I found it very interesting. A novice at the computer, I found the operation nonetheless straight forward. I would definitely encourage this format for future classes.

- What I like most about the case of the "Unhappy Client" is the challenge to understand, read, and respond using two different approaches, i.e. E-Mail/Bad News Document. To find the problem was very challenging.

Student Use of the Learning Platform

Because the focus of this study was to compare student performance and perception of the traditional case versus a multimedia version, no formal data was collected regarding the use of the learning platform's various file options. However, informal observations of students at their computers produced a number of interesting points. Although students were each assigned to individual computers, most students preferred to work in teams of two or three, with one student manipulating the computer while the others dialogued on both the nature of the problem and possible solutions. At times, groups would decide to divide their search tasks, work on their own, and then return to report their findings. Collaborative learning was definitely the method of choice when students worked on the learning platform. Approximately two thirds of the students using computers referred to the Quicktime video "lecture" on how to handle bad news. Providing mini-lectures via Quicktime movies or Powerpoint presentations to be accessed during the problem-solving process appears to be an efficient way of serving the needs of learners. While many students explored the "CoF Information" files, many did not. Providing richer contextual information does not ensure that students will feel the need to access this information. Unless instructed to do so, many students ignore such information which would help them understand the problem at hand. Further study is needed to determine if students receive higher grades on their assignments when they explore the files which provide background material on the telecommunications industry.

Students found little difficulty accessing financial and written data and moved easily from the "office" to the college's word processor. It would be interesting to provide additional access to the Web and to redesign the case so that learners integrate Internet search techniques as part of their problem-solving activities.

When the ESL help function was added, it was thought that students would use this function as most computer users use the help functions found in most software programs, such as the "Balloon Help" option of Microsoft's Word. Typically, users select the help function to find a quick answer to a specific problem or function. Our ESL learners did not use the ESL help function in this way; to our surprise, ESL students used the help function as a language tutorial! Groups of two or three learners would go through each underlined expression and discuss its meaning and use before attempting the case problem. One student from Hong Kong told me that he was as interested in how the English language is used to conduct business as he was in solving the case. For multimedia case developers, language support and language issues are central to ESL learners and provide a gateway to our own linguistic landscapes. In "The Case of the Unhappy Client" ESL students wanted to know how language wraps itself around business and used the help function to achieve this end.

Using the Platform to Integrate Lehigh's MBA Curriculum and Communication

In a recent article published in *Change*, the American Association for Higher Education's magazine, Elaine Hairston describes a structural "metamorphosis" which significant numbers of American businesses have undergone during the 1980s and early '90s as they struggled to remain competitive. Driven by global competition, rising costs, lower market share and profits margins, rapid obsolescence of product lines, and the impact of information technology, companies and whole industries have restructured and consolidated their operations, placing increasing pressures on their employees to meet higher performance goals within shorter time periods. The end result for many companies, Hairston points out, is similar to what has happened to B. F. Goodrich: "the company's whole mode of operating today is more intense, rapid and more productive, and its technological and other systems are better" (1996, 35). What also changed was the type of manager needed to succeed in this fast-paced world where agility and adaptability are revered. The old model of manager, as someone skilled at directing operations within a centralized, hierarchical organization with layers and layers of bureaucracy, was quickly becoming irrelevant. For graduate institutions and programs training future managers, there was a clear and urgent message from American business: today's managers require a restructuring of old competencies, plus new knowledge and new skills.

Part of this new knowledge includes a thorough grasp of an industry's structure and the impact economic and competitive forces exert on that industry's competitive advantage. Managers must also understand the role information technology is playing in the new electronic networked environment where change can be both friend and foe (Applegate, McFarlan, and McKenney 1996). Some MBAs will no doubt work in traditional, highly structured, hierarchical companies which are being forced to change, but more will find themselves in newer corporate structures which are integrated, extended, open, and networked, where activities are focused around multidisciplinary teams capable of crossing departmental boundaries, reaching into every part of their enterprise from suppliers to clients (Tapscott and Caston 1993, 33). Corporations and organizations extend far beyond the traditional boundaries of stone and mortar, extending even beyond the traditional organizational chart. Today we have virtual corporations and organizations which consist of a temporary network of independent companies—suppliers, customers, even erstwhile rivals—linked by information technology to share skills and costs, and to provide access to one another's markets. What is curious about these developments is that while Porter (1980), Tapscott, Caston, and others stress the need for greater skill integration, mastery of information technology, and better ways of achieving what Fuld (1995) calls "competitor intelligence," little mention is made by these authors of the significant role language and interpretation play in these activities. Indeed, communication issues are largely ignored.

As part of Lehigh University's response to the growing number of MBA programs competing for a finite number of students, the changing needs of today's agile companies, and the globalization of American business, its College of Business and Economics (CBE) set about restructuring its MBA and professional education programs and turned to its Center for Business Communication and the learning platform as a possible vehicle for integrating the MBA curriculum and for developing new agile managers. At this writing, the learning platform is being modified to reflect the operations of a major American microelectronics firm whose corporate structure is integrated, extended, open, and networked, and whose activities are focused around multidisciplinary teams who are required to cross departmental boundaries. Working closely with this firm, business faculty representing different functional areas will develop cases to be used in their courses, and faculty from business communication will attempt to integrate writing and communication into each case. The "office" will include links to financial databases and the Internet. Video lectures will also be integrated into the platform, and communication, writing, and ESL support will be added under "Training." A grant from AT&T's Foundation is helping to make this a reality. A major challenge for business education has been demonstrating how the various competencies taught relate to each other and to the workplace. By having students work cases in different courses which refer to a single company, and by integrating communication and writing training into the fabric of the learning platform, it is hoped that the relatedness of what we teach will become apparent and the MBAs we graduate will have a greater sense of how to apply what they learn and how to meet the communication challenges that they will face.

Works Cited

Addams, H. Lon. 1981. "Should the Big 8 Teach Communication Skills?" *Management Accounting* 62.11: 37–40.

Applegate, Lynda M., F. Warren McFarlan, and James L. McKenney. 1996. *Corporate Information Systems Management: Text and Cases*, 4th ed. Chicago: Richard D. Irwin.

Berkenkotter, Carol, and Thomas Huckin. 1995. *Genre Knowledge in Disciplinary Communication*. Hillsdale, NJ: Lawrence Erlbaum Associates.

Britton, James. 1983. "Language and Learning Across the Curriculum." In *Fforum: Essays on Theory and Practice in the Teaching of Writing,* edited by Patricia L. Stock, 221–24. Portsmouth, NH: Boynton/Cook.

Catron, Douglas M. 1984. "A Case for Cases." *Bulletin of the Association for Business Communication,* 47.2: 21–25.

Chiesl, N.E. 1990. "Interactive Real Time Simulation." In *Guide to Business Gaming and Experiential Learning,* edited by J. Gentry, 141–158. London: Nichols/GP.

Couture, B., and J. R. Goldstein. 1985. "Procedures for Developing a Technical Communication Case." In *The Case Method in Technical Communication: Theory and Models*, edited by R. J. Brockmann, 33–46. Lubbock, TX: Association of Teachers of Technical Writing.

Crowe, Douglas, and Janet Youga. 1986. "Using Writing as a Tool for Learning Economics." *Journal of Economic Education* 17: 218–22.

DeLespinasse, Doris. 1985. "Writing Letters to Clients: Connecting Textbook Problems with the Real World." *Journal of Accounting Education* 3.1: 197–200.

Dickerson, Reed. 1978. "Legal Drafting: Writing as Thinking, or Talk-Back from Your Draft and How to Exploit It." *Journal of Legal Education* 29.4: 373–79.

DiGaetani, John L. 1989. "Use of the Case Method in Teaching Business Communication." In *Writing in the Business Professions,* edited by M. Kogen, 187–201. Urbana, IL: National Council of Teachers of English.

Drenk, Dean. 1982. "Teaching Finance through Writing." In *Teaching Writing in All Disciplines,* edited by C. Williams Griffin, 53–58. San Francisco: Jossey-Bass.

Elgood, Chris. 1984. *Handbook of Management Games.* 3rd ed. Brookfield, VT: Gower.

Emig, Janet. 1977. "Writing as a Mode of Learning." *College Composition and Communication* 28.2: 122–28. Reprinted in *The Writing Teacher's Sourcebook*, edited by G. Tate and E. Corbett (1981). New York: Oxford University Press.

Field, William J., Daniel R. Wachter, and Anthony V. Catanese. 1985. "Alternative Ways to Teach and Learn Economics: Writing, Quantitative Reasoning, and Oral Communication." *Journal of Economic Education* 16: 213–17.

Fisher, C. F. 1971. "Being There Vicariously by Case Studies." In *On College Teaching*, edited by O. Milton and Associates, 258–85. San Francisco: Jossey-Bass.

Fuld, Leonard M. 1995. *The New Competitor Intelligence: The Complete Resource for Finding, Analyzing, and Using Information about Your Competitors.* New York: John Wiley and Sons.

Fulwiler, Toby, and Art Young. 1990. *Programs That Work: Models and Methods for Writing Across the Curriculum.* Portsmouth, NH: Boynton/Cook.

Gale, F. G. 1993. "Teaching Professional Writing Rhetorically: The Unified Case Method." *Journal of Business and Technical Communication* 7.2: 256–66.

Haas, Christina. 1996. *Writing Technology: Studies on the Materiality of Literacy.* Mahwah, NJ: Lawrence Erlbaum Associates.

Hairston, Elaine. 1996. "A Picaresque Journey: Corporate Change, Technological Tidal Waves, and Webby Worldviews." *Change* (March/April): 32–37.

Halpern, Jeanne. W. 1981. "What Should We Be Teaching Students in Business Writing?" *Journal of Business Communication* 18.3: 39–53.

Hartman, Larry D. 1992. "Business Communication and the Case Method: Toward Integration in Accounting and MBA Graduate Programs." *Bulletin of the Association for Business Communication* 55.3: 41–45.

Hugenberg, Lawrence W. 1992. "Simulations as a Fundamental Teaching Tool: Striking the Appropriate Balance." *Bulletin of the Association for Business Communication* 55.4: 65–69.

Jameson, Daphne A. 1993. "Using a Simulation to Teach Intercultural Communication in Business Communication Courses." *Bulletin of the Association for Business Communication* 56.1: 3–11.

Knoblauch, C. H. 1989. "The Teaching and Practice of 'Professional Writing.'" In *Writing in the Business Professions,* edited by Myra Kogen, 246–64. Urbana, IL: National Council of Teachers of English.

Orth, Michael, and Carl R. V. Brown. 1984. "Computer Generated Rhetorical Simulations for Business and Report Writing Courses." *Journal of Technical Writing and Communication* 14.1: 29–34.

Pepper, Gerald. 1995. *Communicating in Organizations: A Cultural Approach.* New York: McGraw-Hill.

Porter, Michael E. 1980. *Competitive Strategy: Techniques for Analyzing Industries and Competitors.* New York: Free Press.

Putnam, Linda. 1983. "The Interpretative Perspective: An Alternative to Functionalism." In *Communication and Organizations: An Interpretive Approach,* edited by Linda Putnam and Michael Pacanowsky, 31–54. Newbury Park, CA: Sage Publications.

Rozumalski, L. P., and M. F. Graves. 1995. "Effects of Case and Traditional Writing Assignments on Writing Products and Processes." *Journal of Business and Technical Communication* 9.1: 77–102.

Scharton, Maurice. 1989. "Models of Competence: Responses to a Scenario Writing Assignment." *Research in the Teaching of English* 23.2: 163–80.

Smircich, Linda. 1983. "Implications for Management Theory." In *Communication and Organizations: An Interpretive Approach,* edited by Linda Putnam and Michael Pacanowsky, 221–41. Newbury Park, CA: Sage Publications.

Stine, Donna, and Donald Skarzenski. 1979. "Priorities for the Business Communication Classroom: A Survey of Business and Academe." *Journal of Business Communication* 16.3: 15–30.

Swindle, R. E. 1982. "Making Certain That Graduates Can Write." *Bulletin of the Association for Business Communication* 45.1: 7–10.

Tapscott, Don, and Art Caston. 1993. *Paradigm Shift: The New Promise of Information Technology.* New York: McGraw-Hill.

Teach, R. D. 1990. "Designing Business Simulations." In *Guide to Business Gaming and Experiential Learning,* edited by J. Gentry. London: Nichols/GP.

Tedlock, David. 1981. "The Case Approach to Composition." *College Composition and Communication* 32.3: 253–61.

Wolfe, Joseph, and Michael Chanin. 1993. "The Integration of Functional and Strategic Management Skills in a Business Game Learning Environment." *Simulation & Gaming* 24.1: 34–46.

Zinsser, William. 1988. *Writing to Learn.* New York: Harper and Row.

Resources

Communication Education newsgroup: Bit.Listserv.Commed

Communication discussion groups:

XCULT-L: for discussing intercultural communication
Contact address: Oliver@dhvx20.csudh.edu (Oliver Seely)
E-mail address: listserv@psuvm.psu.edu (Bitnet: LISTSERV@PSUVM)

XCULT-X: for interdisciplinary discussion of communication philosophy, theory, and practice via computer-mediated communication
E-mail address: listserv@umrvmb.umr.edu (Bitnet: LISTSERV@UMRVMB)

Communication research and theory:

CRTNET: A magazine about communication research and theory.
Contact address: t3b@psuvm.bitnet (Bitnet: T3B@PSUVM)
E-mail address: listserv@psuvm.psu.edu (Bitnet: LISTSERV@PSUVM)

Discussion group for instructors of business communications: BIZCOM@EBBS.ENGL

7 Composing Human-Computer Interfaces Across the Curriculum in Engineering Schools

Stuart A. Selber
Texas Tech University

Bill Karis
Clarkson University

In this chapter, we discuss some contributions that technical communication studies might make to electronic communication across the curriculum in engineering schools. One premise of our chapter is that teachers of technical communication, those individuals interested in nonacademic writing issues and communication practices in modern technological contexts, have areas of expertise that can productively influence the teaching of human-computer interface design for World Wide Web pages, multimedia programs, and hypertext applications. Another premise of the chapter is that within the context of an engineering or technological school, these areas of expertise, areas which are rooted in a multitude of humanistic and rhetorical traditions, are often either undervalued or not well understood, and that in many instances technical communication teachers will need to make arguments that demonstrate the pedagogical value of their perspectives. In this chapter, we provide a framework for helping teachers make these arguments in their own institutions.

We begin the chapter with some local context, describing writing-across-the-curriculum efforts at Clarkson University and recent movements toward electronic-communication-across-the-curriculum activities. Next, looking more closely at these electronic activities, we briefly discuss the emerging digital composition practices that we see in science and engineering courses—practices that are not uncommon in other colleges and universities focusing on science, engineering, and technological enterprises. In the main portion of the chapter, we outline five key areas associated with technical communication that relate to communication across the curriculum in an electronic age: interface design practices, usability testing methods, pedagogical issues, humanistic perspectives on computer technologies, and electronic portfolios of professional work. Although we focus on technical communication and engineering contexts, our discussion should be useful to a wide range of teachers and researchers: as other chapters in this collection indicate, teaching about the design of World Wide Web pages, multimedia programs, and hypertext applications is a pedagogical practice that interests many different disciplines.

Movements toward Electronic Communication Across the Curriculum

For a variety of institutional and political reasons, writing-across-the-curriculum activities at Clarkson University have been relatively limited in historical terms. Despite guidance from several WAC specialists, including Anne Herrington, Gail Hawisher, and William Condon, the only formal initiatives that currently exist at Clarkson are in early pilot stages. However, the Department of Technical Communications is expanding these efforts by engaging in three interdisciplinary projects broadly related to electronic communication across the curriculum: supporting the instructional design of two major CD-ROM initiatives in the School of Engineering; developing a master's degree program in electronic communication and rhetoric that includes courses taught by teachers working in other departments; and creating a communication center that can help undergraduate and graduate students from across the curriculum develop a wide range of literacies, including those associated with computer-mediated communication. Increasingly, such centers promote a model of electronic communication across the curriculum that is network-supported and writing-center-based (Palmquist, Rodrigues, Kiefer, and Zimmerman 1995).

The two engineering initiatives represent major funding sources for Clarkson University professors. The Center for Advancement in Instruction for Science and Engineering (CAISE) is developing CD-ROM-based textbooks for the delivery of online engineering curricula. This project is currently funded by a variety of corporations and government agencies: General Motors ($750,000 over three years), NASA ($300,000 over two years) and EDS ($150,000 over three years). The Clarkson Thin Film Multi-Media Development group, funded by the National Science Foundation ($400,000 over three years), is developing hypermedia-based instructional materials for teaching thin-film technologies to engineering students. The role of technical communication in these two projects is in the related areas of interface design and usability testing. Working in these critical development areas is helping the department accomplish two connected goals: positioning itself as a contributing member to dominant research activities on campus; and, in turn, productively influencing the ways in which science and engineering teachers teach human-computer interaction principles to students across the curriculum.

As with many institutions, Clarkson is rethinking its approach to education within the context of shrinking fiscal resources. Operating with budget deficits for the past five years, the university has hired a new president and reformulated its vision of what a Clarkson education should promote: in short, (1) solutions to real-world, open-ended problems; (2) exceptional communication skills; (3) collaborative projects; and (4) instructional computing. Historically, as with many technical communication programs, the department has supported more traditional print-based publications work, work that is still important but not aligned in square ways with the evolving educational goals of many technological institutions in the late 1990s or with the emerging research directions of the technical communication profession. By partially refocusing research and teaching activities around two linked components of the university's new vision statement—developing exceptional communication skills using instructional computing technologies—the department is beginning to revitalize itself in both intellectual and fiscal terms: it has hired a new faculty member, built a new multimedia lab, developed new courses on World Wide Web authoring and rhetorics of the Internet, developed the online writing lab (OWL) on campus, and gained other kinds of material support, both internally and externally.

This new focus on electronic communication and instructional computing is helping the department make contributions to electronic communication across the curriculum. Not only has technical communication contributed to the interface design of CD-ROM-based instructional materials developed on campus, for example, but these contributions, in turn, have encouraged broader pedagogical discussions with the university President, Dean of Liberal Studies, and engineering professors in different departments. In the long run, we hope that our willingness to accommodate the multimedia and instructional design needs of science and engineering teachers will abate their resistance, in many instances, to humanistic and rhetorical perspectives on student writing in online information space. As Spilka (1993) cogently argues, agents of change and social innovation must also be agents of accommodation on some level. Composing in an electronic age at engineering schools, we realize that student writing in science and engineering courses is still often paper-based. Students use word processing, graphics, statistics, mathematics, and other computer programs to create reports, feasibility studies, research papers, journal entries, proposals, and other documents that are laser printed on white paper and handed in for evaluation. And it is a safe assumption, we think, that these paper-based requirements will continue in educational environments: conservative institutional forces—for example, standard curricular approaches, teaching and research perspectives invested in technologies of print, and certification agencies for academic programs—often encourage rather than defy existing discursive practices in classroom settings. Moreover, clear value exists in helping students develop the print-based literacies still privileged in most aspects of corporate and civic life.

At the same time, the projects of science and engineering encourage technological optimism. Despite critiques from rhetoricians of science and from scientists and engineers concerned about human and environmental conditions, the Western, commonsense connection between technologies of all sorts and cultural and educational progress remains strong (Feenberg and Hannay 1995; Smith and Marx 1994). In most disciplines, at least some teachers on our campuses seem interested in computer-based writing and the promise of hardware and software to support new and different ways of learning. And indeed, in many cases a significant number of institutional resources are being shifted in this direction—consider, for example, the grant monies now available on college campuses for instructional computing purposes in all areas. Although as humanists we tend to be more skeptical about the potential of mechanical devices, on their own, to bring about productive pedagogical change in classroom settings, we appreciate the enthusiasm of the science and engineering teachers we see working along a continuum of modest to robust electronic-communication-across-the-curriculum approaches.

In terms of modest efforts, teachers use electronic mail to promote student communication beyond the temporal and spatial boundaries of the classroom, synchronous conferencing sessions supported by local-area networks to provide alternative forums for classroom discussion, and asynchronous conversations supported by wide-area networks to extend both face-to-face and online, real-time discussion. Entire courses revolve around bulletin board applications running on campus-wide servers in which teachers post and collect writing assignments, projects, quizzes, and tests. The electronic writing done in connection with these efforts is often valuable: in many instances, science and engineering students have more opportunities in which to write over the course of a term, more informal contexts in which to write, and more opportunities in which to use writing as a way of collaborating, knowing, and learning. Even when teachers use these computer technologies for reasons of simple technical efficiency, we often see the kinds of positive effects just outlined (although automating course requirements and procedures is not without its pedagogical problems).

For the purposes of this chapter, teachers working in more robust ways are of particular interest. Increasingly, we see teachers asking students to develop World Wide Web pages, multimedia programs, and hypertext applications, and to author electronic course-related projects either in place of or in addition to more traditional print-based assignments. We suspect that this kind of digital composition will become increasingly common in colleges and universities, not just in science and engineering courses but in many other types of courses as well. Indeed, as we draft this chapter (April 1997), AltaVista, a popular search engine developed by Digital Equipment Corporation, finds thirty-one million World Wide Web pages on 627,000 Internet servers, and multimedia projects in both academic and nonacademic instructional contexts are increasingly common (Hodges and Sasnett 1993).

An example of the kind of digital composition project to which we are referring was developed by a student, Mark Cornett. His project describes research expertises existing among Clarkson professors for students interested in learning about these expertises and for corporate sponsors interested in funding research projects.[1] His project discusses sea ice, a sub-field within the area of Cold Region Technologies important to civil and environmental engineering in northern climates. The project includes a wide range of written texts, still graphics, audio clips, and video clips—all designed, developed, and synchronized into a coherent whole for several different audiences with several different purposes. It includes an elaborate navigational structure for users, who can read information nonsequentially by using the toolbar at the bottom of the program, several dynamic maps, hypertext links embedded in key places, search engines, and a bookmarking feature for creating personalized place holders.

In courses encouraging this kind of digital composition, a primary focus is on designing the human-computer interface, in using Internet resources, object-oriented multimedia authoring programs, and hypertext authoring programs to create the ways in which users interact with educational applications in online environments. Such work, even when done in limited ways, often departs from the traditional concerns associated with writing and reading printed texts, requiring expanded textual perspectives and design considerations (Selber 1997; Kolosseus, Bauer, and Bernhardt 1995). As science and engineering teachers encourage their students to create online materials in the form of World Wide Web pages, multimedia programs, and hypertext applications, technical communication studies is positioned to make some important rhetorical and humanistic contributions. The following five areas represent a starting place in which such contributions might be made.

Area #1: Interface Design Practices

Historically, representing human-computer interactions in online information space has been the task of technologists—in many cases, computer scientists and engineers with important programming expertise but also a system-centered perspective encouraging interface designs that fail to consider adequately the needs and complexities of end users. As Johnson (1994) notes, "much of the research in human factors, from its beginnings over a century ago to the present day, places the needs of technology over the human, thus treating the 'human factor' as an unfortunate impediment in the process of developing emerging technologies" (196). Although such a situation might have been less problematic in the 1960s and 1970s, when computer users were most often other scientists and engineers, individuals now interested in computing for educational, professional, and personal reasons are far less specialized and far more diverse. In fact, Duffy, Palmer, and Mehlenbacher (1992) argue that the computer-using population now includes fewer experts in any one software program; fewer users developing expertise in the majority of the software programs they use;

more users using different software programs in the same application area, trying to apply their knowledge of one program to another; and, increasingly, more first-time users of hardware and software (2-4).

This expanded user base, other market forces, and a host of social and technological factors have encouraged new ways of thinking about the interface that are more inclusive. The tasks associated with human-computer interaction, once solely aligned with computer specialists, are now engaged by teachers, artists, activists, and other individuals for whom considering social interactions and human consequences is an important fact of professional life. Interface design teams in both academic and nonacademic settings now commonly include interdisciplinary mixes of product managers, marketing representatives, instructional designers, multimedia developers, graphic artists, subject matter experts, systems analysts, quality assurance specialists, audio/video specialists, filmmakers, software engineers, technical communicators, end users, and others—all workers with varying expertises, educational backgrounds, and ways of seeing the world (Whiteside and Whiteside 1994). Mountford (1990) outlines some specific contributions of creative fields such as film, animation, theater, architecture, and industrial design to interface design practices, and Laurel (1993) provides an extensive framework for envisioning human-computer interactions as dramatic rhetorical moments.

From our perspective, the contributions of technical communication to developing human-computer interfaces across the curriculum relate to rhetorical and social concerns, concerns not always privileged in system-centered ways of teaching digital composition. Two important contributions—naturalistic usability testing methods and humanistic perspectives on computer technologies—are discussed in detail later in the chapter. But in addition to these two critical areas, numerous other contributions exist. As with writing, if we envision interface development as a recursive process situated within complex social contexts, then rhetorical considerations become a central concern on both macro and micro levels.

On macro levels, for example, audience and task analyses are an essential part of determining what kinds of collaborative and individual activities a computer interface should support. Moreover, the organizational, navigational, and contextual structures of an online environment—three core areas supporting human-computer interaction—should reflect the broad rhetorical concerns of users, goals, and time/space frames rather than the formal characteristics of online genres (Selber, Johnson-Eilola, and Mehlenbacher 1997). Two recent graduates of the technical communication program at Clarkson debated this interface design principle as they developed a large-scale multimedia project for the Admissions Office. Both students took the department's hypertext course and were at odds over a particular instance of how best to structure navigation paths for end users. Based on audience and purpose profiles developed in an initial documentation plan, one student argued for as much user freedom as possible, while the other student argued that extensive freedom, in this instance, would only confuse users of the program. From our view, the tensions existing between the rhetorical theories they studied in the course and their actual development practices led to a useful interface design debate, a debate that demonstrated the importance of social and rhetorical perspectives on user-centered design.

And on micro levels in the development process, for instance, there are numerous critical issues associated with composition and balance, from developing an online writing style to achieving visual symmetry on the screen. These are just a few of the areas in which technical communication might make rhetorical contributions to the pedagogical practices of science and engineering teachers teaching interface design practices across the curriculum. Other related areas are discussed in an emerging literature on the rhetorical and social dimensions of design (Coe 1996; Kaufer and Butler 1996; Barrett and Redmond 1995).

Area #2: Usability Testing Methods

A central component of developing a computer interface is evaluating its effectiveness in terms of human performance as opposed to technical or fiscal performance, a task often accomplished with formal usability testing methods. According to Nielsen (1993), usability testing is commonly concerned with five key areas: learnability, efficiency, memorability, errors, and user satisfaction (26). That is, how easily can users learn an interface? Once they learn it, can they use it efficiently? Can they remember how the interface features work over time, even if they only use those features sporadically? Do users make errors using the interface? And, are users personally satisfied with how the software looks and feels? Systematically examining these kinds of questions at key stages in the development process helps designers create human-computer interfaces that are more usable for end users.

Usability testing procedures, as with other research methods, represent ways of framing and seeing a problem. Historically, in many engineering cases, the privileged lenses for examining usability have been experimental: studies are designed for controlled environments, variables defined, and results often derived in quantitative terms. And indeed, there is clear value in this type of empirical work, depending on the questions that a researcher is asking. But we would argue that technical communication, a field that often appropriates ways of knowing from the social sciences, has a different empirical contribution to make. According to Lauer and Asher (1988), empirical research can also be descriptive, employing approaches that restructure the situation or environment under investigation in as few ways as possible (15). In their taxonomy of empirical research designs, a taxonomy which moves from explanations that are less to more quantitative and statistical, Lauer and Asher locate case studies and ethnographies within the realm of descriptive work (16). Unfortunately, these two approaches to understanding user behavior in context and as situated are often devalued in engineering environments: as one teacher told us, "they're too soft and subjective to yield reliable results." Indeed, on at least two separate projects at Clarkson, engineering faculty were reluctant to subject their interface designs to even modest usability testing of a qualitative nature, even when that testing might have yielded useful results.

As opposed to discussing specific procedures for conducting case studies and ethnographies in this short chapter, discussions which already exist in other places (Zimmerman and Muraski 1995; Silverman 1993; Sullivan and Spilka 1992), we provide five key reasons why it is important, in an age of electronic writing and communication, to promote usability testing methods for naturalistic settings. Technical communication teachers can use these arguments to expand the experimental testing procedures that science and engineering teachers often privilege in human-computer interface design projects:

- *Developments of human-computer interfaces are not solely determined by technological possibilities.* Human-computer interfaces are designed within organizational contexts that are subject to a wide range of forces, among them, economic, political, and social. The designs informing human-computer interfaces are therefore ideological, embodying particular ways of knowing and working. Understanding how organizational contexts influence the work of interface designers is an important area of research.

- *Uses of human-computer interfaces are not solely determined by mechanical features.* Computer users approach communication problems with a wide range of complex tasks that are at least partially determined by their work environments and institutional cultures. Often, the tasks of workers fail to align closely with system features, software commands, and interface structures. Understanding how organizational contexts influence the work users is an equally important area of research.

- *Final forms of human-computer interfaces are not solely determined by designers.* In an age of electronic writing and communication, end users will have increasingly more control over the content and shape of their software. Understanding the role of users in modifying human-computer interfaces is a complicated and relatively new area of research.

- *Work contexts are not solely determined by employers.* As institutional downsizing continues and telecommuting increases, more individuals will work at home and at other alternative sites. Corporate offices are no longer considered typical work spaces, just as traditional classrooms are no longer considered typical education spaces. Articulating the nature of these new spaces will be critical to understanding how human-computer interfaces should be structured in the future.

- *Educational activities are not solely determined by local possibilities.* World-wide area networks and the Internet provide interesting opportunities for professional development and instruction. But understanding how particular educational models and institutional cultures might encourage or discourage computer-based learning activities will require naturalistic research perspectives. These five arguments presuppose that interface design practices are bound in complex ways to the social, political, organizational, and rhetorical contexts in which both developers and end users work. Making this case in engineering and technological schools, however, is not always an easy task for electronic-communication-across-the-curriculum specialists.

Area #3: Pedagogical Issues

It is not difficult to find arguments claiming that computer-based learning is better than other types of learning. Indeed, newspapers, magazines, trade journals, and academic journals feature articles on a regular basis describing the ways in which hardware and software will revolutionize education in positive ways, or at least make it faster and cheaper to deliver. And indeed, writing and communication teachers are not immune from such technological optimism. According to Hawisher and Selfe's (1991) survey work, for example, in the late 1980s many teachers preferred teaching writing with computers based on the following claims: using hardware and software, students spent more time working on their writing; peer teaching was common; classes became more student-centered; one-on-one conferences between teachers and students increased; opportunities for collaboration increased; students shared more with other students and teachers; and communication features provided more direct access to students, thus allowing teachers to get to know them better (59).

A decade later, although the technological optimism that Hawisher and Selfe critiqued still exists in both the popular press and professional discourse (a fact we consider in the next contribution area), critical perspectives toward instructional computing seem less isolated. We realize now more than ever, though still not widely and deeply enough, that productive computing in classroom settings is more than a function of creating good human-computer interfaces or eliminating the very real technological inequities that exist across educational institutions at all levels. Rather, for students to learn in productive ways with (or without) computers, additional forces must be considered, among them, their basal needs (Rockman 1995), reward systems in academic units (Strickland 1991), professional development programs for teachers (Selfe 1992), and a whole host of social, cultural, and political factors.

At the same time, we cannot ignore the instructional dimensions of the interface. Too often, software is structured in ways that fail to consider what it means to productively teach and learn, supporting the worst as well as the best of instructional design practices. For example, in 1994 two technical communication faculty members at Clarkson were involved in an initial experiment to develop multimedia instructional materials for an engineering course. Although the technical communication faculty members were included early in the development process and worked with engineering faculty to generate and answer important pedagogical questions about instructional goals and approaches, in the end this work was dismissed as "too time consuming." Instead, the lead faculty member from engineering scripted his own lecture, taking traditional lecture notes and transferring them to an online environment. In effect, he created the computerized equivalent of a film strip, which on occasion he would turn off in order to answer and ask questions.

From our view, part of the problem with the design approach just described relates to pedagogical perspective—misconceptions about learning are simply transferred from traditional classroom environments to online environments. Among these misconceptions, Kay (1991) includes the fluidic theory of education (akin to Freire's banking concept, in which students are viewed reductively as empty vessels waiting to be filled); the notion that education is a bitter pill that must be sugarcoated (in online environments, such sugarcoating includes the game-like images and sounds often found in instructional multimedia programs); the idea that during activities of learning, students can only rely on innate ways of thinking; and the equally disturbing idea that reality is only what the senses reveal (138). As with many literature professors (Latterell 1996), we realize that the education of engineering teachers often provides little formal training in pedagogical areas. And yet such a background seems central to teaching human-computer interaction principles across the curriculum that are instructionally sound.

In this area, technical communication has much to contribute. Social perspectives on writing, reading, teaching, and learning relate to instructional design practices in substantial ways, as do the rich rhetorical traditions informing the communication practices of individuals working and learning in complex cultural contexts for over 2,500 years. When organizing information in a multimedia program, for example, designers must make decisions about the degree of complexity supported by the navigational and organizational structures of their application. These design decisions, for the most part, should be influenced by pedagogical and rhetorical concerns and not by the available technological features of an authoring environment. Moreover, if we expand the domain of human-computer interaction to include the physical environments supporting interface design work, then technical communication has additional contributions to make. Research by writing teachers indicates that the design of a computer lab or classroom significantly influences the teaching and learning occurring in that space (Selfe 1989; Myers 1993). Technical communication teachers, therefore, can also help engineering departments design computing environments in which student-centered electronic communication across the curriculum is encouraged and supported.

Area #4: Humanistic Perspectives on Computer Technologies

In addition to pedagogical issues, we cannot ignore the political and ethical dimensions of the interface in teaching human-computer interaction principles. Too often in science and engineering contexts, however, computers are viewed as neutral tools, machines that support the work of interface designers and users in apolitical ways (Winner 1986; Feenberg 1991). Such a view arose at a recent retreat for Clarkson academic administrators. Although there was wide consensus at this retreat that the first-year program should include, among other things, instruction and experience with computers and communication, the details of what that meant were unclear. Many people interpreted this statement in strictly functional terms: all students should be able to accomplish the basic computer tasks that support the work of scientists and engineers. There was no real recognition of the fact that computers not only support but also influence these tasks in central ways, and that students need to be prepared as both consumers and critical users of hardware devices and software applications.

In the best of cases that we have seen, such an instrumental perspective is modified to account for technological concerns but in a manner that seems little better: although computers can be used for both productive and unproductive purposes, if we just choose the right ones educational and social progress will necessarily follow. On some level, such logic rings true: a hammer can be used either to build a shelter or to commit a heinous crime. At the same time, however, a hammer cannot replace a screwdriver or a saw. In other words, computer technologies, as artifacts of an industrial culture, instantiate particular ways of knowing and working that are far from neutral. But grand narratives perpetuated in Western culture, those linking technological developments with notions of cultural progress, remain an influential force encouraging computer-related optimism in educational settings (Postman 1995).

In terms of the politics and ethics of the interface, a literature informed by humanistic perspectives is emerging. For example, Turkle (1995) describes different orientations informing dominant human-computer interactions in online information space. She aligns the design of her old Apple II computer with modernist interpretations of the world, while her new Macintosh seems more informed by postmodern ways of knowing. Respectively, the design difference here is between depth and surface, between the values of calculation and those of simulation (34). Johnson-Eilola (1995) traces three models influencing interface design practices in online research spaces, arguing that certain cultural tendencies toward valuing information can have the negative effects of technical decontextualization and cultural fragmentation.[2] Selber (1995) considers metaphorical perspectives on hypertext appropriated from a variety of disciplines, claiming that these diverse ways of knowing centrally influence the design of texts, nodes, and links in complex hypertext systems. And Selfe and Selfe (1994) contend that human-computer interfaces, in many popular instances, can be read as maps that value "monoculturalism, capitalism, and phallologic thinking" (486). Although these technology critiques may seem unusual to some because they challenge the commonsense cultural connections existing between computer technologies and notions of educational progress, these critiques provide important political and ethical perspectives that fields aligned with the humanities can provide.

In encouraging humanistic perspectives on computer interface design across the curriculum, technical communication specialists can focus on at least two related areas: the authoring environments that students use to create World Wide Web pages, multimedia programs, and hypertext applications; and the design decisions that students make when using these environments to create human-computer interfaces. From an end user's perspective, these two areas represent a double layer of political choice that structures the field of possibilities in at least partial ways. The developers of an authoring environment determine its operation and how designers work with objects, linking structures, system features, and so on. In turn, designers use these biased environments to build human-computer interfaces for end users, making additional choices about how a program operates, looks, and feels. These layers of interest can be productively scrutinized during the teaching of interface design practices. For instance, students and teachers can critique implicit and explicit assumptions about learning, working, and knowing in a wide range of areas, among them, interface metaphors, default structures, permission settings, composing and editing tools, menu arrangements, and features supporting collaboration.

Area #5: Electronic Portfolios of Professional Work

Professional portfolio development is a final, more practical contribution of technical communication to electronic communication across the curriculum. Writing specialists use portfolios as an alternative to traditional evaluation methods, asking students to participate in the construction of their grading context by providing commentary on their work and by selecting and organizing the writing samples to be graded. Other reasons for using portfolios relate to process concerns: grading is delayed to encourage substantial revision, and whole performance is privileged over the narrow surface features of a final written text. In addition to formative and summative portfolios of writing, however, technical communication, a field aligned with workplace and product concerns, also often requires students to develop presentation portfolios, portfolios that showcase final projects and serve as professional writing samples in job interview situations.

Our earliest experience with presentation portfolios was in 1994, when Peter Deuel, an undergraduate in the technical communication program at Clarkson, posted his portfolio on the World Wide Web. At the time, his portfolio included his resume and links to some sample HTML documentation he had written. This relatively early example of an online portfolio attracted the attention of the Intel Corporation, leading first to a summer internship for Peter and then to a full-time job. Pilot efforts are now under way at Clarkson to encourage all technical communication majors to develop professional electronic portfolios, and campus-wide discussions are considering the issue of extending this opportunity to all Clarkson students. As digital composition practices becomes increasingly central to science and engineering workplace environments, students in all majors will benefit from representing their electronic work in these types of portfolios.

Creating an electronic portfolio of professional work is a complicated rhetorical process. Once content decisions are made and the best electronic samples are in final form, one central concern exists: developing an overarching interface design that integrates the samples into a focused, coherent whole. Before beginning this task, students must select an online environment that can display their electronic projects, which are often created in a variety of programs and contain a wide range of data types (sometimes, file conversions and screen captures are required). In designing the portfolio interface, there are many critical issues to consider, among them, providing a conceptual model for readers; developing front matter that introduces the portfolio and describes its design; organizing and annotating the portfolio entries; developing a linking structure for navigating the portfolio; creating cohesive ties that logically connect the entries; creating aesthetic dimensions and transitional effects; highlighting the most important material; and, perhaps, creating a micro-portfolio of one or two self-running samples that can be left with a potential employer. Although the task of creating an electronic portfolio of professional work is time-consuming, it is a useful project in which engineering teachers and students can consider the rhetorical and social dimensions of human-computer interface design.

Notes

1. In creating his multimedia program, Mark Cornett used Multimedia Toolbook 3.0 running on a Pentium machine with 16 MB RAM, 500 MB hard drive, VGA monitor, mouse, Windows 95, sound board, external speakers, and a CD-ROM drive. In addition, Mark used Paint Shop Pro, PhotoShop, a scanner, CD-ROMs with sound clips and art clips, and a digital camera.

2. We thank Johndan Johnson-Eilola for his helpful comments on a draft of this chapter.

Works Cited

Barrett, Edward, and Marie Redmond, eds. 1995. *Contextual Media: Multimedia and Interpretation.* Cambridge, MA: MIT Press.

Coe, Marlana. 1996. *Human Factors for Technical Communicators.* New York: Wiley.

Duffy, Thomas M., James E. Palmer, and Brad Mehlenbacher. 1992. *Online Help: Design and Evaluation.* Norwood, NJ: Ablex.

Feenberg, Andrew. 1991. *Critical Theory of Technology.* New York: Oxford University Press.

Feenberg, Andrew, and Alastair Hannay, eds. 1995. *Technology and the Politics of Knowledge.* Bloomington: Indiana University Press.

Hawisher, Gail E., and Cynthia L. Selfe. 1991. "The Rhetoric of Technology and the Electronic Writing Class." *College Composition and Communication* 42.1: 55–65.

Hodges, Matthew E., and Russell M. Sasnett. 1993. *Multimedia Computing: Case Studies from MIT Project Athena.* Cambridge, MA: MIT Press.

Johnson, Robert R. 1994. "The Unfortunate Human Factor: A Selective History of Human Factors for Technical Communicators." *Technical Communication Quarterly* 3.2: 195–212.

Johnson-Eilola, Johndan. 1995. "Accumulation, Circulation, and Association: Economies of Information in Online Spaces." *IEEE Transactions on Professional Communication* 38.4: 228–238.

Kaufer, David S., and Brian S. Butler. 1996. *Rhetoric and the Arts of Design.* Mahwah, NJ: Lawrence Erlbaum.

Kay, Alan C. 1991. "Computers, Networks, and Education." *Scientific American* 265 (September): 138–43.

Kolosseus, Beverly, Dan Bauer, and Stephen A. Bernhardt. 1995. "From Writer to Designer: Modeling Composing Processes in a Hypertext Environment." *Technical Communication Quarterly* 4.1: 79–93.

Latterell, Catherine G. 1996. "Training the Workforce: An Overview of GTA Education Curricula." *Writing Program Administration* 19.3: 7–23.

Lauer, Janice M., and J. William Asher. 1988. *Composition Research: Empirical Designs.* New York: Oxford University Press.

Laurel, Brenda. 1993. *Computer as Theater.* Reading, MA: Addison-Wesley.

Mountford, S. Joy. 1990. "Tools and Techniques for Creative Design." In *The Art of Human-Computer Interface Design,* edited by Brenda Laurel, 17–30. Reading, MA: Addison-Wesley.

Myers, Linda, ed. 1993. *Approaches to Computer Writing Classrooms: Learning from Practical Experience.* New York: SUNY Press.

Nielsen, Jakob. 1993. *Usability Engineering.* Boston: Academic Press.

Palmquist, Mike, Dawn Rodrigues, Kate Kiefer, and Donald E. Zimmerman. 1995. "Network Support for Writing Across the Curriculum: Developing an Online Writing Center." *Computers and Composition* 12.3: 335–53.

Postman, Neil. 1995. *The End of Education: Redefining the Value of School.* New York: Alfred A. Knopf.

Rockman, Saul. 1995. "In School or Out: Technology, Equity, and the Future of Our Kids." *Communications of the ACM* 38.6: 25–29.

Selber, Stuart A. 1995. "Metaphorical Perspectives on Hypertext." *IEEE Transactions on Professional Communication* 38.2: 59–67.

———. Forthcoming. "The Politics and Practice of Media Design." In *Foundations for Teaching Technical Communication: Theory, Practice, and Program Design,* edited by Katherine Staples and Cezar Ornatowski. Greenwich, NJ: Ablex.

Selber, Stuart A., Johndan Johnson-Eilola, and Brad Mehlenbacher. 1997. "On-line Support Systems: Tutorials, Documentation, and Help." In *The Computer Science and Engineering Handbook,* edited by Allen B. Tucker, 1619–43. Boca Raton, FL: CRC Press.

Selfe, Cynthia L. 1989. *Creating a Computer-supported Writing Facility: A Blueprint for Action.* Houghton, MI: Computers and Composition.

———. 1992. "Preparing English Teachers for the Virtual Age: The Case for Technology Critics." In *Re-imagining Computers and Composition: Teaching and Research in the Virtual Age,* edited by Gail E. Hawisher and Paul LeBlanc, 24–42. Portsmouth, NH: Boynton/Cook.

Selfe, Cynthia L., and Richard J. Selfe. 1994. "The Politics of the Interface: Power and its Exercise in Electronic Contact Zones." *College Composition and Communication* 45.4: 480–504.

Silverman, David. 1993. *Interpreting Qualitative Data.* Thousand Oaks, CA: Sage Publications.

Smith, Merritt Roe, and Leo Marx, eds. 1994. *Does Technology Drive History?: The Dilemma of Technological Determinism.* Cambridge, MA: MIT Press.

Spilka, Rachel. 1993. "Influencing Workplace Practice: A Challenge for Professional Writing Specialists in Academia." In *Writing in the Workplace: New Research Perspectives,* edited by Rachel Spilka, 207–19. Carbondale: Southern Illinois University Press.

Strickland, James. 1991. "The Politics of Writing Programs." In *Evolving Perspectives on Computers and Composition Studies: Questions for the 1990s,* edited by Gail E. Hawisher and Cynthia L. Selfe, 300–317. Urbana, IL: National Council of Teachers of English; Michigan Technological University: Computers and Composition.

Sullivan, Patricia, and Rachel Spilka. 1992. "Qualitative Research in Technical Communication: Issues of Value, Identity, and Use." *Technical Communication* 39.4: 592–606.

Turkle, Sherry. 1995. *Life on the Screen: Identity in the Age of the Internet.* New York: Simon and Schuster.

Whiteside, Mary F., and J. Alan Whiteside. 1994. "The Successful Multimedia Development Team: Expertise and Interaction." In *The McGraw-Hill Multimedia Handbook,* edited by Jessica Keyes, 7.1–7.21. New York: McGraw-Hill.

Winner, Langdon. 1986. *The Whale and the Reactor: A Search for Limits in an Age of High Technology.* Chicago: University of Chicago Press.

Zimmerman, Donald E., and Michel Lynn Muraski. 1995. *The Elements of Information Gathering.* Phoenix, AZ: Oryx.

8 InterQuest: Designing a Communication-Intensive Web-Based Course

Scott A. Chadwick
Iowa State University

Jon Dorbolo
Oregon State University

A traditional model for a distance education course locates the bulk of the students at satellite campuses receiving electronically transmitted instruction from a teacher at a central location. Of course, that location is central only to the teacher and the handful of students able to attend class in the broadcast studio that serves as the classroom. This type of distance education helps bring education to students physically remote from the campus, but tends not to differ in presentation from the traditional classroom.

A different distance education model incorporates the technological capabilities of the Internet and the World Wide Web, allowing radical changes in the level of interaction among students and teachers while staying true to course content. Classes taught via the Web can be constructed to rely heavily on writing, yet offer flexibility to accommodate other forms of communication (pictures, graphics, sound, etc.) supportable by the students' and teachers' technology.

The InterQuest (IQ) course at Oregon State University is an introductory philosophy course conducted virtually via the Web. The virtual nature of the course allows students to enroll and participate in the course as long as they have a computer connection to the Web. This inter-institutional course accommodates university, community college, and advanced placement high school students simultaneously. These students interact with each other and the teacher by reading course content on the Web and engaging each other, and that content, via e-mail. InterQuest is based on a distance education pedagogy that believes students can learn effectively in a computer-supported communication environment.

This chapter addresses many of the issues associated with developing a Web-based course using e-mail writing as its dominant form of communication. The next section of the chapter provides a description of the InterQuest course. A discussion of developing a communication-intensive distance education course follows, using InterQuest as an exemplar.

Introducing InterQuest

Imagine a university where students satisfy a college core requirement through a virtual course. Students enroll in the course via telephone, log on to the course and read course materials using a Web browser, dialogue with the teacher and other students using e-mail, take quizzes from their home or campus computer lab, and turn in papers electronically. For the Introduction to Philosophy course at Oregon State University that world exists. InterQuest[1] is the name for that course and the name for the research and development team applying IQ techniques to other courses on campus, including CalcQuest[2], a virtual introduction to calculus.

The goal of InterQuest is to guide students through philosophical claims and arguments in a virtual environment. Students enter InterQuest with their own philosophical beliefs and values. The IQ course seeks to change the way students think about some of their own philosophic beliefs and values. The desired change is not to replace the students' beliefs and values or to weaken their conviction in them; the desired changes are in the ways students apply awareness and reasoning to their beliefs and values. Students' thinking, virtually discussing, and writing about philosophy facilitate those changes. Students succeed in the course when they can demonstrate in their writing that they

- are aware of their commitment to a philosophic belief or value of which they were previously unaware,
- can develop a more sophisticated interpretation of their beliefs,
- can provide an explanation of some philosophic claim to which they are committed,
- can provide support for an explanation of some philosophic claim to which they are committed, and
- can demonstrate in writing they are aware of the implications of the philosophic claims to which they commit.

Pedagogy precedes technology in InterQuest. The educational objectives of InterQuest center on teaching philosophic claims and reasoning. Technology used in InterQuest is valuable only to the extent that it increases the likelihood that the educational objectives are reached. We believe it is possible, and appropriate, to use technology to guide students through paths of learning. Students can intellectually walk these paths autonomously, or they can seek assistance along the way. The power of the technology InterQuest uses is its capacity to incorporate thinking, writing, and communicating into all assignments and aspects of knowledge acquisition.

Designing a Virtual Distance Education Course

Modifying any course to keep it current and interesting is challenging. Converting a lecture/discussion course to a virtual course on the Web can be daunting. The following sections explain the key components to consider when converting an existing course to a Web-based course.

Pedagogy Drives It All: Components of a Virtual Distance Education Course

Six course goals were identified prior to designing the technical aspects of the course: (1) student autonomy, (2) active student participation, (3) intellectual community, (4) time and place-independent learning, (5) collaborative learning, and (6) networked instruction. The first goal, student autonomy, seeks to provide students a choice about which perspective they take in engaging the course content. Philosophy readings in IQ are linked to each other, allowing students to choose where to begin their study of the course content (e.g., do they see themselves as moralists, utilitarians, etc.). They do this by reading text associated with five worldviews, then selecting the worldview that best fits how they see the world. (The worldviews are (1) self-interest is central, (2) cooperation is the key, (3) faith is the focus, (4) reality is relative, and (5) knowledge is negligible. See Chadwick and Dorbolo 1997-1[3].) This linking of worldview statements with supporting text, or hypertext design, provides a structure that guides students, placing each student in a framework group where all group members share the same worldview. Future writing and discussion assignments will ask the students to interact with their own or other framework groups. Students using this method demonstrate high levels of commitment to the subject matter and course pursuits.

The second goal, active student participation, puts a premium on student-teacher and student-student interaction. The quality and quantity of student-student and student-instructor discussion is substantially increased over traditional classroom discussions. InterQuest demonstrates that close to universal active participation can be accomplished for classes of over 100 students. Students interact asynchronously, providing them time to craft their written arguments. All IQ discussions and assignments are designed to be iterative to some extent, so students practice and benefit from editing, rewriting, and reformulating their ideas across the entire term of the course. For a sample of InterQuest writing assignments, see Chadwick and Dorbolo 1997-2 and 1997-3. The first sample is a presentation essay assignment where students must write a presentation in which they explain some of their philosophic views. The second sample is a rhetorical precis assignment where students must provide a written summary interpretation of a philosophic text.

Building an intellectual community, goal three, requires creating a cohesive group of student scholars who are equipped with what they need to continue their studies and intellectual conversations after they complete the course. InterQuest provides forms students can use to publicly respond to a text while reading it on the Web.[4] These forms are e-mailed to other students reading that same text, or working on that same assignment. All structured communication in IQ fits one of five discourse models: (1) peer-peer exchange (Chadwick and Dorbolo 1997-4), (2) small group exchange (Chadwick and Dorbolo 1997-5), (3) framework-group to framework-group exchange (Chadwick and Dorbolo 1997-6), (4) chain exchange, where students are linked sequentially (Chadwick and Dorbolo 1997-7), and (5) global exchange (Chadwick and Dorbolo 1997-8). This interface of activities collapses the traditional learning methods of class discussion, reading text, and writing responses into a single activity. This produces active reading and makes course time more efficient.

Goal four, time and place-independent learning, seeks to provide students a learning environment where they are not tied to a time and a place to learn. Class discussions progress around the clock and around the globe. During one term, an IQ student had to return home for a family emergency. The challenge was that home was in Ecuador. Computer connections were made for the student, and of all the courses he took that term, IQ was the only course in which he could stay current and participate during his time off-campus.

Central to all distance education successes is ensuring that students understand what is expected of them and how they can achieve success in the class. InterQuest accomplishes that by providing an online Objective and Requirements Page (Chadwick and Dorbolo 1997-9) and an online InterQuest Orientation (Chadwick and Dorbolo 1997-10). The Objectives and Requirements page explains the course objectives and what students will be required to do. The InterQuest Orientation page provides links to pages covering the syllabus, course objectives, grading criteria, keeping in touch with the teacher, and how to improve Web and Internet skills.

The fifth goal, collaborative learning, strives for a class situation where students must communicate with each other in order to complete their tasks. All InterQuest discussion and writing activities require students to read and consider other students' ideas. Responding to other students is as easy as writing comments on the class conversation form (see endnote 4) or sending an e-mail message to all class members by clicking on the class e-mail list icon. Writing activities set a minimum number of collaborative interactions, but students are free to collaborate more than required. The ease of communicating across time and space makes increased collaboration more likely. That increased ability to communicate also makes collaborative learning projects easier to design and accomplish. (An example of a collaborative writing example can be found at Chadwick and Dorbolo 1997-11.)

Finally, the goal of networked instruction provides a class structure allowing multiple teachers to participate cooperatively, especially when they teach in different schools. Instructors separated in place, time, institution, and discipline may teach collaboratively in new ways. InterQuest allows multiple teachers from several institutions to co-teach the course. In these cases, a form of networked instruction is used which distributes teaching tasks according to teacher expertise. Multiple instructors may require multiple course evaluation forms. InterQuest handles this requirement by using separate forms accessible by students. See Chadwick and Dorbolo 1997-12 and 1997-13 for two such IQ evaluation forms.

Organizing Students into the Course

The mechanics of organizing the course at the start of the term are burdensome. Getting group e-mail lists set up and dealing with late enrollments requires much effort. Having just a few students out of the discourse loop creates major logistic issues for all the structured communication models mentioned above. Online registration tools are currently under development. These tools will handle the registration, recording, and authentication of students and their coursework (Chadwick and Dorbolo 1997-14). Likewise, we are working to develop software that will automate assigning and tracking students in their conversation activities. That conversation management engine is being designed to assign partners, deliver instructions, track progress, and report exceptions to the teacher (Chadwick and Dorbolo 1997-15).

Technology Training for Students

Course designers need to be prepared for the possibility that students lack computer and Internet skills. Differences in skill levels create issues of perceived and real fairness. Because IQ students were not centrally located, early attempts at providing face-to-face computer skill tutorials proved difficult to manage and were largely ineffective. The problem has largely been solved by providing online tutorials in those skills. The IQ Orientation page (Chadwick and Dorbolo 1997-16) includes Web links to pages addressing (1) how to effectively use the Web, (2) how to navigate and search the Internet, and (3) how to use the IQ Move Bar, a navigation tool internal to InterQuest. The IQ Move Bar is particularly useful to students because it allows them to move about the entire IQ course Web site without using any Web browser tools. Students can click on icons to go back one page, forward one page, to the login/logout page, to the IQ Compass page to learn more about using the Internet and Web, or to the IQ Central page, where they can then link to any other Region in the course (Chadwick and Dorbolo 1997-17).

Accommodating Different Learning Styles

InterQuest accommodates different types of learners based on Kolb's (1984, 1985) four learning modes and four learning styles. Kolb claims that learners predominantly use one of these four learning modes: (1) concrete experience, or learning from feeling; (2) reflective observation, or learning by watching and listening; (3) abstract conceptualization, or learning by thinking; and (4) active experimentation, or learning by doing (1985, 4-5). Kolb's four learning styles reflect combinations of the learning modes (1985, 5-7). *Accommodators* learn by feeling and doing. *Assimilators* learn by thinking, watching, and listening. *Convergers* learn by thinking and doing. *Divergers* learn by feeling, watching, and listening.

InterQuest's Dear Author activity (Chadwick and Dorbolo 1997-18) helps students learn through reflective observation and abstract conceptualization. The Dear Author activity pairs students who are reading the same philosophy text. Each student poses a serious question to the author, then e-mails that question to his or her partner. A serious question is a question whose answer will help the student understand some difficult part of the text being read (see Chadwick and Dorbolo 1997-19 for information provided to students regarding how to make a serious question relevant to the discussion at hand). The student receiving the Dear Author question assumes the role of the author and answers the partner's question as best he or she can. This task commonly takes several iterations where students seek and provide clarification of questions and answers. All e-mail is electronically copied to the teacher, who can step in and provide assistance throughout the process. (See Chadwick and Dorbolo 1997-20 for a discussion activity form designed to help students form constructive questions about texts they just read.)

InterQuest's Virtual Conversations allow students to participate in discussions and grow intellectually through relating their personal experiences to the text being studied. Virtual Conversations occur weekly as the teacher poses a discussion question or statement for student discussion. Students create and send e-mail messages responding to the teacher and each other. Students regularly post multiple messages to the class e-mail list as the discussions move forward. The quantity and quality of interaction regularly exceeds similar discussions in traditional classrooms. Students feel comfortable engaging the text and each other in the discussion format. They argue about the text using knowledge they have gained in the class and through their lived experiences. (See Chadwick and Dorbolo 1997-21 for a Virtual Conversation addressing students' worldviews. See Chadwick and Dorbolo 1997-22 for a Virtual Conversation designed to help students improve their argumentative skills.)

The Concept Analysis activity allows students to actively experiment with their newly gained knowledge of philosophy. Here students analyze and argue for their intellectual position on a philosophical claim, such as "God exists."

Similar discussions are often attempted in philosophy courses held in traditional classrooms. Those discussions often fail because students need more time to try their hand at philosophizing than the class period allows. Accomplished philosophers may be able to generate arguments on philosophical claims quickly; students need time to experiment with their ideas, argumentative styles, and methods of articulating those ideas in writing. The Concept Analysis activity gives students that time (Chadwick and Dorbolo 1997-23).

Building a Cohesive Class

Teaching students virtually introduces unique communication situations that need to be addressed. The processes of feedback, trust, sensitivity to others in the class, and relationship-building all require special attention in the virtual environment. Teachers designing and executing a virtual course can benefit from computer-supported communication (CSC) research on those processes. The Web provides a communication channel rich enough to accommodate primary communication goals. Those goals include communicating about (1) the tasks at hand, (2) the relationships created and extended during the class, and (3) the impression students project about themselves to their classmates and teacher (Clark and Delia 1979).

Feedback

Students and teachers need to provide feedback to each other to keep any class running smoothly. This is particularly important during a Web-based course. Persons are more likely to seek feedback, and more likely to do so immediately, when using computer-mediated communication (CMC) than when using face-to-face communication (Ang et al. 1993; Ang and Cummings 1994). Persons receiving positive feedback tend to engage in more subsequent feedback-seeking than persons receiving negative feedback. Also, persons trusting the feedback giver gain satisfaction from a high quantity of feedback (O'Reilly and Anderson 1980). Students are provided feedback opportunities each time they enter and prepare to leave the IQ Web site. Feedback in IQ occurs as students log in and log out during every session describing what they intend to do, what they did, and what concerns and questions they have (Chadwick and Dorbolo 1997-24 and 1997-25). Feedback in IQ also occurs via evaluation forms. Evaluation forms are used to determine how well students are reading the assigned readings (Chadwick and Dorbolo 1997-26) and as overall course evaluations (Chadwick and Dorbolo 1997-27).

Trust

Teachers and students can build trust in the classroom using CMC. Trust arises out of class members' interdependency in achieving positive outcomes and preventing negative outcomes (Kipnis 1995). That trust can come directly from students being able to (1) determine the costs and benefits of their behavior, (2) predict the teacher's and other students' behavior, and (3) identify with other class members' desires and intentions (Lewicki and Bunker 1995; Shapiro, Sheppard, and Cheraskin 1992). Determining costs and benefits, and predicting behaviors is largely driven by the syllabus (Chadwick and Dorbolo 1997-28). Throughout the term, identification in InterQuest is facilitated through interaction with and feedback from the teacher (Chadwick and Dorbolo 1997-29) and from interaction with other students individually, in groups, and as a class.

Tying all of this together is the class constitution. The class constitution is a student-generated set of principles defining acceptable student behavior in the class. Modeled after the United States Constitution and Bill of Rights, the InterQuest class constitution allows students to define the class as theirs, instead of merely following rules given by the teacher. In this exercise, students first learn the principles associated with constitutions and read the Bill of Rights. Then the students create a principle they would like to see in their class constitution, e-mail that principle to the class e-mail list, then discuss all students' postings until a class constitution is agreed upon.[5]

Interpersonal Sensitivity

Teachers in a traditional classroom can often control inappropriate communicative behavior by using nonverbal looks and gestures or by giving verbal reprimands. InterQuest instructions help students build their rhetorical sensitivity skills, adapting their messages to the communicative needs of the receivers of those messages (Hart and Burks 1972; Hart, Carlson, and Eadie 1980). These instructions inform students about how to write to others directly, affirmatively, and ethically. A unique assignment toward that goal occurs in the second region[6] of the course. Region II: Constructing Communication inoculates students against producing offensive communication, or flames, in course discussions. This region asks students to write a summary of their own thinking, then identify "sparks" in their writing. A spark is a statement or argument that works to block productive discussion. Sparks are often inflammatory in nature, leading to future flames. Once students recognize their own sparks, they are instructed to look for others' sparks and discuss the intent and effect of such communication. See Chadwick and Dorbolo 1997-30 for the full text on sparks and flames.

Relationship-Building

InterQuest students' relationship-building skills via e-mail and the Web confirm studies comparing face-to-face and electronic communication. Members of computer-supported groups participate more equally than do members of face-to-face groups (Dubrovsky, Kiesler, and Sethna 1991; Straus 1996; Weisband 1992). Further, e-mail can diminish status effects in the class. Gone are the faces in front of which some students are afraid of speaking. Gone are physical classrooms with their front rows and back rows, each with its own supposed types of students. Students can ignore social roles and demographics, thereby reducing the pressure they feel to fit in. All of this tends to make students write to each other via e-mail as if everyone is of the same status level (Kiesler and Sproull 1992; Sproull and Kiesler 1986). However, when students do know the status of the person they are e-mailing to, such as the instructor, the students create messages respectful of that status hierarchy (Saunders, Robey, and Vaverek 1994).

Once the cornerstones of trust, feedback, and rhetorical sensitivity are in place, the students are ready to begin forming a sense of class unity. And it does not take long to build a cohesive group. Walther and Burgoon (1992) found that persons can develop quality working relationships with others before meeting them face-to-face. Persons interacting exclusively through CMC also use more messages about their relationship with their e-mail partners when they believe they are in a long-term relationship (as short as six weeks) than in a short-term interaction (Walther 1994). In fact, the proportion of relational communication to total communication in CMC increases over time, approaching the proportion of relational communication to total communication in face-to-face interactions (Walther, Anderson, and Park 1994). Within five weeks, persons communicating asynchronously create impressions of their fellow communicators as deep as those created by face-to-face communicators (Walther 1993).

Using E-mail as a Writing Tool

In early IQ trials, student essays were of low quality in both form and content. Few students showed a grasp of basic compositional style and organization. To correct this, assignments now include information about the practice of writing as well as information about the desired content of that writing (see Chadwick and Dorbolo 1997-31 and 1997-32). To further help students use e-mail as a writing tool, InterQuest's Writing Style in E-mail page provides ten tips for successfully using e-mail (Chadwick and Dorbolo 1997-33). Students can also link to Oregon State University's Writing Center Web site for online writing assistance (Chadwick and Dorbolo 1997-34).

A problem being worked on in the current phase of InterQuest is students' tendency to cram their readings and assignments a few days before they are due. This behavior does not take advantage of the capabilities of asynchronous teaching and learning. It is particularly damaging to the flow of computer-assisted conversation. A solution being tested is to include lessons about time management and learning styles as explicit features of the curriculum (see Chadwick and Dorbolo 1997-35 and 1997-36).

Traditional classes offer students products they take with them from the course (e.g., books, journals, class notes, etc.). InterQuest currently only provides students what they choose to print off the Web version of the course, including conversations they have been in. A solution under development is to implement a portfolio system in which students will save to disk their work, their conversations, their teacher's comments, and texts significant to them (see Chadwick and Dorbolo 1997-37)

While determining how to structure e-mail writing assignments, the goal has always been to get students to engage in "hyperpersonal" communication (Walther 1996, 29). Hyperpersonal communication exists when students intentionally select and edit what they communicate to present a unique image of themselves to the receivers of their e-mail. This allows students to exploit the power of e-mail as "editable verbal communication" (36). Students initially use e-mail as a means to quickly jot down a response to something they read. Students must be trained to read, think, and reflect, and then craft a response. When students do this they may still "see" the receivers of their e-mail they are "talking to" but they will take the time necessary to edit that "verbal communication" into quality written communication. This process is not unlike forcing a delay time in classroom discussions. The delay time allows all students enough time to think about a question posed to the class and prevents the "fast thinkers" from blurting out their response, regardless of the quality of that response.

Testing

InterQuest is not an online text book. It is more a succession of activities students perform. Still, students tend to get lost in the course and frequently ask where they are in it and how they are doing. This information must be accessible by the student directly. We are testing a Web quiz tool that gives students instant feedback (Chadwick and Dorbolo 1997-38). The quiz is intended to be a way of helping students organize their reading and to provide a marker of course progress.

Conclusion

Designing a Web course for current technology requires heavy emphasis on writing assignments. In InterQuest even the class discussions are conducted as students write e-mail. The key is to craft a seamless connection between the task, technology, and students so that students can focus on learning course content, not just technology. Most students appear to enjoy taking IQ and find the format intriguing. Many report that they do not feel they are in a "real" class. We interpret this positively, believing that IQ is giving students practice at learning after formal schooling is over, whether that learning uses the Web or not.

Notes

1. The homepage for all InterQuest-related pages is http://iq.orst.edu. InterQuest is written for all Web browsers that can display forms and tables.

2. CalcQuest can be found at http://iq.orst.edu/cq. The CalcQuest site contains Java and Frames. A browser supporting frames, such as Netscape 2.0 or higher, is required to successfully navigate this site.

3. All Chadwick and Dorbolo 1997 citations refer to the InterQuest Web pages located at http://osu.orst.edu/pubs/ecac. The numbers following 1997 correspond to the hyperlinks on that Web page.

4. A form is an HTML element which allows the person using the Web page to enter data into preconfigured spaces, then send that data to a server for processing. A Web form is not unlike any paper-based form you may be used to filling out for a driver's license application. See Chadwick and Dorbolo 1997-39 for the form used to conduct a student survey in the IQ class. See also Chadwick and Dorbolo 1997-40 for the standard IQ Class Conversation form.

5. The class constitution for the spring 1996 version of InterQuest contained these seven principles: 1) To thine own self be true; 2) The ideas and opinions of everyone participating must be respected; 3) Do unto others as you want to have done unto you; 4) There will be no discrimination on the basis of race, class, sexual orientation, marital status, gender, age, or nationality; 5) Participants in our class must be open-minded and supportive to all others; 6) Before criticizing the work of others, we must seek to understand the point of view from which they are speaking; and 7) It is the responsibility of all class members to enforce the above laws by communicating disapproval to those who "get out of line." The class constitution activity involves four Web pages: Chadwick and Dorbolo 1997-41 through 1997-44.

6. InterQuest is organized into regions instead of weeks. The course currently is taught during a ten-week term, where each region usually maps to a week. However, orienting students to regions instead of weeks allows the teacher flexibility in adjusting how much time is spent on each content area. Traditional classes are tied to the working days of the week (Monday–Friday). Students in InterQuest can work at the class at any time on any day. Thus, it makes sense to allow one region to take eight days, another region to take four days, etc., as long as assignments are due during the workweek.

Works Cited

Ang, Soon, and Larry L. Cummings. 1994. "Panel Analysis of Feedback-seeking Patterns in Face-to-face, Computer-mediated, and Computer-generated Communication Environments." *Perceptual and Motor Skills* 79:67–73.

Ang, Soon, Larry L. Cummings, D. W. Straub, and P. C. Earley. 1993. "The Effects of Information Technology and the Perceived Mood of the Feedback Giver on Feedback Seeking." *Information Systems Research* 4: 240–61.

Chadwick, Scott A., and Jon Dorbolo. 1997-1 through 1997-44. Web pages indexed at http://osu.orst.edu/pubs/ecac.

Clark, R. A., and J. G. Delia. 1979. "Topoi and Rhetorical Competence." *The Quarterly Journal of Speech* 65: 187–206.

Dubrovsky, V. J., S. Kiesler, and B. N. Sethna. 1991. "The Equalization Phenomenon: Status Effects in Computer-mediated and Face-to-Face Decision Making Groups." *Human-Computer Interaction* 6: 119–46.

Hart, Roderick P., and Don M. Burks. 1972. "Rhetorical Sensitivity and Social Interaction." *Speech Monographs* 39.2: 75–91.

Hart, Roderick P., Robert E. Carlson, and William F. Eadie. 1980. "Attitudes Toward Communication and the Assessment of Rhetorical Sensitivity." *Communication Monographs* 47.1: 1–22.

Kiesler, Sara, and Lee Sproull. 1992. "Group Decision Making and Communication Technology." *Organization Behavior and Human Decision Processes* 52: 96–123.

Kipnis, D. 1995. "Trust and Technology." In *Trust in Organizations,* edited by R. M. Kramer and T. R. Tyler, 39–50. Thousand Oaks, CA: Sage Publications.

Kolb, David A. 1984. *Experiential Learning: Experience as the Source of Learning and Development.* Englewood Cliffs, NJ: Prentice-Hall.

Kolb, David A. 1985. *Learning-style Inventory: Self-scoring Inventory and Interpretation Booklet.* Boston: McBer and Company.

Lee, Allen S. 1994. "Electronic Mail as a Medium for Rich Communication: An Empirical Investigation Using Hermeneutic Interpretation." *MIS Quarterly* 18 (June): 143–57.

Lewicki, R. J., and B. B. Bunker. 1995. "Developing and Maintaining Trust in Work Relationships." In *Trust in Organizations,* edited by R. M. Kramer and T. R. Tyler, 114–139. Thousand Oaks, CA: Sage Publications.

O'Reilly, Charles A., and John C. Anderson. 1980. "Trust and the Communication of Performance Appraisal Information: The Effect of Feedback on Performance and Job Satisfaction." *Human Communication Research* 6.4: 290–98.

Saunders, Carol S., Daniel Robey, and Karen A. Vaverek. 1994. "The Persistence of Status Differentials in Computer Conferencing." *Human Communication Research* 20.4: 443–72.

Shapiro, D., B. H. Sheppard, and L. Cheraskin. 1992. "Business on a Handshake." *Negotiation Journal* 8.4: 365–77.

Sproull, Lee, and Sara Kiesler. 1986. "Reducing Social Context Cues: Electronic Mail in Organizational Communication." *Management Science* 32: 1492–1512.

Straus, Susan G. 1996. "Getting a Clue: The Effects of Communication Media and Information Distribution on Participation and Performance in Computer-mediated and Face-to-Face Groups." *Small Group Research* 27.1: 115–42.

Walther, Joseph B. 1993. "Impression Development in Computer-mediated Communication." *Western Journal of Communication* 57: 381–98.

———. 1994. "Anticipated Ongoing Interaction Versus Channel Effects on Relational Communication in Computer-mediated Communication." *Human Communication Research* 20.4: 473–501.

———. 1996. "Computer-mediated Communication: Impersonal, Interpersonal, and Hyperpersonal Interaction." *Communication Research* 23.1: 3–43.

Walther, Joseph B., J. F. Anderson, and D. W. Park. 1994. "Interpersonal Effects in Computer-mediated Interaction: A Meta-analysis of Social and Antisocial Communication." *Communication Research* 21.4: 460–87.

Walther, Joseph B., and Judee K. Burgoon. 1992. "Relational Communication in Computer-mediated Interaction." *Human Communication Research* 19.1: 50–88.

Weisband, Suzanne P. 1992. "Group Discussion and First Advocacy Effects in Computer-mediated and Face-to-Face Decision Making Groups." *Organizational Behavior and Human Decision Processes* 53: 352–80.

9 Teacher Training: A Blueprint for Action Using the World Wide Web

Todd Taylor
University of North Carolina–Chapel Hill

In 1989 Cynthia Selfe published *Creating a Computer-Supported Writing Facility: A Blueprint for Action*, an informative overview of the theoretical and logistical requirements for establishing computer-supported writing programs, typically within departments of English. In this chapter I humbly attempt something similar, but I present instead a blueprint for developing electronically enhanced communication across the curriculum—and I describe only one part of such a plan. Perhaps *Electronic Communication Across the Curriculum* as a whole will provide the reader with a complete blueprint, while I map out only one room: using the World Wide Web to support program development and instructor training. And since this chapter does not afford the space to provide as much detail as Selfe's monograph, I want to emphasize in particular one key dimension of my blueprint: I recommend that CAC programs adopt a grassroots approach for creating a Web site, an approach that focuses on specific, local needs. In order to demonstrate what I mean by such an approach, first, I provide a theoretical analysis of some of the ways that the WWW can help overcome obstacles toward establishing successful CAC programs; next, I describe my own experiences using Web pages and HTML with a group of CAC faculty; and, finally, I recommend a "micro" model for other CAC programs to pursue.

CAC Faculty Training and Electronic Communication: How the Web Can Help

In the introduction to *Programs That Work* (1990), Toby Fulwiler and Art Young identify ten key questions that help define each of the fourteen WAC programs described in their now landmark collection (2-5). While Fulwiler and Young do not explicitly answer in their introduction their third question, "What faculty training models have proved most effective?," the collection as a whole does. One pattern that emerges among the fourteen case studies in *Programs That Work* is that retention of faculty interest and participation in WAC programs is poorer than one might hope for or expect. On the one hand, soft (non-ongoing)

129

funding for CAC programs contributes to poor retention, but soft (again, non-ongoing) faculty development strategies are also to blame. A related pattern among these fourteen case studies is that even though faculty-wide one- or two-day seminars—auditorium-filled "cattle calls"—serve to hook some faculty members on CAC programs, in order to keep them involved, these programs must offer constant and consistent additional support.

According to my reading of the Fulwiler and Young collection, the most clearly effective approach to offering additional support is not a series of Friday afternoon seminars or brown-bag lunches (which are somewhat useful, although faculty inevitably begin to skip these meetings in increasing numbers); rather, establishing close, genuinely reciprocal collaborative relationships among WAC faculty seems most likely to promote retention. As Flynn et al. observe in their chapter in *Programs That Work,* the trick to establishing such collaborations is twofold: (1) creating balanced, give-and-take relationships, and (2) finding a common ground. They write,

> Collaboration is, by definition, reciprocal, dialogic. Two or more individuals representing different, though compatible approaches, value systems, or epistemologies come together to create a new solution to a problem. . . . What is essential, though, is that both agents contribute and that one approach, system, or epistemology not be effaced by the other. . . . The collaborative model works well with engineering faculty because it encourages mutuality and respect. . . . The challenge, initially, is to identify a common ground. (168)

I propose that computer technology in general and computer-assisted instruction in particular can provide just such a common ground.

Why use the WWW to promote CAC? Let's be frank, issues regarding instructional technology—along with budget crises and continuing concerns about issues of race, class, and gender—are extremely hot topics in higher education today. As such, why not use technology as an additional focal point toward the development of institution-wide writing programs? The specific combination of writing specialists, faculty members from across the disciplines, and computer technologies seems particularly promising for CAC training programs, not only because it can solve the problem of identifying a common ground but also because it addresses an additional problem related to CAC program administration and development: communication among CAC administrators and faculty who are often separated by severe disciplinary, institutional, and geographic boundaries. In 1990 Fulwiler and Young could not have known that a few years later the Internet would seem to provide an ideal solution to the problem they identified in the following observation: "To date few mechanisms have been available for disseminating information about CAC programs in a systemic or comprehensive manner" (2). Yet even though the Internet is now available, much work will have to be done for it to emerge as an important CAC

resource. I propose that the unique media of the Internet, especially asynchronous technologies such as e-mail and the World Wide Web, can support genuinely collaborative efforts among colleagues who seek to integrate writing in
classes from across the disciplines. And since we already have examples of how
e-mail can help in these efforts (e.g., the WAC-L discussion list[1]), I want to
focus in particular on the World Wide Web.

Beyond providing an effective focal point for CAC faculty training, the World
Wide Web can also address a number of logistical problems. Asynchronous
communication technologies, such as the Web and e-mail, allow busy, often
overworked professionals to exchange information and ideas as their schedules
permit instead of enduring the nightmare of trying to gather everyone together
for a face-to-face meeting. Using the World Wide Web as a hypertextual, online
archive of CAC-related materials (e.g., workshop outlines, grant proposals, both
formal and informal teacher-researcher studies, syllabi from across the curriculum, sample course assignments, etc.) allows program leaders and participants
to create a collaborative collection of texts that documents their work and makes
it accessible to an international audience to be imitated, expanded upon, or even
contrasted. WWW-based resources permit CAC faculty with similar disciplinary interests to collaborate across institutional and geographic boundaries; for
example, an environmental microbiologist may not be able to find a local colleague who is interested in CAC, but he or she may be able to establish connections with a similar teacher/scientist hundreds of miles away. In fact, the bonding
of a local anatomy instructor with colleagues miles away is what actually encouraged me to explore the potential of the WWW to support CAC. I'll explain.

The Accidental Web Tourist

I must admit that I discovered by accident the power of the World Wide Web to
facilitate CAC faculty development. In fall of 1995 I led a graduate seminar
titled "Computers and Literacy." Even though the course was listed within the
department of English, many of the students in the seminar quickly let me know
that they weren't as interested in literacy as they were in instructional technologies. Most of the students in the seminar were community college instructors
with graduate degrees and years of teaching experience looking to satisfy continuing education requirements. These instructors were from a variety of institutions and from all over the curriculum: art history, microbiology, health
sciences, business, communications, etc. Thus, shaping the seminar to focus on
the intersection of CAC and technology seemed not only a logical decision but
also a convenient solution to the problem of making the experience relevant for
all of the participants—a solution that I believe can work in other CAC training
contexts. As you can see, I came to realize through serendipity that computer-
assisted instruction could serve as a way to reach out to faculty who may not

initially be very interested in CAC programs. A word of caution, though: I'm not suggesting that instructional technology should be used as a bait-and-switch tactic to lure faculty members into a seminar or program only to try to sell them CAC—that would violate what I have said about the importance of mutual respect and give-and-take relationships. I am suggesting that instructional technology, particularly the Internet, can be used to bring faculty together to consider CAC, not just literally in terms of communication but also in terms of establishing mutual interests.

Most of the instructors in my seminar had never seen the World Wide Web before, and, like me when I first browsed the Web, they were profoundly struck by its power and potential; they clearly wanted to learn more. At first I was having a difficult time selling the faculty from outside of the humanities on the idea that their students would benefit from courses that were more writing intensive. That is, I was having difficulty until I led these instructors on a guided tour of Web sites created by CAC faculty in other places and in various disciplines. My arguments in favor of writing intensive courses across the curriculum gained credibility because I was able to present objective evidence of the viability of CAC programs in other places. But my success was not without limitations: for example, some seminar members felt cheated because, unlike others, they were unable to locate Web sites that spoke specifically to their academic interests.

The highlight of the seminar, however, was the Web sites created by faculty from outside composition. Interestingly enough, the writing specialists in the seminar all chose to develop conventional academic research papers for a final project. The scientists as well as instructors from art history and literature authored Web sites. An anatomy instructor turned an ordinary, photocopied handout into an lively hypertext with links to some of the most impressive online graphics I have ever seen on the Web: an almost too-lifelike, three-dimensional, cross-sectional, and, in fact, computer-generated illustration of an anatomical man. This instructor used Web technology to solve the problem of duplicating copyrighted work by simply creating links to material made available by evidently talented and apparently well-funded researchers in her field. This instructor was, thus, beginning to create, in effect, her own online textbook. An art historian in the seminar uploaded scanned photographs of her travels that followed the path of an ancient pilgrimage across the Spanish countryside to a sacred chapel. She arranged maps and photographs of her trip sequentially and combined these images with a narrative that wove together her personal experiences with lessons concerning art history. Students can therefore travel along, in a sense, with their teacher as she surveys Spanish art through photographs and text, pausing along the way to interact with the hypertext and perhaps to respond to sequential writing assignments. A literature instructor designed an online lesson on Ambrose Bierce by linking together the full text of "An Occurrence at Owl Creek Bridge," biographical material, excerpts from "The Devil's Dictionary," and writing assignments (by the way, a great wealth of literary material is now available online for free through philanthropies such as Project Gutenberg[2]).

On the one hand, these projects and others like them in the seminar were a rousing success, one of those moments when a group of educators is clearly excited about the advances they made and the work they produced. But, of course, such gains do not come without a price. Perhaps others who take up the blueprint I present in this chapter will gain from the problems we experienced. These problems fall into two categories: negotiating a variety of learning curves and overcoming institutional constraints.

Based upon my experience leading the seminar, I project that those who plan to integrate the use of the WWW into a CAC program will encounter problems regarding learning curves on three fronts. First, a leader within the CAC program must learn how to build Web pages. This requires learning the codes through which Web documents are formatted: currently, this means learning HTML (hypertext markup language).[3] Fortunately, HTML is not very complicated; it is not much more difficult than learning to use the formatting codes in old versions of some word processors such as WordStar. And HTML editors, software that shortcuts much of the coding process, are becoming increasingly more reliable, available, and user-friendly. A second obstacle can be much more troublesome for obvious reasons: learning not just how to use HTML but learning how to teach others how to use it. One possible solution to the problem of getting leaders up to speed on HTML is to encourage some of the more technologically oriented members of a CAC program (rather than those who are primarily writing specialists) to lead a training session. Another possible solution is to seek out junior faculty or graduate students with Web page experience to lead or help facilitate these sessions. Third, those who will be learning HTML are likely to have significantly different technological backgrounds; some will either already know HTML or will pick it up almost instantly, but others will struggle with every step. Probably the best solution to the problem of different levels of experience among the audience members is to have those who are ahead of the curve work one-on-one with those who are struggling. Based upon my experience teaching HTML to literally dozens of faculty members in various workshops, I can say with confidence that, with well-structured training, most novices can independently create rudimentary pages within three hours or less.

Institutional logistics present additional problems. One of the failures of my first experiences with CAC and technology is that the Web sites which the instructors created in the seminar have already been erased. I did, of course, recommend that this work be saved onto floppy disks so that it might be restored later, but, because of institutional constraints, we were granted only temporary access to a file server on which to build these Web pages. As with all programmatic applications of instructional technology, using the WWW to develop CAC requires firm and preferably documented commitments of support from institutional authorities. In order to be effective, such programs require well-maintained and relatively permanent electronic archives. A CAC program supported by the WWW should also secure access to sufficient hardware and software: computers for formatting and uploading, HTML editing software to help flatten the learning curve, and reliable access to a scanner for digitizing images. And, finally, what sort of pages should a CAC program encourage its instructors to develop? What model should a CAC program ask its members to follow? Answers to these questions will depend significantly on the aims and needs of each individual program.

A Local Model Going Global

In closing, I would like to consider two markedly different approaches to building a network of CAC-related Web sites. On the one hand, a top-down, macro approach to such a network might look to an established entity such as the Alliance for Computers and Writing (ACW), the Council of Writing Program Administrators, or even the active WAC-L discussion list to provide a central clearinghouse for models of CAC pages, links, sites, materials, etc. In fact, the ACW Web site already includes a number of CAC-related links[4], and Larry Beason has created a WAC homepage with links to various programs.[5] On the other hand, I would argue in favor of a more micro, grassroots approach. As *Programs That Work* demonstrates, each program and institution has a unique profile, and I contend that CAC programs must build on local strengths and be very responsive to local contexts if they are to succeed. For example, the members of my seminar clearly wanted to develop materials they could use in their classrooms as well as present to others as evidence of innovative work; thus, they created CAC-related Web pages for their students to use. In contrast, a CAC program administrator might want to create a Web site that archives histories, descriptions, policies, and evaluations of the program. This central homepage could, in turn, connect materials that faculty produced during CAC training sessions. Asking faculty to build online resources that are woven together through a local CAC program Web site can serve as an ideal conclusion to a development seminar, as it did in mine, for the act of individually (re)defining a CAC course can synthesize the experiences of the seminar, drive the crucial move from discussion about CAC to a tangible commitment, and record the progress and breakthroughs made by faculty members. Such Web sites also increase the likelihood that CAC faculty who feel alienated because of disciplinary distance from program leaders or other program participants will be able to locate a model that speaks to their idiosyncratic concerns. I recommend in particular that CAC faculty be encouraged to author Webbed versions of individual course principles, syllabi, and other course-specific materials; in surveying the Web for both the seminar and this chapter, I found a surprising lack of such documents.

While there are a number of exemplary CAC pages currently available on the WWW (Northern Illinois University's, for example[6]), I hesitate to foreground what others have already accomplished, even as a template, because, as I suggested earlier, I believe the key to my blueprint is that each individual program should in fact custom build. As before, if close, reciprocal, collaborative relationships among faculty in the program are a priority, it will probably be more effective for a local group to work together to define their program and build a Web site that specifically addresses their own needs. According to the micro as opposed to macro paradigm, the purpose of such CAC Web sites would be first to serve the needs of a local program and second, and almost incidentally, to establish connections to other programs.

In short, I recommend that CAC faculty use the WWW to define themselves as a local community and, instead of relying fundamentally on a national or central organization, allow the individually guided, grassroots tendencies of the Internet to steadily and organically link together autonomous CAC Web sites.[7] My blueprint for action, therefore, is not a detailed plan for a local site or for a national clearinghouse of CAC materials; rather, it outlines an intentionally theoretical and speculative architecture for a local program. As I discovered by working with faculty from outside the humanities in particular, CAC proponents and instructors can take advantage of the excitement and power associated with the WWW to join together and move forward. Again, this is not a gimmick: the vast majority of the information on the WWW is primarily textual, even though one of the tremendous advantages of the Web is the fact that it also supports graphics, audio, photography, and movies. That is, even though the Web is certain to become more audiovisually oriented, it is likely to remain a largely textual, interdisciplinary, literate space—not a mere reflection of electronic communication across the curriculum, but an embodiment of it.

Notes

In the Computers and Literacy seminar we used fifteen multimedia computers; one was a Power Macintosh and the rest were either 486s or Pentiums. The file server was a Sun Sparcstation. Initially, we used the Windows Notepad accessory to compose in HTML, but eventually we moved to HTML Editor. Netscape was our Web browser.

1. Those with e-mail accounts can subscribe to WAC-L by sending an e-mail message containing "subscribe WAC-L <yourfirstname> <yourlastname>" (without quotes) addressed to: listserv@postoffice.cso.uiuc.edu. Do not include anything else in this message, such as a subject line or a signature file.

2. http://www.promo.net/pg/

3. Currently, HTML is the most widely used language for creating and viewing Web documents; however, this preference could change suddenly. For example, VRML (virtual reality markup language) and SGML (standard generalized markup language) have also emerged and may some day replace HTML as the standard. Regardless, learning the fundamentals of a language such as HTML should provide a foundation for whatever languages may be preferred in the future. In order to be able to create basic Web sites, it's not likely that coding for laypersons will become more difficult in the future.

4. http://english.ttu.edu/acw/

5. http://ewu66649.ewu.edu/WAC.html. See also note 7.

6. http://www.niu.edu/acad/english/wac/wac.html.

7. Larry Beason's current WAC Web site is an example of the organic tendencies of the Internet to link together previously separate local interests. See note 5 for URL.

Works Cited

Flynn, Elizabeth A., et al. 1990. "Michigan Technological University." In *Programs That Work: Models and Methods for Writing Across the Curriculum,* edited by Toby Fulwiler and Art Young, 163–80. Portsmouth, NH: Boynton/Cook.

Fulwiler, Toby, and Art Young, eds. 1990. *Programs That Work: Models and Methods for Writing Across the Curriculum.* Portsmouth, NH: Boyton/Cook.

Selfe, Cynthia L. 1989. *Creating a Computer-Supported Writing Facility: A Blueprint for Action.* Houghton, MI: Computers and Composition.

II Partnerships: Creating Interdisciplinary Communities

10 Accommodation and Resistance on (the Color) Line: Black Writers Meet White Artists on the Internet

Teresa M. Redd
Howard University

It happened every year. Every year my all-black composition class would write essays about racism in America.[1] And every year when these first-year students discussed one another's first drafts, the classroom sounded like an "Amen Corner." Sharing a language and history, they seldom questioned what was expressed and often understood the unexpressed. Thus, their essays touted unsupported generalizations about race relations in the United States while hiding unexamined assumptions about whites and blacks. For example, one student wrote without the slightest reservation, "The effects of going to a white school are a dislike for and hostility against whites."

To rein in such overgeneralizing, scholars such as Arthur Applebee (1981), Richard Lloyd-Jones (1977), and Lee Odell (1981) would suggest that my students accommodate a critical or uninformed audience. *Accommodation*, as I will define it, is a writer's attempt to meet the audience's needs. It is not the same as acquiescence, for a writer who *dis*agrees with the audience's feedback can still accommodate that audience by mustering stronger counterarguments. On the other hand, *resistance* occurs when a writer has no intention of accommodating the audience. As long as writers *intend* to accommodate the audience, they are accommodating, not resisting—even if they fail to produce an accommodating text.

Most of my students did not accommodate an audience's need for evidence and explanation, even though I had encouraged them to imagine a challenging audience. Classroom discussion revealed that the topic was so emotionally charged, so personally searing, that they could not recognize a hasty generalization, hidden assumption, or even an offensive tone. But why should they have? Their assigned audience was *imaginary*. Research suggests that we cannot rely upon imaginary audiences to elicit accommodation in student writing (see reviews by E. Oliver, 1995; Redd-Boyd and Slater, 1989). I was the only audience my students were likely to accommodate. However, since I was African American, they were liable to assume that I would understand and accept their sweeping claims about racism.

The Internet Project

The problem I have described is one faced by teachers across the curriculum: to produce informative and persuasive writing in the disciplines, our students need to practice accommodating appropriate audiences (see Schriver's 1992 review). Yet often we are inappropriate audiences. During the summer of 1994, I was still pondering this problem when I received a call from Stephanie Newman-James, an art professor at Montana State University (MSU). Newman-James asked me if our students could collaborate on a project that fall, so I suggested that the project focus on racism. Perhaps, I thought, I have found an appropriate audience.

Since I taught engineering freshmen in a computer classroom, I also suggested that we collaborate via the Internet. With Internet access, our students could communicate quickly and cheaply while mastering a valuable technology. As an added advantage, the personal but faceless nature of e-mail might encourage students to write frankly about a sensitive topic such as racism. At the same time, the direct and informal nature of e-mail would make me a less intrusive audience (even though students would copy messages to me).

Thus, we planned an elaborate series of electronic exchanges. My students would write essays analyzing the causes and effects of a racist incident in their lives. Next, they would send their first drafts to Newman-James's students via the Internet. The MSU students would respond by e-mail, and my students would reply. Afterward, my students would revise their essays and dispatch them via the Internet. Then the MSU students would illustrate the essays and forward their graphics over the network. Finally, my students would e-mail their reactions, and the MSU students would revise their layouts. This process would last one month, allowing students sufficient time for planning, drafting, e-mailing, and revising outside class.

From the beginning, Newman-James had hoped that our Internet collaboration would produce a publication, but she did not know whether we would have enough time or money. Therefore, initially, my students wrote only for Newman-James's class; they did not anticipate a wider audience. Later, however, ten MSU students volunteered to design a formal publication for wider circulation, and my students agreed. So the following semester, as an independent study project, the MSU students produced a thirty-two-page booklet entitled *On (the Color) Line: Networking to End Racism*. Printed in black and yellow, the booklet displays selected e-mail messages as well as the essays and illustrations (see sample pages in the Appendix).[2]

Newman-James and I believed that our students could benefit from this exchange because it crossed so many boundaries: geographical, disciplinary, and cultural. Not only could the Internet join composition and art over sixteen hundred miles, it could unite science and art, as my engineering majors discovered the intricacies of graphic design and Newman-James's art majors explored the complexities of computer technology.

While our students could learn from this cross-disciplinary collaboration, they could also profit from the cross-cultural exchange. My thirteen students were black and mainly urban: all but one of them were African Americans, some from overcrowded schools in the inner city.[3] If by chance they had grown up in the country or in suburbia, they experienced a rude awakening once they hit the hard, cold pavement of Washington, D.C. Living in the heart of a D.C. ghetto, students on our campus saw neighborhoods infested with rats and roaches, winos, addicts, pimps, and gangs. Many students were all-too-familiar with poverty, pollution, and crime.

On the other hand, the MSU students were mainly white and rural. Newman-James described them as follows:

> A surprisingly large number of my students come from one-room schools or had high school graduating classes of less than 10 people. Montana is the fourth largest land-mass state, and the fourth smallest population-wise. This means that MSU students, 90% of whom are Montana residents are often more familiar with land, horses, and cattle than [with] people. According to the 1990 census, less than 0.3% of Montana's population is black. (*On (the Color) Line* 1995, 1)

Because of the cultural contrast, I welcomed the opportunity to bring my student writers "screen to screen" with forty-nine student artists in Montana. While the MSU students gained "live, critical clients" for their artwork, each of my students gained three to four critical or uninformed readers for their writing (*On (the Color) Line* 1995, 1). Such an audience could challenge my students to consider other perspectives as they wrote, while encouraging them to explain their own perspectives vividly and clearly. The MSU students could motivate my students this way because they were a real *rhetorical* audience. According to Lloyd Bitzer (1968), a rhetorical audience consists of readers who are engaged with the topic, readers who might be willing and able to bring about change. Certainly, the MSU readers were rhetorically engaged with the topic, for, as white Americans, they could help eradicate racism in the United States. The MSU students could also motivate my students because they were a *collaborating* audience. Since they were going to illustrate my students' essays, my students needed to express themselves well enough to be interpreted visually.

As I had hoped, when the MSU students received the essays, some challenged my students to consider other perspectives. And as I had hoped, some of my students attempted to provide missing explanations, stronger counterarguments, and more effective language. Thus, in one of his last e-mail messages, Sonny reflected, "It's interesting what ya'll think of my ess[a]y. When I wrote it I saw it only a cer[t]ain way, but after talking to ya'll I see in a whole bunch of different ways."[4] Likewise, some of the MSU students approached their design task differently after reading my students' drafts and messages. For instance, as she came to know her Howard client, one MSU artist's "figures became less stereotypical and cartoony" (Blumenstyk 1995, 35).

However, several Howard students ignored the MSU feedback. Drawing upon e-mail messages, journal entries, and essay revisions, I began to explore why some of my students accommodated their target audience and why others resisted. Seeing my students' patterns of accommodation and resistance led to the following observations—observations that made me question my prior assumptions about writing for real audiences.

A Question of Authority

When asked to write to a white audience about racism, some African American students might have protested, "What for? They won't understand where I'm comin' from." But none of my students expressed such feelings in class discussions, conferences, e-mail, or their journals. They accepted the MSU audience as a target audience. I had assumed that they would eagerly respond to their MSU audience because they thought a white audience would *need* to hear their side of the racism story. I had also assumed that the students would seek to be understood so that the MSU readers could accurately illustrate their ideas. Thus, I had expected my students to respond to criticism from the MSU audience by strengthening or clarifying their essays.

Sheila reacted as I had expected. In her first draft, she had recorded how some white boys had hurled racial slurs and broken bottles at her mother. After reading the draft, one MSU reader wanted to know how Sheila and her mother felt about the incident. So Sheila added several lines about the pain she and her mother had experienced. Then she reported by e-mail,

> I went back and added the majority of the points you made. . . . I hope you enjoy reading it. Let me know what you think and what else I need to enhance it some more. I want my essay to be well explain[ed] so that your drawings will reflect every detail.

Like Sheila, Jameela was ready to accommodate her target audience, even when the feedback was negative. Three of her readers accused her of overgeneralizing about the white race, even though she had used hedges such as "most" and "some." For example, one observed, "You have contradicted yourself throughout your piece. I find that your general message was to state that the white race should not generalize the black race, but the problem is that you have generalized the white race throughout your entire essay." Another student remarked, "I react to the 'blanket statements' made about all whites, or white society. Perhaps this is the experience in your area, but it's hard for me to handle when I don't hold these viewpoints about blacks."

Despite the negative feedback, Jameela responded to the criticism, refuting some points and conceding others. On the one hand, she defended her use of the phrase "working past our abilities." She explained via e-mail, "Yes, I meant to say 'working past our abilities' in the sense that every individual has certain things they can and can't do and each black person would be working towards developing higher than there [sic] own individual abilities." On the other hand, instead of singling out whites for blame, in her second draft she included other racial groups or omitted race altogether. For example, she changed "some whites" to "some people" and the finger-pointing "you" to "they." In her journal she confessed:

> As I read my readers' responses and took a second look at what I had written, I somewhat had to agree with them. . . . Having the Montana State students to reply to my essay was beneficial. It made me realize my mistakes. I made sure to apologize to those students whom I offended and let the others know that I didn't intend to offend anyone. At the time, I was just reacting to my own experiences and allowing the pain to come out.

Unlike Sheila and Jameela, a few students dismissed the MSU feedback. Their resistance would not have been unusual had the MSU readers merely been classmates reviewing their assignments. Studies of classroom peer groups show that sometimes writers do not value their classmates' feedback (Berkenkotter 1984; Freedman 1987). However, the MSU readers were a target audience, readers my students sought to influence. If, as Aristotle (1984) and Chaim Perelman (1969) suggest, the primary goal of rhetoric is to influence the audience, the target audience commands a certain authority: what the audience thinks—right or wrong—is at least worth *considering*. But this was not the case for Arnice.

Initially, Arnice welcomed the MSU readers' feedback because she did "not really like" her first draft. Thus, in an early e-mail message, she wrote to the students, "If you think of anything that is unclear or you do not understand please write me and let me know. When I am writing I appreciate the help."

However, after a student said that the essay needed more facts and less emotion, Arnice announced via e-mail, "Dear fellow students I am very happy with your suggestions and techniques for revision, but I am pleased with my essay now and I intend to keep it the way it stands." Later, in her journal, she explained her decision: "These people are critiquing my paper and they have no experience in criti[ci]sm."

Arnice's position is surprising because she had so openly accepted the MSU students as her target audience. Indeed, in her final journal entry, she lamented, "I tried to write well for these students so they would like my writing." But as her comments reveal, she questioned her target readers' authority. Since they were not professional critics (e.g., English teachers), she questioned their right to critique her essay. Ironically, even though they were the readers who mattered, what they *said* no longer mattered.

Revision or E-vision

Arnice did not attempt to change her readers' opinions about her essay during their e-mail exchange. But some of her classmates used e-mail to debate with the MSU readers prior to revising. During these e-mail debates, the students could learn more about their audience because they had more opportunities to receive comments on their essays. Crafting e-mail messages also gave them more opportunities to *write* for their audience and receive a response to *that* writing as well. Thus, I had assumed that the e-mail dialogue would stimulate revision, as indeed it did in the case of Kevin.

E-mail allowed Kevin to prewrite his revision: in his e-mail he agreed or disagreed with each point that his readers had raised, and many of his responses found their way into his essay. For instance, one MSU reader asked him how his friends reacted after a cab driver snubbed them and picked up some white students instead. In his e-mail Kevin replied, "Your comment on exploring the thoughts of my friends is a good one; I didn't think about that. During the ride back my friends were rather quiet." This last line reappeared in his revision as "During the ride back home we were all quiet."

However, I discovered that the e-mail stifled as well as stimulated revision. Some students responded to their readers' concerns via e-mail—what I call "e-vision"—but not via their essays. Maurice is a case in point. Maurice received a barrage of negative comments from MSU, especially regarding an incident he considered racist. In his e-mail reply, he attempted to counterargue by citing new evidence of racism:

> Last week while watching the Six O'Clock News I saw a white lady plead-ing for the return of her two sons, who were stated to be abducted by a black man. A few days later, I saw the same lady on T.V. being escorted to court by Policemen, where she was charged with murdering her two sons. Do you think this case would have recieved[sic] so much publicity if the suspected abducter was white?

An MSU student shot back:

> How do you think the media would have reacted if she had said a white man had carjacked the kids? I really believe it would have gotten the same amount of attention. The facts remain—people are outraged at crimes against kids and I feel that that was the main focus of the media.

At this point, Maurice admitted that he was not in a position to answer her question about the media since he—a Jamaican—had lived in the United States for less than a year.

None of this debate ever surfaced in Maurice's revision—no rebuttals, no concessions. In his journal he confirms that he did not try to revise his essay to accommodate the MSU readers: "They did not affect my revision because they really did not think that my incident was racist." Ironically, if Maurice had had *less* access to his readers, he might have revised more.

Real vs. Imagined Feedback

The most striking pattern of findings began to emerge when I compared Maurice's planning and revising processes: his anticipation of the MSU audience had a greater impact upon his essay than the audience's feedback.

I had assumed that *real* feedback from readers would count more than *imagined* feedback. However, some students' journals revealed that the MSU audience had figured significantly in their plans but not in their revisions. For instance, although the feedback did not affect his revising, Maurice wrote, "Writing for the Montana State University students affected my planning of this essay because I knew that I had to be very specific and detailed." Rashid reacted similarly. According to Rashid, the MSU feedback was "appreciated but not used." Yet writing to the MSU audience proved useful to him because, he explained, "we had to change our way of thinking and adapt our thoughts to go to an all white audience. The fact that they were the audience caused me to adapt some of the words that I would have used because they may not understand." Likewise, Sheldon wrote, "The students['] responses did not alter my essay," but "in planning the essay I kept in mind the reader's attention."

Conclusion

What can we learn from this Internet project? To elicit audience accommodation in student writing, we might heed the following advice:

- Don't assume that a student writer will listen to readers simply because they are the target readers. Assign a well-respected target audience, or announce that you will take into account the target audience's reaction when you grade. After reading the project e-mail, I considered the MSU comments as I evaluated the content, organization, and style of the essays. However, next time I will *tell* my students that the MSU response will influence my assessment, and perhaps Newman-James will do the same. I might even request holistic scores from MSU readers to count as a percentage of the essay grade. After all, the more authority the audience has, the more students will consider the audience's feedback.

- Keep in mind that e-mail can become "e-vision"—an electronic substitute for essay revision. If you want students to revise their essays, ask them to respond to their target audience "by essay" *before* they respond by e-mail. Or ask students to revise for a larger audience (e.g., the whole MSU campus) after soliciting feedback from a segment of that audience (e.g., MSU design students). Otherwise, after replying by e-mail to a reader's feedback, students may feel that revising their essay is unnecessary or at least perfunctory.

- Encourage students to think carefully about their target audience while planning their first draft. If you plan to publish their work, help students imagine a wide range of possible audiences as well as the final publication's potential uses and the social or cultural changes it may engender. Although some students may not respond to *imaginary* audiences, many will respond to *what they imagine about real audiences*. In fact, what they imagine about a real audience may elicit more accommodation than the actual feedback will.

With these lessons in mind, I plan to maintain the Internet connection with MSU, for it motivated most of my student writers to clarify, elaborate, and persuade an audience. At the same time, it made the MSU artists more responsive to *their* audience. They had to contend with my students' e-mailed questions (e.g., "I like your idea about the scale of justice but what is sitting in the scale?"), corrections (e.g., "The cab driver looks to be oriental. The cab driver of that night was probably east Indian."), and suggestions (e.g.,"I would like to see some Aboriginal art attached."). Regardless of the type of feedback, the MSU artists felt the impact of designing for real clients. "Having a contact," Newman-James explained, "even if the contact didn't say specifically, 'No, I want it this way,' made my students more accountable."

Clearly, the Internet project supported our goals for composition and graphic design. But it accomplished something more. As Hewett and Pattison (1995, 14, 19) discovered in their classrooms, the personal yet faceless nature of e-mail encouraged students to write candidly about their thoughts and feelings. Moreover, because e-mail is direct and informal, it transformed some of my procrastinating essay writers into prolific e-mailers. The frank and frequent exchanges opened several students' eyes, minds, and hearts. Thus, one MSU student wrote to Jameela:

> The experiences you and your friends have gone through is [sic] something I don't have to think about very often and they are startling and painful to read. . . . Your closing remarks seem to acknowledge the basic underlying problem behind racism, namely a lack of knowledge and a basic misunderstanding perhaps on the part of both blacks and whites. . . . I truly hope that being able to work together on this project will result in some new understanding and breaking down of barriers. . . .

And so it did.

Acknowledgments

This research was supported by the American Institute of Graphic Arts and the National Science Foundation's ECSEL program as well as two computer labs (Howard University's CLDC and Montana State University's OSCS). Apryl Motley, Betsy Sanford, and Beth Sorensen also provided valuable assistance.

Notes

1. I use the term *black* because a few students were Afro-Caribbean rather than African American.

2. To produce *On (the Color) Line,* my students wrote their essays on word processors using MS Word for Windows 6.0. Next, accessing the PINE mail application, they attached the essays to e-mail messages. These messages traveled over the Internet via the PC-based UNIX system maintained by Howard University's Computer Learning and Design Center (CLDC). Because my students relied on PCS and the MSU students on Macs, sending the graphics over the Internet was more complicated. First, the MSU students scanned their pen-and-ink drawings, using Ofoto. Then, the scanned images were converted to .tiff files, with the aid of Adobe Photoshop. Afterward, Newman-James turned these Mac files into PC files and ftped them to me. Finally, in CLDC I accessed the xz program on a DEC5000 workstation to change the files to .ps files for printing. The following semester copies of the booklet were printed on a newspaper press. Although the technology was available, we did not publish the booklet electronically because the MSU design curriculum focused on hard-copy print projects.

3. One student, Maurice, had grown up in Jamaica.

4. Throughout this article I have used pseudonyms to refer to students.

Works Cited

Applebee, Arthur. 1981. *Writing in the Secondary School: English and the Content Areas.* Report No. 21. Urbana, IL: National Council of Teachers of English.

Aristotle. 1984. *The Rhetoric,* translated by W. R. Roberts. New York: Modern Library.

Berkenkotter, Carol. 1984. "Student Writers and Their Sense of Authority Over Texts." *College Composition and Communication* 35.3: 312–19.

Bitzer, Lloyd. 1968. "The Rhetorical Situation." *Philosophy and Rhetoric* 1: 1–14.

Blumenstyk, Goldie. 1995. "Networking to End Racism." *Chronicle of Higher Education* (22 September): Sec. A, 35, 38–39.

Freedman, Sarah. 1987. *Response to Student Writing.* Urbana, IL: National Council of Teachers of English.

Hewett, Beth, and Felicia Squires Pattison. 1995 "Computers and Community Building in the Composition Classroom." *CEAMAGazine* 8: 15–25.

Lloyd-Jones, Richard. 1977. "Primary Trait Scoring." In *Evaluating Writing,* edited by Charles Cooper and Lee Odell, 33–66. Urbana, IL: National Council of Teachers of English.

Odell, Lee. 1981. "Defining and Assessing Competence in Writing." In *The Nature and Assessment of Competency in English*, edited by Charles Cooper, 95–138. Urbana, IL: National Council of Teachers of English.

Oliver, Eileen I. 1995. "The Writing Quality of Seventh, Ninth, and Eleventh Graders, and College Freshmen: Does Rhetorical Specification in Writing Prompts Make a Difference?" *Research in the Teaching of English* 29.4: 422–50.

On (the Color) Line: Networking to End Racism. 1995. Bozeman, MT: Bozarts Press.

Perelman, Chaim, and L. Olbrechts-Tyteca. 1969. *The New Rhetoric: A Treatise on Argumentation*, translated by J. Wilkinson and P. Weaver. Notre Dame, IN: University of Notre Dame Press.

Redd-Boyd, Teresa M., and Wayne Slater. 1989. "The Effects of Audience Specification on Undergraduates' Attitudes, Strategies, and Writing." *Research in the Teaching of English* 23.1: 77–108.

Schriver, Karen. 1992. "Teaching Writers to Anticipate Readers' Needs." *Written Communication* 9: 179–208.

Appendix

Two pages from *On (the Color) Line*

"Marvin Donaldson"
<mdonald@cldc.
howard.edu>
Hi Mary, how are you,
it's good to hear from
you. I am sorry that
you felt offended by
my essay, I did not
know that you would
be and I am still try-
ing to determine
exactly why you
were. Personally, I
have not experienced
racism but I do know
however, that it
exists. I am an immi-
grant from
Jamaica,..., where
99.5% of the popula-
tion is black, and I
have been living in
the United States for
about eight months.
The incident that was
outlined in my essay
was adapted...., there-
fore I am simply com-
menting on this inci-
dent which I believe
to be of a racist
nature.

"Mary O'Neil"
<iarsn118@gemini.
oscs.montana.edu>
Marvin, Hi and thank
you for writing back?
I guess I still don't
see how this particu-
lar incident is related
to racism?... Maybe
she was just afraid
given the lateness of
the evening, the
desertedness of the
street and the fact
that her neighborhood
may be affluent but it
is truly an island in a
very dangerous sec-
tion of chicago... Take
care!

"Bryan Paterson"
<iarsn119@gemini.oc
s.montana.edu>
Greetings at Howard
University, here's the

Designed & Illustrated By
Jill Rodgers

Center Spread Designed &
Illustrated By
Mary O'Neil

Essay By
Marvin Donaldson

In his essay "Black Men and Public Space," the journalist Brent Staples describes how he was mistaken for a criminal because of his race. *My first victim was a woman—white, well-dressed, probably in her late twenties. I came upon her late one evening on a deserted street in Hyde Park, a relatively affluent neighborhood in an otherwise mean, impoverished section of Chicago. As I swung onto the avenue behind her, there seemed to be a discreet, uninflammatory distance between us. Not so. She cast back a worried glance. To her, the youngish black man—a broad six feet two inches with a beard and billowing hair, both hands shoved into the pockets of a bulky military jacket—seemed menacingly close. After a few more quick glimpses, she picked up her pace and was soon running in earnest. Within seconds she disappeared into a cross street.* This incident is definitely of a racist nature, which could be caused by various factors including the influence of the media, previous experience and also the influence of peers.

The media have influenced the thoughts of many Americans. Movies like *Birth of a Nation* and *Pretty Woman* portray views that certain physical attributes are related to inferiority or superiority in moral, intellectual, and other non-physical areas. These movies promote belief in sharp division and boundaries: one is either white or black. Movies like these automatically portray blacks, namely young males, as being lazy and violent troublemakers. These movies also portray blacks as having only low-income jobs or being unemployed or gangsters and drug dealers with wives living in the ghetto on welfare. Being exposed to these false portraits could have been the reason why the lady became suspicious.

Previous experience could be another cause of such an incident. It is possible that the lady could have been robbed or assaulted by a youngish black man before. An incident such as this could cause her to have a mental block against all black men, so whenever she sees a black man, she may become scared instantaneously.

Another possible cause for the lady being scared might be the influence that her peers have had on her. Her peers may be all whites who often justify social avoidance and domination by claiming that relevant traits are biologically inherited and thus unalterable. Peers are very influential in instilling certain messages in a person's brain, since people tend to imitate their peers to remain in a group.

Regardless of the laws enacted, treaties and pacts signed and people everywhere striving to end racism, there will be no end to this practice. "Out of many we are one" might be the motto for most people, but as long as hate, greed and a feeling of superiority exist in the world, we will still be prisoners, mentally fighting for freedom.

by Marvin Donaldson
Illustrated by Mary O'Neill

RACISM IN AMERICA
by Marvin Donaldson

Designed & Illustrated By:
Bryan Peterson

---

don't think this is a justifiable case of racism. A white man dressed in a military jacket with funky hair would frighten her in the same way... This woman is terrified of being raped, attacked and battered or even mugged. ...the man's skin comes second to the fright or flight. This is only an opinion, it could be wrong, and that's for you to decide... Where are you from? I can't believe you have never experienced or even witnessed racism... I'd like to hear your responses to my comments. Nice job. Until next time.

"Jill Rodgers"
<iarsn120@gemini.oscs.montana.edu>
Dear Marvin, I am grateful for your attempt to relate to racism. ...Where are you from? Being from Montana, I do not see a lot of racism first hand. However, when I read the incident you portrayed, I felt you were being a little harsh... Being a grown woman should allow her to form her own opinions instead of peer group opinions... If I was in this situation, I would have wanted to distance myself from any individual regardless of their race or appearance. I would like you to consider other possibilities, such as safety, instead of assuming racism. I think your conclusion was strong. Thanks for your time.

11 International E-mail Debate

Linda K. Shamoon
University of Rhode Island

For the past four years at the University of Rhode Island, small groups of American students have had the opportunity to use e-mail to formally debate a variety of topics with peer groups in universities in England, Ireland, Korea, Finland, the Netherlands, India, and other countries. This project, called International E-mail Debate, began with efforts of the University of Rhode Island's College of Business to "globalize" their curriculum, but it quickly evolved into a writing-intensive, small-group project that could be part of any class. In fact, International E-mail Debate has proven to be a particularly exciting way to introduce formal, highly structured writing tasks into any class. Furthermore, International E-mail Debate poses interesting challenges to the current theoretical approaches of writing across the curriculum, and it questions whether or not a fairly deliberative use of e-mail can prompt the same kinds of spontaneity, democratization, creativity, or resistance as other uses of e-mail. The outcome of the University of Rhode Island's three-year test effort with International E-mail Debate suggests that highly focused, formal, topical writing should have a strong place in writing across the curriculum theory and practice, especially when joined with international e-mail communication.

International E-mail Debate Description

International E-mail Debate is a semester-long, collaborative writing project in which students debate with their counterparts in another country about topics related to their classwork. For example, during URI's three-year pilot test, 1992–1995, students majoring in management information systems at the University of Rhode Island debated with students from the University of Bilkent, Turkey, about whether or not the United States would long retain world leadership in the semiconductor industry. As another example, students majoring in business management debated with students from the Technical University, Braunschweig, Germany, about whether or not corporate sponsorship of nonprofit events (such as McDonald's sponsorship of the 1996 Olympic games) improves a firm's success. These students researched and wrote in depth about themes they viewed as important to their professional careers, and the best of these topics were deepened by the international perspective afforded through the e-mail exchanges with students from another culture.

These electronic exchanges were conducted in English and followed the rules of formal collegiate debate. Typically, within classes at each site, groups of three to five students formed into debate teams, and then in response to a debate resolution, each team researched, wrote, and sent via e-mail three long position papers to their international peers. First, each team sent to the other team an opening position or "constructive" essay that either supported or opposed the debate resolution. Next, each team closely read their opponents' constructive essay and responded with the second debate document, the "refutation" essay. Finally, each team wrote the third document, their "rebuttal" or reconstruction of their original position, one that also accounted for criticisms and responses received during the refutation. Along the way, each team also produced an "executive summary" of their position and a list of the definitions of key terms in the debate.

General Results of the Three-Year Test Period

During the three-year test period, which was sponsored by the Fund for the Improvement of Postsecondary Education, the project leaders monitored the instructors' plans and procedures, the students' writing, and the students' overall responses. These sources of information, which are elaborated below, helped us to understand much of the excitement and many of the difficulties specific to International E-mail Debate. By way of preview, on the positive side, students were excited as well as a little intimidated by the prospect of communicating with peers in foreign countries, and during the debates students wrote extensively and deeply on their debate positions. The more problematic side of International E-mail Debate emerged later in the debate process, when some teams responded rudely and insultingly to their peers' arguments, an occurrence in keeping with others' experience with e-mail communications and some forms of argumentation (Frey 1990; Hawisher and Moran 1993, 631, 634).

The typical faculty experience during the pilot study was most eloquently summarized by Albert Della Bitta, professor of marketing, whose class debated with a team from the Manchester, England, School of Management on the resolution "The nature of marketing research needs to change little across Western cultures in order to be successful." In general, and typical of other instructors' experiences, Della Bitta found that his students participated enthusiastically and wrote extensively, and some developed a sustained interest in other cultures. "The success story of the project," says Della Bitta, "is seen in one student who had no international awareness at the beginning of the class. After the project she started to communicate with other international students and then she spent a year in Israel." He also found that throughout the debate his students' assumptions about life in England were corrected, such as when the Manchester students informed the URI students that people in England do not need to shop every day for fresh food or that many Britons do not view themselves as European in culture or lifestyle. On the other hand, Della Bitta noted that while his students wrote a lot for the debate exchanges, they did not necessarily deepen their knowledge of marketing as a discipline. "Next time, I would be much more careful about the topic of the debate, limiting it to a resolution that is really variable in consumer behavior and, in that way, helping students learn more about marketing."

Della Bitta's report of the students' experiences is confirmed by the students' own responses. Chai Kim, professor of management information systems, frequently solicited written feedback from his URI students and from the students on the opposing team. Most of the responses confirm the students' excitement noted by Della Bitta:

> This [International E-mail Debate] is a great idea, much more fun than a term paper. In fact, I think I got more out of the research and communications required for this project than I would have by any other means (paper, studying for test, case study, etc.). And my teammates were great about sharing the work and meeting when necessary. All in all, it was fun. (An American student)

> First of all, debating with a counterpart was enthusiastic. I learn a lot from that study. . . . We spent weeks making research, then eliminating unnecessary documents. We spent more weeks reading and summarizing, finding statistical evidence. Through this process I learn to differentiate related issues from unrelated ones. Also I learn how to cooperate with group members efficiently. This project leaves me self-confident. . . . (A Turkish student)

Not every student gave blanket approval, however. Some of the students' criticisms confirmed the importance of carefully selecting topics for the debates:

> Although the concept is excellent, I do not think that we received their true views on the subject we were debating. . . . This program would work more effectively if the debate were over topics which the two countries were passionate about. Americans may be passionate about NAFTA, but most Turkish students are not. This format would be superb if we were debating Israeli students on the issue of Israeli-Palestine territorial issues, etc. . . . We should have debated the Mexican students on the NAFTA issue. (An American student)

This American student's insight about the importance of choosing topics that are under debate by real people around the world is consonant with the conclusions of Della Bitta and other instructors.

This commentary from participating faculty and students was further confirmed and elaborated in the observations and data gathered by project leaders.
The leaders noted that the students' writing exhibited three striking outcomes:
the amount of writing was impressive; the attention to evidentiary material in
the debate documents was notable; and the quality of peer critique was high.

One of the most noticeable outcomes of the pilot test was the high amount of
writing. During International E-mail Debate, the debate teams produced at minimum about thirty pages of text and, more typically, upwards of sixty pages.
This level of production compares favorably with writing in other classes at the
University of Rhode Island. Two Faculty Senate surveys have shown that in
lower level courses students write on average from zero to about fifteen pages,
and in upper level courses from zero to about thirty pages. Classes engaging in
International E-mail Debate easily outstrip this amount of writing while remaining enthusiastic about the project. Furthermore, this high amount of writing was also produced by the student teams abroad, all of whose English language
ability was notably well developed and whose faculty were often looking for an
opportunity for English language practice.

The second positive outcome concerned the highly focused, deeply elaborated style of writing prompted by the collegiate debate format. International E-
mail Debate retains all of the conditions of formal collegiate debate. Thus, the
topics are chosen ahead of time by the faculty and are stated in the form of
resolutions; for example, "Resolved: Sponsorship can improve a firm's success"; or, "Resolved: Direct foreign investment in American technology should
continue without restraint." Each team assumed either an affirmative or negative stance toward the resolution. From a writing perspective, this means that a
team's central focus or thesis statement is provided for them, and the challenges
for the team are to gather evidence and reasons to support that thesis and to
elaborate each supporting idea with more evidence and reasoning as the debate
becomes increasingly refined. For the most part, during the pilot test students
rose nicely to these challenges, especially during the constructive portion of the
debate, when most teams usually piled up numerous reasons to support their
stance. In fact, in the debate about direct foreign investment in American technology, the affirmative team supplied at least nineteen reasons to support their
stance that unrestricted foreign investment is a good idea. Most of the supporting ideas were, in turn, supported by references to journal articles, expert testimony, or examples from the business world. By and large, all of the teams
researched their topics extensively and produced a highly focused, deeply elaborated constructive essay in a relatively short period of time.

The third noteworthy result of the pilot study related to the thinking and
writing prompted by the refutation portion of the debates. During refutation,
each team has a chance to read their opponents' constructive essay and to write
an essay which points out the weaknesses, inconsistencies, and errors in their

opponents' argument. The teams routinely pointed to the inadequacy of examples or statistics, bias in supposedly authoritative testimony, out-of-date research, and illogical chains of reasoning. By offering these kinds of responses about content and argumentation, the teams were also pointing out weaknesses in writing and providing good peer criticism which could be used to guide the rebuilding of a position during rebuttal. For example, in the debate about whether or not marketing techniques may be standardized across Western countries, the team against the resolution, the Turkish team, accurately critiques the affirmative team's logic:

> The grouping of [Western] countries into broad categories, based on studies by Szymonshi et al. (1993) and by Huszagh et al. (1982), does not lead to the implication that marketing research can be standardized in those countries. . . . the consumer price index and unemployment figures vary significantly from country to country. [Data follows in the passage.] Therefore the [affirmative team's] categories contain countries which have wide variations and must be researched on an individual basis . . . before any market research can go ahead. Using standardized techniques on the basis of "low-risk" categorization glosses over the cultural differences which exist whether or not there are economic similarities or differences. . . . These include differences in linguistics, religion, geography, climate, communication and distribution networks, legislation, customs and many others.

Here the Turkish team is accurately pointing out the inadequate and incomplete evidence in the URI team's affirmative constructive. This is good peer criticism. A second example comes from the debate on the most desirable kind of corporate structure—should corporate ownership be separate from corporate management? The team from the Netherlands refutes several points made by the URI team. Notice that in these excerpts, the students point to places where the logic and the writing fail to establish a strong connection between the evidence and the supporting reasons:

> There exists no relevant relationship between this [summary of a journal article] and the resolution. The research does not support the argument that the most desirable corporate structure is one in which ownership is separated from control. . . . The argument [that firms which make the correct decisions prosper and firms which do not make the correct decisions are disciplined] is not restricted to a system of separate control and ownership. An owner-controlled corporate structure likewise allows the firms which make the correct decisions to prosper and the firms which do not make the correct decisions to be disciplined. The affirmative team does not state any supportive evidence for this argument. There is no reason to believe that a corporation with separate control and ownership will recover more quickly from market declines and crashes than an owner-controlled corporation.

In these passages the writers have again provided good peer criticism. They have pointed out exactly where the original text needs more evidence, more explanation, and improved coherence. If the other team is able to "listen" to this peer criticism and revise the argument with this critique in mind, they could not only rebut the refutation but rebuild their original argument into the strongest possible case. Clearly, International E-mail Debate's sequence of construction, refutation, and rebuttal formalizes the writerly tasks of drafting and revision while keeping the process exciting.

These positive outcomes prompted many of the instructors to be satisfied with the project. Other instructors, however, addressed themselves to problems that surfaced most clearly during the refutation and rebuttal portions of the debate project, problems which raised core issues about argumentation and about writing for e-mail. During the test period, some students had a hard time accepting the opposition's refutation as valid peer criticism. Instead, they saw the refutation essay as their opponent's attempt solely to discredit and destroy their argument. Also, some students misunderstood the nature of rebuttal, taking it instead as an opportunity for continued attack against the opposing team. Here is a sequence from the negative team's rebuttal portion in the debate about standardized marketing research among Western cultures (italics mine):

> Our opponents claim that "The statement the con team presented deals with the researcher (the person) not the nature of marketing research which is the subject being debated." *Our opponents seem to be laboring under the ridiculous assumption* that the market researcher is not involved in the process of marketing. They then proceed to agree with our argument by saying, "A researcher cannot assume things about the population being researched." . . . *Our opponents appear not to understand* one of the fundamental purposes of marketing research, which is to inform the researcher about consumer behavior and attitudes. . . . *Our opponents have failed to understand a vital function* of marketing research. [Our opponents write] that one of the statistics we used was thirteen years old and that this is therefore irrelevant. This *objection is pathetically weak.* . . .

These rebuttal passages, typical of passages from some refutation and rebuttal essays, resemble the e-mail phenomenon of *flaming* in their insulting tone and personalized attack. In fact, in the original debate just sampled the ad hominem objections and flaming served as the rebuttal, since the negative team merely added to these attacks by repeating some unimpressive material from their original constructive rather than rebuilding their case.

Several instructors in the project were distressed at these outbursts, and during a three-day face-to-face faculty conference held in Braunschweig, Germany, in 1994, they set about explaining this problem to themselves, finally viewing its occurrence as due partly to the students' lack of skill with argumentation and partly to the tendency toward flaming on e-mail (providing examples from their own electronic discussion lists!). During these discussions, some instructors attributed such outbursts to the increasingly competitive aspect of the debate process, a competition which they found to become a little more intense with each document exchange. They also agreed with composition specialist Olivia Frey (1990, 511 ff.), who notes that even in written debate of academic journals, where authors concentrate on establishing a set of apparently incontestable principles buttressed by supposedly sound reasoning and evidence, they are also tempted to discredit those who espouse opposing principles. International E-mail Debate faculty agreed that these ad hominem tendencies exacerbated the possibility of any kind of e-mail discussion to erupt into flaming. Thus, the pilot study faculty also agreed with Gail Hawisher and Charles Moran's explanation (1993, 631, 634) that the electronic environment may encourage such outbursts because e-mail conversations offer the spontaneity of a conversation while providing a degree of protective anonymity and distance; thus, e-mail messages are frequently critical and confrontational.

Given these problems, many of the faculty engaged in the International E-mail Debate project have now made adjustments to their International E-mail Debate instruction and assignments as well as to their own views of the purpose of debate. The simplest changes some instructors have adopted is to limit the length of the essays and to choose debate topics extremely carefully, warning students to be cautious and polite in their exchanges. Some instructors now also include a special lesson on the refutation essay and the rebuttal essay, helping students to see the refutation essay as a form of peer criticism, and urging students to use the critique as a prompt for improved writing, logic, and evidence in their rebuttal essay. Most interestingly, however, a few instructors are teaching their students that debate is not about winning (or not solely about winning). In these instructors' view, International E-mail Debate is valuable because it challenges students to explain the specific cultural conditions and the contexts which make their particular claims, evidence, or appeals more compelling. These instructors select debate topics that are widely and currently debated in the discipline. Students are then challenged to construct a particular argumentative thread to support their stance *and* to explain why, among the many possibilities, that thread seems most plausible to them. In this way International E-mail Debate is transformed from a pro/con exercise in argumentation to a rhetorical problem in cross-cultural communication with sophisticated applications to topics currently under debate in any discipline.

Transportability to Other Institutions

International E-mail Debate originated at URI, but it is easily transported to other institutions. First, the technology requirements are not complex: International E-mail Debate simply requires that each team have access to a computer with a modem and an e-mail address. Second, the major phases of the project follow the widely known sequence of formal collegiate debate. Third, students are usually very receptive to the prospect of communicating with students in other countries and welcome the project to their classes. But even with these features, International E-mail Debate will be more successful if project leaders at other institutions take note of a few important lessons from URI's pilot study.

A first lesson that emerged was that contact with faculty at universities around the world can probably be developed by networking among faculty at one's own campus. For example, during the three-year pilot study, the faculty abroad whose business classes participated in the three-year pilot study were recruited through the personal contacts of Chai Kim. In fact, Kim remains as a primary source at URI for technical information about International E-mail Debate and its applications to business courses (chaikim@uriacc.uri.edu.; see also http://www.cba.uri.edu/faculty/kim/globalclass.html). Several sources at the University of Rhode Island have also proven helpful in establishing other contacts abroad and in pursuing e-mail projects. Faculty in a variety of the foreign languages and in international study areas (such as business, law, and foreign relations) helped establish contact with institutions and with individual faculty abroad, and faculty in communications studies helped with debate procedures and provided useful suggestions for cross-cultural communications.

Another lesson from URI's pilot study pertains to topic selection. Faculty must attend to topic selection just after they have made contact with each other and have agreed to try International E-mail Debate in their classes. Faculty would do well to select topics and debate resolutions that are of current disciplinary interest but that are not too difficult for students to understand fairly quickly since the debate process is so fast-paced. Furthermore, the topics should not be divided into rigid oppositions. Instead they should invite the teams to develop one of many possible positions on the resolution. For example, instead of the either/or resolution, "Direct foreign investment in American technology is good and should continue unrestrained," the more open-ended yet debatable resolution might be, "When and under what conditions is foreign investment beneficial to the development of a country's technology?" Such attention to topic selection will help ensure that the debates are compelling to students and faculty, and do not degenerate into a flame war.

A third lesson from the pilot study involves cautionary words about writing for debate combined with writing for e-mail. Faculty at URI learned that the electronic debate forum can provoke the kind of inflammatory reactions that are counter to the best goals of International E-mail Debate. To counter this tendency, student teams should be encouraged to use e-mail to communicate informally throughout the debate. Faculty must also help students understand that the refutation essay is an opportunity for polite peer criticism and that the rebuttal essay provides an opportunity to rebuild a position while recognizing the validity of others' points of view. This kind of instruction helps students to understand the constructed nature of each debate position and to appreciate the differences of perspective rooted in divergent cultural experience.

Theoretical Challenges

These lessons from URI's pilot study suggest that the rhetorical, social, and topical aspects of International E-mail Debate make it a particularly appealing writing-across-the-curriculum and e-mail activity. The challenge of persuading readers in another country about a truly debatable issue helps students to understand the constructed nature of most chains of argument and the rhetorical nature of most stances. International E-mail Debate helps students recognize what Don H. Bialostosky calls an "authentically situated voice" (1991, 17). As Bialostosky explains, students should wrestle with the formal discourses of academic disciplines, not because such writing leads them to discover who they are, but because the confrontation with new, difficult, even foreign-sounding languages holds these discourses at a distance, underscoring that each discipline offers a particular, constructed perspective and pattern of expression. He continues:

> As part of a college education designed to initiate students into reflexive use of these authoritative languages, the study of college writing should not permit students to retreat from the challenges presented by these demanding languages to languages with which they are already comfortable or to conform without struggle to the new academic languages. It is more important to cultivate students' understanding of their ambivalent situations and to validate their struggles to remake themselves and the languages imposed on them. If they see that they do not possess a finished authentic identity and an authentic language, which the new alien languages threaten from without, they may also see that the new languages do not promise to provide such an identity but only offer new resources for seeing and saying. (1991, 17)

When students engage in International E-mail Debate they are, indeed, struggling with authoritative languages. They contend with topics that have an immediate disciplinary urgency, and they observe specific representations of that topic as written by authors who are presenting themselves to particular audiences in specific ways, and whose writing has disciplinary consequences. International E-mail Debate challenges students to appropriate a particular thread among those representations and to explain to an audience in a different cultural setting the conditions and the context which make that construction of the topic more compelling.

Thus, a project like International E-mail Debate is best understood from a social, rhetorical view of writing. Instead of private, exploratory, or personal writing, some writing across the curriculum activities ought to be framed by topic, from deep within the discipline, and they should have as their goal helping students to become active users of disciplinary discourse while also helping students to become critically aware of the constructed natures of these endeavors. Projects like International E-mail Debate also challenge proponents of computers in composition to acknowledge that some formal writing activities with e-mail, especially those that help students develop an authentically situated voice, may also be framed so as to contribute to a community-engaging, democratic electronic environment.

Future Prospects

International E-mail Debate has proven to be a very appealing project at URI with interesting variations emerging each semester, suggesting interesting prospects for the future. Some variations occur on a class-by-class level and some occur at the program level. For example, some instructors are expanding the role of technology in the debate process. Della Bitta plans to have teams explore the World Wide Web for data and other information to support their debate positions, and another instructor has proposed holding a MOO as part of the debate experience. Thus, through these instructors' various uses of technology, each class project is becoming more individualized, yet each is still within the identifiable boundaries of International E-mail Debate.

At the same time a recent collaboration between Chai Kim and Norbert Mundorf, professor of communication studies, has led to a new, stand-alone course on International E-mail Debate which allows students to conduct their debates while also studying problems in cross-cultural communications. Not only are the colleges of both departments pleased with the collaboration, but the cross-disciplinary emphasis may shape International E-mail Debate projects in the future, throwing more of an emphasis on successful communication while highlighting the differences and difficulties that may be ascribed to culture. We surmise that as other disciplines will become engaged, new variations will emerge and add even more facets to International E-mail Debate.

Finally, at URI writing across the curriculum and International E-mail Debate will continue to drive and shape each other. Since students in any course using International E-mail Debate tend to write more than in other courses, we help promote and extend the use of International E-mail Debate across campus. In some classes, therefore, a schedule of drafting and revising is as important to the project as is the sequence of constructive-refutation-rebuttal. On the other hand, because International E-mail Debate is a formal writing project, we find ourselves broadening our philosophical bases from an expressivist-process orientation to include more rhetorical, social, and disciplinary concerns. We are nurturing this interaction, in particular. It seems to us that as International E-mail Debate continues to develop, we will, too.

Notes

Computer technology: the University of Rhode Island provided IBM Model 55 computers for the project during the three year pilot study, 1992–1995. The debate documents were composed using Microsoft Word for Windows 2.0. Eudora was used for all e-mail transmissions.

E-mail addresses and URLs for International E-mail Debate: For technical information about International E-mail Debate and its applications to business courses, contact Chai Kim, professor of management information systems: chaikim@uriacc.uri.edu.; see also http://www.cba.uri.edu/faculty/kim/globalclass.html. For information on collegiate debate and on the adaptation of collegiate debate to International E-mail Debate, contact Stephen Wood, professor of communication studies: docwood@uriacc.uri.edu. For information on problems in cross-cultural communications, contact Guo-Ming Chen, associate professor of communication studies: cqm101@uriacc.uri.edu. For information on writing across the curriculum and International E-mail Debate, contact Linda Shamoon, professor of English: shamoon@uriacc.uri.edu.

Works Cited

Bialostosky, Don H. 1991. "Liberal Education, Writing, and the Dialogic Self." In *Contending with Words: Composition and Rhetoric in a Postmodern Age*, edited by Patricia Harkin and John Schilb, 11–22. New York: Modern Language Association of America.

Cooper, Marilyn M., and Cynthia L. Selfe. 1990. "Computer Conferences and Learning: Authority, Resistance, and Internally Persuasive Discourse." *College English* 52.8: 847–69.

Della Bitta, Albert. 1996. Interview by author. Kingston, Rhode Island, 7 August.

Frey, Olivia. 1990. "Beyond Literary Darwinism: Women's Voices and Critical Discourse." *College English* 52.5: 507–26.

Hawisher, Gail E., and Charles Moran. 1993. "Electronic Mail and the Writing Instructor." *College English* 55.6: 627–43.

Spooner, Michael, and Kathleen Yancey. 1996. "Postings on a Genre of Email." *College Composition and Communication.* 47.2: 252–78.

12 E-mail in an Interdisciplinary Context

Dennis A. Lynch
Michigan Technological University

Introduction

Cynthia Selfe and Gail Hawisher have argued that the stories we tell one another about our successes using new technologies in the classroom tend to blind us to actual or potential failures, as well as to the possibility that all this new technology can serve in many ways merely to reinscribe the worst aspects of traditional education. Selfe and Hawisher worry especially that the plethora of success narratives found in the literature might forge an unconscious link in our minds between, for instance, networked classrooms and progressive or liberatory goals (Hawisher and Selfe 1991, 56). They are quick to point out that there is nothing inherently progressive or liberatory in these new technologies, and, in that light, they call both for continued critical reflection on how we use computers in the classroom and also for more balance in our storytelling. Accordingly, in this chapter, I will describe using e-mail in a writing-across-the-curriculum setting—a use, I think, that failed—and offer critical reflection from my and my students' perspectives on why e-mail did not work for us and how we might improve its use in educational settings.

The Class(es)

During the past two years, humanities and biology faculty at Michigan Technological University (MTU), with support from their departments and the university administration, have twice tested what began on the drafting table as a version of writing-in-the-disciplines—intensified writing instruction in conjunction with a first-year biology course—but which later evolved into a more fully interdisciplinary educational experiment. Initially, the idea was to link five sections of Humanities 101 (our first-year rhetoric and composition course) with Biology 101 (a lecture and lab course required of all first-year biology majors), and to place all of the first-year biology majors into both classes, in order to create more space and time within which to study—with the biology students—how biologists write and communicate. But as we worked through our reasons and motivations for engaging in the project, we began to see broader connections—as well as "productive tensions" (Leff 1987, 35-36)—between our respective disciplinary goals, which led us to realize that we were integrating more than the skill of writing with the study of biology (Mahala 1991; Russell 1992). We were, we found, integrating two worlds of activity: two ways of teaching and learning, and two sides of campus with different histories. In the spirit of our shift into working more consciously with those broader connections, we decided (the second time we offered linked classes) to connect our students via e-mail in order to create a social space with the potential to enhance the interdisciplinary atmosphere.

Since our courses were not computer-based by design, the possibility of, and possibilities for, using e-mail came to us slowly and incompletely. Past research in computers and writing had suggested to us that an e-mail list might serve several useful functions, especially in an interdisciplinary context (Hawisher and Moran 1993, Herrington and Moran 1992): a list might broaden and complicate the social dimension of the educational process, enhance collaboration and invention (Herrington and Moran 1992), provide a less threatening forum for some students—especially those who are traditionally underrepresented in the sciences (Spanier 1992)—and create a flexible, ambiguous space in which students could discuss questions such as what it means to "become a biologist." Computers were neither our original nor our primary focus for these courses, however, so our goals stayed within that list of possibilities, but not as clearly articulated as they should have been—the consequences of which will be discussed below.

The First E-mail Assignment

We gave two assignments connected with the use of e-mail: (1) an assignment that linked a small group of students from one section to another small group in another section, via a "list"; and (2) an assignment that asked the biology students in the "honors" section (HU 101H) to act as participant-observers and to evaluate the successes and failures of the e-mail discussion format. We based the grades for the first assignment on the frequency of each student's entries—we asked for at least two a week—and on the quality of their entries—we asked them to turn in, at the end of the quarter, four entries they felt represented their most thoughtful contributions to the list-discussion and to briefly explain why they chose these four. The students in the honors section were told that their projects would be graded on the design of their evaluation procedures and on their follow-through, analysis, and recommendations. I will here describe the

first assignment, and in the following sections I will describe the second assignment and what we learned from it.

Since we wanted e-mail to serve as a forum within which students could talk
about the connections between humanities and biology, or about issues that
might come up in biology lectures or in their humanities classes, we kept the
groups small enough to allow sustained discussion of the issues, and we linked
groups from different sections to encourage them to compare experiences from
what might be different classroom perspectives. We had arranged for biology
lab groups to stay together in their humanities classes, so each of our five humanities classes was composed of four or five lab groups, depending on enrollment. We then set up twelve e-mail lists that linked each lab group in one class
to a lab group in a different class. As biology majors, the students have access to
a computer lab on campus, so all they had to do was to stop in regularly, check
their mail, and respond. Some of them were already online; others had to learn
how to open up e-mail and join a list.

Once everyone was securely online, the instructors then offered a series of
prompt questions, a new one each week, in order to facilitate discussion but
with the explicit proviso that students should "feel free" to move beyond the
prompt questions into other areas that concerned them. We tried various kinds
of prompts, from specific questions asking why students thought scientists used
the passive voice so much, to more open-ended questions about the ethics of
secrecy (governmental and economic) in scientific research and about what it
means to "contribute" to science.

As said, we instructors were new to the pedagogical uses of e-mail, and we
were redesigning other aspects of our integrated program at the same time we
planned this first e-mail assignment. We thus made what seems to us now some
bad decisions, such as to initiate discussions ourselves and sometimes either to
"lurk" or to participate on the lists. That those decisions were problematic became clear during the quarter as some students complained or resisted the assignment, but the full extent of the problem only emerged as the honors section
prepared their final reports, the conclusions of which will be discussed in the
following sections.

The Second E-mail Assignment

The idea to have the honors section perform an evaluation of the e-mail assignment came about indirectly. Students in honors sections at MTU are required to
do a research project in order to justify the extra units they receive for the class
(and to justify their exemption from further first-year writing requirements).
We wanted to make sure the added project would not interrupt the goals of our
course, and it occurred to us that if we asked the honors students, as their project,

to evaluate the effectiveness of the e-mail assignment and make suggestions regarding changes, they could contribute to the experimental nature of the course and stay engaged with the other sections. We were careful, needless to say, to explain that they were evaluating the assignment, and not the other students.

From the start the evaluation assignment went well because the students, as one said, "had complete authority over its design and operation." The authority I exercised was to ask them to work collaboratively in their lab groups: they were to invent a way of assessing or evaluating the effectiveness or usefulness of using e-mail as we used it; to write up a proposal describing their planned assessment and present it to the class for feedback; and to then perform the assessment, write up their results, and turn them in at the end of the quarter. When they asked me how to start, I suggested they might "brainstorm" as many different possible goals that might be accomplished by using e-mail in this way, and then invent different ways they might go about determining if we achieved those goals.

The Second E-mail Assignment: Student Evaluation Procedures

The most pivotal moment in the evaluations assignment turned out to be when I refused to articulate my version of the goals for which the students should test. As I explained, this was their assessment and by articulating the goals for themselves and by coming up with their own ways of measuring success, they would determine how we see and understand the results and thus ensure, as best they could, that we make the changes they deem necessary. I hoped they would discover as a group the connection between choosing one's objectives and defining the range of possible outcomes.

The first indication that the evaluations assignment would be successful came when the groups first presented their proposals in class, and we listened to the range of potential goals and the different, creative ways they suggested for testing their achievement. The groups quickly focused on dimensions of the e-mail assignment we instructors had overlooked or assumed were unimportant. For example, their lists questioned the quantity, quality, and pacing of the prompts, the weekly time frame we had established, the effects of teacher participation, and the virtual isolation of students at their terminals. The students also proposed to investigate the quantity, quality, and pacing of the responses, the role that different student backgrounds might play, the nature of e-mail as a medium of communication, and the connection between the e-mail assignment and our interdisciplinary goals.

The methods the students used to answer the above questions also varied. Some groups relied primarily on numerical data. For instance, one group joined all of the e-mail lists and counted the number of responses per prompt, per week, per person (no names were used), and then looked for discourse markers to determine the degree of disagreement present on the lists and the extent of cross-referencing. The groups sent questionnaires out over e-mail (which had them questioning whether their actions would affect what they were trying to observe); they designed intersubjective ways to judge the "quality" of the discussions (such as "intensity of expression" and "connection to what had been said by others"); and they conducted written, oral and online interviews (and designed "before and after" surveys) to inquire into the backgrounds of students, their previous experience with e-mail, their evolving interest (or disinterest) in the assignment, whether e-mail helped with shyness, and so on. Finally, one group chose an extreme participant-observer strategy: they joined in various discussions and used charged language in order to test the effects of strong emotional display on e-mail discussion.

The Second E-mail Assignment: Students' Results, Conclusions, and Suggestions

The students' results reconfirmed observations by now familiar in the literature on networked classrooms and e-mail. The students reported that when they conducted their interviews, other students quickly said they felt less pressure or in a better position to respond over e-mail than they did in face-to-face classroom discussions, even though in some ways they missed the responsiveness of face-to-face conversation; the other students also said they were uneasy about their instructors' presence on the list. The students' results questioned the parameters of e-mail exchange in other ways, as well: they reported the trouble some students had finding a balance between emotional display and intense engagement, their trouble deciding how much or how little to write (what the "essence" of an e-mail message is), and their frustration with having to wait "sometimes days for a good response."

The students' strongest conclusions directly targeted our use of prompts, including their form, content, pacing, and above all, the way they positioned students. The evaluation reports all indicated that students across the lists felt stymied by the prompts. Students felt out of control, able only to respond to what instructors had initiated, yet somehow "expected" to do something more. They felt the instructors' presence(s) everywhere and nowhere, and so our intentions to use e-mail to free the students not-so-paradoxically placed them under even greater burdens—what were they to do, given that they were still "just students"?

In response to these problems, the honors students made two suggestions: first, that e-mail participants play more early on, perhaps exchange names and create "faces" or persona for self-conscious exploration of different communicative possibilities (for instance, one student said she "kind of enjoyed" being "the mean one" for a change); and, second, that we find ways to encourage "spill-over", a chance to move discussions beyond the bounds of e-mail: "another reason we believe the secrecy prompt [one of the prompts used to initiate discussion and mentioned earlier] was so successful was the discussion about this issue in class."

Instructors' Results, Conclusions, and Suggestions

There were serious flaws in our use of e-mail (though fortunately we did not base the success or failure of the entire humanities/biology project upon it). The instructors agreed, in other words, with the conclusions reached by the honors students. We had anticipated that students would collaborate, working thickly through questions, issues, and matters of concern connected to class. Instead, as the assessment groups reported, the interactions between students on e-mail were caught somewhere between "epistolary" and off-the-cuff, neither of which were conducive to what we had hoped for. The students felt out of control because they *were* in fact out of control—because we thought e-mail in and of itself would provide the proper social and interdisciplinary space within which they could come to terms with our course(s).

But what we had hoped for did indeed show up, through the second assignment, and in several ways. First, the second assignment contributed to the interdisciplinary goals of our curricular experiment: the assignment encouraged the students to merge their methodical tendencies and previous scientific training with a subject matter—social and academic communicative interaction—that did not easily adapt itself to quantitative or scientific methods of measurement. As one student explained to me, "This was difficult because we could not just measure success like we could measure data in our experiment. We had to change the way we thought about what experimentation was before we could even start." We had several good discussions about the desire for, problems with, and limitations of "outcomes assessments" throughout the quarter, as an unexpected byproduct of the assignment.

The first suggestion I pull from this experience, then, is that ". . . a pedagogy that includes e-mail will be inevitably project oriented and perhaps cross-disciplinary . . . ," as Hawisher and Moran predicted in their article "Electronic Mail and the Writing Instructor" (1993, 633). The connections between cross- or interdisciplinary education and project-based instruction have already been worked through at a number of educational sites, as Julie Klein so thoroughly documents in her 1990 book, *Interdisciplinarity: History, Theory, and Practice.* Many of the problems that our Humanities/Biology students stumbled across (as a result of our decisions)—problems regarding the loss of face-to-face orientation and the odd intimacy of e-mail exchange, problems stemming from the awkward timing between "send" and "reply," and problems with placing the whole e-mail exchange in a larger picture—can be alleviated in part by integrating the use or uses of e-mail into a larger project.

But there is also a second set of observations I would like to make, coming out of the second assignment. The instructors—and the students—all agreed that the students' evaluation process embodied, in several ways, what we finally came to see was most missing from the first assignment. The second assignment gave students a stake in the assignment itself and a critical angle on what was happening. There were of course flaws in the evaluation assignment, but they were more self-correcting than the flaws in the e-mail assignment precisely because the evaluation assignment, in its goals and design, elicited from the students a greater degree of critical involvement. The worst overall mistake we—I—made, then, was to limit access to such a critical angle only to "honors" students, thereby reinforcing what is already more than a questionable institutional division.

The main suggestion I make for any use of e-mail, then, is to build a critical dimension into any project or assignment involving e-mail, not necessarily as we did here, but in one fashion or another. It might be as simple as beginning the course, as Ira Shor in *Empowering Education* (1992) so passionately argues we do, with a critical discussion of the educational choices being made, i.e., the assigned use of e-mail. Perhaps this could become the basis for the first e-mail exchange—just so that it becomes clear to the students that what they, together, say they want to happen can happen, if everyone is willing to think it through together, listen, and adjust.

The conclusions we all reached, students and instructors together, thus show us even more what Selfe and Hawisher were arguing, that e-mail in itself, or in isolation from other teaching and learning strategies, is not necessarily empowering or liberatory. E-mail, in short, is a means to an end, not an end in itself, pedagogically or otherwise; it can, as we originally assumed, provide a less threatening forum within which students produce knowledge together; it can become a flexible, creative space within which students invent solutions to problems; and it can enhance the social dimension of the educational process; but it can just as easily become a tool for education as usual, by positioning students passively, uncritically, and without ways to resist or respond imaginatively to the assignment or to the framework within which the assignment unfolds. E-mail, in other words, is a possible strategy within an experimental or liberatory educational program, but not a strategy for empowerment in itself.

Works Cited

Faigley, Lester. 1992. *Fragments of Rationality: Postmodernity and the Subject of Composition*. Pittsburgh: University of Pittsburgh Press.

Fulwiler, Toby, and Art Young, eds. 1990. *Programs That Work: Models and Methods for Writing Across the Curriculum*. Portsmouth, NH: Boynton/Cook Publishers.

Hawisher, Gail E., and Charles Moran. 1993. "Electronic Mail and the Writing Instructor." *College English* 55.6: 627–44.

Hawisher, Gail E., and Cynthia L. Selfe, eds. 1991. *Evolving Perspectives on Computers and Composition Studies: Questions for the 1990s*. Urbana, IL: National Council of Teachers of English.

———. 1993. "The Rhetoric of Technology and the Electronic Writing Class." *College Composition and Communication* 42.1: 55–66.

Herrington, Anne, and Charles Moran. 1992. "Writing in the Disciplines: A Prospect." In *Writing, Teaching, and Learning in the Disciplines*, edited by Anne Herrington and Charles Moran, 231–45. New York: Modern Language Association of America.

Klein, Julie Thompson. 1990. *Interdisciplinarity: History, Theory, and Practice*. Detroit: Wayne State University Press.

Klem, Elizabeth, and Charles Moran. 1991. "Computers and Instructional Strategies in the Teaching of Writing." In *Evolving Perspectives on Computers and Composition Studies: Questions for the 1990s*, edited by Gail E. Hawisher and Cynthia L. Selfe, 132–50. Urbana, IL: National Council of Teachers of English.

Leff, Michael. 1987. "Modern Sophistic and the Unity of Rhetoric." In *The Rhetoric of the Human Sciences: Language and Argument in Scholarship and Public Affairs*, edited by John S. Nelson, Allan Megill, and Donald N. McCloskey, 19–38. Madison: University of Wisconsin Press.

Mahala, Daniel. 1991. "Writing Utopias: Writing Across the Curriculum and the Promise of Reform." *College English* 53.7: 773–89.

McLeod, Susan H., and Margot Soven, eds. 1992. *Writing Across the Curriculum: A Guide to Developing Programs*. Newbury Park, CA: Sage Publications.

Petersen, Linda H. 1992. "Writing Across the Curriculum and/in the Freshman Program." In *Writing Across the Curriculum: A Guide to Developing Programs*, edited by Susan H. McLeod and Margot Soven, 58–71. Newbury Park, CA: Sage Publications.

Russell, David R. 1992. "American Origins of the Writing-Across-the-Curriculum Movement." In *Writing, Teaching, and Learning in the Disciplines*, edited by Anne Herrington and Charles Moran, 22–45. New York: Modern Language Association of America.

Shor, Ira. 1992. *Empowering Education: Critical Teaching for Social Change*. Chicago: University of Chicago Press.

Spanier, Bonnie B. 1992. "Encountering the Biological Sciences: Ideology, Language and Learning." In *Writing, Teaching, and Learning in the Disciplines*, edited by Anne Herrington and Charles Moran, 193–213. New York: Modern Language Association of America.

13 Creativity, Collaboration, and Computers

Margaret Portillo
University of Kentucky

Gail Summerskill Cummins
University of Kentucky

In the preface to their anthology, *Landmark Essays on Writing Across the Curriculum*, Charles Bazerman and David Russell (1994) articulate the original reasons for studying writing and rhetoric in the disciplines: "How do students learn (or fail to learn) the specific kinds of writing they will need in their future activities, professional and otherwise? And how can pedagogical arrangements improve that learning?" (xv). At the end of a writing-across-the-curriculum workshop at the University of Kentucky, two professors—one in interior design and one in English—modified these questions to find answers to similar cross-disciplinary concerns: (1) If undergraduates across disciplines are in continual dialogue about the creative processes they use to do their work (written and not written), will they learn about and enhance these processes?; (2) What pedagogical techniques can be used to make this dialogue a significant learning experience?; and (3) How can the use of electronic mail facilitate this exchange?

In order to answer these questions, students in a creative design foundations class and a freshman composition class were paired for e-mail conversations. After completing the same assignments, students e-mailed one another about the creative processes used to do their work and their reactions to the experience.

This creative partnering worked well because of the expressive and inventive space of e-mail as well as its interdisciplinary pairing. E-mail facilitated student exposure to creativity because e-mail can immediately provide someone else's perspective. Mark Zamierowski (1994) notes in *The Virtual Voice of Network Culture* that the voice generated through electronic media is a virtual voice which is

> a matter of linkages and assemblages, arrangements that may not last beyond the space of their cooperation. A virtual voice is inherently a disputable fact. It should never be, but should always be a becoming-voice. It

should never be thought of as existing anywhere but in-between, in the very reciprocating structure of discourse itself. As such, a virtual voice cannot be the sole possession of anyone, nor the dispensation of anything. In this respect, it is nothing more than a desire to express and invent, a desire that simply is expression and invention itself. (291)

The professors, Margaret Portillo in interior design and Gail Cummins in rhetoric and composition, and their students in both interior design and composition learned a great deal about the expression and invention of creativity through their e-mail partnering, as well as with its interdisciplinary pairing and the common work not in the content of the specific disciplines. In addition, the project concluded that raising to consciousness the creative processes necessary to complete disciplinary work via e-mail is a pedagogy worth incorporating into every class.

Creativity Partnering

After working together at the University of Kentucky Writing Across the Curriculum Workshop, marveling at the similarity and difference of pedagogy, research, and creative process, we were inspired and encouraged to find a similar conversational forum for our students. In philosophical agreement about the capacity to create and our students' ability to develop this potential, we two professors shared disciplinary-specific theory to ground our study. Understanding creativity in a developmental context is central to Portillo's work (Dohr and Portillo 1989, 1991; Portillo and Dohr 1989). In addition, Portillo had just discovered Elizabeth Goldsmith-Conley's (1992) dissertation and was excited by her rhetorical approach to teaching literature and painting. Goldsmith-Conley presents a case for raising critical thinking across disciplines through questioning processes. Cummins's dissertation focused on how writers question their relationships between themselves, texts, and audiences (1994). Since the developing nature of creative processes—in both interior design and composition— are central to Portillo and Cummins, the developmental aspects of creativity and voice guided our joint study.

Together, we developed a series of five creativity assignments for an introductory design class and an English course. We attempted to raise creativity to consciousness by exposing students to persons, processes, products, and places. This 4Ps framework for understanding creativity, coupled with a rhetoric and compositional approach, guided the pedagogy in both classes. Engaging students in active learning and self-discovery focused this engagement on student creativity.

After completing assignments, students considered the following questions: (1) How do I do an assignment; what creative processes do I use? (2) What works in creating an assignment? and (3) What doesn't work in creating an assignment? The intent was to make the students aware of creativity and their own creative processes to better realize their potential.

 E-mail was the chosen interdisciplinary platform because it readily maintains lively discussion across classes. Marilyn Cooper and Cynthia Selfe (1990) describe technological sites as

> reduced risk space, [where] students can discover or evolve amongst themselves different patterns of power and linguistic exchange to facilitate these discussions, patterns which may run directly counter to those that have become habitual in our classrooms. (867)

Using e-mail, therefore, we created an interdisciplinary Creativity Partnering Project, a student forum for discussion of creativity.

Students from the two classes were paired and, over the course of the semester, electronically mailed responses to their cross-disciplinary partners. The Creativity Partnering Project began with an assignment that emphasized creativity through life experience. The purpose was to create and write about symbols that represented a significant learning and/or creating event for each year of the student's life. For inspiration, the students were shown a photograph of a Lakota Sioux Stepping Stone Calendar that illustrated seventy-two years in the life of a tribal warrior (1801–1873) through symbols.

The ensuing assignments emphasized creativity in art and poetry: students viewed a film documentary about Georgia O'Keeffe and attended a poetry reading and an informal question-and-answer session by poet Rosemary Klein. The next assignment emphasized the creative process involved in transforming nine non-objective line drawings into recognizable images that were then appropriately titled. The students completed the line drawings in class and then shared their responses with each other. The final experience involved visiting an exhibit of electronic media by Nam June Paik and a photography exhibit by James Baker Hall, both at the University of Kentucky Art Museum.

While issues of creativity could be explored individually within interior design and English, the purpose of collaborating was to underscore commonalities between two fields that emphasize process—a process that is enhanced through creativity. After completing the project, we returned again to the student writings to look for patterns in their responses.

On a first reading, the students' e-mail responses sorted into 3 categories: (1) those who responded emotionally, recording their subjective impressions, (2) those who responded informationally, presenting literal facts, and (3) those who responded contextually, looking beyond their own experience to answer in a larger context. These responses suggested different styles and developmental levels of processing information. Lester Faigley (1986) describes three ways rhetoricians pattern information about writers and writing: "an expressive view including the work of 'authentic voice'. . . , a cognitive view including the research of those who analyze the composing processes . . .," and the social view which "contends that processes of writing are social in character instead of originating within individual writers" (528). The student responses generally sorted into Faigley's categories.

Similarly, a multidimensional stance is found in theoretical descriptions of the creative person. That is, the study of the creative person has encompassed expressive and cognitive views, typically examined in terms of personality and motivational traits, cognitive characteristics, and biographical experiences (Davis 1975; Rothenberg and Hausman, 1976). However, the study of creativity also more recently invited a social view, exploring process, product, and place (Stein 1968; Tardif and Sternberg, 1988). These facets are, of course, interrelated. Paul Torrance (1988) reflects,

> I chose a process definition of creativity for research purposes. I thought that if I chose process as a focus, I could then ask what kind of person one must be to engage in the process successfully, what kinds of environments facilitate it, and what kinds of products will result from successful operations of the processes. (47)

The inherent complexity of creativity defies reaching a universal definition easily; however, people, when asked to define creativity, seem to be able to intuitively identify key aspects of the creative person. Robert Sternberg (1988) probably has done the most work studying how people conceptualize creativity, focusing on "what kind of person one must be to engage in the process successfully." Sternberg's studies indicate that people maintain fairly consistent conceptions of creativity (called "implicit theories") and employ their theories to evaluate or judge others.

We wondered if our students held implicit theories that guided their articulations of creativity. Would students consider creativity as person, process, product, and place? Would they see relationship among these components? Would an interdisciplinary lens, conducted through e-mail, help make this clear?

Again, the interdisciplinary theory guiding this study enhanced the questions and answers it generated—both by professors and students. For example, Portillo speculated that like the student coming to the study of color expecting only to find hue and then discovering nuances of value and chroma, the design student had implicit theories about creativity that could be brought to consciousness through interdisciplinary dialogue. Cummins wondered if the processes of student writers would change if, as Toni Morrison would say, writers could name and claim them.

When analyzed, many of the students' discussions of their creativity processes related to personality traits and characteristics. The traits could be discerned in part because of the comparisons provided by the two disciplines and also because of the informality and open-ended nature of discussion generated by e-mail. Additionally, by looking at someone else's creative process—another student and a "master" artist or poet—students were able to dissect their own method. For example, one student said,

> [The painter Georgia] O'Keeffe had a different style of doing things than I do. Georgia was an abstract artist. She liked to paint things a little out of the norms of society. I prefer things more "normal," not because it is normal, but I can associate with these things easier. . . . Coming up with something no one else has ever tried is not only a brave thing to do but a difficult thing as well.

This inherent tension between the creative self (person) and society (place) relates to the affective side of creativity—the struggle, determination, tenacity inherent in delivering new ideas regardless of the content area—which slides into one's "aesthetic taste and imagination" (process). Aesthetic taste and imagination fuel finding a good problem and realizing its possibilities (product).

Another student discussed his affective side of creativity:

> Georgia O'Keeffe's creative process is similar to mine in that she sees what she is going to create before she brings it to life. Words come to me just as shapes fill her head. I also sometimes have trouble fitting all I want to say into one paper, just as she struggles to put all of her thoughts on a canvas. I don't, however, require the amount of independence and isolation she does to create. I like to have someone close to critique my work.

The creative process of writing does require varying combinations of writer (person), text (product), process, and context (place). One given is that all four elements must co-exist for communication to occur, as exhibited by the previous student's remark. As James Moffett (1965) says, "There is no speech without a speaker in some relation to a spoken-to and a spoken-about" (244). How a creator combines and varies these relationships is what makes the creative process individualistic.

The combination of person, product, and place is discernible when creators discuss their revision practices. When artists and writers revise, they are in constant relationship with the audiences who will see and hear their texts. Cummins has argued in her article "Coming to Voice," "The complicated juggling of relationships—between author and text, author and language, author and other authors—forces us into roles we may not be prepared to take, roles we may not be able to make conscious" (1994, 50). Studying the revision practices of successful artists and writers, students can begin to relate these processes to their own. One creativity partner said:

> O'Keeffe painted 8 variations of the evening star and 3 variations of the Grand Canyon while living in Texas, each one focusing on different perspectives. This, to me, is very similar to a writer's editing and revising methods.

It is essential, therefore, to help students make explicit theories that guide their creative work. A starting point is to tease out the differences between intuitive and rational approaches to creativity, and interdisciplinary conversation is a good way to do this. Responding to Georgia O'Keeffe's painting, some students in the creative partner project found O'Keeffe's process intuitive; others recognized a more rational method. The advocates for intuition related to O'Keeffe's description of shapes flooding into her mind, shapes whose origin she could not place or determine. Students appeared in awe of, even envious of, her creative muse:

> O'Keeffe can begin with a blank canvas and produce a masterpiece while I have to spend hours sketching and starting over.

> O'Keeffe never started a project until she had thoroughly thought out her ideas and processes she intended to carry out.

Regardless of their stance on the accessibility of the creative process, many students connected the creative person with his or her process, product, and place. Calvin Taylor (1988) acknowledges that "To many in the arts, including poets and creative writers, the highest degree of the creative process is almost a combined total-human-being response, involving all aspects of such a person's response repertoire" (99). The students implicitly recognized the multiple forces defining creativity. One student remarked:

> What [Rosemary Klein] said about her life experiences appealed to me because I like to think about how my life and childhood have shaped my creativity . . . I think her [poetry] was a part of her life.

In their writings and dialogue with each other, the students evidenced implicit theories that distinguished among "spontaneous," "forced," and "extended" creativity. That is, they understood that creativity could be manifested as a reverie, occur within constraints, or show elaboration of an idea. The implicit theories of students paralleled extant, sometimes competing, theories of creativity.

The students' implicit theories also echoed the nature versus nurture polemic that exists in the realm of creativity (MacKinnon 1962). Undeniably, creative genius exists. Different levels of creativity exist. But it is the responsibility of the educator to shift the emphasis from "Is one creative?" to "How is one creative?"

In *The Making of Meaning: Metaphors, Models, and Maxims for Writing Teachers*, Ann Berthoff (1981) says

> I learned to come to class not thinking of a territory to be covered [with a map] but with a compass . . . making the raising of consciousness about the making of meaning [my] chief strategy in teaching . . . and in developing a "pedagogy of knowing" (15).

This project made creative processes conscious—both in the professors' pedagogy and research and in the work of their students. Through cross-disciplinary collaboration, the professors and students found new perspectives on their own fields. For example, watching Portillo hold and critique a student's design of a scaled paper furniture component, Cummins was reminded of how easy it is to get away from a hands-on-approach to teaching. By listening and talking to a poet and artists, students learned about and enhanced their creative processes. They considered how their own processes and the processes of those in other disciplines guide their creativity:

> I thought that [Rosemary Klein] was an extremely interesting person. Everyone in my class [interior design] seemed to enjoy her and her poetry. I am sure that your class perceived her in a different way. I guess when you're in an English class, you respond differently to things. I know we were interested in her creative process, while your class questions seemed to center around how Klein knows what art is.

> It was obvious that [Klein] is very moved by her work, and that had quite an effect on the audience. It was a reminder that creativity can sometimes be a risky, brave thing to do. It must take a lot [of] faith in what you are doing to stand up there and do that. I hope that, in my career, when I need to present my work to people, that I can do it as well as she did.

> I think it is very helpful to constantly be exposed to the creative process of others, while you're still learning yours.

Conclusions and Implications

We asked (1) If undergraduates across the disciplines are in continual dialogue about the creative processes they use to do their work (written and not written), will they learn about and enhance these processes? (2) What pedagogical techniques can be used to make this a significant learning experience? and (3) How can the use of e-mail facilitate this exchange?

The Creativity Partnering Project began with self-reflection through symbol and word and moved to consider creativity within the context of art and poetry. In response to these assignments, the students discussed creativity passionately. Their implicit theories of creativity were rich and multidimensional, yet personality of the creator appeared central to their creativity constructs. Again and again, they related personality traits to process, product, and place. It seems that exposure to various highly creative persons encourages students to experiment with creative processes. Further, there appeared to be more similarities than differences in how the students viewed creativity across disciplines.

This entree into fostering a conscious creativeness through shared experiences and dialogue raised several issues that deserve further study. How might implicit theories of creativity change through pedagogic intervention? Subsequent work could examine critical junctures in the creative process. This knowledge would help identify ways to restructure the learning process to facilitate creativity.

Further, this collaborative experience between disciplines could be both further refined and expanded. More focused conversations could occur with an electronic newsgroup or chatline. Partnerships could be extended to other disciplines. Creativity that occurs within formal constraints, for example, could be explored with disciplines such as music, kinesiology, architecture, or communications. Even within an interior design or English program, conversation about creativity could be encouraged between class levels.

How did the e-mail exchange fit into the context of the first-year design and composition courses? How did it relate to the overall course objectives? Most important, this exchange on creativity took students outside their disciplinary boundaries to gain new knowledge and a new way of learning. Students saw the possibilities of innovative, blue-sky thinking by learning from individuals who were not only highly creative but also greatly committed to their work. E-mail made their insights immediate. They learned from each other and found that even as "novices" enrolled in foundations courses, their responses to and thoughts on creativity were listened to and valued.

Additionally, this exchange revealed that mastery of knowledge engages process as well as content. For example, many course objectives emphasize subject matter content, yet another important objective is to introduce and refine processes required for conceptualizing and developing this content. A shift in focus to process and the insights gained about the self and the processes of others can make the students more cognizant learners, better able to realize their creative potential.

How did e-mail support this project? This study contends that using e-mail in an interdisciplinary conversation about how we know our creative process was a worthwhile pedagogy. Reflecting upon people, product, process, and place electronically created what Christina Haas (1996) calls, in *Writing Technology: Studies on the Materiality of Literacy*, "[an] embodied practice . . . a practice based in culture, in mind, and in body . . .—a pedagogy we would all benefit from practicing" (xv).

Note

The e-mail exchange was done using a POP server that the students were able to access at a number of computer labs across the University of Kentucky campus. The model was HP 9000 K200 with the following hardware: 128 megabytes of RAM; 6 Gigabytes of hard disk space; software included Qualcomm's QPopper 2.13; PopPassd; Sendmail 8.7.3. The network employs FDDI and Ethernet connections.

Works Cited

Bazerman, Charles, and David R. Russell, eds. 1994. *Landmark Essays on Writing Across the Curriculum.* Davis, CA: Hermagoras Press.

Berthoff, Ann E. 1981. *The Making of Meaning: Metaphors, Models, and Maxims for Writing Teachers.* Portsmouth, NH: Boynton/Cook.

Cooper, Marilyn M., and Selfe, Cynthia L. 1990. "Computer Conferences and Learning: Authority, Resistance, and Internally Persuasive Discourse." *College English* 52.8: 847–69.

Cummins, Gail S. 1994. "Voices on Voice." In *Voices on Voice: Perspectives, Definitions, Inquiry,* edited by Kathleen Blake Yancey, 48–60. Urbana, IL: National Council of Teachers of English.

Davis, Gary A. 1975. "In Furious Pursuit of the Creative Person." *Journal of Creative Behavior* 9.2: 75–87.

Dohr, Joy H., and Margaret Portillo. 1989. "Creative Behavior and Education: An Avenue for Development in the Later Years." In *Introduction to Educational Gerontology* edited by R. Sherron and D. B. Lumsden, 201–27, 3rd ed. New York: McGraw-Hill.

———. 1991. "Associative Design Framework for Education." In *Design Pedagogy: Themes of Design,* edited by Jordi Periocot, 173–90, trilingual edition. Barcelona, Spain: Elisava Publishers.

Faigley, Lester. 1986. "Competing Theories of Process: a Critique and a Proposal." *College English* 48.6: 527–42.

Goldsmith-Conley, Elizabeth. 1992. *Art as Argument: A Rhetorical Approach to Teaching Literature and Painting.* Ph.D. diss., University of Illinois at Urbana-Champaign.

Haas, Christine. 1996. *Writing Technology: Studies on the Materiality of Literacy.* Mahwah, NJ: Lawrence Erlbaum.

MacKinnon, Donald W. 1962. "The Nature and Nurture of Creative Talent." *American Psychologist* 17: 484–95.

Moffett, James. 1965. "I, You, and It." *College Composition and Communication* 16.5: 243–48.

Portillo, Margaret, and Joy H. Dohr. 1989. "Design Education: On the Road toward Thought Development." *Design Studies* 10.2: 96–102.

Rothenberg, Albert, and Carl R. Hausman, eds. 1976. *The Creativity Question.* Durham, NC: Duke University Press.

Stein, Morris I. 1968. "Creativity." In *Handbook of Personality Theory and Research,* edited by E. F. Borgatta and W. W. Lambert, 900–42. Chicago: Rand McNally.

Sternberg, Robert J. 1985. "Implicit Theories of Intelligence, Creativity, and Wisdom." *Journal of Personality and Social Psychology* 49: 1589–96.

———. 1988. "A Three-facet Model of Creativity." In *The Nature of Creativity: Contemporary Psychological Perspectives,* edited by Robert Sternberg, 125–47. New York: Cambridge University Press.

Tardif, Twila Z., and Robert J. Sternberg. 1988. "What Do We Know about Creativity?" In *The Nature of Creativity: Contemporary Psychological Perspectives,* edited by Robert Sternberg, 429–40. New York: Cambridge University Press.

Taylor, Calvin W. 1988. "Various Approaches to and Definitions of Creativity." In *The Nature of Creativity: Contemporary Psychological Perspectives,* edited by Robert Sternberg, 99–121. New York: Cambridge University Press.

Torrance, E. Paul 1988. "The Nature of Creativity as Manifested in Its Testing." In *The Nature of Creativity: Contemporary Psychological Perspectives*, edited by Robert Sternberg, 43–75. New York: Cambridge University Press.

Zamierowski, Mark. 1994. "The Virtual Voice of Network Culture." In *Voices on Voice: Perspectives, Definitions, Inquiry*, edited by Kathleen Blake Yancey, 275–97. Urbana, IL: National Council of Teachers of English.

14 COllaboratory: MOOs, Museums, and Mentors

Margit Misangyi Watts
University of Hawaii at Manoa

Michael Bertsch
Butte and Shasta Community Colleges

Walden3 is a virtual online community in which students are able to interact dynamically with other students from around the world. They construct museum exhibits, share service learning experiences, and collaborate on the process of communicating ideas, information, perspectives, and meaning. This virtual community allows electronic communication to cross disciplines and fosters an academic environment which engages a variety of learning strategies. Walden3 is an integral component of a much larger educational initiative called COllaboratory at the University of Hawaii at Manoa.

The Program

The University of Hawaii at Manoa Rainbow Advantage Program (RAP) is a tightly woven learning community based on the coordinated studies model developed at Evergreen State College in Washington. It restructures the core curriculum in order to offer a supportive academic environment which promotes a sense of community and shared values. Students are actively engaged in their education and participate in a variety of approaches to learning. Education in this program is seen as the process of open-ended inquiry, and students are challenged to view learning as the development and building of connections. Therefore, the focus is on collaborative teaching strategies, cooperative learning techniques, a wide use of technology, and a variety of links to the wider community.

In order to produce lifelong learners, the teacher-as-bearer-of-knowledge image is replaced by the collaborative teacher-learner model, allowing for an environment which encourages students to be creative, original thinkers, asking questions and continually analyzing and evaluating their own learning. Providing a small college atmosphere within the larger university framework, RAP is one of a collection of programs offered to first-year students in Hawaii to ensure them a successful beginning at the university.

The University of Hawaii is a research institution with approximately 15,000 undergraduates. Its student body is possibly the most ethnically and culturally diverse population in America. The students are primarily from culturally diverse Hawaii, representing a multitude of Asian, Pacific Island, and European cultures, with additional students from the mainland, including African American and Hispanic students. The students who choose to apply to the Rainbow Advantage Program are as various as the whole student population.

RAP students take fifteen to eighteen credits together during their first year (twenty-four credits is considered a full-time load). They enroll in core courses such as American studies, journalism, art, and English, and they take a year-long foundation course which serves as the forum for teaching communication and research skills, the class for which the project COllaboratory serves as the centerpiece. COllaboratory is an international initiative bringing together students of all ages from around the world. To date students from Canada, California, Pennsylvania, Guam, and Washington, D.C., have participated, working with museum staff and teachers on interpretations of ideas. These partnerships culminate in the installation of museum exhibits, amazing testimony to a variety of learning styles, to cooperative teaching and learning, and to the use of multiple media to interpret ideas, showing students that school is not contained inside the four walls of any classroom.

The guiding philosophy behind this project is twofold: (1) education is bound by neither time nor place, and (2) the student must be at the center of any curricular planning. Thus, students are involved in a multiplicity of activities all directed at allowing them to construct meaning from their experiences, heeding Neil Postman's call (1995) for a guiding narrative for schooling in general and students in particular.

The concept of a global classroom also informs the philosophy and activities of this learning environment. Students are linked with the wider community in three very distinct ways. The first type of connection is with corporate and community leaders who act as mentors and who offer experiences beyond the classroom, varying from Chamber of Commerce breakfasts to mornings spent shadowing a corporate president in her day-to-day activities. These mentors are committed to engaging the students in active discourse about the relationship of a liberal education to the rest of their lives.

Another community connection is service learning. All RAP students are required to do two hours of community service weekly. They have a variety of choices, such as working for the library, humane society, social agencies, and churches; however, they are strongly urged to participate in Kid's Kitchen, a project initiated by the RAP program. In partnership with Harbor House, Inc., a subsidiary of the Foodbank, Kid's Kitchen feeds dinner to latchkey children

Monday through Friday evenings. RAP students help serve the food, but more important, they serve as mentors and companions to the children, helping them with homework, playing games, and generally giving them what they need most: time and attention.

COllaboratory provides the third connection to the community. The goals of this project are to develop international partnerships, to foster collaborative research, to use appropriate and varied technologies, and to discuss ideas with others around the world. Students work in teams to further their critical thinking skills, broaden their base of knowledge, and enhance their understanding of culture. In each local community, a team or teams of college and K–12 students work together for a year toward an interpretation of culture that can eventually be developed into a museum exhibit. Partners in this project also commit to doing a variety of service learning activities throughout the course of the year. For instance, this past year the third graders of Le Jardin Academy who worked with RAP students on the GenX exhibit also spent their year adopting grandparents from a local senior center.

During COllaboratory's three years of operation, the exhibits installed in the Bishop Museum (a natural history museum) have varied. Students in the first year concentrated on Hawaiian culture and created large exhibits that displayed ancient Hawaiian games called the Makahiki; the art of net fishing in the town of Hana, Maui; and a model of a home destroyed on Kauai by Hurricane Iniki. In the spring of 1996, the students concentrated on a theme of community. The six exhibits ranged from a glitzy computer room asking the question, "Can you have a community on the Internet?" to a look at the changing Waikiki community. In the cyberspace community portion of the exhibit, they enlarged John Barlow's *Declaration of Independence for the Internet* and were delighted that Barlow came to the museum opening. Another exhibit showed the changing face of Waikiki over the past fifty years and asked visitors to envision the future. Small wooden blocks were placed in baskets next to a map of Waikiki. These blocks represented hotels and other buildings, and visitors were encouraged to place or remove blocks as they saw fit in their own perception of how Waikiki should look in the future. Another exhibit looked at how various modes of communication might have changed the way in which people view the size of their communities. For instance, did the telephone change our concept of space and time? Participants in this project began with the concept of the pony express and ended with new computer technologies.

The Project

The most recent exhibit, focusing on Generation X and how the media perpetuated a negative image of this group of people, was the biggest challenge to date and illustrates well how COllaboratory operates. University of Hawaii (UH)

RAP students worked with third-grade students from Le Jardin Academy and sophomores from Waimea High School on the island of Kauai on the planning, research, and design of a 2,400-square-foot exhibit. In early September the students got together at UH and began brainstorming on questions such as "Who am I?" and "Who are we?" They created poster collages of their ideas and then continued their discussions over electronic mail. In early November these students joined the RAP students at UH for an overnight activity. They spent the afternoon doing creative projects learning about the design and visual representations of ideas. This was followed by a potluck dinner, a trip to a UH volleyball game (several of the players were students in RAP), and an overnight event at the Special Events Arena at which time the students presented their afternoon projects to the whole group.

The rest of the year was spent working in teams, over electronic mail and face-to-face. The result was an exhibit which showed a roadway beginning at a chaotic wall filled with graffiti and images of body piercings, drug use, and drive-by shootings. However, visitors who followed the road found themselves in a totally different environment at the end, a hopeful one that depicted Gen Xers filled with promise, holding religious beliefs and dreams, working as volunteers, going to college, and participating in other productive endeavors. The third graders created sets of footprints with drawings and essays depicting their view of Gen X and their hopes for the future. These footprints were distributed on the walls throughout the exhibit to show that a younger generation is following behind, paying close attention.

Each year, one component of COllaboratory has taken place in a text-based online environment, a MOO (Multiple-user Domain, Object Oriented). Students learn MOO protocol and commands. They then enter a virtual world called Walden3. In this synchronous Internet community, students meet to share their ideas about exhibits, to try their hand at describing themselves to others around the world, and to hold discussions about their work with others working on similar projects. Members of the Walden3 community develop MOO text files to make rooms and useful objects, to dialogue and provide verbal cues, and to create a virtual environment displayed completely in text. A MOO enables all users to converse with each other at the same time, if everyone is in the same virtual room, or space. However, users may also construct their own spaces which can be designated either public or private. Students may discuss any interests in these rooms, from surfing to cooking.

Of the many advantages enjoyed by MOO users, perhaps the most significant is the increased control over their learning options. People can find reference materials via the Internet and engage in conversations public or private about what has been found. For example, one tool, a text-based Web browser similar to Lynx, allows students to call up Web text from anywhere and then manipulate it on the MOO. The same is true with gopher text. These tools are called webbers and gopher slates, respectively. Once called up, Web or gopher text is viewed privately by the user unless she chooses to share it with others. The premise in all of this is simple: give students a variety of options to gather, discover, analyze, synthesize, create, rearrange, share, and finally display information. The use of MOO technology is clearly one way to enhance this process.

The success of the MOO has varied from year to year and has been dependent on the amount of connectivity available to the K–12 students. During the first year, a team of high school students in Chicago worked with museum staff at the Museum of Science and Industry and created a virtual representation (in text) of the U-505 submarine which is actually on display at the museum. Students from Hawaii, Canada, and California would often join these Chicago students and take an online virtual tour of the submarine. At other times the RAP students would log into Walden3 and seek help from a librarian, meet with program staff, or chat with students in other states about their community service work or their projects. Or students might post to a MOO list and review a project or the entire exhibit. The following is an excerpt from such a post:

> First we walked past the chaotic wall and I got a chill as I realized what violence exists in our world today and how much generation Xers are exposed to it. The drive by shooting took me by surprise because it is not something that one would think of in Hawaii, but they happen so often on the mainland. The sounds coming from the sound booth did not sound too inviting so I did not go in. The sounds added a dreariness to the negative side. The dead tree added a dead ambiance to the scene and the choices gave me a scary feeling. I hope that I never have to make a decision that could lead to one of those choices.

Many of the online conversations were not logged, as one does not necessarily need to record the activities of the students when on the MOO. Just knowing that they are actively engaged in "talking" to others as well as communicating in text is sufficient. After all, one must write when logged into a MOO environment; otherwise, one is only silent.

Communicating a Community

The University of Hawaii requires that each student take a minimum of five writing-intensive courses before graduation. These small classes require at least twenty pages of writing per course, peer editing, and many revisions. Students participating in COllaboratory fulfill two of these requirements within their year-long foundation course. Students talk to each other online about their projects, they share ideas leading up to their exhibits, they post to lists on the MOO (such as specific lists on philosophy, or visual representations, or museums), they write weekly electronic journals detailing their work in teams and their progress both on the exhibits and on their community service, and finally they write reviews of the exhibit itself. At the end of the year they all write reflective pieces on their community service endeavors as well as a lengthy course rumination paper on their personal growth, team collaboration, museum exhibits, and other insights. Throughout the first semester students develop an autobiographical portfolio that serves as their database for the eventual design of their museum exhibits. This project prepares them well for their exhibits, teaches them about information retrieval and critical reading of text, and hones their research skills. Critical reading and writing skills are integrated in every aspect of their COllaboratory experience: these students are engaged with text through in-class writing, long autobiographies, or online dialogues with students elsewhere.

Here is an exchange between two students working on a short story:

> Roberta says, "Ah, speaking of 'Melissa', I found a neat turn of phrase you did in there, the words of which might work in a title. I flagged them. Hang on."
>
> ----------------------------------Roberta (#112)------------------------------
> sigh of relief. "I thought I was drowning in darkness!"
>
> *potential title words
>
> ----------------------------------Roberta (#112)------------------------------
> Rosa nods.
> Roberta says, "There: drowning in darkness. I liked how it sounded."
> Rosa says, "I haven't given much thought to titles. . . ."
> Roberta says, "Still, you might call it Melissa, though that's not super either."

This ability to share text across the ocean, in this case between Hawaii and California, enables students from different states to work together using the MOO for discourse, learning, sharing ideas, and developing text-based communication skills.

Text Immersion

One way to understand the value of text immersion is to think of a musician—a piano player or guitarist, for example. Fluency derives from facility and familiarity. The fluent musician has spent many hours playing scales in different keys, improvising, and practicing from sheet music. In the same way, students participating in COllaboratory are immersed in many forms of text, sometimes following grammatical conventions and other times allowing creativity to flow. The key, however, is that at all times they are practicing *how* to communicate ideas through text. Like all of us, COllaboratory students already intuitively understand the influences of context on communication. A MOO platform allows the student to change the manner of presentation to reflect the present context, helping them develop fluency while being immersed completely in text.

A rich context enables one to make comparisons more easily, a vital part of language (Nilsen and Nilsen 1978, 157). Continued practice evaluating contexts and writing within them hones the writer's judgment regarding language use. On Walden3 as students write to each other, the immediate situation revolves around the acquisition of critical thinking, collaborating, and writing skills, but these are hidden behind the students' desires to complete various projects. The students are being guided toward specific goals, and they acquire these other skills as a consequence of being members of the virtual community. Therefore, students immersed in communicating via written language naturally acquire more readily those conventions peculiar to such discourse, especially in the hands of an aware and intrepid instructor who models these conventions: "The first essential constituent of learning is the opportunity to see what can be done and how" (Smith 1986, 101).

Learning to write via text immersion can be perceived as making sense of more and more kinds of language in more and different contexts. When the instructor models the writing process and offers students the opportunity to imitate, students develop the intuition necessary to become independent writers and to develop what William Irmscher (1987) calls "syntactic maturity" (137). Text immersion helps to provide that experience. As communities tend to make and enforce their own rules, when proper language conventions are encouraged, the community learns to police itself quite quickly, and the remaining time is spent actually communicating. Walden3 and similar educational MOOs should be seen as safe learning environments where participants can and do make mistakes. In the virtual community of a MOO, the targeted skills are used in classroom activities where students become comfortable using them in real life.

The Community

Members of Walden3 create a sense of community in many ways. For example, the MOO allows people to "look" at each other, and everyone writes his or her own description. These range from the concrete, ". . . is five foot two inches tall with blue eyes and blonde hair," to the ethereal, ". . . seeks balance among all things"—and everything in between, the result of granting some measure of autonomy to students, unlikely in regular classrooms. In addition, the MOO provides students with the opportunity to develop a sense of self in a text-only environment. This systemwide feature allows more writerly freedom, which in turn is a tool of discovery and revelation (Ueland 1987, 133).

Another aspect of student autonomy is the ability to control levels of communication on the MOO, and this affects student language acquisition. There are several ways to communicate on the Walden3, and we can subsume them under two broad categories: synchronous and asynchronous. We'll look at synchronous, or real-time, communications first.

Briefly stated, users control who sees what they write on the MOO as well as how it is seen. For example, in a virtual room filled with ten other people, the student can say something to everyone by typing, "Hello." Everyone sees this text. But just as in face-to-face encounters, it is likely that the writer will want to say something directly to another individual. In a normal situation we would look at the other person, get his or her attention, then say something directly to that person. On the MOO, we would type "to Fred hello," which would appear on the computer monitor as, "Samantha says, [to Fred] 'Hello.'" Everyone in the room can read what Samantha says to Fred, but Fred knows it is being directed to him. Such an option is necessary in collaborative work when several people must work together toward a common goal. But there is another, private level of communication where any user can communicate to another without anyone else being able to read it—only the sender and the receiver of the message can. And this is different from face-to-face environments when such privacy is nearly impossible in a small group working collaboratively. One could lean over and whisper to the other, an action which has a certain social stigma attached, but only if the other person sits adjacent. The MOO provides this extra level of communication without an accompanying social stigma and thus is an even richer and more fertile context with regard to the use of written words than is a face-to-face environment.

Asynchronous, or outside-of-time, communications comprise MOOmail, lists, e-mail, notes, and the use of tools such as blackboards and shared note boards. We have discovered that the tendency so far is for students to write rather more formally in situations designed to be read asynchronously, and it is likely that this is as it should be. Writing which is designed to be read outside of time shall have been revised for efficiency in communication, for unity and flow, and to achieve the writer's purpose. Such components are not as likely to be present in synchronous MOO communications—these writerly skills are not inbred but must be learned contextually, and a text-immersion environment is ideal for their acquisition. "Readers must bring meaning to texts. But obviously writers make a contribution too. And there must be a point at which readers and writers interact. That point is the text . . ." (Smith 1986, 167).

Writing a Community

What is compelling about this project is that students around the world can be simultaneously involved in local projects as well as in sharing their ideas globally. They can collaborate with students near and far and discover together some interpretations of their world. In the end they can look at themselves and discover who they are. Students become the center of their own education, and participation in COllaboratory extends this by putting them into the center of their own cultures. All discussions on Walden3, through e-mail, and around the Internet are carried out in text under the watchful eyes of experienced writers and result in documents designed to make solid the self-discovery and creativity embraced by the program. Such text-immersion helps instill appreciation for language, fosters and supports the development of critical thinking skills, and engages students in the exploration of the possibility of a global community.

Works Cited

Boyer, Ernest L. 1987. *College: The Undergraduate Experience in America.* New York: Harper and Row.

Gardner, Howard. 1983. *Frames of Mind: The Theory of Multiple Intelligences.* New York: Basic Books.

Goodlad, John T. 1994. *Educational Renewal: Better Teachers, Better Schools.* San Francisco: Jossey-Bass.

Irmscher, W. 1987. *Teaching Expository Writing.* New York: Holt, Rinehart and Winston.

Nilsen, Don, and Alleen Pace Nilsen. 1978. *Language Play.* Rowley: Newbury House, Inc.

Postman, Neil. 1995. *The End of Education.* New York: Alfred A. Knopf.

Sizer, Theodore R. 1992. *Horace's School: Redesigning the American High School.* Boston: Houghton Miflin Company.

Smith, Frank. 1986. *Understanding Reading.* New Jersey: Lawrence Erlbaum.

Ueland, Brenda. 1987. *If You Want To Write.* St. Paul: Greywolf Press.

Web References

Composition Sites
http://www.urich.edu/~ritter/CompLink.html
http://webserver.maclab.comp.uvic.ca/writersguide/welcome.html

MOO sites
(through these sites, people can get everything about MOOs, from papers written about them all the way to an actual core, complete with instructions)

House of Words: Designing Text and Community in MOO Environments
http://www.harbour.sfu.ca/ccsp/People/JQMaxwell/MOO/HouseofWords.html#intr

What Can You Do in the MOO?
http://mason.gmu.edu/~epiphany/docs/dointhemoo.html

Necro's MOO Page (source code)
http://www.mcc.ac.uk/~necro/moofaq.html
VA Core Information
http://miamimoo.mcs.muohio.edu/vacore.html
Bibliography of Electronic Sources
http://www.cas.usf.edu/english/walker/bibliog/html
Server Related Site
http://www.ccs.neu.edu/home/fox/moo/moo-faq-l.html
ThesisNet FAQ
http://www.seas.upenn.edu/~mengwong/thesisfaq.html
Distributed Collaboratory Experimental Environments Initiative
http://www.mcs.anl.gov/home/stevens/labspace/root.html
Core Site
http://aldan.paragraph.com/mud/0302.html
More About MOOs
http://www.itp.berkeley.edu/~thorne/MOO.html
Indexes of /pub/virtreality/servers/Moo/Mac-MOO/
ftp://eeunix.ee.usm.maine.edu/pub/virtreality/servers/Moo/Mac-MOO/
http://ftp.tcp.com/pub/mud/servers/moo/
http://moo.cas.muohio.edu/~moo/vacore.html
IMI Client/Server Implementation Services
http://www.infoman.com/database.html
Walden3 MOO
telnet kauila.k12.hi.us 7777

15 Weaving Guilford's Web

Michael B. Strickland
Guilford College

Robert M. Whitnell
Guilford College

*There is no Final Word. There can be no final version, no last thought.
There is always a new view, a new idea, a new interpretation.*
—Theodor H. Nelson, inventor of the term *hypertext*

Introduction: Student Empowerment and Responsibility

About the time that the World Wide Web exploded out of its original niche in
the scientific research community, the business community, the general academic community, and many individual users realized its power for the provi-
sion and acquisition of information. Like many institutions, Guilford College
recognized the need to have a presence on the Web in order to provide information to its diverse audience: current and prospective students, their parents,
alumni, donors, and other friends of the college. However, like many small
colleges, the human resources that could be devoted to the development of a
site were limited. How then could Guilford create a presence that would truly
reflect the college, its students, staff, and faculty?

The answer lay in the collaborative, hands-on approach to learning and the
tradition of student empowerment that is characteristic of the college, and here
we perceived a rare opportunity. In January 1995, we proposed a course which
would have as one of its goals the complete creation of the Guilford College
Web site. The students would work with the administration, the faculty, and
other students to develop the site, from top to bottom. Even given the unlikely
nature of this class—an English professor and a chemistry professor collaborate to teach a course on communicating with computers and ask that the students in that class be given full responsibility for the image the college presents
on the World Wide Web—the administration (president, provost, academic dean,

dean of admissions, head of computer services, etc.) accepted this idea not just willingly, but enthusiastically. So in August 1995, twenty-three students and one librarian came together in our course, "Communicating with Computers: Spinning the Web." In the ensuing four months, they would construct a site for Guilford College (http://www.guilford.edu) that surpassed what we thought was possible. And they would do a lot more in the process.

In the following chapter we first describe the history of this project. We then discuss the class itself and how the discussion of the broader, interdisciplinary issues of electronic media studies, especially as they encompass new technologies such as the World Wide Web, ended up being reflected in the site that the students produced. We also explore the implications of courses such as this that exploit the potential of the Internet for communication across the curriculum (CAC). Finally, we look to the future and how we intend to continue this project as we adapt to developing technologies. Throughout this process we were mindful of the dynamic influence of electronic media on the traditional classroom environment, and tended to agree with George Landow's claim that

> Electronic text processing marks the next major shift in information technology after the development of the printed book. It promises (or threatens) to produce effects on our culture, particularly on our literature, education, criticism and scholarship, just as radical as those produced by Gutenberg's movable type. (1992, 19)

From Campus Community to Virtual Community

One of the many strengths of Guilford College in the real world has always been its sense of community. That community crosses many of the natural boundaries that often separate students, faculty, and administration, and is reflected in our tradition of students and faculty being deeply involved in all facets of the college's operation, from curricular policy to hiring a new president. Guilford has always sought not just to create such a community here, but to find practical applications on a larger scale for its values orientation and mode of teaching as well— thus its rich history of social involvement. As we began to examine how to take Guilford into the virtual world of the World Wide Web, we wanted that sense of community and student empowerment reflected in the Guilford College Web site. After all, as more and more students do research for prospective colleges online, a Web presence becomes one of the most ubiquitous and dynamic ways an educational institution can present itself. But the course and project that we describe here is not just about teaching HTML or surfing the Web for credit. Throughout, our goal was to help our students examine what it meant to be communicating and providing information in the face of rapidly changing rules: where the control of the time and means of access to information is shifting from the provider to the consumer. Certainly any course that utilizes hands-on content production for the Web can explore this, but in this instance we perceived a chance to channel the interests of an entire community through the activities of a class. What we hoped to accomplish was to make this class become the dynamic interface between traditional liberal arts learning, interdisciplinary project-based education, and real-time inquiry into computer-supported communications (CSC) and how it is changing the world. We therefore had a unique opportunity: we would work with our students to construct the official presence of Guilford College on the World Wide Web. The result of a semester of hard work was a site that represents much of what makes Guilford a unique institution. But it was also a site that belonged to the entire community—not to the administration, not to the Information Technology and Services department, not just to a limited group of faculty.

The Course: A Shaping Influence

From the beginning, we were adamant that the students study what these new methods of CSC meant and not just the mechanics of doing it. To that end, we designed a rigorous semester reading list based on the theme of the role of visionaries and the problems inherent with the implementation of new technological ideas.[1]

Our first task was to quickly provide the students with the context for the World Wide Web. Our readings in this area were three-pronged. First, articles from *Internet World* and *Wired* provided a history of the Internet and the World Wide Web. Second, Nicholas Negroponte's *Being Digital*, by exploring the implications of digitizing information, allowed the students to see a vision of where this medium might go.[2] We wanted the students to realize from the outset that our focus on making information accessible through the Web was merely an illustration of much deeper and more comprehensive issues involving digital forms of communication. As Negroponte points out,

> Being digital will change the nature of media from a process of pushing bits at people to one of allowing people (or their computers) to pull at them. This is a radical change, because our entire concept of media is one of successive layers of filterings which reduce information and entertainment to a collection of "top stories" or "best sellers" to be thrown at different "audiences." (1995, 84)

Finally, we traced back through the history of hypertext and communication using the writings of Vannevar Bush ("As We May Think") and Ted Nelson ("As We Will Think"). The historical readings were important both to our students who were quite familiar with the Web, as they needed to see that the underlying ideas are ones that have been around for fifty years or more, and to our students who were just beginning to explore the medium and needed to see that the Web represents a natural continuation of a line of inquiry into better ways of accessing and providing information. For example, we introduced our students to the notion that the footnote or endnote is an example of hypertext since it is a link which the reader follows to another part of the text to find information whose relevance may be high or merely tangential.[3]

We then turned to the question of why the World Wide Web was so effective and became so popular while previous attempts to improve the accessibility of information, such as gopher, were only adopted by the cognoscenti. One area to which we paid particular attention was the ease of use of the Web. The interface is, for the most part, highly obvious. Click on some blue text and you go to someplace new. Our readings in this area took us to the discipline of the psychology of industrial design, as explored by Donald Norman's *The Design of Everyday Things* (1990). Again, the Web becomes a single illustration of a much larger issue in this field: how do we achieve our stated goals? If we want people to be able to access our information, how can we design our site to make that access efficient and painless—even enjoyable? The lessons learned from Norman's work and from putting his concepts into practice will be used by our students repeatedly no matter what field they pursue. In fact, the epithet "bad design" became quite common during late-night work sessions. Negotiating this complex matrix of purposes and multiple audience needs became a rhetorical exercise that is one of the benefits of project-based education. Students are all-too-accustomed to satisfying the expectations of a teacher, but when you add to the mix the responsibility of fulfilling the needs of a bevy of administrators and peers and a true audience of global dimension, you raise the rhetorical stakes immensely. As WAC programs have known for years, having students "publish" for an external audience raises student investment and improves writing. The Web lowers the bar (financially and technologically) to publishing, and the electronic audience offered is both broader and often more impressive for students—communicating to the global village.

In an age where electronic media constantly bathe us in a wash of information, teachers often find that students have a much greater facility with media technology than educators do. However, these same students often lack the critical tools and training for analyzing such media and their pervasive influence. Still, many may question the pedagogical value of reading Marshall McLuhan today. By the time of McLuhan's death in 1980, the transformation of human life by media, especially television, was taken for granted, and McLuhan's often quirky and incoherent writings had lost their influence.

Now, however, the explosion of the Internet and World Wide Web, and of other innovative electronic media, have caused fresh cultural anxieties about the impact of computer-supported communications (CSC). We have again become conscious of our media environment, and in the confusion of the digital revolution McLuhan is once more relevant. We chose *Understanding Media*

(1995) for our reading list, and were excited about bringing his work into our course to help our students establish a critical base of operations. Ironically, our students are now realizing one of the more prescient McLuhanesque mantras of '60s students: indeed, "the whole world is watching."

Our next set of readings led us to the critics of using computers in this fashion. We read selections from Sven Birkerts's *The Gutenberg Elegies* (1994) and Neil Postman's *Technopoly* (1993) as examples of some of the concerns that were being raised. Both works deal with issues beyond the Web. Birkerts is concerned with the way in which the nature of reading might be changed by hypertext, books on CD-ROMs rather than on paper, and the trend toward nonlinearity in writing and reading (that is exemplified quite well by the Web).[4] Postman's concerns are more with the seductiveness of the tools and how that can make us less critical consumers of the information being fed us or of the claims that the purveyors of technology make. As Postman, in his typical understated fashion, puts it, "Information has become a form of garbage, not only incapable of answering the most fundamental human questions but barely useful in providing coherent direction to the solution of even mundane problems" (1993, 69).

But we raised a more subtle concern with our students as well. If we accept that CSC is a valuable path to explore, can the dreams which these visionaries so easily and seductively promulgate be achieved? The history of Ted Nelson's ill-fated Xanadu project, a concept which is much more full-featured than the World Wide Web, indicates that it might not be so simple for several reasons.[5] The technological difficulties are often exacerbated by the hubris that puts the beauty of the idea above any practical considerations. Interestingly, our students often went for simplicity in the construction of their Web pages to avoid exactly these problems and kept a constant concern for the viewing capabilities of their diverse audiences.[6] This was a point in the course where the diverse backgrounds in our class paid off in heated discussion both in class and on the Vaxnotes conference. We encourage instructors from many different disciplines (sociology, history, engineering, etc.) to construct interdisciplinary courses that use the Web to explore these social/philosophical intersections, as we intend to do in future versions of this course.

These warnings about what might go wrong informed the discussion of the future of the technology that the remainder of our readings covered, from Brand's *The Media Lab* (1987), describing the history of current innovations by Negroponte's group at MIT, to Kelly's *Out of Control* (1994), examining how biological evolution can inform technological evolution, to Stephenson's novel *Snow Crash* (1993), portraying a future where innovation has progressed remarkably, yet things still aren't working the way they should. Throughout the discussion of these works, the students were able to apply the concepts developed in their study of the Web to their thinking about how the cyberworld might eventually work. Again the diverse disciplinary backgrounds of the students also added to the discussion, as the management major often saw a particular issue very differently from the education major or the neo-Luddite English major.[7]

One primary strength of the course was in the combination of the reading and discussion with the hands-on element of producing information for the Web. The students were divided into eight groups and asked to produce two sets of Web pages for the college site. The first set of pages done by the students provided the core of the site. Several groups worked with assigned campus units (Admission, Center for Continuing Education, etc.), while other groups worked on pages describing the academic departments or on the underlying infrastructure of the site. On these projects especially, collaboration and a spirit of community were essential to success. It wasn't just that everyone's grade depended on the product (that is usually the case in group projects), but that the audience for the group's efforts was so vast it was almost impossible to shirk or ignore the enormous responsibility. In the second set of pages, the students were given more personal freedom to extend the site in a way that they felt also reflected the nature and spirit of the college.

Several of these pages are especially worthy of note. One student produced a virtual tour of the Guilford College Woods, a campus icon with historical roots in the Revolutionary War and the Underground Railroad. Using a digital camera, she took pictures of various sites of current and historical interest and wove them together into a self-guided Web pathway through the woods (http://www.guilford.edu/woods/woodstemplate.html). Other connections to the roots of the college are evident in the "Quakerism at Guilford" pages (http://www.guilford.edu/Quakerlife/Quaker.html) which explore how the Quaker heritage of Guilford continues to affect the academic and social life of the college.

Throughout the construction of the site, the college kept a strong interest in what was happening, but in a very supportive yet hands-off manner.[8] It was the willingness of the administrators to work with our students and to turn over much of the construction of their pages—the way their department was presented to the outside world—to our students that was an important key to the success of the project. Examples of this collaboration are particularly evident in the pages for the Admission Office (http://www.guilford.edu/admissionfolder/admission.html) and the pages for the Center for Continuing Education (http://www.guilford.edu/CCE/main.html).

With the Admission project, for example, the administrative staff was very busy with developing new print materials for their office, the most important of which was a new viewbook. After meeting with the group assigned to the project, the staff were more than willing to allow our students free rein in designing their pages. In an independent act of creative decision making that neither we nor the Admission staff had previously noted, the team took a photo offered as a promotional image (students walking across campus on a glorious spring day) and used Photoshop to airbrush out the prominent "NAVY" from one student's sweatshirt. With the Center for Continuing Education (CCE) project we had three traditional-aged students designing pages for an audience of older students who make up about one-fifth of our student body. This, of course, took careful research on our students' parts and fostered a new sense of understanding as they met with representatives of the CCE staff and student government.

But it was the pages for the Hege Library that perhaps best represented the type of collaboration and community we truly wanted to encourage. Betty Place, the head of Information and Reference Services at the library, participated in the course at the same level as any other student, doing all the readings and taking part in all the discussions. She joined a group with other students whose task was to build the library and art gallery pages. Betty's ability to deliver detailed information about the library in the context of building pages for the Web, while at the same time participating as an enthusiastic peer in the class, led to a set of library pages that are excellent in both design and content (http://www.guilford.edu/LibraryArt/Hege.html).

Another example of an "insider" helping to open awareness in others as they crossed disciplinary boundaries was the Academic Skills Center (ASC) project (http://www.guilford.edu/ASC/ AcademicSkillsCenter.html). A senior in our class who had been a staff worker and tutor in the ASC for her entire four years led the team that designed the pages for the center. Several members of the team had little prior knowledge of the ASC and its operations, or of the growing presence of such writing centers on the Web. Since the class, and even after graduating, this student has gone on to train others in Web page construction and has extended the ASC pages.[9]

In all of this collaboration the only hitch with the administration involved "creative use" of the college's "tree" logo.[10] Early in our design phase of the site, our students realized that they wanted a consistent visual element on almost all the pages that would say "This page is part of the Guilford College Web site." The element that they hit upon almost immediately was the tree that is part of the official logo, and several of them started doing interesting design work with that tree as a centerpiece (see Figure 15.1). Here is where the conflict appeared. A rigorous application of the Trustees' guidelines would not have permitted this liberal use of the logo. We took this issue to the administration and argued that adhering to such strict guidelines would not be in the spirit of this medium, where anything can be borrowed and modified and put back out on the Web in a new form. This conflict led to the formation of that most wonderful of institutions, the task force, in order to study how the logo policy should be changed in light of the new technology. Suffice it to say that our students were allowed to make their desired modifications provided that the official logo was present in sufficiently obvious places on the Web site. Trivial as this might

Figure 15.1. Images from the Guilford College Web site.

seem, the real-world lessons for our students were very important as they saw us spending time being called into meetings to discuss this issue. The contrast between the shiny new technology and the slow-moving bureaucracy was made very clear and informed our class discussions of ethics and regulation in a manner we could never have artificially created.

This was the most serious issue the administration raised, and we know we were fortunate in having an administration willing to hand over so much of the responsibility to the students. We realize some of this trust came about because

Rob had so much experience in constructing and maintaining a Web site, and the administration in Guilford's Information Technology and Services Department was willing to learn from us and with us as a community enterprise about how best to set up our site. As a result they were also willing not to micromanage the site and to let us and the students discover how to make it work best. Our students rose to the challenge of constructing this site completely and responsibly. We were recently asked by a reporter what we would have done if something had gone on the site that was "questionable," that we or the college were not sure should be there. And we honestly replied that we couldn't provide a definitive answer because the issue never really came up. Our students were presented with an opportunity to show the world their view of the college. There was little authority to rebel against because they had essentially all the power. The result is something that proponents of student empowerment can point to as an unqualified success. Our experience in the cyberworld mirrored our experience in the real world here: when trust is placed in our students, they respond in a fashion deserving of that trust. But we are well aware that we could not have placed that trust in our students had there not been a long tradition of trust and student empowerment at Guilford. For institutions where that does not exist, or where those who run the computers are unwilling to give up that control, doing this kind of project on the college-wide level may not work. However, that would not preclude work on a departmental or even divisional level.[11]

Yet our class was not just about handing things over to the students. It was about continuing to strengthen the Guilford College community. The site is a product of students, faculty, and administration, and as such will never belong solely to any small group on campus. The expectation is that the entire community will continue to use the World Wide Web to portray the dynamic totality of Guilford College and as an educational tool for exploring the impact of CSC. Indeed, we were both surprised and pleased to be walking through the ASC computer lab one day the next semester and find one of our students (a chemistry major) demonstrating the pages she had independently built for the new interdisciplinary major in women's studies. Her audience consisted of assorted faculty and students from this program, most of whom had little experience with the Web.

This sense of community building belies many worries about how the virtual world can upstage the real world. In the college's perspective, one of the most important results of this project is that it has shown how, to use Howard Rheingold's term (1994), "the virtual community" can help reinforce communities that already exist. Guilford's strong sense of community engendered a mutual trust between the administration and the students that allowed this project to proceed: the students knew that the administration would trust them to portray Guilford in an interesting and positive fashion. In proceeding, the class members then found themselves reifying the community's basic academic principle, most notably our commitment to innovative student-centered learning, engagement in the ethical dimension of knowledge, and emphasis on global perspective.

The Electronic Classroom: Theory into Practice

While much of the work for this course went on late at night in various computer labs around campus, our classroom atmosphere was truly an electronic one. Held in our telecommunications building, the class met sitting in a huge "U" shape around tables. The center focal point was not a podium, but a wall screen connected to a projector, connected to an AV Macintosh, connected to the Internet. The instructors sat to one side and entered the center of the "U" only periodically to drive the computer. More often a student was at the helm, navigating the Web or demonstrating a group's project for review.[12]

Of course there are many things we need and hope for if we are to continue this community educational venture. Most of these hopes involve institutional expense, and in times of shrinking budgets such costs are difficult, especially for the small liberal arts college. We need more portable data projectors so multiple classroom settings can become electronic classrooms. We need network connections for all faculty offices, classrooms, and student dorm rooms so the electronic classroom can extend beyond the restrictions of class schedules. We need a dedicated multimedia teaching lab and a staff proficient in multimedia for training both students and faculty. Indeed, though no one in our art department expressed interest in our class the first time, once they saw the results and heard from former art graduates about the potential for their students, faculty began to take notice. The latest version of the class now has three art majors. While we have no major on campus for this express purpose, we do have an interdisciplinary major, integrative studies, in which students, with the guidance of a faculty committee, can design their own course of study. We now have two sophomores in our present course constructing majors around computer-supported communications.

What we propose for the future of this project is to focus on the radical center of the monumental vortex of change which now characterizes the media and, by extension, human consciousness generally as the world prepares to enter the twenty-first century—a state which Walter Ong describes as a "new age of secondary orality" (1982, 135). In a nutshell, we seek to continue work which has already begun here, work which involves taking control of and humanizing the World Wide Web by bringing the Web squarely into the arena of humanistic studies. This activity includes both theory and practice. Theory in this context means outright study of the new technological phenomena in relevant educational contexts. It means coming to understand both issues and ethical applications and how traditionally based education can use and control the new technologies (how, for example, to make the resources which the Web offers serve the purposes of liberal arts education). Like a WAC program, we hope to extend electronic media literacy issues to other courses across many disciplinary lines, and we have already seen evidence of this from the number of classes in a variety of disciplines (chemistry, management, physics, English, and the college's interdisciplinary First-Year Seminar program) where constructing Web pages is being integrated into the course requirements. This would not yet be happening without the fully featured Web site created by our students.

Practice, on the other hand, takes a special student-driven form in our approach. Already, in the first version of our course, Guilford students were empowered to create the college's own Web site. They are now taking the final steps toward putting the campus newspaper online. In doing so, the students are learning both how to take charge of the new technology and how to shape its applications. Finally, the Guilford College World Wide Web site is now an online laboratory for our students. As we teach this course in the future, our students will recognize from the outset that the work they produce here can be placed in a medium that can be accessed from almost anywhere in the world.[13] They are not producing material just for us, or for their classmates, or even for the local community. This sense that their projects had a scope outside of the one class gave our first group of students a tremendous drive to produce work that was of a particularly high quality. We expect these students to carry that drive not only into their other classes but into their future lives.

One of our favorite anecdotes from the class concerns the opening image on the college's homepage. Less than twenty-four hours before unveiling the new site for an audience of selected administrators and students, the class had yet to decide on an image for the opening page. In desperation we made a move of professorial authority and placed several possible images online so the class could view them and cast electronic votes on the Vaxnotes conference. We asserted that if the class couldn't come to consensus, we would step in and make a choice in time for the presentation. Two chemistry majors from our class happened to be working in chem lab on different projects for finals that day. Suddenly they both began obsessing about the front page, dropped their chemistry assignment, and began to collaborate on putting together a design. When they stepped back from the computer they knew they had it. They posted their image online and the class reaction was the same as ours—"That's it!"

We like to think of the Web site as an ongoing interdisciplinary laboratory with the biggest windows in the world. When anyone can look in and see what you've produced, your incentive to collaborate and do well is greatly increased. This is a heady sense of empowerment and ownership. The official Guilford College Web site is a wonderful illustration of how students can rise to that challenge. The challenge for us, as educators, will be to adapt rapidly and dynamically to the influence of computer-supported communications and to remember, as Lanham reminds us, "The electronic classroom has a different motivational mix from the print classroom. And it has a different sense of 'finality' too" (1993, 127).

Notes

1. This course was, in fact, two courses with the same title. One group of students received two credits and met for the equivalent of two class sessions each week. Their reading list included the books by Negroponte and McLuhan as well as a number of articles, some of which are mentioned herein, and they worked in groups on two sets of pages for the Guilford College site.

The other students were part of the Guilford College Honors Program and received four credits for the course. They met for an additional class session each week, and their reading list was expanded to also include the books by Norman, Brand, Kelly, and Stephenson in addition to the other readings. Their assignments also included a paper at mid-semester discussing the impact of computer communication on some aspect of society (narrowly or broadly interpreted), and a final project that could take the form of a paper or a set of pages for the Web site or another hypertext project. They also worked with the other students on the construction of the site itself. One of the driving forces behind the reading list was to give our students the ability to use their skills more successfully because they have a more complete understanding of issues underlying these methods of communication and their potential social impacts.

2. It is significant that the words *World Wide Web* don't appear in the index to Negroponte's book, and he mentions Mosaic (from which Netscape evolved) only briefly, even though every issue that he discusses is somehow relevant to the Web.

3. We found this a very fruitful analogy, and one our students quickly adopted. Bush, Nelson, Lanham, and Landow all make this connection. For more in-depth discussion of the similarities between hypertext and the footnote/endnote of scholarly discourse, see Landow 4-5.

4. Again, Landow and Lanham provide elaboration here. See also Bolter. We have consciously tried not to be proselytizers for CSC. We always attempt to stimulate discussion about the adverse effects of such technology—past, present, and future. In the fall 1996 version of the course we added readings from Clifford Stoll's *Silicon Snake Oil*, and Mr. Stoll came to campus to address us and further such discussion.

5. For an excellent discussion of Nelson and the Xanadu project see Gary Wolf's very readable story from *Wired*, "The Curse of Xanadu." The story is also available online (minus photos) at the *Wired* archives at http://www.hotwired.com/wired/3.06 /features/xanadu.html. See also Nelson's responses at http://xanadu.net/ararat and http: //www.hotwired.com/wired/3.06/features/Xanadu/nelson_letter.html.

6. The "browser wars" continue. Our students often took their Web pages around campus to view on different machines using various browsers. We found this a controversial but useful issue, especially when discussing the battles between Netscape and Microsoft and the problems such battles create for developers.

7. The twenty-six students in the class ranged from first-semester sophomores to graduating seniors. They represented fourteen different academic majors. (See http://www.guilford.edu/Who's who/Who'sWho.html for more information on this first class. Pages for the fall 1996 class are also now available on the site.)

8. Support came from the administration in two fashions. First, they provided us with the server hardware and software (the college server is a Macintosh Workgroup Server 8150 running the Webstar server software) as well as various software tools for constructing images and editing HTML. On a less concrete level, they provided us with access: to archives of photographs, to large chunks of information (such as the text of the college catalog in computer files), and to themselves. While during the course, the administration of the site was primarily left to us and our students, the site is now overseen by one of us (RMW), the Director of College Relations, and a representative from Information Technology and Services. However, these individuals represent departments that were strong supporters of this project from the very beginning and will continue to work with the students in a very positive fashion.

9. Karen Rowan graduated in May 1996 and decided to postpone graduate school for a year while going to work full time as assistant to the director of the ASC, Sue Keith. In that role she has continued to supervise the front desk staff and to tutor, but has also greatly extended the ASC pages and is presently constructing an ASC OWL (Online Writing Lab) for the Guilford site.

10. The Guilford College "tree" logo had been a subject of much debate among the administration and Board of Trustees because the logo had been used in a variety of nonstandard and non-approved ways. The "Guilford Tree" is a venerable icon which in the minds of many represented the college on many levels. As a result, a rigid (for Guilford) set of rules had been developed governing the appearance and use of the logo (including requirements about minimum size, colors used, using the logo in its entirety, etc.). However, these rules had been developed at a time when print was the primary use of the logo, in college brochures and on stationery, for example.

11. We don't want to sound too breathlessly upbeat here— there were of course many problems with this project. First, because such a course didn't exist before and wasn't on the books or on our teaching schedules for the upcoming semester, we both taught the first version of our course as a teaching overload. This was especially exhausting. Since until that point Guilford had no Web site, there was no Web manager and limited technical support. Our technical staff did their best to help when absolutely needed, but in essence this project was beyond their already stretched capacities. Getting our students twenty-four-hour access to capable computers and keeping the equipment running became an extra duty for us, often meaning much late night overtime. There is no multimedia resource person on our staff yet (though hopefully this is changing) so researching, buying, and learning the necessary software packages became our responsibility also. Of course, these are all problems encountered whenever a "new" kind of project is undertaken, and the latest version of this course is encountering fewer hurdles.

12. Two very important discourse community tools were e-mail and an electronic bulletin board/conferencing system called Vaxnotes. We used this program for class discussions, announcements, and as a place to post ideas and drafts. On a couple of occasions, when one instructor couldn't be in class, his responses to a set of paper drafts were placed on the conference and during the class discussion the comments were scrolled through as the drafts were discussed. Questions of clarification and elaboration were sent via e-mail which he answered in real time from home—the virtual professor.

Outside of class, the students were provided with a number of tools for accessing the Web and constructing their pages. Several public Macs at Guilford (of the LC III, Quadra

605, and LC575 vintage) were equipped with Netscape Navigator 1.1, and FolderBolt was used to make this program available only to students in our course. The primary tool for HTML editing was HTML Web Weaver 2.5 (although we switched to PageSpinner 1.2 and Netscape 2.02 in fall 1996). Students had access to image generating, manipulating, and processing programs such as Adobe Photoshop 3.0, Aldus Freehand 5.0, Fractal Painter 4.0, GIFConverter 2.3.7, JPEGView 3.3, and Transparency 1.0. The students were given direct access to the Guilford Web server via AppleShare and could therefore upload and edit their pages as necessary. Some students who were not as Mac-centric as the instructors found freeware and shareware software for Windows so that they could use their PC-compatible computers.

Our students were also provided access to a digital camera (Apple QuickTake 100) as well as a facility dedicated by the college to faculty use for multimedia production. This facility contained a Macintosh Quadra 660AV as well as a slide scanner and a print scanner and much of the software described above. Students could therefore use any images they wanted, whether they took them themselves or got them from the college archives, and put them on their Web pages.

13. Indeed, many students were surprised (as were many faculty and administrators) when we checked the hit list only a couple of weeks after the site went online and found we had already been accessed by curious surfers from many exotic locations, from Estonia to Thailand.

Works Cited

Birkerts, Sven. 1994. *The Gutenberg Elegies: The Fate of Reading in an Electronic Age.* Boston: Faber and Faber.

Bolter, J. David. 1990. *Writing Space: The Computer in the History of Literacy.* Hillsdale, NJ: Lawrence Erlbaum.

Brand, Stewart. 1987. *The Media Lab.* New York: Viking.

Bush, Vannevar. 1945. "As We May Think." *Atlantic Monthly* 176 (July): 101–108.

Kelly, Kevin. 1994. *Out of Control: The Rise of Neo-Biological Civilization.* Reading, MA: Addison-Wesley.

Landow, George. 1992. *Hypertext: The Convergence of Contemporary Critical Theory and Technology.* Baltimore: The Johns Hopkins University Press.

Lanham, Richard. 1993. *The Electronic Word.* Chicago: University of Chicago Press.

McLuhan, H. Marshall. 1995. *Understanding Media.* Cambridge, MA: MIT Press.

Negroponte, Nicholas. 1995. *Being Digital.* New York: Alfred A. Knopf.

Nelson, Theodor H. 1991. "As We Will Think." In *From Memex to Hypertext*, edited by J. M. Nyce and P. Kahn. Boston: Academic Press.

Norman, Donald. 1990. *The Design of Everyday Things.* New York: Doubleday.

Ong, Walter. 1982. *Orality and Literacy: Technologizing the Word.* London: Methuen.

Postman, Neil. 1993. *Technopoly: The Surrender of Culture to Technology.* New York: Vintage.

Rheingold, Howard. 1994. *The Virtual Community: Homesteading on the Electronic Frontier.* New York: Harper Perennial.

Stephenson, Neal. 1993. *Snow Crash.* New York: Bantam.

Wolf, Gary. 1995. "The Curse of Xanadu." *Wired* 3: 142–52, 194–202.

III Classrooms: Electronic Communication Within the Disciplines

16 Pig Tales: Literature Inside the Pen of Electronic Writing

Katherine M. Fischer
Clarke College

I have two stories to tell you. One is about pigs, the other about bewitchment. My museum-director husband has a penchant for garage sales. "Just collecting the material folk culture," he claims when I razz him, but the gold elongated porcelain pig candle holder that sits on the back of our piano, Liberace-style, squeals on him. We may start out on a five-mile run on a spring morning but almost always end up following the flags directing us to another lawn sale, another purchase of old Mason Proffit record albums, a collection of Louis L'Amour western novels, or, if he's lucky, a true find like the Green River knife he discovered in a "buck grab box" a few years back, the seller, no doubt, mistaking it for a rusty kitchen knife.

The other story, the one about spells, is my own story. When I was a new teacher of literature, I felt that if we could *think* enough about literature, we would come to *know* it. In those earlier years, students and I charted the elements of plot, delineated static and dynamic characters, and counted out iambs. With the writing-across-the-curriculum movement to make even literature courses writing intensive, I encouraged my students to write often in order to think, in order to know. To a degree, my methods worked. By writing journals, by responding to entrance and exit prompts, by writing letters to characters, students grew more able to interpret and appreciate the novels, poems, short fiction, and drama we studied. But in recent years I have come to feel that this is not enough, this kind of knowing. I share Dan Morgan's (1993) belief that literature interprets life and that "the greatest literature is about *how to be*" (492). How can I know a person if my only entrance to the knowing is through my thinking? How do I anticipate his laughter? How can I finger the edges of his soul? How can I know him unless I feel him, breathe him in—in short, become so engaged with him that I am enchanted? And how can I know literature, alive and energetic, unless I am similarly enthralled?

Terry Tempest Williams (1994) tells us "writing becomes an act of compassion toward life, the life we so often refuse to see because if we look too closely or feel too deeply, there may be no end to our suffering. But words empower us, move us beyond our suffering, and set us free. This is the sorcery of literature" (57). To this I would add that in interacting with the text through electronic writing, students also empower themselves to feel literature pulsing through their veins, truly knowing it, cognitively and emotionally. Only a few of my students, usually those already bewitched by the page, experienced this level of knowing when our writing took place on paper alone.

What does the sorcery of literature have to do with the tale of the pig? Just this. In what I call department-store writing, journal writing is kept as safely apart from feeling passion as women's lingerie is distanced from men's boxer shorts; the price of the page is as fixed to academic language as is the price of plaster pigs in the china department, neither of them open for haggling; and the overly familiar format of essays in print and teacher-determined prompts restricts what we will find within the margins as much as coupons restrict which size cereal box we may buy on sale. In the garage-sale nature of virtual spaces, however, students may find greater opportunity for reaching beyond buying off the rack into writing which so inhales the lives within literature that they feel their hearts race. Like garage-sale buyers who may have some idea of what they hope to purchase beforehand but are quite flexible as to what they actually bring home, writers using e-mail, networked software, and MOOs are freed to explore the bargain boxes of literary interpretation with one another online, emerging with the greatest find of all, a nearly inebriating sense of knowing, of living what they have read. Sellers who had no intention of parting with the lawn chair may, on impulse, barter it away right out from underneath themselves at the first inquiry of "how much?", just as students writing in electronic landscapes are prone to read, write, and learn what they may have otherwise kept safely locked in interior storerooms marked "not for sale." When neighbors shop on a neighbor's lawn, even the roles of buyer and seller may turn on the head of a dime; when students write in the virtual lawn, they may join with authors to become co-authors of literature itself. Perhaps it is this openness to expectation that conjures internalized ways of knowing. One is never quite sure what to expect when walking up the driveway.

By Paper Alone

Before crossing the threshold into electronic media for writing about literature, I had always assigned traditional, safe, department-store journals and writing assignments. "Write journal entries to Antigone expressing whether you agree or disagree with her decisions in the play" or "Describe Vonnegut's writing style," or "Reveal the secrets the unicorn knows about Laura in *The Glass Menagerie*." Although such assignments encouraged students to analyze their readings and to think both critically and creatively about them, I was always dissatisfied with the distance from literature exhibited in their writing, the sense of "jumping through hoops" to please me, the teacher. They wrote to think about literature, but not to know it as organic, as alive. I longed for them to hear characters' voices, to feel the heartbeat of the complex lives they were reading, as well as to sense the soul in a writer's style.

When Internet access and other computing technology became available on our campus outside of the computer science and science departments, I wondered if this might be a way for us to cross over from the tidy rows of compartmentalized thinking into the messier but fuller piles and heaps. My late-night jaunts through the campus computer lab had shown me another side of the students who appeared in my literature classes with eyes at half-mast, intellectually flaccid, unable to catch the wind of enthusiasm over literary lives I attempted to blow their way. But on chat lines and the Internet near midnight, they were at full throttle, eyes aglow, hooting excitedly about discoveries they'd come upon while surfing the Web. Clearly they caught the waves on this ocean with much greater alacrity and energy than they did in the classroom. If I could use this medium in teaching literature, I reasoned, we might really sail.

Getting Wired

The first time I used computers to assist in teaching literature was with an Approaches to Literature class of twenty-three honors level first-year and sophomore students. Clarke is a small private college where interactive learning is strongly promoted and students are accustomed to small-group work in a relaxed atmosphere where most faculty, students, and administrators are on a first-name basis. Classes like this general education course are intrinsic to the core of the liberal arts focus even in professional programs like physical therapy and nursing. In these earlier years, however, few classes outside of the computer science, math, and science departments used computers for course work other than for word processing. The Approaches to Literature course was divided into three units—drama, short fiction, and poetry. Students had written traditional paper journals during the drama unit, but even with this class of bright, motivated students, the writing seemed as bound as the spiral wire holding their entries together. Although they sometimes traded and read one another's journal entries or wrote to other audiences like mayors, newspaper editors, or literary characters, I was their main reader. With e-journals, however, their audience would be the entire class, and each of them would become a reader. After teaching them e-mail, I formed them into one large online discussion group and required them to write three to four times per week about the current reading "in place of regular journals." They sent these posts to all classmates and to me.[1]

The initial entries in the e-mail journals were similar to entries in their paper journals—students constructed interpretations without interacting with the literature. Perhaps this was because they had written notebook journals at first or perhaps it was because I labeled the writing "e-journals." But then it is entirely possible that students new to this electronic writing format just needed time to become accustomed to its immediate audience, its capability for dialogue, and the opportunity for recursive reading and responding.

Slowly they became more aware of an audience beyond just the teacher, however. In discussing T. Coraghessan Boyle's "Greasy Lake," one of the students[2] offered a provocative challenge to his classmates:

> *Jack*: I disagree with what Ellen says about the narrator from "Greasy Lake" being a jerk just because he tried to rape a girl. Though I do not condone rape, I don't think you are justified in saying that he is a jerk just because he was doing this. This young man and his friends were quite high, drunk and in any other state alcohol or drugs could possibly put someone in. His actions were being determined by the drugs, they were really not his own. If you want to say he is a jerk because he uses drugs, that's fine, but it's unfair to say he is a jerk for actions he is not directly responsible for.

Jack's entry caused a stir with his classmates, most of them young women. Not only did two of the students stop me in the hall that day—"Katie, you have got to see what Jack wrote on e-mail today. You won't believe it!"—but word spread fast among them, and the number of entries multiplied rapidly. Immediately, others posted to discuss an issue they related to their own lives:

> *Patricia*: Jack, I cannot believe you do not think that the guy in Greasy Lake is not a jerk. It does not matter if the man is sober or not, rape is rape. I hope your opinion changes. I know this is an ethical issue and probably doesn't belong in this journal, but I think it is to important to ignore, especially in this day when women have a right not to be victimized.
>
> *Ellen*: First off, I agree with Patricia. Anything you put into your body is YOUR responsibility. I suppose killing someone with your car while drunk does not deserve indictment or imprisonment? Compare him to Sammie in A&P. Sammie has the hots for those girls but he doesn't go out and try to rape them!

Haggling over a character's ethics engaged students emotionally with one another and with the text, even though at first they felt unsure about becoming so involved, wondering whether this was even an acceptable topic to discuss in an academic forum. Out in the garage-sale world of cyberspace without the neat price tags and tidy sales clerks—without the verbal and physical cues of the teacher—they were left to negotiate thinking and writing independently. But with Jack's challenge before them, they plunged into what Michael Basseches (1989) calls "metapositions," places outside the typically accepted confines of academic writing (28). Certainly their writing in direct response to Jack's pinprick was far different than if I had coaxed them to "write about how you feel about the attempted rape." Students returned to the story to find textual evidence to support their comments about the narrator, something they had not attended to earlier despite my usual English teacher incantation, "Please use textual evidence to support your assertions." Purpose? They wrote to change the thinking of their classmates. Audience? They wrote to people they perceived as "real" rather than just to a teacher who, they believed, already knew it all, an audience Fulwiler (1987) so adroitly labels as "no audience at all" (50). As a result, they walked alongside characters, hand in hand. After a few weeks of this discussion, Jack confessed:

> *Jack*: This is my formal apology to all of you for something I did. My comments about the narrator from Greasy Lake were not true. I do not think he was justified in what he did. But I wanted to see what would happen if I threw a wrench into the works of our discussion. Thank you for not taking pot shots at me personally because of my words. I apologize if I offended anyone, but I am not sorry I did this. WATCH OUT in the future! You never know when I (or someone else) will do this again.

Along with students who knew Jack well, I had wondered about his initial inflammatory posting since it was so out of character for this young man known for his gentle spirit and straight-as-an-arrow lifestyle. Some had even wondered if writing on e-mail had changed Jack. We were relieved to find Jack was still the Jack we had come to know; yet we learned a powerful lesson about e-mail's ability to whip up a controversy and enliven writing by providing an audience engaged by more than just impressing a teacher who would grade the journal.

By interacting socially online to develop interpretation, students moved to interacting socially with the text. They saw their writing delight and agitate other students in ways they perceived as more real, more lively than merely writing *about* literature as students outside the experience between the pages. Thus, as they inhaled literature, they exhaled meaning-making collaboratively through e-journals.

Re-wiring

Although this was a fairly successful project, I realized that I would need to make changes in the e-journal assignment next course around. The whole-class discussion left students with enormous amounts of e-mail. Confusion as to who had said what (fairly common in e-mail conversations) was compounded by the large-group format which made it easier for some students to hide, or "lurk," by refraining from writing. Since our classes are relatively small and students are used to small-group work, smaller e-journal groups made good sense. In the next go-round I arranged e-journal groups of five or six; these smaller groups are more manageable for students, with fewer entries to respond to, and they encourage further depth in exploring texts. Although students had fewer entries to read, I still read all their entries and was included on the mailing list for all groups. Of course, they were aware I was "listening in."

I also felt that the initial virtual garage-sale writing project, which occurred entirely outside of class time, was not holistically enough blended with class-period activities. In subsequent literature courses, I encouraged more spillover from e-journals into class and back again. For example, in a later class, role-playing activity from the drama unit flowed into the e-journals. In class, students had assumed the roles of characters like Minnie Wright (*Trifles*), Mommy (*Sandbox*), and Titania (*A Midsummer Night's Dream*). Although their e-journals had been less interactive than the honors class entries had been the year before, their classroom role-playing was lively, perhaps attesting to different learning styles; they engaged in thinking more analytically, deciding what a character should answer to a given question. Following the success of this in-class activity, I reshaped their outside-of-class journal writing, requiring that each student sign up to "become" one of the characters from the drama unit. During the fiction unit, then, they were to write *as* that character about the stories assigned.

Because I borrowed from their in-class success but shifted from the oral mode to one of writing, students took on literature by taking on voices other than their own. As these personas, students not only had to consider what the current short story reading meant, but also what their own persona thought about that story. As they responded to one another, they added yet another layer of thinking; as their personas, they had to engage with other personas in talking about a third set of characters and stories.

The more students spoke in the voice of their assumed roles, the more interactively they engaged with other voices and with the stories—and yet progress was slow at first. Within a few weeks, however, they came upon two real Green River knives. The first surfaced when Rita decided not only to think like Shakespeare's Titania, but also to sound like her as she wrote about Kate Chopin's "The Storm":

> *Rita* (as Titania):
> Shame on Calixta and Alcee'
> For they committed adultery.
> I don't agree with either one,
> Even if they had tons of fun.
>
> Poor Bobinot, Bibi,
> Clarisse, and baby.
> They don't deserve'st such dishonesty.
> I'm sure they hold trust for thee.
>
> The damage done is permanent now.
> Continue, they may not know how.
> Responsibilities are well on their way
> But things will get harder day by day.
>
> Hope is in the air,
> I know they still care.

Although she did not use perfect sonnet form, Rita became more sensitive to Shakespearean style than had any of the students during the study of *A Midsummer Night's Dream* a month earlier. As Meredith Sue Willis (1993) suggests, this imitation of text allowed Rita to "write her way into literature" (127). With her approval, I forwarded to the entire class the sonnet she had posted to her small group. Others soon began writing more carefully, attending to word choice, sentence length, and rhythms from the original text. They were playing and loving the pitch and timbre of their characters' speech. This was distinctly different than the meaningless charting and identifying they had done when students wrote about style and submitted it to me. Obviously, too, rather than simply dropping the first part of the course as "done," they were carrying along with them the full shopping bags of literature gleaned from earlier weeks.

The second treasure surfaced when Tom as Daddy in Albee's *Sandbox* wrote about Sammy (John Updike's "A&P" narrator); Krysta, as Daddy's wife, responded to him:

> *Tom* (as Daddy): This "A&P" story reminds me of my first job and how I met Mommy. Like that boy at the counter, I was hard at work stocking shelves at the local Dominick's. Mommy came in and was arguing with the manager and practically every employee there because she felt the sales price on the melons wasn't marked down very much and "a sale was a sale so things should be cheaper." Somehow I caught her eye and she came up to me and said that if I was gonna support someone like her, I better quit and get a real job. Of course, how could I turn down that kind of offer. And now look at me! Too bad that Sammy kid never connected with that girl in the halter top.
>
> *Krysta* (as Mommy): AAAAARRRRRRH! Daddy, you can't even remember a damn thing! That wasn't me you met in the grocery. Musta been in your dreams. Now listen here to me. That kid in the store was a fool. It was just all lust. He was hot for that girl and couldn't stand it when his boss kicked her out of the store. He was a fool to give up a good job. You have to be realistic in this world. When something like this happens, you have to look the other way. So don't get any ideas, Daddy, about getting all soft and getting "principles" at this point in the game or you may find YOUR dinner in a bowl under the stove!

Krysta and Tom not only imitated Albee's writing in Mommy's craggy voice and Daddy's placating tones, but also spontaneously interacted with each other online, extending the original text. They reached beyond "revisionist literature" (Willis 1993, 133) by adding to Albee's manuscript, suggesting what *could have been*, thus co-creating the text with the playwright. They became both seller and buyer, breathing new life into Albee's characters and relating their experiences to those of Updike's narrator. And they managed all of this without any prompt or teacher intervention.

Not only did we accomplish a more holistic blending of writing inside and outside of class when role-playing took center stage in the e-mail groups, but daily lessons and assignments on paper were changed by the e-journals. Occasionally in class students would respond to discussion prompts as well. "I'm going to speak first as my e-mail persona and then as myself"; or they would comment, "Jordan, this doesn't sound like you. This sounds more like that character Jim Sieg in *Madras*." They also took more initiative in shaping their own learning, requesting that writing assignments be changed to more fully explore in multiple-draft formal essays certain issues raised briefly in the e-journals. No longer content to purchase the advertised specials, they bargained for and negotiated their learning. And I became more sensitive to opportunities arising out of students' online writing to re-route according to the paths they were choosing. In my upper division Science Fiction course, I found a student asking others in her e-mail group, "Can you imagine if Neal Stephenson had written 'Cinderella'?" Following her cue, I asked students to brainstorm the differences between science fiction and fantasy genres and then to write, revising either "Cinderella" or "King Midas" in the style of cyberpunk. Cindy's response was typical of what others wrote:

> She had a friend by name of Fairly Gigmother who worked for the Mafia and had invited her to a Mafia party in the Metaverse pavilion. Anyone who was anyone would be there. With F. G.'s help, she designed a new avatar out of an old word processor program and a Donky Kong video game. She knew Big Al and her slimy co-workers would be there. F. G. told Cyberella that she had to be out of the metaverse by midnight because they would cut the power to the Laundromat she lived in at 12 and the computer would shut down.

This was a far more engaging way to approach literary style than my originally planned assignment to "describe the style of cyberpunk comparing it to other genres." Certainly students could have transformed the style of one story into that of another on paper, but the essence of this experience was that the student created the assignment altogether because the e-journal put her brainstorming conversations with others online. Students knew that their user identification appeared on their e-mail posts, yet there seemed to be more ease in assuming other voices, other personas in this medium. Just as Jack posted an entry contrary to his own feelings about rape and just as Rita mimicked the language patterns of Titania, these science fiction students were immediately comfortable shifting style when writing one another in e-mail. Through the electronic writing, then, students claimed more of a voice in forming their own learning. Although others teaching without computer support may undoubtedly be more imaginative in assigning writing than I was, I found that the dialogical student-student writing encouraged by the presence of electronic writing elicited a flexibility in me as teacher and in each student as learner-teachers.

In referring to a Freirean agenda for the learning process, Ira Shor (1987) notes that in the problem-posing classroom, teachers need to move between the "art of intervention and the art of restraint" (23). The dynamic nature of dialogue between students with the teacher as eavesdropper encouraged such movement. I was privy to their shopping—observing which items they were picking up, testing the weight of in their palms, turning over to see prices on the underside, chatting to one another about in considering whether or not to buy. And because their needs were immediately apparent in the e-journals (rather than being something I realized only upon reading their paper journals at the end of a unit), I could adjust responses and assignments accordingly. I could more easily pace my intervention and feel more secure about my restraint.

Journals on e-mail, read daily rather than only four to five times per semester, encouraged an immediate sense of audience and purpose; there was also an immediate sense in students of writing regularly rather than dashing off entries in various colors of ink the night before the journals were due. Yes, in my classes previous to e-journal, students had written letters to one another of an interpretive nature and we had found, as Toby Fulwiler (1987) suggests, that "when students write to one another, rather than to teachers, a certain pretension necessarily drops away" (51). The e-journal, however, established that which was lacking in paper notebooks; through the ongoing dialogue where no entry is complete until it is "sent" emerged that community of writers Peter Elbow so often mentions as key to thinking and writing in the composition classroom.

Responding to other treasures unearthed from accidental circumstance has also worked well in literature classes using networked software other than e-mail. One of our best finds at our virtual garage-sale writing occurred one day in class when students responded with complete confusion when I asked them to orally discuss "Harrison Bergeron," the short story assigned for that day; it turned out that their text was missing two crucial pages. Fresh from having given a workshop to faculty about using prediction in journal writing in science classes, I suggested we write through the networked synchronous software hypothesizing what the missing pages included. Unlike the more linear oral class discussions where students wait for one another to finish speaking before speaking themselves, synchronous online writing gives each student a writing space to express her views even before hearing those of others. Upon cue from the teacher, she "sends" her writing to the network, which puts it on all student screens in first-come, first-served order, like a transcript of a conversation. Although students could have written their guesses in paper journals before discussing as a class, thus maintaining initial independent thinking, it is unlikely this approach would have worked as well for all students. Some, upon hearing ideas they deemed "more correct" from classmates who spoke first, may have chosen not to share their own ideas. They could have traded and read such paper journals, but chances are they would not have had access to everyone's writing; and then there is also the problem of wrestling with penmanship.

In the early minutes of written discussion on the day we discussed "Harrison Bergeron," hypotheses represented wild first thoughts:

> *Seymour*: What happened in the missing pages? Sort of reminds me of
> Nixon's elusive 18 minutes. I'll bet Harrison and the ballet dancer leaped
> out of the TV studio and took over the government.

As the discussion continued, students questioned how textually based their original guesses had been and kneaded the parts of the text they had read into, giving
rise to those parts that had been missing.

> *Samantha*: Vonnegut says that handicaps were directly proportionate to
> physical and mental ability of the characters. Since Harrison had more
> handicaps mental and physically than any human ever, he must have been
> super human. I suspect he broke out of his handicaps in some clever way,
> partnered with the ballet dancer, and found a way to overcome the control-
> lers. On the last page of the story in our text, we see his mother crying.
> Why would that be?

When they finally read the missing pages I handed out, they were able to review
the printout of their online discussion for comparison's sake and laugh with one
another and with the author. I have come to see this laughter as a very serious
and crucial part of the dialogical writing process. Whether it occurs orally or in
print as "hahahaha" or online as emoticons, this laughter establishes a sense of
community in which students write to know literature beyond just the heady
stuff of academic cognition.

Stretching the Wire

One semester when I taught two sections of Science Fiction, students were able
to use electronic writing to engage in dialogue between classes rather than only
within one class. One section, populated by 18-to-22-year-old students, met at
the crack of dawn, garage-sale time; the other, filled with nontraditional students, met two evenings each week. Day students were full-timers, all but one
living on campus; night students worked full time at jobs during the day and
lived in town and in outlying areas. Although their assignments were similar
and their readings identical, their perspectives varied considerably. I wondered
how the online technology could broaden each group by bringing them together
through writing in virtual space since doing so in physical time and space was
impossible.

When we wrote about Vonnegut's *Slaughterhouse Five*, the day students, a
generation born after the Vietnam War, experienced difficulty understanding
Billy Pilgrim's postwar mental condition. As students grew impatient with Billy's
Trafalmadorans, their e-journals discussed how "nuts" he was. When the night
students entered the e-journal discussions some days later, they were able to
reveal insights into Billy based on their own postwar experiences, the recollec-
tions of pacifist marches, and accounts of losses left in the wake of wars:

> *Dave* (from the night class): I came back from Vietnam, but a lot of my friends never did. My own brother came back but never really returned. He looks normal to outsiders at the bank where he works, but he's the most wounded person inside you'd ever meet. And he drinks a lot. For me, it's pretty hard to see what all the killing gave us anyway and I lay awake wondering about that.

> *Cheryl* (from the day class): I guess maybe having visits to another planet is sort of understandable given what you say Billy's been through, Dave. Gee, I wonder if he didn't wish he could have just died in that slaughterhouse in Dresden rather than having to re-live all the horror for years.

Although we could have invited an "outsider" to speak with the class, these two groups formed a writing community using electronic technology in which they shared the stories from real life that enlivened literature for one another. It was a bit like listening to a grandmother at a garage sale explaining to her grandson as they finger saltcellars, "We used to use those the way you use salt shakers now."

Shor suggests that teachers establish a Freirean situated pedagogy where learning is seated in students' own culture (1987, 24). Through their dialogue online, students positioned themselves this way without direction from the teacher. Not only did the evening students inform the day students; just as the grandson at the garage sale may turn to inform his grandmother about the Atari game they find alongside Monopoly, so the day students took their turn. When we studied Neal Stephenson's cybernetic novel *Snow Crash,* the day students helped their nighttime classmates feel the lure of rollerblading and virtual reality interactive video games. Many other experiences with e-journals—like the one in which I found students liken Marilyn Monroe in Judy Grahn's poem "The Marilyn Monroe Poem" to Madonna, an envoy from the student culture rich in MTV and rock music—further suggest that writing with computer support encourages students to see relationships between the lives they live and the lives they read.

For students in both classes, the perimeters of their own culture expanded to include the World Wide Web, used initially to research background on literature and authors. When Bobbie chanced upon a state senator's homepage (Harkin 1996) revealing that he had been involved in investigating the inhumane treatment of prisoners of war in Vietnam, she shared the find with both classes; this sharing resulted in a flurry of e-mail letters between them and the senator's account. Through the dynamic capability of online writing with its varied audience a given, the world of student reading and the world of student living merged. Billy Pilgrim's narrator and his views of the treatment of war prisoners were no longer the mere fictional creation of Kurt Vonnegut. The issues became real, political, and contemporary for students.

In searching for "doublespeak" on the Web when we studied *1984*, students came across a Web page tirade about politically correct language and "these feminist war mongers" ("Political Correctness, the Doublespeak of Today" 1996). The students' interpretation of the novel conflicted strongly with the author of those Web pages, a man who called himself "Bob." Cynthia Selfe and Richard Selfe (1994) suggest that writing and learning are political acts where we may analyze motives for the use of language (483). Just so, writing in the electronic environment compelled several students to write Bob in an attempt to challenge his use of Orwell's novel as justification for his somewhat vigilante purposes. None of this was assigned writing. On their own, through the electronic environment, students moved to a level of knowing the character of Winston Smith and of realizing how language control results in thought control. For the rest of the term, whenever oral or written discussion smelled of censorship, I heard students whisper "Big Brother Bob."

Over the past five years working with literature classes with a variety of writing-to-learn assignments on computers, I have been continually surprised by the golden pigs and Green River knives that emerge in students' writing both inside and outside of class. Unlike earlier literature classes where my students wrote only between the margins in print, the writing my students now produce using e-mail, networked synchronous software, and the World Wide Web results in wonderfully wild, unpredictable directions of a more dialogical nature encouraging greater attention to text alongside more independent interpretations of reader response. Best of all, students visiting electronic garage-sale writing internalize—know— literature in ways deeply affecting relationships within their own lives. I believe their success is due primarily to three phenomena intrinsic to online writing: (1) my role as teacher is far less intrusive in their engagement with literature and results in more student-centered learning; (2) students form a more active community of writers which fosters an audience of peers rather than the audience of teacher, a community that elicits spontaneous and independent interaction with the text; and (3) blending the characteristics of dialogue borrowed from oral modes of discussion with the recursive and recordable capabilities of writing results in a more dynamic interaction within the community of writers than does either mode alone. Once this community establishes a social construction for interaction, they move on to interact with the literary text itself. As Michael Spooner and Kathleen Yancey (1996) suggest, e-mail and other synchronous software offer, instead, a curious new way "of representing intellectual life" (254).

I am not advocating the abandonment of traditional, non-electronically produced writing-to-learn practices. But in concert with these department-store writings, I find students are able to write directly into the heart of knowing literature when their pens are electronic and they experience the plaster pigs alongside the Green River knives. Responding enthusiastically to the power of writing online, students in these courses grew to remind me of another story, the story of Margaret Atwood's (1985) heroine in *The Handmaid's Tale*. Ironically in Offred's story, where even the use of paper and pen are reserved for men alone and are, therefore, the cutting edge writing instruments of her world, it is not the computer which enables her to feel the energy of words. When she is given a pen to use for the first time in three years, Offred finds "the pen between my fingers is sensuous, alive almost. I can feel its power, the power of words" (241). With computers—the electronic pens of the story my students wrote—the power of literature is as sensuous, as powerful, as alive.

Notes

1. In our classes, we used both Macintosh and IBM platforms. Word processing was mainly in MS Word 5.1 and WordPerfect 6.0. Students used a variety of Web search engines including Excite, Yahoo, Lycos, and Magellan. Versions of Netscape ranged from 0.9 to 2.1. Our e-mail package is Pine running on an IBM RS/6000. Macintosh computers included everything from an SE30 to a Power Mac 7100. IBMs were 486s.

2. Pseudonyms have been substituted for all student names.

Works Cited

Atwood, Margaret. 1985. *The Handmaid's Tale*. New York: Fawcett Crest.

Basseches, Michael. 1989. "Intellectual Development: The Development of Dialectical Thinking." In *Thinking, Reasoning, and Writing*, edited by Elaine Malmon, Barbara Nodine, and Finbarr O'Conner, 23–45. White Plains: Longman.

Flynn, Elizabeth A. 1986. "Composing Responses to Literary Texts: A Process Approach." In *Writing Across the Disciplines: Research Into Practice*, edited by Art Young and Toby Fulwiler, 208–14. Portsmouth, NH: Boynton/Cook.

Fulwiler, Toby. 1987. *Teaching With Writing*. Portsmouth, NH: Boynton/Cook.

Morgan, Dan. 1993. "Connecting Literature to Students' Lives." *College English* 55.5: 491–500.

Selfe, Cynthia L., and Richard J. Selfe, Jr. 1994. "The Politics of the Interface: Power and Its Exercise in Electronic Contact Zones." *College Composition and Communication* 45.4: 480–504.

Shor, Ira. 1987. "Educating the Educators: A Freirean Approach to the Crisis in Teacher Education." In *Freire for the Classroom: A Sourcebook for Liberatory Teaching*, edited by Ira Shor, 7–32. Portsmouth: Boynton/Cook.

Spooner, Michael, and Kathleen Yancey. 1996. "Postings on a Genre of Email." *College Composition and Communication* 47.2: 252–78.

Williams, Terry Tempest. 1994. *An Unspoken Hunger*. New York: Vintage.

Willis, Meredith Sue. 1993. *Deep Revision*. New York: Teachers and Writers Collaborative.

Resources

Harkin, Thomas. 1996. "Tom Harkin's Biography." http://www.senate.gov/~harkin/
     bio.htm (21 Mar. 1996).
"Political Correctness, the Doublespeak of Today." 1996. http://www.bob.com/
     doublespeak.html (17 Jan. 1996).

17 E-Journals: Writing to Learn in the Literature Classroom

Paula Gillespie
Marquette University

Roses and jasmine were in bloom. Hummingbirds careened past us as they made for the trumpet vine. We were dreaming in California. Suddenly my daughter Leigh took me back to the cold Wisconsin winter and the semester I was about to face back home in Milwaukee. "Don't forget your engineers, Mom," came her Silicon Valley voice.

"What?"

"When you start teaching your lit course this fall, don't forget that you have students just like Torrey in your class." Torrey is my son-in-law, an engineer. For many years, for all the years of his undergraduate and graduate training, he never read for pleasure. He never read fiction. In fact, he considered it frivolous, a waste of time. He'd only recently come to see it as a form of education and pleasure. But I was well aware that in every class I taught, there were students like Torrey, keeping quiet about it, but feeling frustrated, feeling defeated by the subject matter. I also knew that there would be students in my class who read the way I did: for pleasure, for the joy of the language, for the intensity of the involvement with plot and character. And I also knew that to be able to read for pleasure was to be able to experience, to inhale, to live with and love the prose rhythms, the rich, evocative sentences, the irony, the complexity of language, the cleverness of wit, the play of words of great writers. I felt, going into this class, that exposure to these structures and forms and genres would influence the thinking of students, make possible to them new forms, and through those forms new and increased complexity of ideas. Learn to interpret a text and you will know more about interpreting the world. Lofty goals? Yes. Aspirations; inspirations, even.

But I had other, simpler goals too, goals that were closer to the ground in a sense, but that related to those loftier ones, that made them possible. One goal for my literature class was to make it truly writing-intensive, to use as many of the writing-to-learn techniques as I could adapt from their two-semester first-year writing sequence and from writing-across-the-curriculum (WAC) workshops I'd attended and conducted. I was trying to address two problems I'd encountered at Marquette: I'd found that literature teachers who assigned two

221

papers and gave two essay tests considered their courses writing-intensive. I'd also found through working in the writing center with students from these literature classes that a number of them, as they wrote literature papers, had lost sight of many of the heuristics they had found helpful as first-year students; they became one-draft writers in their literature courses. They attempted to fit old five-paragraph theme forms from their high school writing into the literature class. They wanted to summarize or write biographies.

This meant, though, that they had to forget our entire first-year sequence, two rigorous semesters that taught them an awareness of audience and purpose, a sense of style, sound argumentative strategies, appropriate supporting arguments, and research methods. Our first-year sequence has built into it many revisions of drafts and many invention techniques that adapt well to the literature classroom. I wanted to integrate as many of these writing elements and strategies as I could into my literature classes so that I could report back to the director of undergraduate studies about those that had worked and those that hadn't. I wanted the word to get out about how to tap into what students already knew so that they could keep their writing skills current and apply what they knew, to write to learn on their own, in all courses and for all writing, in and out of college. These sophomore-level literature survey courses, required for most majors, including engineering, are our last chance to reach some of these students with writing-to-learn strategies. I taught one section of Introduction to Fiction during the fall and again the following spring semester. The texts were six novels, all with the theme of the maturation of a young protagonist. But far from being a course in the bildungsroman, it was simply a non-major's course in fiction with a theme I hoped they could relate to.

I couldn't have predicted it, but the electronic journal turned out to be the centerpiece of the course, the one element that, more than any other, really moved my students ahead, that facilitated their learning about literature and about writing about literature. It fit into a matrix of other writing-to-learn exercises and techniques, but it outshone them. I incorporated a few of my favorite writing strategies, some my students had ranked as very helpful. One was the technique of structured in-class group brainstorming for paper topics. Another was peer critiques. Students offered feedback on drafts, as they had learned to do in their writing course the year before. Then I collected drafts and had conferences with students on the ungraded papers. Then they revised. I encouraged some of them to continue their discussion of their work with tutors at the writing center. They did proofreading workshops the day papers were due. And there was plenty of in-class freewriting. But the online or e-journal was the highlight of the course, the element that helped my students come closest to my goals for them.

My initial goal for the e-journal was to have the students learn from one another. I wanted the resistant readers to learn from those students, majors in every discipline, who read for the joy of it and who have a sharp critical reading ability, an ability to interpret texts shrewdly. And regardless of their approaches to literature, like it or hate it, many students would come to class hoping I would give them canned interpretations they could learn and be tested on. But learning a single privileged interpretation, of course, is not the goal of a good literature course. The goal, in addition to initiating the students into the tradition and forms of literary interpretation, is to get students to venture interpretations of their own, a goal that fits into the mission of the college and of the university, to foster independent critical thought.

My colleague and friend in the math department, George Corliss, had first introduced me to e-mail by convincing me that he could extend his office hours and increase his contact with his math and computer science students by inviting them to e-mail him. He considers e-mail at least as important as lectures and office hours, especially for those students who are still intimidated by office visits. Depending on the project, he sends messages and assignments over e-mail. This, he finds, gets the students hooked on reading their mail and makes them more likely to communicate with him. His students submit their computer programs to him over e-mail so he can run them and verify their results. He also finds it useful to be able to verify from which account the programs originate. And because he is compiling a database of article summaries in his field, he collects certain assignments only electronically. He sent me my first e-mail message and has been a valuable resource for me as I find my way electronically.

I found my inspiration for the e-journal in a peer tutoring course taught by Virginia Chappell, another Marquette colleague and friend. She had her class of fifteen write an electronic class journal once a week. Each week a different student would pose the week's question about the readings or the tutoring they were observing. Each student was expected to read all the entries. She found that the e-journal fostered speculation about writing center theory and practice. (Chappell 1995).

Although my literature class had forty students rather than fifteen, I still thought they would benefit from one another's literary interpretations. My students were responsible for reading all the posts from their classmates that preceded theirs. This was a lot of reading for them and for me, but it was not overwhelming, except for those students who put it off and had to read all thirty-nine at once before they could reply. They would, I hoped, get used to the idea that there are alternative readings of texts, and that the answers do not always or only come from the instructor. I wanted them to build on the reflexive nature of the journal but to take it further. I knew, as all instructors do, that some paper journals are written the night before they are due and are done meticulously in different handwritings and different colored inks. So I wanted a weekly deadline for the e-journals. I felt that since the entries were coming to me over the course of the week, I would find them easier to read than a stack of paper journal entries. And I felt no need to comment on them, since the other students would be responding to their entries. I sent the class a prompt during the weekend, and their responses were due by midnight of the following Thursday.

The rules were simple: it was to be freewriting, one screenful. The entry had to respond to a prompt, and it had to show me that the writer had done the reading. To be sure they understood what was expected of them, I brought in a few fine posts on overheads so they could see what features made the entries successful. In the rare case of the post being vague or general, I would send it back to the student and ask him or her to re-do it. I also sent praise, private and public, for good work.

The reward for keeping up with the e-journal was substantial: they could raise their final grade by a full letter if they met the requirements. The punishment was substantial too: since the e-journal was a course requirement, if they missed more than two they did not pass the course. (This of course led to a few frantic Friday morning phone calls, but I was lenient with them; I knew that access could be a problem and felt that students who forgot once should be forgiven.)

I wrote the prompts because I wanted to direct the week's emphasis and coordinate it with class discussion. E-mail conferences are a fine way to free the students of the tyranny of the instructor, but I wanted no pretense here: we had work to do, and I wanted to guide this discussion. We began with *Pride and Prejudice*, looking at elements of character development, then plot structure, then narrative features. Austen set a high standard. As we read such novelists as Henry James, Oscar Wilde, and James Joyce, who set innovative new standards for fiction, we had a baseline from which to move and with which to compare. As we looked at the work of contemporary writers Margaret Atwood and Bobbie Ann Mason, we would have a rich social matrix and sets of norms against which to look at current issues of coming of age.

Because many students had never used e-mail, I scheduled a session in our computer lab during the first week of class and had one of the technicians there introduce students to their accounts and to the techniques they needed to know to maintain them and mail to the class. Those who had already sent me an e-mail message were allowed to skip this class. Bob Ferguson from our computer services division set up a distribution list for me based on my class list and sent me instructions to forward to those students who did not attend the e-mail session with him, simple steps that let them access the list.

Although some students simply could not make it work at first, soon the project was off the ground. Initially, the students were acutely aware of their peers and of me as they freewrote. When they started, they used a stilted mini-essay approach in their posts, but as they began to feel comfortable with one another and with me, they switched to a free-and-easy slang and bantered briefly with one another at the beginnings or endings of their posts, initially apologizing for clumsy e-mail use, but then wishing one another a good weekend, setting a relaxed tone. Students often started by specifying which part of the prompt they were responding to. My prompt usually included a number of questions; when one topic would start to feel "used up" to them, they would shift to another. Laura used a colloquial style as she changed the subject:

> Please excuse my last failed attempt at a message. Anyway, I agree w/ basically what everyone said about Char's marriage to the idiot, so I'm going to talk about Lydia and Wick. It is pretty obvious as to why W. married Lydia. First, Darcy really gave him no choice, as no one would let him get away w/ruining L.'s life. . . .

Charlotte had become Char, Wickham became W or Wick, and the Reverend Collins was "the idiot." Laura had started using abbreviations as well as nicknames, but though students continued to have fun with nicknames, the monogramming trend did not continue, as students seemed to find that spelling out the words worked better for them, for clarity. Laura concluded: "Well, that's that. I really liked this book, which surprised me." Being able to speak in their student voices helped them relax with one another and risk alternative interpretations.

Students were also aware that they had to make a case for their claims. This had been one of the goals of their first-year sequence, evaluating evidence, and I'd made it clear that they would need to carry it over into the literature class. Jennifer was the first to incorporate quotations and page numbers into her posts. This was one of her early posts on *The Picture of Dorian Gray*:

> I believe there are a couple of reasons for Dorian's initial coldness Toward Sybil. First of all, she has made him out to be a liar to Basil and Lord Henry, whom Dorian so eagerly wanted to impress with this talented young woman he'd fallen in love with. Dorian brags to his friends, ". . . she is divine beyond all living things. When she acts you will forget everything" (86). This description hardly portrays the Sybil Vane on stage however, ". . . the staginess of her acting was unbearable, and grew worse as she went on. Her gestures became absurdly artificial . . . it was simply bad art" (88). Dorian was well aware of the discontent of his friends with her performance. "She seemed to them to be absolutely incompetent. They were horribly disappointed" (88). A lot of dorian's bitterness evolved around the fact that she had embarrassed Him greatly in front of his friends.

When I saw her do this on her own, I posted to the list as well, pointing out how helpful this had been.

> *Subj: Great post*
> Hi, everybody. Look again at Jennifer Metcalfe's post; if you deleted it, email me and ask me to forward it to you. It's a sort of model response to the question. It refers to specific passages in the text, and even quotes them,

> with page numbers. Try to be specific, the way Jennifer is; try not to be too
> general. Jennifer, this is great work. PFG

Soon other students began quoting and citing, some even apologizing to the
others for not having their books with them when they posted. In their desire to
be clear to one another, they had stumbled upon the elements of a good literature paper: quotations from the text, page numbers, interpretation of quotations.

I knew that audience would make a difference in journal writing, but I had
no idea that it would tie in so well with the goals of the course. Students began
engaging with one another as well as with the texts. Early in the semester, Jeremy, who had identified himself to me as learning disabled, found it more comfortable to agree with others than to disagree. Most of his posts took the previous
positions and added to them. Here is his post in October:

> Pansy. When I first met Pansy I agreed with Jessica Taylor in that I too
> thought that Pansy was a little kid instead of a 15 year old girl. The author
> even refers to her as "the child" on page 188. I would also have to agree
> with a previous statement in someone elses response (sorry I can't remem-
> ber who it is) that the auther named her Pansy to strengthen her charater of
> being like a "wimp or pansy."

This post shows not only the way students took seriously my request to be
specific and use textual evidence, but an engagement with other students, including an apology for a forgotten name. By November, answering a question
about *A Portrait of the Artist as a Young Man*, Jeremy feels comfortable disagreeing, and he supports his position well:

> After reading all the prompts, the majority of the people responded to why
> it is so hard to get to know stephen. The only problem is that it is not hard
> to get to know stephen at all. From the first page in the book you could tell
> that stephen is a child by the way he jumps from thought to thought. He
> would be thinking about one thing and then ramble on to another. this is
> extremmly typical of a child; rambling on about everything and anything.
>   A major point raised in the prompts was that because their is no set
> narrator or family to describe stephen we have a hard time getting to know
> who he is. Well that fact is is that Stephen doesn't even know who he is so
> how could the narrator know who he is. As Tara Strauss pointed out stephen
> is growing and maturing as we go along in the story. We are learning about
> stephen as stephen is learning about himself. Karen Talbot points out that
> stephen jumping all over the place is getting to know him. I couldn't agree
> more, the more I read the clearer picture I get of stephen. We are learning
> of stephen character thru himself which I think is a well needed change of
> pace then having the character hand fed to us.
>   I like the way that this book is written and the way that stephen think
> because it reminds me a lot of when I was a kid and the way that I would
> change my thought process every other second. Quit complaining and start
> enjoying the book.

Even in his disagreement, Jeremy shows respect for his classmates, mentioning them by name, showing what a thorough job he has done in his reading of their entries.

Students used the e-journals, too, as a way to communicate to me. One was confused by the Hugh Kenner introduction to our copy of *A Portrait of the Artist*. I addressed her question in class, taking issue with Kenner myself, setting a tone of respectful disagreement over interpretations. Another student wanted me to explain who Parnell was, so my class lecture/discussion on Irish politics felt to the students as if it had started with their inquiry to me. Sometimes they just vented: "Does any of this make sense? I fear I may have lost some brain cells during the celebration of halloween (smile). Jennifer"

Sometimes their engagement with the texts led to statements about their own experiences:

> Getting to know Stephen is so different because I feel like I am inside of Stephen—he is more real to me than the characters in past novels and I can relate to the vacillating emotions he experiences. I am enjoying this book because I can see a lot of myself in young Stephen. When asked if he kissed his mother before going to bed, Stephen first says "I do" and when everyone laughs, he switches his answer to "I do not" and everyone laughs again. Stephen, in a state of confusion, asks himself, "What was the right answer to the question?" (26). YES—I CAN RELATE!!! I am glad to finally read a book with characters I can relate to! So many students have said that this book is confusing and hard to understand. Isn't that the whole point of the book— LIFE IS CONFUSING, UNFAIR, AND HARD TO UNDERSTAND— ESPECIALLY WHEN YOU ARE A YOUNG ADULT OR AN OLD TEENAGER!
>
> Sara

By the end of the semester, the posts astonished me in their sophistication. Sometimes they led students to paper topics. Sophia developed her query here into a very fine final paper on Atwood's *Cat's Eye*:

> I will be responding to the prompt about whether this book is written in a child's voice or Elaine's adult voice.
>
> I have thought about this question long and hard and I've searched the book to find passages that are telling as far as this question is concerned and I have come to the conclusion that we are seeing both points of view at the same time. That's why in chapter one, Atwood is explaining to us how she wrote the book. She says, "Time is not a line but a dimension, like the dimensions of space. If you can bend space you can bend time also, and if you knew enough and could move faster than light you could travel backward in time and exist in TWO PLACES AT ONCE." Later on, we get to the chronological point where Elaine gets this from her brother, but there's a reason why she begins with this. It's because that's exactly what she is doing throughout this entire novel. Elaine is existing in two places at once and taking us along with her. We are in the place where the child Elaine is telling us what she is seeing and also the place where the adult Elaine is

tellin us what she remembers. THere is evidence throughout the novel that both of these points of view are existing simultaneously. some of the evidence that we are listening to a child's voice has already been mentioned, the references to scabs and snot and farts and the like. but one thing I noticed is that Elaine, in these childhood memories doesn't always use these childhood words. sometimes she says "pee" and "turds" and sounds like a child, and sometimes she says "piss" and "shit" and sounds more like an adult applying adult language to her childhood memories. Refer to these quotes. "Sometimes he writes in pee, on the thin edge of sand or on the surface of the water . . . . By the end of the summer he has done the whole solar system, three times over, in pee." (72).

Students were required to write only one screenful of text, but Sophia did not stop at that. She went on from here to detail example after example, writing the draft of a mini-essay that was to become her final paper for the class. She used an informal student voice, but was doing serious text-searching and analysis of narrative structures, the sort of work that would normally appear in a formal paper, but that students would never get to see from their peers, unless they were doing peer critiquing or editing. Students were not required to take the journal to these lengths, but many did, outstripping my simple goals for the engineers who might hate novels.

The two classes that tried this e-journal wrote very similar online posts. But the classroom carryover was striking in its differences. The first class was the most talkative I had ever taught. Everyone had ideas. Hands were up all over the room as we elaborated on issues raised in the journals. And even those students who, I feel, would have been hesitant to talk in a traditional class joined in. Class was relaxed, since the students all knew one another from their online discourse. I was feeling heady about the generalizations I could make about class discussions.

But then I tried the e-journal again for the second semester, sure that the students would respond the same way in class. I threw questions at them, just as I had in the first class. Silence. To my surprise, they were reticent, not shy with one another, but hesitant to offer answers. I had to vary my pedagogy and allow for them to try out their ideas on paper first. If I let them freewrite in response to my questions, they were as free and experimental, as unrestrained as the first class. They had, as a group, simply become reliant on writing as their means of thinking questions through. I think that it was unusual and lucky that I had two classes that sorted themselves out in this way, because I feel that the more usual class would be made up of some students who feel ready to hazard an interpretation right away while some others would need to write out an answer first and then discuss. Now I'll be more attuned to those students who prefer to write before they speak.

I ran into one technical problem that I needed to address after the first few weeks. I gave feedback to those students who were approaching the limit of the posts they were allowed to miss. When I warned them, they claimed that they had sent posts in every week. Clearly I had to have an accounting system that would keep this from becoming a problem. Here was what I worked out. Every time I read a post, I saved it in a folder in my mainframe account (I had to get some extra memory to do this). Then every Friday morning I would bring to class the printed-out directory of the folder. Students were to check it to make sure their names were on it if they had sent a post. They were to keep a copy of their own posts so they could re-send them if necessary. Once I began circulating those lists, there were no further problems with missing entries.

Another modification I will make the next time I teach this course is to divide a class of forty into two journal groups, so there is less volume for them to read. I will bring in the best posts from both groups and show them to the class so they all have the opportunity to see these or, as the year goes on, forward posts to the other group. I will still have forty entries to read, but so far I have never found the task too demanding, even at 11:55 on a Thursday night.

I've often asked myself why reading e-journals seemed like less work than collecting and commenting on paper journals, and there are several reasons. For one thing, students comment on one another's posts. I don't have to. When I do send back written feedback to an individual, it's instantaneous and doesn't require class time to hand out. And entries come in over the course of the week. I would post the prompts on the weekend, and usually by Sunday night the first entries would appear. Sometimes there would be a rush on Thursday night, when they were due, but that would be rare. I'd often be up late, reading e-mail, and sometimes I'd get a personal note from a student racing to finish up: "Sorry this is so late: my week was so crazy." Occasionally a post would just make it in at 11:59 and then the student and I would laugh about it together online.

Earlier this year our experienced WAC enthusiasts had a series of brown bag lunches for interested Marquette faculty. We were each asked to describe our uses of WAC techniques. In a joint presentation, George Corliss and I each spoke of the way we had used online journals or e-mail class communications. We could tell from their responses and questions that faculty from all the departments present could see an application of the online journal for their own disciplines. George has set up e-mail discussion groups for his students who work as computer consultants with area businesses. These groups include him and sometimes the business contact person. The groups do much of what my e-journal did: allow ideas to become refined, allow input from everyone, keep all group members informed. He has now moved his database onto the World Wide Web. This prospect is tempting, but until my building is hard-wired, I am still confined to e-mail for my discussions. The other faculty members, especially those who use paper journals, have been very enthusiastic about picking up the ideas, and the staff at our computer service division is very cooperative and interested in seeing computers being used to advance learning.

The e-journal not only allowed students to write to learn, but it allowed them to see how others wrote to learn. I received a letter at the end of the spring semester class from a student who felt at the start of the term that he would never understand literature. He was discouraged and hostile, he said. But by the end of the semester he felt he could master any fiction, and he felt he would enjoy it. His letter took me back to that California afternoon when my child reminded me to do my job and when I resolved to use Silicon Valley technology to get the job done.

Work Cited

Chappell, Virginia A. 1995. "Theorizing in Practice: Tutor Training 'Live From the VAX Lab.'" *Computers and Composition* 12.2: 227–37.

18 E-mailing Biology: Facing the Biochallenge

Deborah M. Langsam
University of North Carolina at Charlotte

Kathleen Blake Yancey
University of North Carolina at Charlotte

How can one use e-mail in a large introductory science class? Why would one? Does it work? What do we mean here by "work"? These are the questions that guided an experiment in an introductory biology class for non-majors, one with two hundred students, some of whom wanted to learn, and some of whom . . . well, you've probably met them before.

What we'll share here is a report in progress, the story of e-mail usage in two sections of this biology course: one in fall 1995, another in spring 1996. Not surprisingly, what was learned in the fall experiment shaped the e-mail design in the spring, and the success enjoyed in both semesters encourages us to move forward and use our experiences to shape next year's iteration. Just stopping to review what's been done, to listen in on the students' perceptions, and to articulate for ourselves and others what we think is happening, as Lee Shulman (1996) reminds us, helps us to understand our classes and the learning that takes place there.

The basic question, then: Can e-mail work in a large general education class in science? Yes. How does it work? And specifically, does e-mail writing facilitate learning the subject matter of biology? Can it become an exercise in writing to learn? Those questions take longer to answer.

The Course

The class, taught by one of the authors (Langsam), is the first semester of a two-semester introductory biology sequence offered at the University of North Carolina at Charlotte for non-majors. The students taking the course are typical of the increasingly diverse student populations at many mid-size comprehensive institutions: there are full-time and part-time students, residential and commuting students, and students representing a broad spectrum of ages, educational backgrounds, and ethnicities. The common denominator here is that the vast majority of the students in the course "have" to take it to fulfill their science requirements in general education. Not surprisingly, the students often bring with them negative attitudes toward science and to the course in general, and some of them seem almost science-phobic. More often than not, they come to the course convinced that they can't succeed in science: it's too hard, too technical, too detailed, too boring. Many display fragile commitments to the course; they give it a low academic priority, right after courses in their major, outside commitments, and life in general. As they claim, "it's just a general education course"; "it's not in my major"; "it's general education so it shouldn't be hard." And what science faculty have said for years is also true: many students simply have poor science backgrounds.

Because the goal of the course is to help students become "biologically literate" so that they can understand biological issues as these impinge on their lives, questions related to personal and civic life are at the heart of the course. Do you understand enough about biology, we ask, to be able to ask informed questions about your health? Why are antibiotics generally ineffective against viral infections, we query? Why is the appearance of resistant forms of tuberculosis an "evolutionary" issue? Do you understand enough about biotechnology to make informed decisions about state funding for biotechnology-related research? How does the decimation of the rain forest contribute to global warming? The aim of the course, then, is to provide students with the type of background that they need to understand current biological events.

The course is designed to follow a "micro" to "macro" approach. It starts with cells and the chemistry needed to understand cell physiology. The students begin by working their way through "typical" plant and animal cells, contrasting them with cancer cells, bacteria, and "noncellular" entities such as viruses. This involves discussions about cell structures and metabolic processes such as photosynthesis and sugar breakdown, as well as what these activities imply about broader ecological issues such as global warming. And the course also includes material on cell reproduction and genetics which forms the basis for discussions about gene manipulation and its impact on medicine, the environment, and in industry. The course syllabus (available at http://www. bioweb.uncc.edu) suggests the kinds of tasks required in the course: primarily, four multiple-choice/short answer/essay tests and an optional portfolio used to award extra credit.

The Fall Experiment

Initially, the goals in using e-mail in this biology class were modest. Simply put, they centered on access. First, we simply wanted students to have another means of communicating with the instructor, and we thought e-mail could provide that. Online, students could (1) ask questions, (2) clarify information from the course, and (3) raise issues—in biology—which they might see as peripheral to the course proper. In addition, we expected that students might find e-mail access to the instructor more efficient access than tracking the instructor down. Posted office hours don't always coincide with student schedules, especially given the urban setting and commuter population of the university; and even phone calls can deteriorate into telephone tag. We also expected that students might find e-mail less intimidating than talking face-to-face with an instructor or raising a hand in a lecture hall of two hundred students, where even extroverts fear that they'll sound stupid. And with the e-mail, we wanted another kind of access—a means for Dr. L., as the students call her, to find them, to give them extra material (in the way of study tips, thought questions, assignments, reminders, whatever) beyond what might be given in the classroom—and without running off reams of handouts or taking up yet more class time.

But even when we started, we knew that eventually we would want to use e-mail as a springboard to other things: to promote critical thinking skills and to introduce students to other online resources. So getting them online was really the first step toward beginning to develop a whole new generation of assignments, ones which could use the World Wide Web to promote student learning. As we began, our main concerns were thus related to the purpose of access: time, time, time. Could e-mail from students be handled in a timely fashion? Would answers reach students fast enough to make those answers relevant? What purposes would they find for this voluntary use of e-mail? And would students respond to a program which, by definition, was "voluntary"?

Ironically, the uses students found in this first e-mail experiment matched all too well what we had planned: they found access and little more. Over the course of the term, far fewer than 50 percent of the students used the e-mail, and nearly all who did employed it to "convey," to inquire about administrative or procedural issues, generally to acquire information that had been provided to them already: when would the exam be given, for instance, or at what time would the extra study session take place? Perhaps more troubling than this instrumental, nonintellectual use of e-mail was the tendency of students to use it to talk about their grades, or more accurately, about their unhappiness with low grades. On the other hand, even this use of e-mail was useful in giving students a voice which could then be translated into mid-course improvements and corrections. In the fall, student concerns communicated via e-mail contributed to the development of a new grading option which we thought would boost student morale by providing an added incentive for students to study hard and do well on their cumulative final:

Here's a once-in-a-lifetime opportunity for Biology 1110 students. . . .
Currently, there are two ways to improve your grade in this course.

First, you can submit a portfolio of items at the end of the semester. These items include your responses to questions assigned from your text and to questions which accompany case studies and other readings. As you will recall, the portfolios will be used to determine whether students with borderline grades (58, 68, 78, 88) will receive the next highest grade. Everyone is eligible to do this.

Second, you have the option of taking a make-up exam on the last Friday of classes. This exam will be given at 2 p.m. in a room to be announced.

Third, and this is a new option. You may opt to allow your final exam score to count twice (if that final exam score is higher than your lowest grade). You may not use both option 2 and 3. You can *either* take the make-up exam on the last Friday of classes or you can opt to have your final exam score count twice.

What do you all think? Any takers on option #3?

Dr. L.

And students appreciated this option, as a student here suggests on e-mail:

I think the new idea you've proposed is a great one. I missed taking the third exam today, but did well on the first two. I was going to have to take the make-up exam on the last Friday of classes, but this new option will work out really well for me. Now I can take one test instead of two, which makes my life a little easier. Thank you. You've gone out of your way to make this class more convenient for us students, and I for one really appreciate your efforts.

Sincerely,

KH

But as the semester closed down and we reviewed e-mail usage over the fall 1995 term, it was pretty clear that what we exchanged on the e-mail was more in the way of information around the class rather than information deriving from or focused on the intellectual work of the class. It was also clear that the usage—under 50 percent of the students—was low. If we wanted e-mail to do more than provide access, we would need to design that more into its usage.

The Spring Experiment

In the spring, in addition to keeping e-mail a venue of access, "biochallenges" were introduced: questions that asked for applications of the material under study. Also, in order to motivate students, the biochallenges—which were still voluntary—"counted" for 1–5 extra credit points on an exam. So in attempting the biochallenges, a student had little to lose, much to understand. And if the understanding were persuasive, the student's grade could reflect that. This e-mail design seemed much more likely to produce the kind of writing to learn and, through it, intellectual exchange that we'd hoped for from the start.

For many students, about half of them, this too "worked": they took on questions that were new to the course, questions that students hadn't really thought of before. Also, the e-mail permitted an iterative process between student and instructor; as students wrote, the instructor would comment back and ask them to expand their answers or to think in a new direction or from a new perspective. The students comfortable on e-mail were also comfortable enough to "write aloud," to write on the e-mail in an informal, noncorrective mode; thus, we could often see evidence of their thinking as they talked through a biochallenge. Asked why rain didn't soak a raincoat but did soak a cotton shirt, for instance, one student responded:

> There are two types of fatty acids, which make up the lipids along with the glycerol molecule. One type is (poly)unsaturated. This means that there is only one double covalent bond in the fatty acid. This one double bond means that the hydrogens are less compacted, these fatty acids are liquid at
>
> Okay, I need to start over because I think that I was confused on what the question was asking. Lipids are insoluble in water because they are made of non-polar covalent bonds. Water is made up of polar covalent bonds. In order for a substance to be soluble in water the substance must have some charged ends (also be a polar molecule). . . .

The student continues with relevant information, finally ending with this observation:

> Rain does not soak through a raincoat because it has a waxy or oily coating. As I just explained lipids are insoluble so the materil of the rain coat does not get wet. The waxy or oily coating protect the material, this is much like the oil on a duck's feathers or the wax on your car. Ducks feathers do not soak up water ("water off a ducks back") and when your car is properly waxed then the rain beads up. A cotton shirt does not have this lipid layer therefor water soaks through.
>
> Again I am sorry about the beginning when I was answering a different topic.
>
> Deray Krueger

Here the student seems to write the e-mail as though it's a journal entry—with misspellings, a dearth of punctuation, and even a few biological misconceptions mixed in with solid knowledge—but the writing is both for self and for other. As important, the other is not James Britton's teacher-as-examiner (1975), but teacher-as-coach, teacher-as-fellow-biologist. The e-mail welcomes different kinds of information, both the academic—*lipids*—and the *non-academic* that suddenly, in the act of learning, is germane—*water off a duck's back*. Perhaps most interesting, when the student takes a "wrong" turn, she doesn't start over: the *process* of arriving at the right answer is itself part of the right answer.

We also used e-mail as the springboard to introduce assignments which asked students to access information from the World Wide Web that was too current to be represented in their text. In one assignment, for example, students were asked to gather information about the fat substitute *Olestra*. They reported back with summaries of their readings and the appropriate URL's used to gather their information. And at the end of the semester, a number reported positive experiences with the technology that was new for them:

> Doing the internet was my first experience; I'm glad she assigned it. I used it in research for another class and got a 100.
>
> More than just "busy-work"—thought provoking and relevant.

Even for those students who simply had questions—and there were many— the e-mail was instructive; it provided (1) a place to try to articulate the questions, (2) a person who would respond, and (3) an opportunity to learn just in the asking of the question. And as the e-mails show, students had to know enough to phrase the question that stumped them:

> I'm confused about the amino acid Tyrosine. I understand that it is inside the melanocytes, but what does it have to do with melanin? Also, I'm confused about phenylalanine. Could you explain it a little better? Thanks for your help!
> S. A. S.

Or from another student who is interested in the same topic, but carries the question beyond the confines of the classroom and into a "real life" situation:

> Dr. Langsam,
> I have a question concerning melanin. I am taking melatonin pilss that are 3mg. They also contain 25mg of B26. I was wondering if this would really help to boost my melanin? I am very pale and am scared of the sun. I brought them over-the-counter but when I run ot of them I am going to have them prescribed to me in a stronger strength. Is this ok for me? HC

In this instance the student has actually made a logical, but erroneous connection (between melatonin and melanin); the e-mail, however, provides a venue for the question that might have gone unasked in the large-lecture classroom setting.

Other student questions are less detailed, but again they are related to content:

> Dr. L.:
> In osmosis, diffusion, Active transport, exocytosis, and endocytosis, is equilibrium the main objective? Or am I totally confused?

This second time around, then, e-mail worked better. Using it with a new, e-mail-explicit task—the biochallenge—encouraged learning in two ways: the students could attempt the task without risk to their grade if they failed; and they could earn higher grades. And beyond the value of the biochallenges specifically, just incorporating them into the e-mail helped define it as a place to learn, a place to write about what students were thinking, a place where real questions and even confusion were welcome, a place where a real person would respond. With this version of e-mail, writing to learn was migrating online.

But there was a downside: not all students participated, and upon reflection, a number of issues may be at play. For one thing, our students are not technically proficient, nor are they scientifically literate. Asking them to acquire literacy in a field and in a medium both of which they find strange and forbidding compounds the learning problem. This is especially so when the "techno-phobia" is coupled, for many students, with "techno-access" problems. As one student noted, again, in end-of-course evaluations:

> I never used e-mail because it is too much of a hassle to get to computer
> lab.

The majority of our students have no home access to e-mail and must make a special trip to the biology lab, where computers are available, or to the campus computer labs, where they may have to wait or where they may be frustrated by glitches in the system:

> I only used e-mail twice, the first time was in lab and the second time I
> went to Colvard and I couldn't get my email, so I did not use it anymore.

It's also possible that the rewards being offered (a few extra credit points) may not be perceived as generous enough to warrant the time it would take to be persistent: to go to the computer lab, or to gain technical proficiency, or to respond to the challenges.

But it may be misleading to conclude that techno-hassles were the only obstacles to student participation. If technical proficiency and aversion to e-mail were the only issues, then it would follow that more students should have taken advantage of a number of nontechnical extra credit opportunities connected with the course. But participation was sporadic there as well. Indeed, 25 percent of the class took advantage of none of the extra credit assignments offered in the spring semester. These included the "computer related" activities of e-mail and World Wide Web assignments, but they also involved writing an article for the school newspaper based on material they'd learned about sunscreens, developing a study guide for one of the exams, and answering a series of questions about a "human interest" essay in their text. These activities could be e-mailed to the instructor or done in standard low-tech pen and paper mode. It is true that the e-mail activities elicited the lowest percentage of participation, and here's where the techno-phobia and lack of access problems rear their heads. But the bigger issue here may be the students' fragile commitment to the course because of a lack of interest or the presence of competing activities of higher priority.

And it's also likely that the actual design of the e-mail component requires a little "tweaking" in order to engage more student interest. To be sure, students who responded to instructor-posted messages or who initiated e-mail communication with us could count on a timely reply to their queries. But those who were just "listening in" to the general messages posted to the list might only be rewarded with a new message every two to three weeks, at a rate which didn't captivate students or communicate a sense of urgency about the list to convert the casual participant into a more active user.

Addressing these issues is the next (bio)challenge.

E-mailing and Learning

Still, reviewing the year, we see e-mail as an important addition to any class, but particularly to a large lecture class. While it cannot transform a class of hundreds into a class of even seventy-five or forty, it does change the tenor of the class. Certainly, it gave a voice to some students who might not have communicated with the instructor in other ways:

> Email was great especially if you are a shy person and didn't want to ask the professor questions in front of a big class.

Others didn't have to fear a one-on-one, face-to-face conversation. They could write their thoughts and take as much time as they needed to compose what they wanted to say, so they weren't caught off guard; this could have special significance to some of the students whose language of origin isn't English. And those who wrote got a more thoughtful response to their queries since typing was much less tiring than writing out comments by hand. Also, it freed all of us from the endless sheaves of papers that seem to envelop us.

It's also true, however, that a minority absolutely hated e-mail:

> I did not like E-Mail, it is very impersonal.
>
> I hated email. It's just one more way of introducing technology into our lives. And I don't like being a guinea pig!

Most students, however, expressed the opposite view. They felt this was a more personal approach and that the instructor was more accessible.

> I enjoyed e-mail—I felt I was always in touch with the professor.
>
> It was a great source of information. Extra credit over E-mail a great idea.

Ironically, many of those who commented had never written a private e-mail note, so it's not clear if the perception was based merely on "knowing" the instructor was there, or monitoring the messages sent out to the group.

But particularly encouraging were several messages expressing sentiments along these lines:

> A wonderful use of time management. A great way to drag people (kicking and screaming!) into the 21st Century.

So at the least, even the fall e-mail usage enhanced students' overall general education experience.

And the spring usage delivered more:

- the integration of another mode of learning—a writing to learn that is e-writing, not quite writing, but not quite speech either (Spooner and Yancey 1996) that many students seem comfortable with;

- an opportunity for a kind of communication that we don't usually see in large lecture classes, with chances to ask questions, where even the phrasing of the question is a learning act, a real writing-to-learn activity; and

- through the biochallenges, a chance for students to apply what they were learning, to connect it to everyday experience, and to link understanding with the processes through which we achieve understanding.

Recommendations

In some ways, the introduction of e-mail is no different than the introduction of any new course initiative: you have to be clear about why you want to do it, related assignments have to fit your agenda, and, if you want students to take you seriously, you have to assign credit to the assignments. But there are issues specific to e-mail, particularly as it relates to large classes. On the basis of our experiment, we'd like to offer some recommendations for its use in these settings:

- Start small; it's wiser to be less ambitious and experience limited success rather than be too ambitious and "fail."

- Factor in the techno-hassle time; unless you are unusually proficient and have abundant time, secure technical support.

- Develop a regular schedule for e-mail assignments so that students receive them early in the term and at regular intervals throughout. This creates a kind of expectation and routine that helps students, especially those not technically proficient, to enter into the system.

- Be ready to respond personally (and in a timely fashion) to e-mail messages—or else students will quickly believe that e-mail is just another black hole from which they're ignored.

Perhaps most important, and these are issues we are still contending with:

- We mentioned before a concern: time, time, and time. This concern is still alive. The model that we have outlined here is student-teacher, with some student-student interaction, and it is very teacher-labor-intensive. Both to reduce the time and to increase time students spend working with students, we are currently considering a two-model system: the first model would be the access model, used for disseminating information and providing another venue for administrative access; the second model would be comprised of multiple listservs where student groups would work together and present a single response to the group at large. One question we are pondering as we consider this change is the impact on student learning in switching to a group-based rather than individual-based list.

- It's important to include in any e-mail design reward/exigency/urgency. Students in our large general education classes won't participate in any activity if we don't assign some value to it, and this maxim is true for e-mail also. How we do assign value to the e-mail tasks—in terms of moving to e-mail that is not optional but required and integrated and in terms of how we assess student response without losing the benefits of e-writing to ask and to learn—is the second part of our next (bio)challenge.

Note

Techno-hassles comprised another category of concern. The first was focused on setting up a list, but a laboratory manager who knows computer systems inside-out took over that burden, among others—students not getting their e-mail, e-mail addresses being confused, the list not working properly, to name the incidents that happened the first three weeks of class. The second techno-hassle involved the students more directly: training them to use e-mail. Since there were too many students for a single instructor (even with the help of a lab manager) to train personally, we trained TAs to train the students in their laboratories (within the first two to three weeks). They explained the e-mail system while in their labs, sat with students while they logged on to e-mail, and provided written directions (which need to be clear and user-friendly). Although this training model worked fairly well, some students didn't catch on to the training. In some cases, it may have been poor training by the TAs; in other cases, the students were so techno-phobic that they were willing to let that part of the course go rather than face the computer.

Works Cited

Britton, James N., Tony Burgess, Nancy Martin, Alex McLeod, and Harold Rosen. 1975. *The Development of Writing Abilities (11–18)*. London: Macmillan Education.

Shulman, Lee. 1996. "Course Anatomy: The Dissection and Transformation of Knowledge." Plenary session speech given at the American Association of Higher Education Conference on Faculty Roles and Rewards. Atlanta.

Spooner, Michael, and Kathleen Yancey. 1996. "Postings on a Genre of Email." *College Composition and Communication* 47.2: 252–79.

19 Computer-Supported Collaboration in an Accounting Class

Carol F. Venable
San Diego State University

Gretchen N. Vik
San Diego State University

A communication course has been part of the accounting curriculum at San Diego State University since 1980. In 1995, we began teaching an expanded version of this course that includes more oral presentations and emphasis on small-group communication, reflecting changes in accounting education to emphasize critical thinking, interpersonal communication, and problem solving. In the late 1980s, the professional accounting community joined with educators nationwide to stimulate accounting education reform aimed at developing skills and abilities for a changing environment. As a result, the School of Accountancy at San Diego State University undertook a complete revision of its undergraduate upper division program. The culmination of this effort was the replacement of traditional accounting courses with three mandatory six-unit accounting courses, all team-taught; two accounting electives; and one expanded communication for accountants course.

San Diego State University is a large regional university with a nationally known business school. Our accounting graduates typically have a very high national pass rate on the annual Certified Public Accountant's (CPA) exam. Our accounting curriculum, revised to meet the Accounting Education Change Commission goals, now uses teams extensively both in and out of class to teach students problem-solving and interpersonal skills. One objective in revising our courses was to demonstrate the interrelated nature of various accounting subdisciplines. Another objective was to show how accountants are part of a larger, dynamic environment where they must anticipate, understand, and respond both orally and in writing to the information needs of a variety of constituencies. A third objective was to create a learning environment that included students as interactive participants. Computer conferencing is used in the re-engineered accounting curriculum for student/instructor questions and comments, homework problems, case discussions and write-ups, and working with other team members. Spreadsheet templates for projects that previously had been distributed by copying floppy disks are now stored on the server, and students can upload these to workstations.

This chapter discusses how the Reporting for Accountants four-unit course uses computer conferencing, collaborative learning, and team teaching to strengthen a formerly more traditional course. The three-unit course offered since 1980 required a number of papers and two presentations, but students had only one team project. Reports were written and revised; text material and cases were discussed in class after lectures on professional communication topics.

In the revised course, students receive more practice in team writing and presentations and write on some topics based on actual accounting practice, in addition to observing teamwork between instructors and using computer conferencing to exchange information. We recently changed the computer conference program but need to continuously evaluate new options as technology evolves. In the past, students tended to communicate on the conference only when required. We find, however, that more user-friendly systems encourage more and more varied online communications between students.

Internet Research

We use information searches extensively in company/industry reports. Students attend a lecture by a business librarian that demonstrates online Internet research and electronic library holdings research so they can access various sites, including Hoover's On-Line and EDGAR (Electronic Data Gathering Analysis and Retrieval), the Securities and Exchange Commission (SEC) electronic filing database. Students are also introduced to Lexis/Nexis (available only in the library itself to registered students), and various public company Web sites.

One important point we make to students is that financial information for SEC-registered corporations downloaded from the Internet from company, commercial, and government sources may not be identical, since the detailed requirements for format and disclosure in government filings do not apply to postings made by the company or by commercial organizations that evaluate and summarize financial information. In addition, hard-copy company annual reports sent to shareholders look very different because of color and illustrations as well as differences between detailed SEC filing requirements and less comprehensive annual report requirements.

Because many sources exist that are not available on Lexis/Nexis, students need to use the full range of services available in the school library rather than relying on just one. For the company/industry reports, we require that students use at least the annual report and the 10-K (annual SEC filing) plus other business press sources to give a picture of the company and its place in the industry it represents.

Computer-Supported Writing of Team Reports

Computer-aided writing helps students work collaboratively and makes the teacher a "learned coordinator" rather than a lecturer. Like Lanham (1990, xiv), we find that computer collaboration helps balance class contributions (people who may be silent in class can contribute anonymously via computer), gives students a chance to both create and analyze writing, and adds the ease of electronic text (easy changes, varied typography, cutting and pasting). Revising documents on a computer also helps students see writing as a process rather than just as an end product, recognized by Maxine Hairston as a paradigm shift in English composition classes (Kemp 1993, 161).

Boiarsky has compared classroom computer writing to collaboration among journalists in a newsroom, as long as students can make substantive comments on documents (1990, 59). The computer can be used to record team activity and comments so no member has to take notes of team meetings (Cyganowski 1990, 70). One idea that comes up often in the literature about computer classroom writing is that the teacher becomes a coach (Langston and Batson 1990, 147) rather than the rule maker.

Once our students learn the positive points of writing as a team activity, they resist reverting to the solitary model of writing that Handa fears (1990, 175). Even students writing drafts on their own computers can work on a final document as a team by cutting and pasting together, which is a great improvement over one person having to type a final copy of the paper for the group. An added computer-supported feature of many e-mail systems is the ability to attach files. Students can e-mail copies of their individual papers to one another for easy consolidation and editing. Revision via computer can also be faster and can teach students about the search function, for example, as Cyganowski mentions (1990, 82). We stress that technology can help writers but not produce good writing without careful use.

Accounting Topics for Team-Taught Writing

One area of improvement in the expanded course is that two people teach it nearly every day, a communication specialist and an accounting professor. Students have more "guided participation" and "shaping context" (Freedman 1995, 134) because the written and presentation assignments are, for the most part, on accounting topics.

Early semester assignments ask for library and Internet research on accounting and business frauds (some good recent company examples are Phar-Mor Corporation and Bausch and Lomb) or on funding of not-for-profit organizations. These reports are similar to ones written in many business communication courses and ask students to gather information and then discuss the implications of their research for a professional audience. Another successful team topic is business dress codes. Students are interested in how the real business world operates and enjoy finding out how the new relaxed dress codes, such as casual Fridays, fit into professional accounting firms. The real test of accounting student writing is whether it can both convey the facts (usually easy for our students) and do so in a way useful to a specific audience (often a difficult task). In the following short examples of facts put to use for an audience, note how the tone and emphasis show a good grasp of audience analysis. The amount of detailed factual information given (here edited for space) varied depending on audience needs.

- With our search for a computer system in mind, I found an article in *Business Week* that describes a system fitting our specific needs. Since we are a small company, finding a system within our budget, user-friendly, and with working software has proven difficult. According to Stephen Wildstrom, most dealers would rather sell their products to large companies. However, Hewlett Packard now has a computer product line directed at small businesses.

  The Hewlett Packard Vectra 515MX comes equipped with Microsoft Office—a program that we all know how to use. The system also manages voice mail and comes with its own audio system and headset for hands-free use. . . . Hands-free headsets would also permit us to search for information in the computer more easily while conversing with a customer. . . . This sounds like a good deal to me. Let me know what you think.

- The enclosed article highlights some of the changes we can expect over the next few months. Other than the migration of our financial data from our old accounting systems to STARS-FL, we have not felt the full impact of the 1990 CFO Act and other recent initiatives, such as the 1993 Government Performance and Results Act (GPRA) and the 1994 Federal Financial Management Act. This is likely to change beginning in fiscal year 1997. How we manage this change is of upmost importance. . . .

  Plan of Action and Milestones
  We need to take action now to ensure that our employees are ready to meet the challenges presented by these coming changes. Upon your approval, I will formulate a plan of action and milestones to train our staff members for their new roles in the government financial management world.

- To increase the company's sales, profits, and market share, we should implement a travel policy similar to the ones recently implemented by Charles Schwab and Grubb and Ellis, who are now allowing their employees to spend a little more money and be more comfortable, thus raising morale.

These employees are allowed to rent bigger cars than compacts, stay in hotels with computer hook-ups and comfortable conference rooms for client meetings, and fly business class while keeping the frequent flier miles for themselves.

Later assignments include payroll workpapers and company/industry business risk analysis. Integrating technical material from real-world exercises allows students to see the course as an integral part of their accounting program. We agree with Freedman that "writing can be more effectively taught in ways that supplement what is going on in the disciplinary classes" (1995, 140) and are developing more assignments that tie in with the six-unit accounting courses where feasible. A company-industry report is an excellent way to have students research and write an individual report and then build on that assignment by continuing to research the same industry segment in a team project. The four team projects give students a number of chances to read others' work and comment on it, and our new technology classroom will make this even easier as students can edit work during class.

In an effort to provide students with enough writing and speaking practice and keep the grading load from becoming too large as class size approaches sixty, we are using a combination of individual and team assignments. We are still meeting our goals of improving student writing and having students write to different audiences, but we are doing this by having students critique each other's work, and requiring students to tolerate more ambiguity in their assignments.

Grading of collaborative writing is an important pedagogical issue. Enough assignments are graded individually so that we can confidently judge student work. In-class (controlled writing) communication case exams are one important segment of the final grade in the class, since the class is a graduation writing requirement mandated by the California State University system. Peer review of writing as students work in teams is a valuable tool, as students learn a great deal from seeing how others handled the same or similar communication problems.

Mentored Online Seminar

Several of our accounting courses require online activity to help students get through the course readings and to summarize/critique current professional publications. Often used in distance learning, the online activity ensures that students are doing the required reading by having part of the class requirement to respond to open-ended questions posed on a conference or list server. Students can be required to respond a minimum number of times weekly to discussion threads covering some of the course objectives. The instructor monitors the discussion to make sure that course objectives are fulfilled. "This format presupposes that motivated students with access to information sources and who are capable of interacting in a community of scholars are capable of educating themselves on the course content" (Albrecktson 1995, 103).

In our accounting communication course students initially learn how to write summaries of technical material. Later, in an advanced course, they are required to critique authors' assumptions and conclusions. Other students respond to the critiques and a dialogue ensues on the issues. Each student must, at a minimum, post during the semester one summary/critique and two replies to other student postings. Building in reactions to the reading is important, because less class time is available to discuss readings now that a lot of time is used for small-group interaction to teach team-building and leadership skills in the accounting courses. The following excerpts from a discussion of Martin Feldstein's "Time to Privatize Social Security," *Wall Street Journal*, March 8, 1996, shows typical interaction. Student 1 (Patricia) summarizes and critiques a current article. Note the more personal "voice" in the critiques and the comments that follow. All comments were edited for brevity—people tend to write at length on the computer.

> Mr. Feldstein illustrates that the current Social Security system cannot sustain the growing number of retirees past the year 2020 unless the system is seriously revamped. The U.S. Advisory Council on Social Security has suggested that shifting to a funded program with individual retirement accounts or 401(k) plans would permit employees to earn a higher rate of return if invested in stocks and bonds. (the summary was two screens long and detailed methods of saving the Social Security system)
>
> I thought that this was a very enlightening article. Most of us at some point have thought that Social Security benefits would probably not exist by the time we retire, so we know that we have to look into other means for saving for retirement. Many view this tax as our obligation to support the retirees of today, our grandparents and parents, despite the fact that we may never reap any benefits when we retire. I think that this is a valid point, but if we can do the job with private investments, why not? My only concern is the fluctuation of stock and bond prices. Will the U.S. Government back these investments? I would definitely like to know more about this proposal and to see this plan or something similar become effective.
>
> *Student 2* (Deborah): Is this good for all? Patricia, I found your article summary to be really interesting. The Social Security debate is a hot issue for most Americans, especially older voters. I often wonder if the money I pay in for Social Security will ever benefit me. However, the proposal for self-saving does not seem to be the most favorable answer for everyone. I agree that responsible individuals will benefit from the proposal because they will have more money after each paycheck, and if they save properly, more money in the future for less cost. . . . Not everyone will save for the future, so then what will the government do? . . . I do know that an alternative to Social Security is needed sooner than we think, but Feldstein's pro-

posal seems too easy to me, and it does not take into account all those individuals involved.

Student 3 (Jennifer): no title. I think that what Debbie said is true; people generally will not do what is best for themselves, with regard to saving for the future, and similarly to the welfare situation, taxpayers have to step in and foot the bills. . . . Education seems to be the best hope for offsetting future bills, by providing information to employees about what is needed for their retirement living.

Student 4 (Eric): Social Security Rip-Off. The Social Security system is not giving the young people of our country a fair shake. Those receiving benefits now are getting out much more than they contributed. The politicians will simply raise the rates on us again to prevent the system from going bankrupt unless some changes to the system are made. . . . I think that this proposal has merit but as with anything else it must be implemented properly to insure that the risk level of invested funds is not too high and that another bloated wasteful bureaucracy is not created.

Student 5 (Shuang): People Need to be Responsible. Good intentions may not always produce good results. I agree with Debby and Jennifer that education will help employees to understand the importance of saving. . . . Why do Asian countries have a high rate of saving? Because in these countries, people tend to rely on themselves and their families, not their government. . . . I am all for taking care of our elderly, but the system really needs to be restructured.

Student 6 (Cindy): One Solution to the SS Problem. I agree with the frustration that those currently on SS benefits are receiving more than they put in. But we can't just put them out on the streets! People like my Mom put in an honest life's work knowing that SS would be there when they retired. We need to consider benefits for someone at home raising kids, so if divorce occurs, the non-working spouse has some money to fall back on in an IRA or other savings plan.

Shuang: In Reply to Cindy. Oops! I didn't mean to step on your toes, Cindy! I am absolutely in favor of helping those in need. The point that I made was that no matter what is out there, we are the only people who can help ourselves.

Student 7 (Chaomei): Privatize Social Security? Patricia, interesting thoughts. It seems to me that for the benefit of new job opportunities alone, this is a very attractive proposal. We can certainly make a far better rate of return than the 2.5% current rate of return on Social Security. As you said, investing in stocks and bonds will earn 8-9% on average, even if the market price fluctuates over the years. An increased Social Security tax rate will, however, have a detrimental effect on the economy.

Patricia: Reply to Chaomei. Chaomei, I think privatization would be a good thing as long as each individual can choose which funds in which to invest their money, so each individual is responsible for choosing good long-term investments rather than risky funds. . . . I still think there should be some sort of Social Security system because you cannot be sure that everyone will invest.

> *Student 8* (Susan): SS and Medicare Abuses. Patricia—I cannot help but add another angle to your article ideas. If the current system were revamped to a needs-based calculation, it might become a more fair and stable system. . . . A note on Medicare—the abuses of this system are probably beyond what we can fathom. . . . Unfortunately, a system run by the government is wide open for abuses.

Students learn to summarize for the initial part of the assignment and then are able to discuss the article online. As this discussion illustrates, students' comments are based on both personal opinion and on their knowledge of how investments and savings grow and how alternative retirement plans work.

Through team teaching and collaborative classroom pedagogy, assignments are designed to incorporate changing technical areas in the field, as well as the move by the Big Six public accounting firms to specialize in industry groups, a move addressed by our company/industry reports. We have also added more material on team work and on critical thinking.

Sample Assignments

Summaries of Published Professional Articles

One assignment has students research, write, and turn in a typed memo summarizing a professional article for an accounting audience, for example, the accounting staff members in a controller's office or public accounting firm. The article summarized must be from a professional publication dated within the last few months and must be of interest to both accountants and their clients (for public accounting) or managers (internal accounting). Each summary is graded as part of an individual's grade.

Meeting in teams, students read each others' summaries and discuss any points that are unclear. They then choose one of the team member's summaries and revise it for a different audience (either clients or non-accountant managers within a firm). This revised team-written summary is then posted on the computer conferencing system, and the team prepares a presentation for the class. All students read all the summaries and prepare for a day of oral presentations designed to occur in an office environment. After reading the posted summary, the other class members are required to prepare written questions that a client might ask. These are handed in and are part of an individual's grade. Teams present their summaries and field questions from other class members. The pre-class conference posting and the prepared questions encourage active participation in class and promote the development of communication skills.

Documentation of Personal History

A more traditional assignment in business writing classes is preparing a resume. In our class, students write a biographical sketch the first day of class explaining what job they would prefer if for some reason they had to change from actual accounting practice. After discussing this sketch in pairs, they use it to introduce each other to the class. Then they post a short biography on the computer conference that is used for later class discussion on the creation and use of business biographies or resumes. For the last step, they write their resume, which is peer-reviewed in draft form by members of the student's team and the instructors and then rewritten for a grade.

Company/Industry Report Assignment Integrating Accounting

A major late-semester project involves individual analyses of companies (chosen by the instructors from industry groupings used by the Big Six public accounting firms) followed by team analysis of the industry group. As discussed in the Internet Research section, students need to find out from print and electronic sources what the company does, how well it does compared to competitors, its financial strength, management and operating characteristics, risks, stock and industry trends, future prospects, and so on. Keeping both the individual company and the team industry reports under three pages each while giving a professional reader a full picture of the company is a very good assignment, because it makes students sort and synthesize information, evaluate sources (and cite them correctly), plan helpful graphic attachments, and analyze and explain what they know rather than just list facts.

Potential industry groupings used by the Big Six accounting firms include financial services, health services, entertainment and media, government and not-for-profit, retail merchandising, computers and software, and communications. Using different subgroups and different companies gives the company/industry assignment a different flavor every term (and encourages students to produce new work). For example, one semester we might use banks as a financial services segment and another semester use credit card companies or automobile credit companies. Entertainment has segments such as theme parks, recreational equipment, television cable companies, and golf club manufacturers.

In addition to teaching business research skills (among more traditional sources, students use the SEC electronic filing Web site), this assignment integrates accounting course information into the communication course, reinforces teamwork skills, and gives students real-world experience in preparing information for business audiences. Report writing, document design, graphics development, and other communication topics become more relevant to students when they apply this material to accounting topics.

Computer-supported communication skills that students learn include the use of presentation and spreadsheet programs to depict complex financial data in a form that non-accountants can readily understand.

Interviewing Skills and Systems Documentation

One team project has students plan an interview, visit a local firm, and interview the firm about its payroll process. Students must prepare accounting workpapers to document the payroll process through computerized flowcharts, written narratives, and other formats such as tables. Students must assess the strengths and weaknesses of the internal controls and processes.

Communication skills learned include computerized graphics used in team presentations similar to those used by a professional accounting firm doing a presentation to a client. Students learn how to import helpful graphics to add value to their reports, such as producing a slide from an existing spreadsheet or adding a product photograph to a slide or report. The excellent team presentations on this payroll project have covered local companies of all sizes from three to three thousand employees.

Typical semester assignments include computer conference posting of short biographies, team memos, and reports on accounting issues such as fraud auditors; oral interviews and presentations with visuals; and observations of businesses and evaluation of the workplace. Because the course is not lecture-based, a handout (see Appendix) shows students where to find more information on important professional communication topics.

Innovative Classroom Aspects

In addition to using computerized feedback on papers, we are using computer conferencing, e-mail, peer editing, computer presentation packages, and Internet research using Web sites to access various financial and accounting material. A new "smart" classroom containing team computers connected to the Internet for in-class research will also help with team editing and teaching teamwork. This will come close to the newsroom environment Boiarsky writes about (1990, 47–67).

The computer-communication supported Reporting for Accountants course is now an even more integral part of the revised accounting curriculum. Team teaching by Information/Decision Systems and Accounting faculty encourages technology use and allows for more cross-discipline topics for real-world writing assignments. In addition, team teaching may provide useful role models for building students' team skills in preparation for jobs in the contemporary accounting workplace.

Works Cited

Albrecktson, J. Raymond. 1995. "Mentored On-Line Seminar: A Model for Graduate-Level Distance Learning." *T.H.E. Journal* 22.3: 102–5.

Barker, Thomas T., and Fred O. Kemp. 1990. "Network Theory: A Postmodern Pedagogy for the Writing Classroom." In *Computers and Community: Teaching Composition in the Twenty-First Century,* edited by Carolyn Handa, 1–28. Portsmouth, NH: Boynton/Cook.

Boiarsky, Carolyn. 1990. "Computers in the Classroom: The Instruction, the Mess, the Noise, the Writing." In *Computers and Community: Teaching Composition in the Twenty-First Century,* edited by Carolyn Handa, 47–68. Portsmouth, NH: Boynton/Cook.

Cyganowski, Carol Klimick. 1990. "The Computer Classroom and Collaborative Learning: The Impact on Student Writers." In *Computers and Community: Teaching Composition in the Twenty-First Century,* edited by Carolyn Handa, 68–89. Portsmouth, NH: Boynton/Cook.

Feldstein, Martin. 1996. "Time to Privatize Social Security." *Wall Street Journal,* 8 March, Eastern edition.

Freedman, Aviva. 1995. "The What, Where, When, Why and How of Classroom Genres." In *Reconceiving Writing, Rethinking Writing Instruction*, edited by Joseph Petraglia, 121–45. Mahwah, NJ: Lawrence Erlbaum.

Handa, Carolyn. 1990. "Politics, Ideology, and the Strange, Slow Death of the Isolated Composer or Why We Need Community in the Writing Classroom." In *Computers and Community: Teaching Composition in the Twenty-First Century,* edited by Carolyn Handa, 160–85. Portsmouth, NH: Boynton/Cook.

Hirsch, Maurice L. Jr., Rob Anderson, and Susan Gabriel. 1994. *Accounting and Communication.* Cincinnati, OH: SouthWestern Publishing.

Kemp, Fred. 1993. "The Origins of ENFI, Network Theory, and Computer-Based Collaborative Writing Instruction at the University of Texas." In *Network-Based Classrooms: Promises and Realities,* edited by B. Bruce, J. K. Payton, and Trent Batson, 161–81. Cambridge: Cambridge University Press.

Langston, M. Diane, and Trent W. Batson. 1990. "The Social Shifts Invited by Working Collaboratively on Computer Networks: The ENFI Project." In *Computers and Community: Teaching Composition in the Twenty-First Century,* edited by Carolyn Handa, 140–60. Portsmouth, NH: Boynton/Cook.

Lanham, Richard A. 1990. Foreword to *Computers and Community: Teaching Composition in the Twenty-First Century,* edited by Carolyn Handa, xiii–xvii. Portsmouth, NH: Boynton/Cook.

North, Alexa B., Joan Hubbard, and Jack E. Johnson. 1996. "Inquiry-Based Learning via the Internet." *Business Education Forum* 50.4: 47–50.

Vik, Gretchen N., and Jeannette Wortman Gilsdorf. 1994. *Business Communication.* Homewood, IL: Richard D. Irwin.

Wilson, Gerald L. 1996. *Groups in Context: Leadership and Participation in Small Groups,* 4th ed. New York: McGraw-Hill.

Appendix: References on Selected Communication and Teamwork Topics

Audience Analysis

Hirsch, Maurice L. Jr., Rob Anderson, and Susan Gabriel. 1994. *Accounting and Communication.* Cincinnati, OH: South-Western Publishing: 37–49.

Vik, Gretchen N., and Jeannette W. Gilsdorf. 1994. *Business Communication.* Burr Ridge, IL: Richard D. Irwin: 5–10.

Basics of Business Communication

Hirsch 17–37.

Vik and Gilsdorf 3–30.

Documentation and Evaluation of Sources

Hirsch 65.

Vik and Gilsdorf 592–602 (briefly covers differences among MLA, APA, and University of Chicago styles), 129–49.

Graphics

Hirsch 66–72, 105–108, 124.

Vik and Gilsdorf Chapter 7.

Intercultural Communication

Chaney, Lillian H., and Jeanette S. Martin. 1995. *Intercultural Business Communication.* Englewood Cliffs, NJ: Prentice-Hall Career and Technology.

Varner, Iris, and Linda Beamer. 1995. *Intercultural Communication in the Global Workplace.* Chicago, IL: Richard D. Irwin.

Victor, David A. 1992. *International Business Communication.* New York: HarperCollins Publishers.

Leadership

Wilson, Gerald L. 1996. *Groups in Context: Leadership and Participation in Small Groups,* 4th ed. New York: McGraw-Hill, Inc.: Chapters 8, 9, and 10.

Listening and Nonverbal Communication

Vik and Gilsdorf 465–86.

Wilson Chapter 6.

Professional Writing Techniques (includes emphasis techniques)

Hirsch Chapters 4 and 5.

McClaran, Jeanne L., and Judy Stopke. 1988. *Do's and Don'ts of Desktop Publishing Design,* 2nd ed. Ann Arbor, MI: Promotional Perspectives.

Vik and Gilsdorf Chapters 2, 3, and 4.

Williams, Robin. 1992. *The PC Is Not a Typewriter: A Style Manual for Creating Professional-Level Type on Your Personal Computer.* Berkeley, CA: Peachpit Press.

Proposals

Clark, Thomas D. 1994. *Power Communication: Plan, Organize, Write, Edit, Revise.* Cincinnati, OH; South-Western Publishing: 247–50.

Vik and Gilsdorf 102–28.

Resumes

Vik and Gilsdorf: 386–409.

Revision and Editing

Hirsch Chapter 6.

Huckin, Thomas N., and Leslie A. Olsen. 1991. *Technical Writing and Professional Communication for Nonnative Speakers of English,* 2nd ed. New York: McGraw Hill, Inc. Chapters 28–37. Appendix A.

A Nit-Picker's Guide to Proofreading: How-to Procedures, Tips, and Cautions. Ann Arbor, MI: Promotional Perspectives.

Vik and Gilsdorf Chapter 3, Appendix B.

(An office handbook such as Clark, James L., and Lyn R. Clark. 1994. *A Handbook for Business Professionals.* Belmont, CA: Wadsworth Publishing Company, could also be helpful.)

Small Group Communication

Wilson Chapters 2–5.

Summaries

Hirsch: 62–65.

20 Electronic Tools to Redesign a Marketing Course

Randall S. Hansen
Stetson University

This chapter presents reasons from the business community why communications skills are vital, historical information about the WAC movement, and suggestions for ways instructors can combine writing projects with newer technologies, such as e-mail and the Internet. The end result is a revamped marketing course that satisfies basic core content competencies while also incorporating electronic writing assignments that produce advanced thinking and communication skills employers seek of college graduates.

Introduction

The importance of good communications skills for success in business—and in marketing in particular—is recognized as an important asset for anyone who hopes to succeed in a business career (e.g., Collins 1982; DiSalvo 1980; Latimer 1982; Meister and Reinsch 1978; Myers 1991; Wolvin 1984). Indeed, Brownell (1987) suggests that effective communication is essential to effective management. However, the lack of good communications skills by entry-level college graduates and employees is frequently mentioned by businesspeople and educators as a serious problem in business (e.g., Aby, Barr, and Sterrett 1991; Chonko and Caballero 1991; Hahn and Mohrman 1985). Part of this increasing awareness, according to Dingle (1989), is the decline in the quality of writing in schools and the workplace as perceived by educators and the media. Another reason is pure economics: unclear writing in the business profession is expensive. Unclear writing costs American businesses in excess of an estimated one billion dollars annually (Dingle 1989). Furthermore, Waxler (1987) argues that "writing is central to the creation of meaning in the business world" (42).

Poor writing is not the only complaint business leaders levy at business school graduates. Other complaints include the following:

- business graduates do not perform adequately in the areas of oral and written communication;

255

- business school curricula are too "tools-oriented" as the expense of qualitative thinking;
- business school graduates cannot tolerate ambiguity and bring order out of seeming confusion;
- business school graduates do not know how to recognize common themes in business situations;
- business school graduates have not learned how to see the relationships among things that seem very different;
- business school graduates are not capable of the type of thinking that comes from the many ways to look at the world. (Chonko and Caballero 1991)

Further, in a study of chief executive officers (CEOs) of 200 of the largest U.S. corporations and deans from 200 business schools, two of the five key learning areas considered to be most important for graduating business students included oral and written communication skills and the ability to think, to analyze, and to make decisions (Harper 1987).

The need for business school graduates—for marketing graduates—to have strong written and oral communications skills as well as the ability to analyze and synthesize is increasingly apparent. In fact, Chonko (1993) suggests that developing critical-thinking and strong communications skills should be two objectives for business school education. How can this be accomplished? Business schools can instill a communication-across-the-curriculum (CAC) mentality, particularly in marketing departments.

Writing Across the Curriculum

A great deal has been written about the broad and growing influence the WAC movement has had in American higher education over the past twenty years (see, for example, Russell 1991). The WAC literature suggests that writing plays a powerful role in the production, as well as presentation, of knowledge, and that writing is a tool that enables people in every discipline to wrestle with facts and ideas (Zinsser 1988).

Wolfe and Pope (1985) propose that writing is an important way of realizing, clarifying, defining, reflecting, imagining, inventing, inquiring, organizing, interpreting, discovering, decision-making, problem-solving, and evaluating—in short, an important part of thinking and learning. Knoblauch and Brannon (1983) reinforce the use of writing in all courses when they state,

> Presumably what every classroom seeks to nurture is intellectual conversation, leading to enhanced powers of discernment. Since writing enables both learning and conversation, manifesting and enlarging the capacity to discover connections, it should be a resource that all teachers in all disciplines can rely on to achieve their purposes. (473)

Electronic Delivery of Information

For many companies, electronic delivery of information has become the prominent communications system (Hawkins 1990)—mainly because it addresses a
real problem facing large organizations: how to operate in multiple locations
and still achieve timely and cost-effective interpersonal communication
(Crawford 1982). These organizations have discovered that e-mail offers five
essential advantages over traditional communication modes: (1) an overall cost
reduction; (2) reduced paper handling; (3) faster communications; (4) improved
communication effectiveness; and (5) integration of data communication with
records management (D'Souza 1991).

Furthermore, educators describe electronic communications as a combination of skills: verbal and written functions, critical thinking, and computer and
telecommunications (Hansen 1994). Including electronic communications in
content area courses such as marketing actually can make teaching more effective.

Redesigning an Introductory Marketing Course

The typical introductory marketing course focuses on introducing students to
the marketing discipline and marketing terminology. To facilitate these objectives (and often large class sizes), most of these marketing courses require objective tests and quizzes. Some instructors will incorporate a term paper or project
(usually due at the end of the term) or case studies.

The redesigned marketing course is based on writing assignments that em-
body the following assumptions: (1) writing is a critical process of thinking and
learning; (2) students become empowered by building thinking and analytical
skills through writing; (3) not all student writing must be read and evaluated by
the instructor; (4) students may and should help each other in writing assignments through the use of peer reviews; and (5) some student writing is for the
writer alone, whereas other writing is intended for sharing (Coker and Scarboro
1990).

The redesigned marketing course is also based on the following assumptions
about electronic communication: (1) it offers students speed in communicating
ideas; (2) it provides a forum for feedback of ideas and interests; (3) it provides
a "safe" place for shy students to express their opinions and ideas; and (4) it
offers students the opportunity to experience and partake in communication
with people different from themselves.

The redesigned marketing course includes a number of different writing
projects that occur electronically, including participation in a "local" marketing
discussion group, an Internet electronic discussion group (listserv), and case

write-ups and reaction papers, as well as others described below. Specific guidelines for the Marketing Discussion Group can also be found below. The revamped marketing course takes a great deal more preparation on the part of the instructor, but the results make it well worth the effort.

Possible Electronic Communications Assignments

- Local Marketing Discussion Group. Moderated by the professor and teaching assistant. Purpose is to stimulate discussion and learning of marketing-related issues.
    —minimum of one entry per week
    —maximum of five entries per week
- Case Write-ups/Reactions. Groups of students (sometimes working with students from other universities via the Internet) analyze and write a case analysis. The case can then be forwarded to another group of students for reaction analysis.
    —utilize local e-mail or Internet for group discussions
    —case analysis and reaction can both be used in marketing discussion group
    —use of Internet is encouraged for case research
- Country Project. Individual project that involves student becoming an expert on a particular country, then developing a product/service to market in that country.
    —utilize Internet/Web for country background and research
    —utilize marketing discussion group (or e-mail to professor) to test ideas
    —abstract and outline e-mailed and peer-reviewed via e-mail
- Internet Discussion Groups. Students are required to join three Internet discussion groups, with at least one being marketing-related. Many join Market-L, the oldest and most respected of marketing-related electronic discussion lists.
- Electronic Journal. Weekly journal entries are sent to professor's e-mail account. Some assignments are assigned (formal), but most are writer's option (informal).
- Study Guides. Students work in groups electronically preparing chapter study guides. Group then electronically submits one version to professor's account.
- Chapter Reviews. Similar to study guides, class members work in electronic groups developing chapter reviews, with one version sent to professor's account.

- Market Research. Students are responsible for finding information on the World Wide Web (using browser software such as Netscape or Microsoft Explorer) on a particular subject. Students have found the best search engines to be Infoseek, Lycos, and Magellan. More information can be found in the forthcoming book by Hansen and Hansen, *Write Your Way to a High GPA*.

- Web Homepage. Students design and create their own Web homepages, with a clear understanding of the marketing/advertising value of the Web. Students design their pages through HTML coding or specialized software, such as HTML Assistant Pro Lite.

The Marketing Discussion Group

Point Value: 100

Rationale: To summarize, to argue, to take issue with, to respond, to relate, to contemplate, and to question issues dealing with marketing and you.

Requirements: Starting as soon as you get an e-mail account, you will be placed into a local (Stetson) marketing discussion group. The dialogue in this group will be moderated by the professor, but the goal is unlimited marketing discussion.

Several specific topics will be discussed, but beyond those assigned by the instructor, you are on your own to discuss anything at all.

Many of the specific topics raised in the discussion group will pertain to the class. These topics will be assigned weekly, but include such possibilities as:

1. Reactions to chapter readings;
2. Discussions of trends/current events in marketing;
3. Responses to ethical issues/discussions;
4. Brainstorming ideas for term paper;
5. Developing marketing vocabulary;
6. Creating press releases and advertisements;
7. Writing memos and letters;
8. Preparing individual work for group projects;
9. Gender issues in marketing.

You must be prepared to log on to the discussion group at least once a day so that you can monitor current debate/discussion.

Grading: Grading will be done according to the extent to which you actively participate in the discussion group.

Evaluation of Electronic Communications

After using e-mail in a principles of marketing class for several semesters, students' overall evaluation is positive. To a high degree, students accept using electronic communications; students tend to be more enthusiastic about the course; students have a clearer understanding of different forms of writing; students often complete assignments before deadlines when a project is being submitted electronically; and initial comparisons with prior classes where electronic communications were not used show that grades are generally higher in the redesigned classes. On the negative side, there is still some degree of computer phobia among students not familiar with computer or electronic communications; there is the problem of access and availability of computers; there is the potential of technical support problems, depending upon the quality of the school's computer services department; and there is a new set of technical excuses relating to why assignments are not completed by due dates.

Results from student evaluations specifically about the use of electronic communications in a marketing class can be found in the Appendix.

Conclusions

While the results are preliminary, they speak for themselves. Incorporating electronic writing into a WAC-redesigned marketing course achieves all goals and expectations. The use of writing— electronic writing—improves analytical and critical-thinking skills, betters problem-solving abilities, and strengthens communications and technical abilities. These results are shown through the quality of discussion, higher grades, and a deepened interest and understanding of the subject.

There are, however, some downsides for teachers who use this type of CAC approach. First, there is a greater amount of time spent before the class begins preparing for many of the electronic assignments. Second, more technological knowledge is needed by the teacher—and by the students—and often spills over into classroom discussion. Third, no matter how good the system, there will be technology-related snafus. Fourth, there are new technology-related excuses from students, such as power surges destroying files on floppy disks. Finally, the teacher is much more dependent on an outside group—the school's information technology/academic computing department.

Still, educators have an obligation to both students and employers to develop essential skills, including communications and technological skills. The rewards for students are a better understanding or course content and a higher value in the job marketplace. The rewards for faculty using the communication-across-the-curriculum techniques described in this chapter are intrinsic: more successful and more satisfying teaching.

Note

More specific information about what the final redesigned courses look like can be found on Randall Hansen's Web site: http://www.stetson.edu/~hansen/courses.html.

Works Cited

Aby, Carroll D. Jr., Saul Z. Barr, and Jack H. Sterrett. 1991. "Do Business Schools Prepare or Placate Students?" *Business Forum* 16 (Fall): 6–9.

Brownell, J. 1987. "Communications in the Business Curriculum." *The Cornell HRA Quarterly* (August:) 56–59.

Chonko, Lawrence B. 1993. "Business School Education: Some Thoughts and Recommendations." *Marketing Education Review* 3.1: 1–9.

Chonko, Lawrence B., and Marjorie J. Caballero. 1991. "Marketing Madness, or How Marketing Departments Think They're in Two Places at Once When They're Not Anywhere at All (According to Some)." *Journal of Marketing Education* 13.1 (Spring): 14–25.

Coker, Frances H., and Allen Scarboro. 1990. "Writing to Learn in Upper-Division Sociology Courses: Two Case Studies." *Teaching Sociology* 18 (April): 218–22.

Collins, Bertha B. 1982. "Are You a Listener?" *Journal of Business Education* 58.3: 102–103.

Crawford, Albert B. Jr. 1982. "Corporate Electronic Mail: A Communications-Intensive Application Technology." *MIS Quarterly* 6 (September): 1–13.

Dingle, Doris D. 1989. "Two Alien Tasks: Writing and Writing in a Certain Way." *Business Education Forum* 43.5: 3–5.

DiSalvo, Vincent S. 1980. "A Summary of Current Research Identifying Communication Skills in Various Organizational Contexts." *Communication Education* 29 (July): 283–90.

D'Souza, Patricia Veasey. 1991. "The Use of Electronic Mail as an Instructional Aid: An Exploratory Study." *Journal of Computer-Based Instruction* 18.3: 106–10.

Gaedeke, R. M., and D. H. Tootelian. 1989. "Employees Rate Enthusiasm and Communication as Top Job Skills." *Marketing News* (27 March): 14.

Hahn, R., and K. M. Mohrman. 1985. "What Do Managers Need to Know?" *AAHE Bulletin* 37.2: 3–6+.

Hansen, Randall S. 1994. "Using the Internet in Marketing Classes." *Marketing Educator* 13.4: 3, 11.

Hansen, Randall S., and K. S. Hansen. Forthcoming. *Write Your Way to a High GPA.* Berkeley, CA: Ten Speed Press.

Harper, Stephen C. 1987. "Business Education: A View from the Top." *Business Forum* (Summer): 24–27.

Hawkins, Donald T. 1990. "Information Delivery—Paper and E-mail." *ONLINE* 14.2: 100–103.

"How Businesses Search for Qualified Candidates: Trying to Bridge the Skills Gap." 1992. *Measurements, a Supplement to the June 1992 Personnel Journal*: 102.

Knoblauch, C. H., and Lil Brannon. 1983. "Writing as Learning Through the Curriculum." *College English* 45.5: 465–74.

Latimer, M. 1982. "If I'm Smarter than Joe, Why Didn't I Get the Promotion?" *Supervision* 44: 5–7.

Meister, Janis E., and N. L. Reinsch Jr. 1978. "Communication Training in Manufacturing Firms." *Communication Education* 27: 235–44.

Myers, W. S. 1991. "10 Steps to Good Writing." *Women in Business* 43.4: 18–20+.

Russell, David R. 1991. *Writing in the Academic Disciplines, 1870–1990.* Carbondale: Southern Illinois University Press.

Waxler, Robert P. 1987. "On Process." *Journal of Business Communications* 24 (Winter): 41–42.

Wolfe, D., and C. Pope. 1985. "Developing Thinking Processes: Ten Writing-for-Learning Tasks Throughout the Curriculum." *Virginia English Bulletin* 35.1: 11–17.

Wolvin, Andrew D. 1984. "Meeting the Communication Needs of the Adult Learner." *Communication Education* 33: 267–71.

Zinsser, William. 1988. *Writing to Learn.* New York: Harper and Row.

Appendix: Electronic Communications Evaluations

I. Quantitative Results
   (Seven-point scale, where 7=strongly agree, 4=neutral, and 1=strongly disagree)

Evaluative Statement	Mean	Std. Dev.
1. I found the overall process helped me learn more material about the class.	5.48	1.37
2. I found the process a convenient and efficient method to do assignments.	5.95	1.09
3. I would prefer to do assignments on e-mail rather than more traditional ways.	5.14	1.42
4. I would have preferred more tests than the e-mail case analyses.	2.38	1.84
5. I believe participating and using e-mail will be beneficial to me as an employment skill.	6.19	0.91
6. Overall, I found the e-mail exercises to be useful.	5.81	1.05

II. Qualitative Results

(Verbatim)
1. The biggest benefit of using e-mail in this class was:
    - Instant communication with instructor and other class members.
    - The easy availability and quick transfer of information which it allowed for.
    - Expressing ideas and mailing (communicating) faster.
    - I like the convenience. E-mail is an effective way to do the assignment.
    - The information that was available on a daily basis. I felt it was a good way to keep on top of things.
    - Not having to print out papers—just push a button and it was sent to the instructor.
    - The biggest benefit of using e-mail in this class was the convenience it provided for both the student and the professor.
    - Communication of the whole class, yet no nervousness about it. The e-mail system allows everyone to view their opinions about the cases and class.

2. The biggest problem of using e-mail in this class was:
    - The fact that it does not work in the same manner as a normal word processing program.
    - Trying to work around the computer lab hours, especially on weekends.
    - The fact that you cannot save it, go back to it, or edit the line above.
    - If you don't check your mail often, you lose out on things, fall behind.

21 Network Discussions for Teaching Western Civilization

Maryanne Felter
Cayuga Community College

Daniel F. Schultz
Cayuga Community College

Background

If literacy is, as Charles Schuster (1990) has said, "the power to be able to make oneself heard and felt, to signify . . . the way in which we make ourselves meaningful not only to others but through others to ourselves" (227), then literacy is not simply a matter of learning to read and write. It is, in fact, a complex process of communication that cuts across all disciplines in the academy and, as such, should be a primary focus of all courses, not just those which focus on rhetoric and composition. Collaboration between disciplines, especially between members of English departments and members of departments where the teaching of composition has not traditionally been a focus, should be fostered and encouraged in an attempt to spark innovation, creativity, and flexibility as well as to improve productivity and assessable outcomes. Our Western Civilization project is an attempt at such cross-curricular broadening of scope. We have designed a course that uses computers to support the concepts of collaborative learning and writing to learn, methods by which our students can, using technology already available on campus, develop literacy skills. We used three technological "tools" to help us implement our writing across the curriculum ideas: networked discussion sessions, e-mail, and Internet access. Before we focus on goals, we need to discuss at least two institutional barriers to setting up and implementing communication-across-the-curriculum projects such as ours: students' limited access to technology and the relatively inflexible structure of community colleges.

Studies indicate that the use of technology has far-reaching social implications, the impact of which is apparent at public institutions, particularly community colleges, whose students are typically technologically disenfranchised (Forman 1994, 133). The community college is the only place where many disadvantaged students can access the current technologies. The political, socioeconomic, and cultural implications of this are enormous: we are witnessing the development of a "war between the 'techno/crats' and the 'techno/peasants'" (Selfe 1990, 97). And as professionals committed to the mission of the community college, we must foster, across the curriculum, student access to the technologies they will need to compete in the marketplace of the 21st century.

Such a project requires college-wide commitment to writing across the curriculum with appropriate funding that provides both time and access to equipment. In community colleges, which claim to be teaching institutions, the structure of the college itself often works against creative pedagogy, including such systemic problems as the fifteen-hour credit load for teachers, and the fact that there is no release time and no reward for creative effort since most community colleges do not have rank systems.

Because community college teachers often find themselves arguing for student access and facing heavy teaching loads, we have come to the conclusion that the most important ingredient in collaborative teaching efforts is the commitment on the part of the faculty.

The Plan: Goals and Methods

We had a number of goals in mind when we first started our projects. Our first goal was to incorporate more writing into the syllabus, and we designed the networked discussion sessions to facilitate this. Since many students come to a community college with limited writing backgrounds, we wanted to give them more writing experience in a content area to help them understand, synthesize, and analyze issues, topics, and information in a collaborative learning mode. We assumed that the more writing was encouraged and mentored by faculty in non-composition disciplines, the more students would make the transition from their writing classes to their other courses. More experience with writing using computers would alleviate the two major obstacles for disadvantaged students: their lack of experience with the modes of academic discourse and their unfamiliarity with technology.

Our second goal was to give students the benefit of having the opportunity to try out their ideas in writing before they are asked to write formally on a topic. Collaborative, networked discussions on the computer would minimize the punitive aspect of grading and provide constructive criticism prior to the submission of a final paper and/or exams. Most important, we wanted students to use writing to learn about the concepts they were studying in class and clarify issues before they found themselves in academic trouble. To achieve this goal, we developed twelve discussion sessions for the students to use as a study group, one for each unit studied. These consisted of writing exercises loaded into the network using software (Norton Textra Connect)[1] that allowed students to discuss the topics asynchronously in groups. The class was randomly broken into discussion groups, each group working together for the entire semester, building a sense of collaboration in their learning experience. Questions we designed for each topic help students to focus on key ideas, concepts, individuals, and events with a goal toward seeing these in a historical, cultural perspective. We used the discussion function of the software in two ways. Before the semester began, we loaded fairly formal essay questions for students to think about and write about with members of their groups. We might, for example, define a topic and then ask them to do something like this:

> Based on the readings in McKay, the handouts, and class discussion, choose two examples of scapegoating from two different centuries and discuss the following in a minimum of 350 words (to count your words, click on Utilities, then statistics):
> - The perceived external threats to the society
> - The perceived internal divisions of the society
> - The social reaction to the real or perceived threats
> - Why specific individuals and groups were chosen as scapegoats

We reminded students to cite their sources using MLA form and to generate a Works Cited page to practice these skills for formal writing. Then each week we would send out, through the messaging system (much like e-mail) that is built into the software, more conversational, informal, chatty kinds of questions that helped them synthesize each week's lectures into their thinking/writing about the topic. These weekly messages encouraged a kind of informal, conversational tone, freeing students to question and challenge each other and their professors. A sample from the same unit follows:

> FROM: dan schultz and maryanne felter TO: CLASS 9/22/95, 1:57 pm
> OK, gang—things SHOULD be falling into place for you about now. . . . In the meantime, here are some more things to think about—and write about if you have the chance.
> 3. Who benefited from the witchcraft crazes? Otherwise phrased: who had what kinds of vested interests in keeping what going? think Greece, think medieval Europe, think Salem.
> 4. Why do you suppose Schultzie went off on the little tangent about 1960s America?—any parallels you can draw from that time period that might help you pull this all together.

The discussion sessions trained students to use the sources they were assigned in class—handouts, textbook, films, and class lectures—to formulate their ideas about the various topics. They learned to read sources carefully to respond to the questions, to use the sources to support their theses, and to document the sources correctly. Their collaborative writing discussions prepared them for the six exams (three each semester) that had also been loaded onto the network. The culmination of these efforts was the transference of the accumulated knowledge and skills into a final research paper. Deadlines for work could be controlled by shutting the system off when the deadline passed. Completion of assignments was the students' responsibility, focusing on the skills necessary for successful school-to-work transition.

We also developed twelve mini-lessons in writing strategies as backup instructions available on the network, including reading and writing strategies as well as test-taking and studying hints. Eleven bibliographies on works of literature corresponding to the historical topics were also included. These lessons reinforced instruction given within the English department and supported in skills centers and writing labs. Writing strategies as applied to the particular discipline provided models for students to follow as they worked their way through their own ideas on various topics. Each mini-lesson explained the particular kind of writing, took students through the process, gave a sample of what that process could produce, and then explained the strengths and weaknesses of the sample. The mini-lessons used the course content to show the process. So the lesson on developing details, for example, discussed the idea of development and showed various methods of generating ideas, such as brainstorming:

> For example, if you were writing an essay about witchcraft as scapegoating, you might make a list like this:
> • Salem witchcraft trials/ neighbors fighting, inexplicable natural phenomena
> • Dreyfus/ set up to protect army
> • McCarthy/ blame it all on communists
> • Socrates/ daring to speak the truth no one wants to hear, etc.

This was followed by an explanation on how to develop ideas further. We then supplied students with a model paragraph, parts of which are reprinted here:

> For example, if we were writing up the paragraph on the Salem witchcraft trials, we might come up with something like this:
>> In 1692, the town of Salem experienced a wave of accusations of witchcraft and the resulting trial and execution of 21 people (McKay 484). At the time, the residents were sure that they were doing God's work in ferreting out Satan's helpers and saving their community from the devil. . . . Historians have different ideas of why the witchcraft craze happened, including theories about ergot and porphyria that caused people to hallucinate (Watson 119). But whatever sparked the initial accusations, many believe that the witchcraft trials were an example of scapegoating. When farmers couldn't explain strange occurrences such as the death of cattle or the failure of crops, the accusation of witchcraft became a convenient explanation for an inexplicable phenomena. It was much easier to blame someone who was consorting with the devil rather than try to find some natural cause that they probably couldn't have found anyhow (Watson 121). When neighbors, holding longtime grudges about property boundaries and ownership, wanted redress, what better way to "stick it to" the other person than accuse him of witchcraft (Watson 124)? . . . Because witchcraft was a supernatural phenomenon

and not subject to the laws of reason and close scrutiny, it provided an almost foolproof method of "getting even" or explaining what could not be explained. Who could contest it when there were "eyewitnesses" who could accuse the witches?

After the paragraph and the Works Cited, we highlighted for students what we wanted them to see about the paragraph:

Notice a few things about this paragraph:
- it uses two examples: property questions and inexplicable natural phenomena
- it offers alternative explanations that historians have given for the witchcraft
- it connects the idea of witchcraft with the historical period
- it explains how the accusations were connected with the idea of scapegoating
- it gives enough background from McKay to show that you have done that reading as well
- it uses in-text citations to show Dr. Schultz where the ideas came from, proving to him that you have done your work in reading sources, listening to lectures
- length: it is not that long necessarily means good, but it takes more than two sentences to explain an idea such as the one explained above. Take your time to explain. Don't try to just get it done quickly.

Near the end of the spring semester, we administered a student survey in order to ascertain the number of students using these backup instructions. The survey indicated that students used many of them. Of the nineteen students completing the course, eleven used "study guide exam #1," seven used "reading exams carefully," "documenting sources," and "bibliographies," and five selected "prep for exams 2 and 3," "basics about essays," and "comparison/contrast essays." One student responded, "I printed them all out at the beginning of the semester and reprinted them as updated. The info contained in most items benefits not only Wes Civ but other courses as well." Apparently, this aspect of the program was relatively successful in assisting students with the mechanics of writing assignments. And the student who printed them all off at the start of the semester did what we had hoped all of the students would do: use the background information for support all semester, not only in this class but in other classes as well.

Our third goal was to encourage a team-centered approach to learning. The technology facilitated this. Lab facilities tend to be open and accessible to students at most times of the day and evening, and networking allows students to join the study group on their own time, increasing flexibility in terms of participation. At community colleges, study groups are commonplace but usually restricted to day/time/place. With the network, the teacher and/or designated students within the groups could control topics and keep groups on task. The networked discussions fostered collaboration, a mentoring among students ("I do not see where Socrates fits into all of this."), helped them develop critical thinking skills (writing about the spread of AIDS: "I understand that when the first people came over here and exposed the Native Americans to smallpox they didn't realize what was going on. But what about in the late seventies and early eighties when gay men left and right dragged their feet until it was too late. . . . I'm not saying our government purposely committed genocide but looking back now they didn't do everything they could have to prevent it."), and gave them practice in synthesizing sources and using proper documentation. The technology also facilitated collaboration with the professor. This alleviated the problem of student schedules that often conflict with office hours, as well as constraints of the typical community college student—jobs, family, external situations. Messages could be sent daily and responded to immediately.

Another goal, consistent with the content of the course, was to encourage cross-cultural exchange and a multicultural perspective. Giving students access to e-mail and Internet accounts (including Netscape, Lynx, and Gopher) not only facilitated research but also broadened their perspectives about what information is accessible for a variety of learning purposes outside the specific classroom context. We encouraged students to join listservs to gain access to a multicultural perspective on the topics, at the same time expanding their ideas and reinforcing writing skills. We also encouraged their use of Internet research, including a Web-research project as one of several take-home exam options. Such Internet connection increased student access to scholars, journals, and other students in other countries interested in similar problems and issues. Student participation in these various discussions was encouraged via reward of in-class credit, making it an integral part of the students' final grade. We considered ourselves relatively successful in this. Research papers included topics on Cheyenne Indians, the Sikhs, Tamerlane, Haiti, voodoo, Duvalier, female genital mutilation, Chiang Kai-Shek, and Vietnam. Much of the information students found on these topics came through research on the Internet.

The Reality

We worked out all of these ideas over the summer, and they sounded great. But come fall, we found some obstacles to their implementation. Those problems we had anticipated did not materialize, while others caught us unprepared. One anticipated difficulty was time taken away from instruction. However, class time spent on teaching the use of e-mail and network software amounted, surprisingly, to not more than two class days, and the students generally responded positively. Asked to rank order (1=high, 4=low) which items they found most useful, 41 percent of the students indicated "access to Netscape for research" was extremely useful; 35 percent said they would use Netscape more often. One stated further, "If there was more access to Netscape besides the library, I would use it more." Eight students out of nineteen responded they would use e-mail more, one going so far as to say, "I only kept [this course] because of the e-mail account, but now I enjoy the great learning experience I have acquired."

Initially, we feared that technological problems inherent in the computer systems—viruses, network difficulties, crashing systems, failure to observe appropriate precautions in saving materials—might create student and faculty frustration. However, we found that the failure was not rooted in the computer system itself; rather, it stemmed from the students' unwillingness to utilize the system, especially the discussion questions. In fact, when asked to rank which items were least helpful and why (questions 7 and 8), the overwhelming choice was the discussion component. In general, students disliked these questions because of the extra time commitment they required: "it was too much of a hassle"; "there were too many essays [that] needed to be done." We found that it was an issue of time or their perception that the networked sessions were not user-friendly that seemed to be the problem; it was not the concept per se to which they objected. Hence, responses to question 8 ("If you used discussion on connect, do you believe it has helped you succeed on exams?") were gener-ally favorable. For example, one student indicated such questions were helpful not only for exams but also with the research paper. Another noted, "Yes . . . if you are not on the right track, another student or Dr. Schultz will help you. So when the test comes, you already know the info." Students who utilized discus-sion and e-mail to discuss items with their instructor (question 13) found them very useful. Similarly, their response to using e-mail/connect with their discus-sion group was extremely positive.

Although we have made a vast array of technological tools available, we find students lacked motivation. Despite doubling the number of in-class lab instruction days and having additional lab hours scheduled for their use, only a handful of students became involved. For example, in the fall 1995, of the twenty-eight students who remained for the entire semester, for each discussion ques-tion required there was an average of twenty-one responses. In the spring, there were only six responses for the nineteen students who finished the class. Per-haps the combination of too many options and too little structure was over-whelming for our students. During the second semester, we were remiss in specifying deadline dates for the discussion questions; hence, there could be no cut-off dates. When students were asked to evaluate themselves as students, of nine options, the third largest response was "procrastinator." In the final three weeks of the semester, we were inundated with student responses to discussion questions. So our lack of structure did play a major role in students' lack of response early on. What we found, not surprisingly, was that the good students took their work seriously and got right down to it; weaker and average students put it all off until the end. As teachers, we may also have overestimated stu-dents' interest in technologies, their commitment to the course and its requirements, and their trust in our knowledge that this could help them overcome the burdens of synthesizing materials and not simply add to their workload.

Perhaps the most devastating statistic came when comparing withdrawal from the four classes in Western Civilization over a two-year period. Course content had not changed significantly from the academic years 1994–95 to 1995–96 except for the addition of the technological component in the second year. During the fall of 1994, there were 5 Withdrawals, representing 13 percent of the enrolled students. During the spring 1995 semester, there were 8 Ws, or 26 percent of the students withdrawing. During the fall of 1995, there were 14 Ws, or 29 percent of the class. For spring 1996, there were 16 Ws, or 46 percent of the students withdrawing. High drop-out rates are often part of the community college experience, and we suspected that the time and job constraints of community college students were problems limiting their participation. Our suspicions were confirmed by our institution's Middle States Report citing the students' need to work and their family responsibilities (1994 MSPR, 167–74) as reasons for withdrawing.

There may have been other forces at work. The student survey confirmed that homework is often not required on the high school level; anything that must be done outside of class will probably not be done. When asked if they felt "intimidated by the computer element of the course," the respondents were about evenly divided. The "yes" respondents said there was "too much out of class commitment," outnumbering the second largest by an almost two-to-one margin. Lack of time was the main response. Such problems could be alleviated, as several students noted, by scheduling more in-class time in the lab. Of those who responded to the research paper issue, two were positive about it ("I like to write and it gives me a chance to become acquainted with a topic of interest."), but a plurality were against it either because they don't like to write or because it took too long to do. Perhaps there was resistance to the idea because, as one student stated succinctly, "In other [introductory] courses, a term paper was not required."

Whereas the writing and the technology components created minor problems for our students, the most significant obstacle was getting students to use the technology to write in a non-English/non-"writing" course ("This is a history course, not a writing course."). Recent research has revealed a significant increase in the use of information technology in courses, especially at the community college level ("Technology Use," 1996, 2). Faculty are using technology to enhance their curricula, and more and more students are coming to expect such a component in their courses, especially as they become more commonplace at the secondary level. Connecting technology to writing assignments is a natural link; our student sample was not put off by a "writing intensive" course label if a writing lab experience were a scheduled part of the program for which they received credit (four vs. three credit hours). Some sample responses: "An hour in the lab with discussion due dates would be a tremendous help. Four credits is a big incentive also"; "This is the way you have a scheduled time to work on assignments and you don't have to stress over whether you're going to get everything done." These kinds of comments indicate that the expectation to go above and beyond class time is outside the realm of community college students' experience. The students come to class unprepared, and they admit it. The implicit expectation is that they will be "given" information rather than be held accountable for their own learning. And they want to have time scheduled into their classes for the writing work they need to do. But if given the time and when shown how the technology can facilitate writing-to-learn activities, students generally recognize both the importance of and the benefits of such a program. A number of students who experienced past difficulty with writing and who used the network on a regular basis demonstrated an improved ability to synthesize materials and to communicate their newly gained knowledge effectively. One student, for example, who had previously failed Freshman Composition and repeated it only to get a D, subsequently earned a well-deserved B+ in this class.

Conclusions

Given our limited experience with this collaborative model, it appears that if writing across the curriculum and technology are to be effective, there is a need for a "carrot-and-stick" approach. Students must come to see writing as an integral part of the learning process, be rewarded for taking courses that develop their writing skills (Writing Intensive designations, extra credit for courses that have a writing lab component, for example). We are fairly certain that our high drop-out rate in Western Civ stems not from the use of technology but from time constraints coupled with student expectations that they will not be required to write in non-composition courses. Hence, a commitment to writing to learn on the part of the faculty and the institution is essential. We suspect that many people across the disciplines would gladly include more writing in their courses if they were given some guidance in establishing goals for their disciplines, given some help in constructing effective writing-to-learn activities, and given some support by the institution to have the time and the facilities to work on projects such as this one. Faculty workshops on the WAC process, coupled with institutional support in the form of grants, equipment, course scheduling, time easements, establishment of teams/courses/collaborators may prove ways of encouraging such experimentation. Such items are essential if the program is to be effective, especially given the time commitment entailed in planning unit topics; writing the discussion questions, bibliographies, and exam questions; and establishing deadlines and the like. Given our experience, initial faculty reaction has been one of suspicion and concern, given the realities of student enrollment, job security, the restrictive wording of union contracts, and departmental in-fighting. Hence the imperative for a nonthreatening technical and institutional environment under which such innovations could be encouraged. With the increasing interest in and use of information technology on the part of students and faculty come financial, technological, and pedagogical challenges—replacing hard- and software, training, and improving the infrastructure to facilitate its use. All this questioning of methods and results is not an admission of failure but rather an exploration of what the education process is all about, that good teachers are perpetual students. It must be utilized by all segments of the academy if its full potential is to be realized.

Note

We used for this project Norton Textra Connect, a "networked writing environment," as the editors call it. It is an interactive, collaborative word-processing program that can be run through DOS or through Windows and is compatible with major word processing programs such as WordPerfect and Word for Windows. It can be used with Novell, NFS, LANTASTIC, OS/2, Vines, and PATHWORKS networks. Students need only buy the access number so that they are licensed to enter the program on the network; it is free for the institution that installs it. The price (as of summer 1996) is modest for students: approximately $30.00 allows them access to the software which includes a word processor with an online handbook, a collaborative discussion facility, and an internal e-mail system. Further information is available through W. W. Norton.

Works Cited

Forman, Janice. 1994. "Literacy, Collaboration, and Technology: New Connections and Challenges." In *Literacy and Computers: The Complications of Teaching and Learning with Technology,* edited by Cynthia L. Selfe and Susan Hilligoss, 130–43. New York: Modern Language Associaion of America.

MSPR (Middle States Periodic Review). 1994. Cayuga Community College.

Schuster, Charles. 1990. "The Ideology of Illiteracy." In *The Right to Literacy,* edited by Andrea A. Lunsford, Helene Moglen, and James Slevin, 225–32. New York: Modern Language Association of America.

Selfe, Cynthia. 1990. "Computers in English Departments: The Rhetoric of Techno/Power." In *Computers and Writing: Theory, Research, Practice,* edited by Deborah H. Holdstein and Cynthia Selfe, 95–103. New York: Modern Language Association of America.

"Technology Use on the Rise in Classrooms." 1996. *NEA Higher Education Advocate* 13.4: 2.

22 Math Learning through Electronic Journaling

Robert Wolffe
Bradley University

Walls to Learning

> I have been pretty confused this week because I am very math illiterate.
> Math makes me nervous and I think that I am going to have some difficulty
> with this class.
>
> I have always tried to stay away from math because it is not a subject in
> which I ever did very well.

In statements like these we see problems that teacher education students, particularly females, bring to their mathematics courses (National Research Council 1989). Many prospective elementary and early childhood teachers are uncomfortable with their own ability to learn mathematics. Their prior experiences have been all-but-encouraging, so new encounters with math are entered with trepidation and fear, further hindering new attempts to learn math (Fennema & Hart 1994; Williams 1988). Educational applications of neuroscientific research call this type of phenomenon "downshifting" of the brain. Most people are familiar with downshifting from high-stress level situations, tests and the like where the brain seems to "freeze" instead of processing knowledge or information, although the material might be well learned and immediately accessible after the stress is removed (Hart 1986; Jensen 1995; Sylwester 1995). Preservice teachers' negative emotions are interfering with their learning of mathematics. This interference is problematic, for it occurs at a time when the philosophy of and curriculum for precollegiate math education is being revised and new demands are being placed on teachers' mathematics knowledge base (National Council of Teachers of Mathematics 1989). These revisions require that these students must study mathematics if they are going to be able to implement best practices in their classrooms (National Council of Teachers of Mathematics 1991). As we strive to empower young learners, we need to mathematically empower those who teach math with both an intrinsic motivation for the subject and the ability to engage in genuine dialogue (Cuevas 1995). The problem then is how to accomplish two tasks:

- to help reluctant students overcome their fear of the subject, and
- to raise to an acceptable level the mathematical knowledge base of these same students.

One component of the answer I have explored is the use of e-mail journals. The students taking the required math course for elementary, early childhood, and special education majors submit electronically a weekly journal entry. What follows describes this pedagogical exploration.

A Plan for Passage

The decision to use e-mail journals in the math cognate course was based on my experience as a teacher and my reading of several areas of research. After teaching preservice teachers math for several years, it was clear to me that their attitudes were interfering with students' ability to engage the course material. It appeared that the students had placed a wall between themselves and the course. The intuitive-affective barrier described by Lozanov (1978) in which the learner rejects everything which fails to create confidence and a feeling of security was a clear factor influencing the students' mathematical development. A portal through that wall was needed.

During my first three years of teaching this course, I began to connect the problem of math anxiety with writing across the curriculum, the benefits of metacognitive thought, and the effective use of telecommunications. Advocates of writing across the curriculum suggest that by having students write in the various disciplines they will make stronger connections between their current learning experiences and previously developed knowledge schemata (Kelly 1995; Smagorinsky 1995). "One learns by writing. Writing is an integral part of the learning process because it enhances and supports what one reads and thinks about. One way to help remember something is to write it down: The act of writing reinforces what is spoken aloud or pictured in the mind" (Grinols 1988, 15). Literature also suggests that the inclusion of reflective practices promotes both a deeper understanding of the subject being studied and of the learning process itself (Henderson 1992; Schon 1987). The use of e-mail held the potential for enhancing the effect of a writing/reflecting activity (Sumrall & Sumrall 1995; Slovacek & Doyle-Nichols 1991). Female students brought to the class a higher propensity to be involved in language activities than in activities involving mathematics. Informal polling of my class showed that, if given a choice, most of the students would not take additional math classes. The use of a journal activity looked like a means to link these ideas. The writing process would allow the students to relax as they used their favored means of communications in a manner which had them engaging the content of the course and reflecting upon their experience. Possibly, journaling would be a key to opening a gateway to more productive learning.

Constructing an Opening

The journaling process I use today is somewhat different from the procedure I first tried. Initially, the students chose to use either paper and pencil or e-mail to summarize what had been studied in that day's class. The purpose of requiring summaries was the constructivist, brain-based theory that by revisiting current experiences, the building of knowledge constructs is enhanced (Wolffe & McMullen 1995; Brooks & Brooks 1993). Students were also encouraged to reflect on their learning experience. During class I suggested that they could discuss how they were learning, addressing both the nature of their frustrations and their successes. This metacognitive aspect was not required. Analysis of the first semester entries indicated that nearly 80 percent of the time the students adequately summarized the new content and nearly two-thirds of the students chose periodically to reflect upon their experience. As I will illustrate here, the content of the reflection showed that this aspect of the journaling process was crucial and needed to be made mandatory instead of being optional. It also became apparent that the writing should done using e-mail. For example, only 19 percent of those students communicating with paper and pencil ever used their journal entry as a means of posing questions. This was compared to 44 percent of those using e-mail who asked for further clarification about something being studied in class when they journaled. This first semester of journaling made it clear that the use of e-mail provides immediacy of dialogue between teacher and student. Next to private face-to-face meetings, e-mail seems to be the most effective means to communicate between teacher and student. The use of e-mail enabled the sender to articulate questions and concerns in writing. The receiver could then read and respond to the message quickly. This process could take place at any time of the day or night, rather than just during class, on the phone, or during a scheduled meeting. As one student who switched from paper-pencil journaling to using e-mail put it, "I think you should make e-mail journal entries mandatory. They are more prompt. Even though you always got paper journals back by the next class period, I had forgotten my questions. They just aren't as meaningful." (Wolffe & McMullen 1995, 27). What is most important is that the e-mail journals provide an ongoing opportunity to elicit thoughts about math content and the learning of this subject which might not have been expressed otherwise. With so many females reluctant even to take math courses, moving them to be reflective about the experience can be problematic. Through the use of e-mail, the teacher is able to work individually with each student, and through the energy created by this interaction move toward deeper and deeper thought.

The requirements for the first journal assignment were quite loose; the idea was that by providing a fair amount of choice, the students would be comfortable with the assignment. While no one expressed concerns with their ability to write the journals, it should be noted that a certain portion of the students did not value this course requirement. They saw twice weekly entries as imposing on their time and/or as "busy work."

Since this first attempt, I have made three changes in the journaling. It did appear that having the assignments be a bit more defined did not take away from the students' attitude regarding the assignment and that there was potential for improving the effect. Therefore, the assignment now requires not only a summary of what was learned but also asks the students to talk about some aspect of their recent learning experiences which either went well or was problematic. Students no longer have a choice of using either e-mail or paper-and-pencil entries; all of the entries are to be sent electronically to me. Last, to decrease the dissatisfaction with doing this assignment, students may journal either after each class or at the end of each week.

A Door Worth Opening

The use of electronic journaling as just described has reaped many more benefits than I initially expected. The journal entries provided students an opportunity to express themselves in relationship to growth in content knowledge, self-image, understanding themselves as learners, and the ability to connect their own experiences to their futures as teachers. It is quite likely that many of these thoughts would not have been realized if they had not been required to formulate the ideas in their journal entries. The web shown in Figure 22.1 depicts the many areas being connected by students as they wrote their journals.

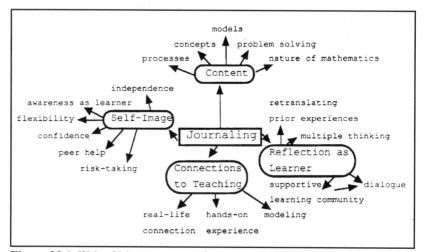

Figure 22.1. Web of ideas generated from student journals.

The summative aspect of the journal entries has motivated students to keep up with their readings and other assignments. While some students are not sold on the advantages of this requirement of reviewing what they have just learned, others have commented on the benefit of doing this as a part of their studying process. In addition, journals which include questions show how the students have used their entries to build their content knowledge. With some prodding by the instructor, the students have learned to ask questions within the context of what they already know. They pose questions related to concepts:

> Is this the correct procedure for differentiating the arithmetic sequence from the geometric ones? When the numbers increase by a common differ-ence, it is an arithmetic sequence. While in geometric sequences, the num-bers increase by the same ratio. Please correct me if I'm wrong.

and processes and models:

> I just had a question about the charged fields. I need to get something straight. When your adding and subtracting numbers, just when your add-ing, you cancel out the positive and the negative, but you don't cancel them out when your subtracting. Does that make any sense?

The questions also relate to content in the areas of problem solving and the nature of mathematics.

As students asked questions, they came to understand that even though they still have questions, they know a great deal. This is an important part of improv-ing the students' self-image. The reflections also have worked well in bringing to a conscious level the writers' attitudes about themselves as math students. As the students reflect, the instructor reacts to the comments and poses questions to help the students expand their thoughts. The students' statements fall into a number of categories.

Some students express a new found awareness of themselves as risk-takers. One student commented:

> What I learned about myself from Wednesday's class is that I need to be more brave. The people in my group were having problems with that prob-lem concerning marbles. I was able to complete it, but I wasn't exactly sure if I got the right answer. I didn't want to explain what I did to my group just because I was afraid I did it incorrectly and I would confuse them more. Later, you came over and showed us how to do it. It turned out that I did the problem right and it felt pretty good. I think I learned that I should be more willing to try even if I turn out to be wrong.

Other students' improved self-image is apparent in their reflections about working with their peers. Two students filed the following entries:

> *S1*: When we were going over the homework I felt pretty good about my-self because the others at my table were asking for my help which not only

made me feel smart, but it also made me feel like a leader and it tells me that I have a good grasp on the subject.

S2: I would also like to thank you for taking the time to explain #16 on section 1.2 with our group. I actually understood where each preceding answer arrived from while working backwards. How am I sure of this? Because I was able to help someone in another group with this identical problem at the end of class.

Some students seem shocked that they actually can learn mathematics: "The sections that we covered for class this week I actually think I understand." This revelation may be somewhat shocking for some students because they have little to no prior experience constructing their own knowledge of math. Female students more than males are often given less help when they encounter difficulties in precollegiate math classes. This entry above and the one which follows speak directly to the students' increased confidence and an emerging belief in themselves as independent learners:

I feel more comfortable with the math problems now. I am learning shorter ways to get the answer, but it takes a while. I always start with the long way first, but then the light comes on later. I am a lot neater with the solving of the problems. I am also coming out of that math phobia that I had.

Finally, the students' journals relate to their enhanced self-image as they write about their newly constructed awareness of the need for flexibility when solving math problems. One student wrote, "I am glad that I am learning to work these problems in a new way. I finally am starting to feel comfortable in solving a problem in more than one way."

Connected to the students' expressions of improved self-image are the insights they gain about themselves as learners as they think about their experiences in this math class. As was the case with self-image, the entries related to reflections on being a learner fall into several categories.

One area discussed in a number of entries is the need to retranslate one's prior learning experiences into more effective learning practices. The students recognize that how they learned in the past can impede their current progress. Two comments are indicative of this type of thought:

S1: The problems assigned in this section proved to be challenging to say the least. I am trying to look at the integer relations from a teaching perspective, but I seem to keep falling back on the notion that "I know the rule so this is the answer." In other words, I tend to want to just give the answer than show why or how I know the answer. It's tough!

S2: I had a hard time at first with chapter one, but after working through the problems with my group I have come to realize that the reason I have trouble with these problems is because I am not used to thinking in the way I am required to in order to solve these problems. It is as if I have to train my brain to a whole different way of thinking.

Students also communicated the need to consider multiple thinking strategies if they are to be successful learners:

> By building the problem, I was able to see visually the rows and columns of the triangle pieces and how they fit together to form a rectangle. Building helps you to move the pieces around and manipulate the shape to possibly come to new conclusion or equation. In the future I won't be afraid to build and then rearrange a problem in different ways until finding a solution.

Furthermore, the students reflect their own learning processes in relationship to setting their own pace so they can have the time to understand new material. This idea is apparent in the following journal entry:

> The use of the cubes definitely influenced me positively as a learner. The use helped me because the cubes made the problem "real." We could see it. I was able to do my homework and understand it better because of the cubes. The activity made me slow down and think of why I was doing what I was doing rather than just rush through just to get an answer. I actually took time to understand the homework and thus I believe did a better job.

The reflections on being a successful learner show insights concerning the need for a supportive learning community and for dialogue. One student writes, "I have trouble when I am trying to do my homework alone, but if I can talk out the problem then it seems to be easier." Another entry recalls,

> I'm feeling more confident this week about understanding the material. I find it helpful to know the different strategies that could help lead to an answer to the problem. I talked to another girl in the class, who lives on my floor, and she understands the material pretty well. She said she would be willing to help me work through the problems if I needed help. We worked on the homework together. She helped me understand some of the problems. I think that if I learn how she knows what strategies to try, eventually I will be able to see the strategies by myself.

Some of the students expanded their reflections regarding their own learning experience and discussed how their own efforts to comprehend mathematics would influence their actions as a teacher in the future. The students' writings capture how important it is for teachers to provide learners real-life connections, hands-on experience and a chance to work with models. By thinking and writing about their own experience, they are becoming aware of what Peltonen (1985) reports in his research about learning. Within total learning 10 percent is learned through hearing; 30 percent through seeing; 50 percent through seeing and hearing; 70 percent through talking, seeing, and hearing; and 90 percent through doing, talking, seeing, and hearing. The more multimodal learning experiences are, the more effective learning will be. Two students came to the following conclusions:

S1: Wednesday we played with the flats, longs, cubes and singular thingies which I can't remember the name for! We built a multiplication problem out of them and dissected the pieces to see many different multiplication problems within. It was the first time I had ever done this, so I was a little confused at first, but I think I'm cool with it now. In my opinion, I think it's really good that we're learning in OUR class how to use these items to solve OUR problems, so we can use them in our FUTURE classes to help our students learn as well.

S2: Wednesday's class was especially good because we got to play with the manipulatives. It was very helpful to have those when we are trying to understand the concepts. Everyone in the class knows how to add, subtract, multiply, and divide, but it makes everything so much clearer when we can make and have our own sets right in front of us. When I teach, I am definitely going to make math more of a hands-on experience for my students. I remember learning math by working on probably hundreds of dittos. I learn better by doing and I am sure that the children I teach one day will be the same way.

It is clear from the comments reported above that having students record through e-mail journals both what they are learning about math and reflections on the learning process can lead to many intertwined positive effects. As students submit their entries and read the instructor's responses, they are stimulated by purposeful thought which makes it more likely that they will become cognizant of their successes as learners and will become aware of how they came to be successful. The importance of the fact that the students' self-esteem is enhanced should not be underestimated. As they become aware of their own learning styles, they become more effective learners and they begin to connect their collegiate course work with their future aspirations. There is no reason to believe that the positive impact journaling has had on these math students could not be repeated in courses in other disciplines. The interactions between attitude, metacognitive analysis of one's own learning, and the ability to project one's learning onto future goals is not specific to any particular discipline. E-mail journaling is a beneficial way to foster these interactions in a manner which is efficient, effective, and empowering. All students can benefit from a better understanding of their image of themselves as learners, of their learning processes, and of how their present efforts connect to their future dreams and aspirations.

Works Cited

Brooks, Jacqueline G., and Martin G. Brooks. 1993. *In Search of Understanding: The Case for Constructivist Classrooms.* Alexandria, VA: Association for Supervision and Curriculum Development.

Cuevas, Gilbert J. 1995. "Empowering All Students to Learn Mathematics." In *Prospects for School Mathematics: Seventy-five Years of Progress,* edited by I. M. Carl, 62–77. Reston, VA: National Council of Teachers of Mathematics.

Fennema, Elizabeth, and Laurie E. Hart. 1994. "Gender and the JRME." *Journal for Research in Mathematics Education* 25.6: 648–59.

Grinols, Anne B., ed. 1988. *Critical Thinking: Reading and Writing Across the Curriculum.* Belmont, CA: Wadsworth.

Hart, Leslie. 1986. "A Response: All 'Thinking' Paths Lead to the Brain." *Educational Leadership* 43.8: 45–48.

Henderson, James G. 1992. *Reflective Teaching: Becoming an Inquiring Educator.* New York: Macmillan.

Jensen, Eric. 1995. *Brain-based Learning and Teaching.* DelMar, CA: Turning Point.

Kelly, Leonard P. 1995. "Encouraging Faculty to Use Writing as a Tool to Foster Learning in the Disciplines through Writing Across the Curriculum." *American Annals of the Deaf* 140.1: 16–23.

Lozanov, Georgi. 1978. *Suggestology and Outlines of Suggestopedy.* NY: Gordon and Breach.

National Council of Teachers of Mathematics. 1989. *Curriculum and Evaluation Standards for School Mathematics.* Reston, VA: National Council of Teachers of Mathematics.

National Council of Teachers of Mathematics. 1991. *Professional Standards for Teaching Mathematics.* Reston, VA: National Council of Teachers of Mathematics.

National Research Council. 1989. *Everybody Counts. A Report to the Nation on the Future of Mathematics Education.* Washington, D.C.: National Academy Press.

Peltonen, Matti. 1985. *Koulutusoppi (Pedagogy).* Helsinki: Otava.

Schon, Donald. 1987. *Educating the Reflective Practitioner: Toward a New Design for Teaching and Learning in the Professions.* San Francisco: Jossey-Bass.

Slovacek, Simeon P., and Adelaide R. Doyle-Nichols. 1991. "Enhancing Telecommunications in Teacher Education." *Journal of Research on Computing in Education* 24.2: 254–64.

Smagorinsky, Peter. 1995. "Constructing Meaning in the Disciplines: Reconceptualizing Writing Across the Curriculum as Composing Across the Curriculum." *American Journal of Education* 103.2: 160–85.

Sumrall, William J., and Carrol M. Sumrall. 1995. "Introducing Electronic Mail Applications within Preservice Elementary Science Methods Courses." *Journal of Computing in Teacher Education* 11.4: 23–30.

Sylwester, Robert. 1995. *A Celebration of Neurons: An Educator's Guide to the Human Brain.* Alexandria, VA: Association for Supervision and Curriculum Development.

Williams, W. Virginia. 1988. "Answers to Questions about Math Anxiety." *School Science and Mathematics* 88.2: 95–104.

Wolffe, Robert J., and David W. McMullen. 1995. "The Constructivist Connection: Linking Theory, Best Practice, and Technology." *Journal of Computing in Teacher Education* 12.2: 25–28.

23 Electronic Communities in Philosophy Classrooms

Gary L. Hardcastle
Virginia Polytechnic Institute and State University

Valerie Gray Hardcastle
Virginia Polytechnic Institute and State University

The Problem

There are at least two problems with traditional lecture courses. First, signifi-cant numbers of students find this format intimidating and consequently neither ask questions nor offer comments. Formal written work suffers as a result, for students put a greater effort into courses in which they feel they are significant participants. The lack of fruitful dialogue (both oral and written) is of special concern in a humanities course, where intellectual *exchange* is supposed to oc-cur. In particular, philosophy courses are dialectic; their goals are to raise ques-tions and acquaint students with issues. Intellectual transformation—not skill development—is the typical aim.

Second, traditional lecture courses make it difficult to accommodate the ex-traordinary range of student readiness and the variety of learning styles. Most students in our introductory courses have had no previous exposure to philoso-phy, and while some find the pace too fast, others find it too slow. Many fall by the wayside as a result: drop rates of 20 to 30 percent and failure rates of 8 to 12 percent are not uncommon. Variations in background and learning styles have been addressed in the past by attending to students individually, but this is not feasible in a large lecture course.

Such concerns are familiar, but in 1994 at Virginia Tech we found ourselves facing them squarely. As a humanities department in a land-grant university of 23,000 students, and one recognized for the education of future engineers, our introductory philosophy courses have always figured prominently in the under-graduate core curriculum and enjoy high demand. But when, in 1994, state-mandated budget cuts coincided with a renewed emphasis on teaching excellence, many members of our department found themselves standing not in classrooms of twenty or thirty students, but rather before audiences of two hundred, with the additional expectation that the teaching of these students would be *improved*. The familiar problems of the large lecture format became pressing; we simply *had* to teach more students more effectively.

Our Approach

Our approach to the problem was, and continues to be, extensive use of computer-supported communication (CSC) in our philosophy classes. Several factors contributed to this decision. Budgetary factors and the fact that we continued to be a research department precluded two obvious solutions: hiring new faculty or graduate teaching assistants, or increasing our teaching load. Our department-wide belief that philosophy classes could not be taught purely as lecture courses barred the elimination of discussion from our classes. Most significantly in retrospect, though, was an initiative of Virginia Tech's Office of Educational Technologies, which placed in the offices of Tech faculty fast Apple computers connected to the Internet via Ethernet. Simultaneously, initiatives of Tech's Computing Center and the Blacksburg Electronic Village, a consortium devoted to promoting electronic community in Blacksburg, quickly made our students and faculty among the best-wired university populations in the world. Shortly we and others at Tech began to ask if this technology, new to all of us, might help our courses.[1]

The technological turn fit well with a pedagogical outlook which aimed to free students and faculty from a "credit-for-contact" model of instruction, which prizes the raw time teachers and students spend together in the same room. The concrete effect of the rejection of this model and the use of CSC has been philosophy courses centered upon a set of small ongoing electronic discussion communities through which students participate in conversations with peers, teaching assistants, and professors. Students are invited to read the contributions of other students in several electronic discussion groups and to contribute to the discussion themselves.

Specifically, we have developed a World Wide Web-based forum for our philosophy classes which we have termed the class "running commentary." This running commentary consists of a series of Web pages which students may view with a Web browser from anywhere on the Internet, and through which students navigate to read other comments and submit their own.[2] The main part of the running commentary is the "main menu" page (see Figures 23.1 and 23.2), which gives the students an opportunity to browse comments by forum or category, to browse the most recently submitted comments, or to submit their own comments.

The taxonomy of forums is flexible; we have oriented ours around class topics such as Free Will and Determinism. To contribute a comment, a student

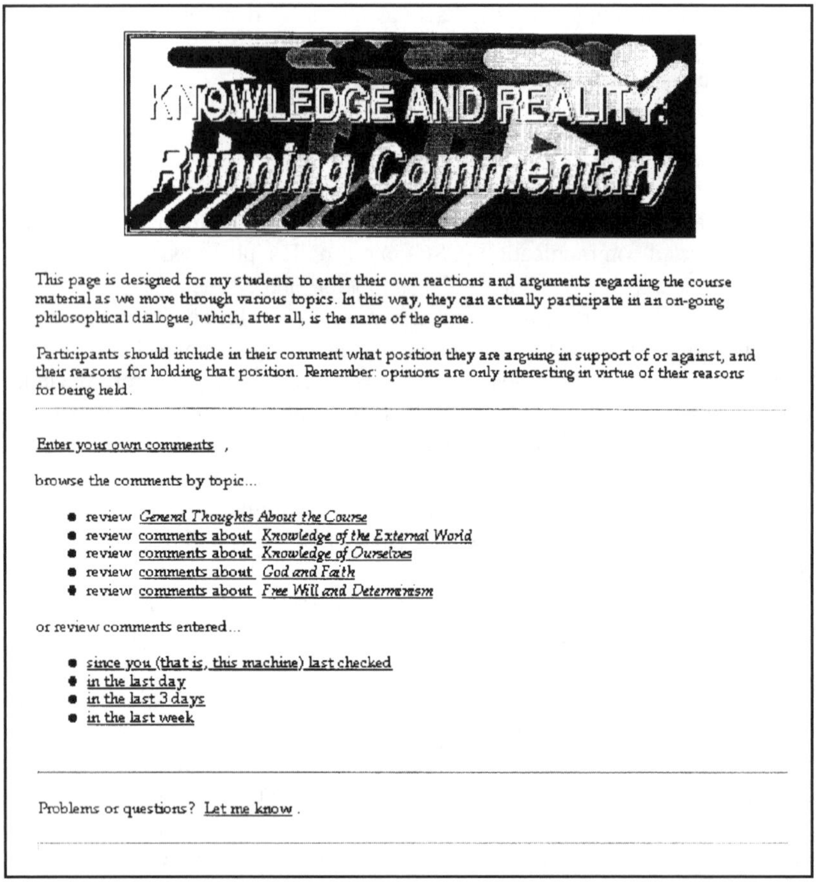

Figure 23.1. Running commentary menu page for Philosophy 1204.

completes a running comment entry form (see Figures 23.3 and 23.4). Although a student is prompted here for her name and e-mail address, the entry of an e-mail address is optional and any text string will serve as a first or last name. Thus the running commentary provides some degree of anonymity from other students, and from the instructor if the student uses a computer other than her own. Anonymity cuts both ways in this context—an issue we have addressed by providing information to our students about running commentaries. We caution students on an instruction page not to violate any official university honor codes or the standards of simple decency.

Note that from such comment pages students have the option of entering a reply which is then linked to the original comment. The effect is to create discussion "threads"—series of comments, each addressed to one that precedes it.

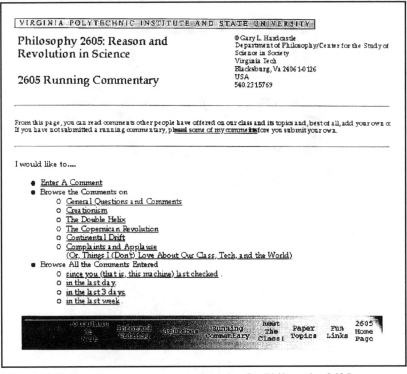

Figure 23.2. Running commentary menu page for Philosophy 2605.

As is familiar to readers of newsgroups, this structure makes for easy identification of the comments in which one is interested (see Figures 23.5 and 23.6).

Once submitted, the new comment's title appears in a listing of the comments which pertain to a given topic. Over the course of the class, comments and their replies accumulate, and that accumulation comprises a philosophical discussion. This is the standard (and perhaps best) way to learn philosophical concepts: students take the ideas and issues presented to them by others, apply them in different contexts, and then through an exchange with their instructors and their peers, revise and refine their claims. The argument-counterargument-revision dialectic is the heart of philosophy itself.

It may help in describing our running commentaries to compare the idea to other instances of CSC. Most important, informal commentaries are asynchronous, meaning that the discussion does not take place in real time. Thus what we do is unlike a MOO or the increasingly popular real-time conferencing platforms, and more like a newsgroup or electronic discussion list. Unlike electronic discussion lists, however, running commentaries organize comments

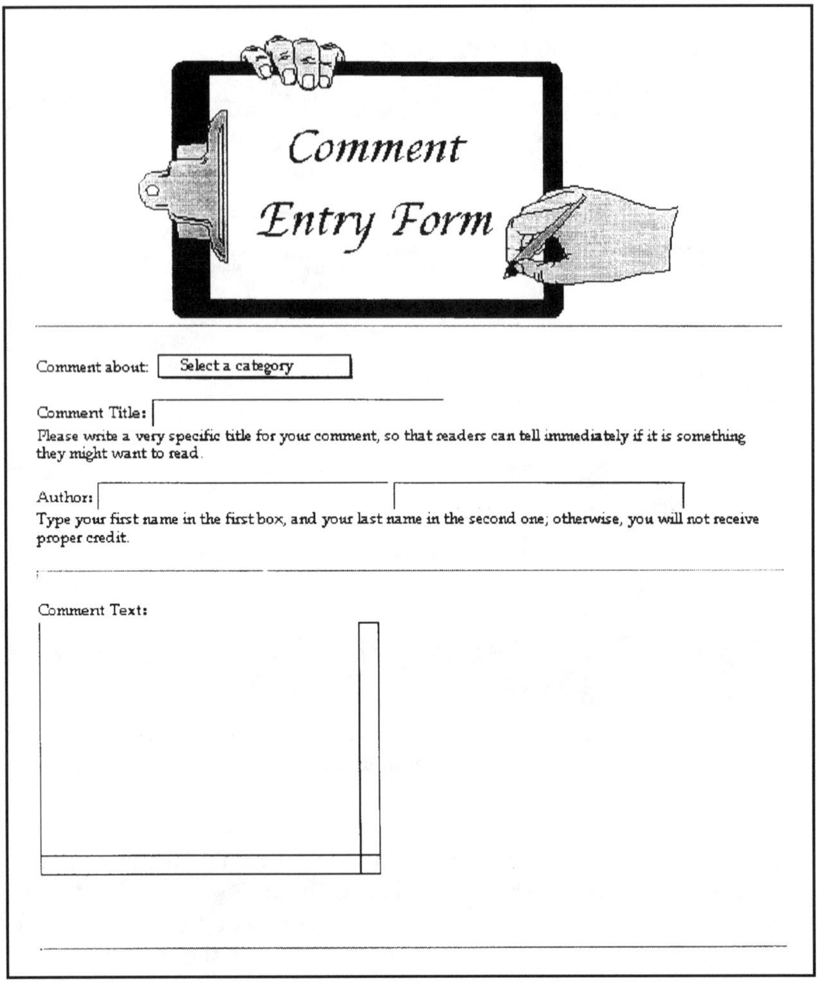

Comment Entry Form

Comment about: [Select a category]

Comment Title: |

Please write a very specific title for your comment, so that readers can tell immediately if it is something they might want to read.

Author: |

Type your first name in the first box, and your last name in the second one; otherwise, you will not receive proper credit.

Comment Text:

Figure 23.3. Running commentary entry form for Philosophy 1204.

around threads, preserve and organize comments on a central server, and do not require the use of e-mail. At the moment, USEnet-style newsgroups are less readily available for desktop platforms, while our running commentaries can be readily implemented on a variety of World Wide Web servers.

In many respects, our approach is not novel. Many teachers in other philosophy classes in other departments have used electronic discussion lists, e-mail, and Web pages. In most cases the pedagogical underpinnings of these efforts match ours—namely, the conviction that the exchange of real ideas among real people is essential to a philosophical discussion. We see our contribution as

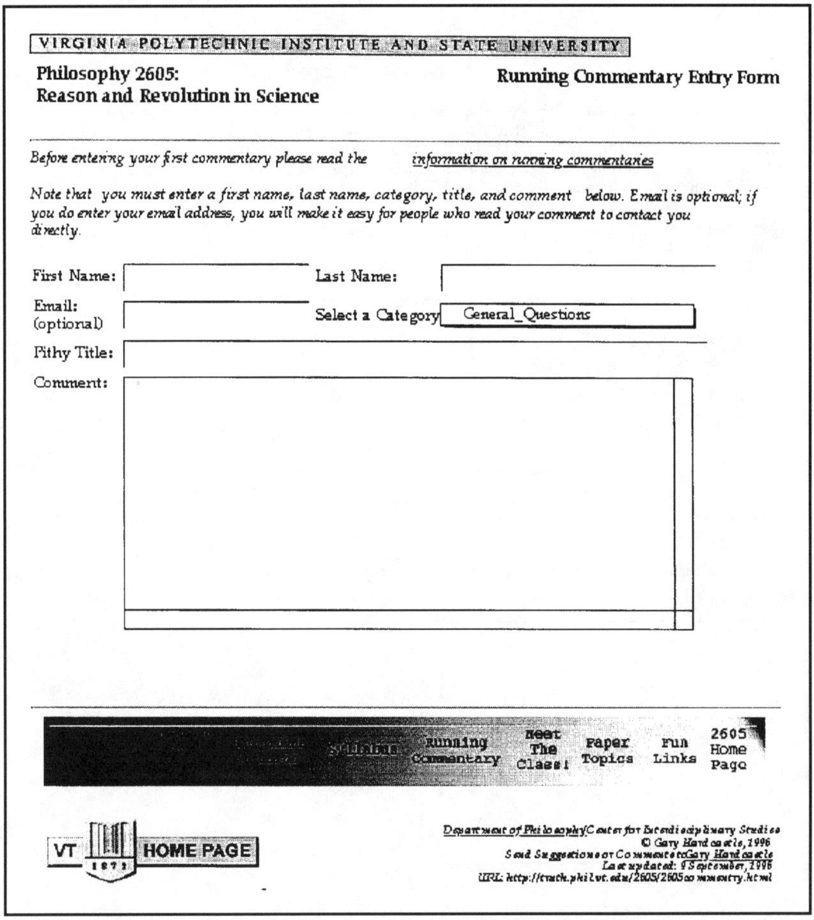

VIRGINIA POLYTECHNIC INSTITUTE AND STATE UNIVERSITY

Philosophy 2605:
Reason and Revolution in Science

Running Commentary Entry Form

Before entering your first commentary please read the *information on running commentaries*

Note that you must enter a first name, last name, category, title, and comment below. Email is optional; if you do enter your email address, you will make it easy for people who read your comment to contact you directly.

First Name:

Last Name:

Email: (optional)

Select a Category: General_Questions

Pithy Title:

Comment:

Syllabus | Running Commentary | Meet The Class! | Paper Topics | Fun Links | 2605 Home Page

VT 1872 HOME PAGE

Department of Philosophy/Center for Interdisciplinary Studies
© Gary Hardcastle, 1996
Send Suggestions or Comments to Gary Hardcastle
Last updated: 9 September, 1996
URL: http://truth.phil.vt.edu/2605/2605commentry.html

Figure 23.4. Running commentary entry form for Philosophy 2605.

another way of promoting philosophical discussion without overburdening instructors.

Our goal in using running commentaries is not to eliminate personal interactions, but to transform and improve them. We want to nourish an intellectual community by providing an electronic "virtual campus" on which students and faculty can exchange ideas among each other in groups of various sizes. In this manner we aim to both break the credit-for-contact model and make it possible to have philosophical discussions in classes of over two hundred students.

The running commentary promotes this goal in another way: only the most confident can contribute to a class taught in a traditional lecture format, but on

---

Ways of Worship

by Jennifer Herman   (5/1/96)

Why is it that some people say they worship their God by praying on Rosary Beads, or by praying in the direction of the son (something like that)? What is it about our cultures that have brought up so many different patterns of worshiping a God? I know a lot of religions were created at different times in history. Is it due to their geographical location or a need for adjustments in believing? I mean as time goes by, people begin to see their own views don't they?

Next Article
Previous Article
Return to Topic Menu

Here is a list of responses that have been posted to this comment...

- Mass (5/2/96)
- Necessity (5/2/96)
- many ways (5/2/96)
- I don't know (5/1/96)
- twelve-I don't know (5/1/96)

If you would like to post a response to this comment, fill out this form completely...

Title of Response:

Author:
Type your first name in the first box and your last name in the second box.

Response Text:

Original Comment: | Ways of Worship | (Don't change this field!)

Forum: | God and Faith | (Don't change this field either!)

Figure 23.5. Sample running commentary for Philosophy 1204.

the Internet one can participate more freely. Our students recognize this on occasion:

> Just a few moments ago I got off of the [computer] . . . and I must say that it is worth the time to get to talk to someone and express your ideas without having to sound like a crazy and be embarrassed. It is not just talking to a computer also. It was like I was talking face to face to someone but not actually knowing who they were. I recommend that everyone try this out.

> At the beginning of class . . . I was a little intimidated. But, after the initial shock I was rather excited. . . . [This] gives students the chance to really be

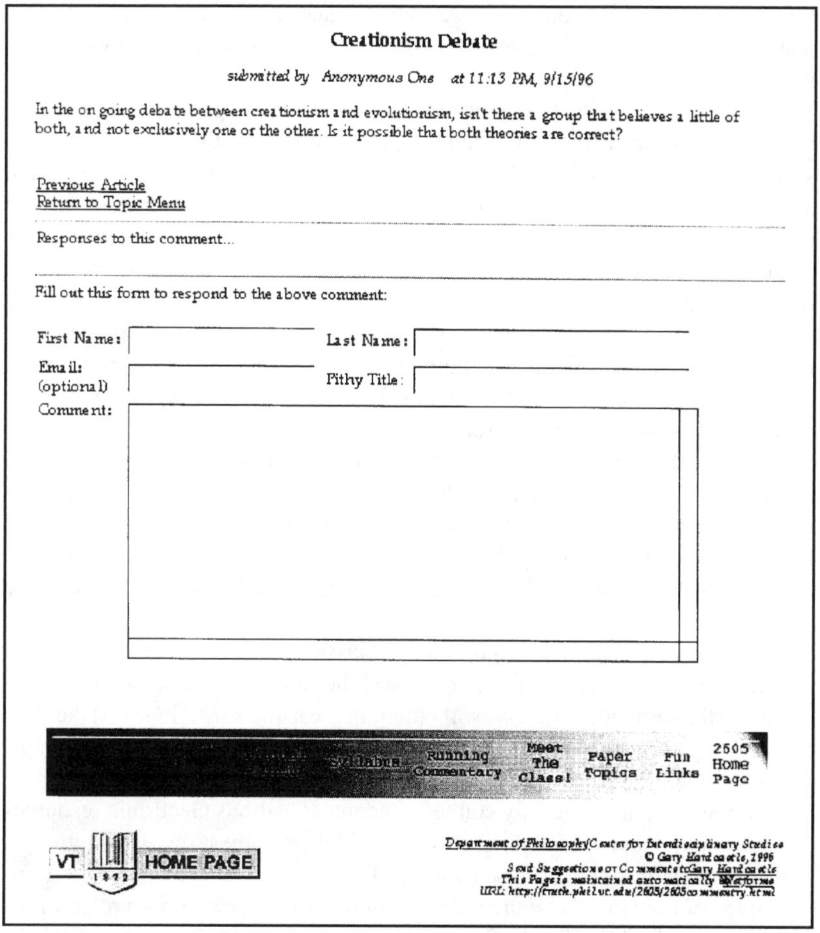

Figure 23.6. Sample running commentary for Philosophy 2605.

> heard. Not only by the teacher but other students as well. Don't you think
> that well outweighs just sitting in a class wanting to say something but
> there are ten other hands up and only fifty minutes in class?

As we sometimes express it to our colleagues, we aim to foster sophisticated written conversations to which the tongue-tied, the shy, the unfashionably dressed, and the easily intimidated will contribute equally.

The Web orientation of our courses has brought some ancillary benefits worth mentioning here. For example, because the course "takes place" on the Web, it is easy to arrange for students to download other supplementary materials. We maintain our syllabi, lecture notes, and homework assignments on homepages for courses such as Epistemology, Knowledge and Reality, Introduction to Humanities, Science and Technology, Reason and Revolution, Philosophy of Mind, and Pragmatism and Logical Positivism.

The advantage of using electronic storage instead of photocopied packets, beyond cutting lead times and saving student money, is that it allows the instructors to include additional materials as the need arises. Professors can make available documents that pertain to the interests of the particular class instead of trying to second-guess how their class will unfold before it ever meets. For example, in one course, discussions of the Internet and its relation to various philosophical theories of community became important. Coincidentally, that spring *Time* magazine published a special issue devoted to the Internet and the changes it might bring about, including of course changes in our society. A few phone calls to *Time* made it clear that the issue would not be on the shelves for several weeks (subscribers had received it early), and so it seemed that our class would miss the opportunity to incorporate that issue of *Time* into the week's readings. Until, that is, a student thought to search the World Wide Web and discovered that the entire issue, including graphics and advertisements, had been placed on line by *Time*. The issue was linked directly to the course page, and as a result everyone in the class had easy and immediate access to the entire issue.

This sort of freedom is important for class discussion, since even though different discussion-based classes may read the same materials, they rarely focus upon the same ideas or follow them up in the same ways. In short, the Web lets instructors be sensitive to the ebb and flow of the various discussion groups, thus encouraging further exploration of the ideas raised.

The Web also lets us easily connect students to various electronic resources related to philosophy, including glossaries, bibliographies, discussion groups, and historical information of high quality, that are not available in libraries. For examples of how these resources can be pulled together as a research tool for students, see the Mind/Brain Resources page and the Philosophy of Biology homepage. The Web has allowed us to introduce students to the worldwide philosophical community in a "user-friendly" format, thus painlessly expanding their intellectual contact with various academic groups and promoting greater intellectual participation with their cohorts worldwide. One student, as he realized that his material could be read by anybody in the world, began ending all of his commentaries with:

> Attention reader: I am a . . . student who is working to understand philosophy of biology and develop my own views on some major issues in philosophy of biology (and to a lesser extent philosophy of science). As such, these . . . [contributions] should be considered works in progress. Any comments regarding content, from basic misunderstandings on my part to reactions to my arguments, would be greatly appreciated. Please e-mail comments and questions to me at [e-mail address omitted].

Our use of the Web in promoting written communication in class has not been limited to Running Commentaries. In Knowledge and Reality, Philosophy of Mind, and Pragmatism and Logical Positivism, students also submit brief informal essays via the Web. In Knowledge and Reality and Philosophy of Mind, in addition to standard formal essay assignments and the Running Commentaries, students respond to a set of short questions for each week's worth of readings by entering their answers directly onto a Web "form" and then e-mailing their answers to their instructor with a keystroke. The instructor responds by e-mailing the correct answers to the student. In this way, the students receive feedback on their work while it is fresh in their minds and they are prepared to engage in the class electronic discussion. In Pragmatism and Logical Positivism and Philosophy of Biology, students are simply required to respond to a more general set of questions about the week's readings. These weekly class contributions then form the basis for a portion of that week's online discussion.

These electronic repositories and homework assignments enable us to move definitions, textual exegesis, brief explanations, and recapitulations out of the lectures and into the context of written discussions. Appropriately prepared study questions and electronic links to supplemental material would supplement this. Answering study questions as one goes along increases retention and comprehension, better preparing the students for subsequent interactions. Ties to contemporary readings, illustrations, and issues help underscore the relevance of class work. Finally, hypertext links among materials posted to the Web allow for students who need additional help to get it without interfering with the progress of students who are further along.

Preliminary Results

While our evidence is typically anecdotal and not systematic, our preliminary results are very positive. With a mix of CSC and human instruction, it is possible to individualize and personalize the courses for our students while increasing the amount and quality of written class interactions. Since participants interact with one another through a medium both personal and public, communication and instruction can be tailored to meet individual needs. This flexibility allows the high achievers to accomplish more and the low achievers to get the attention they require, all without demanding that students with incompatible learning styles be thrown together in lecture classes and forced to endure instruction designed for someone else. This more holistic approach has resulted in a more significant classroom experience; in one current way of putting it, it is more "meaning-making" for the student. As one student in Philosophy 1204 wrote:

> I have to admit that when I first learned that we had to do [a computer assignment] . . . I was dreading it. . . . I was actually surprised when I first entered the [Web site] . . . Most all of the entries and responses have been so interesting. I am just amazed at this whole . . . process. . . . Surprisingly, I have even logged on to the Internet just for fun—if that is what you want to call it!

> I am excited about this class because it is the first class I get to work on the Internet with. I think this is great to be able to converse with other class members through computers because one does not really get to talk with each other in class.

On the face of it, the Web format encourages participation, for students can access the course materials at any time. At any time of the day or night a student can submit an original commentary; similarly, the instructor or other students can read and respond to the submitted commentaries at any time. With the Web one has the immediacy of a telephone call but the freedom of a written letter to read, compose without pressure, and respond to when desired.

Furthermore, the wide visibility of contributions to this community means that a certain degree of peer judgment directed toward all aspects of a contribution is inescapable. We have observed that students in these courses tend to be better spellers and grammarians, and are especially more coherent. They must write, and, "before" their peers, they write more carefully. But they don't have to hurry, or to worry about their voices. This sort of electronic community changes the pressures on students; it does not remove them. Our experience indicates that, overall, better writing results.

Finally, by altering the social patterns that govern the hesitant exchange of ideas, faculty develop new and better skills for sharing information. In lecture courses certainly, these technologies drastically change the classroom dynamic. We have become participants, rather than more detached (albeit expert) lecturers, guiding our students to their own ideas and specializations. Lectures complement the electronic interactions by informing student discussion and setting the intellectual agenda, while allowing the students to take the initiative in their Running Commentaries and pursue avenues that interest them. We lead classes now solely to create a framework for student discussion to fill in and flesh out.

What follows are some excerpts from student commentaries submitted during the spring 1996 semester of Knowledge and Reality that illustrate just how students can teach and learn from one another, if given the chance and venue. In particular, notice that the students raise the issues they want to pursue and then try to sort them out among themselves; we only assigned the relevant readings.

Simulations: Real or Not? (3/21/96)
... It is obvious why many people believe computers to be intelligent and in many cases alive. This is because they produce answers identical to that of

humans. For instance a computer may talk back to you with simulated reasoning and show simulated emotions. But Searle points out that we must not fall into this trap of simulation, believing the computer to be alive just as we would not feel wet when in a computer simulated flood or become hot in a computer simulated fire, although this flood and fire are identical to the real occurrence.

Could Feel It (3/22/96)
If the simulation were real enough, our mind would be tricked into thinking it was real. Therefore, if we were in flood simulation and to our mind everything was simulated to perfection I think we would then feel wet. The Holodeck on Star Trek is a simulation, and even though that is just TV, if we were to create something that real, what happened inside would feel real.

Virtual Reality (3/25/96)
. . . Virtual reality in itself is a simulation of life. Could people "live" in a computer world and not be able to tell the difference between the computer world and the real world?

Similar (4/17/96)
I also can see why some believe computers to be human, but there are several things which cannot be simulated. For instance, a computer can sense heat but cannot feel pain. It can simulate the feeling of pain and show signs of the pain, but this is not the same as a human feeling pain.

Programs, Brains, Same Thing! (3/22/96)
. . . So, here's a more interesting question . . . let's not ask if machines can duplicate human behavior, but rather, are we simply machines by the definition everyone has been giving in this class? After all, it seems as though *everything* we think and do is based merely on an extremely powerful processor running constantly that interprets and refines as it goes along. . . . Perhaps we need to modify our definition of "human" and "machine" to distinguish a bit less, instead of more.

Here you can see the refinement of initially cloudy ideas in light of reflective discussion, which, as we mentioned earlier, is the traditional way of learning philosophical material.

In sum, we have observed that using CSC in our introductory philosophy courses:

- *makes more efficient use of our physical, technological, and human resources* by reducing temporal and spatial constraints on class time while nurturing more and better student discussion and writing.
- *improves the efficacy and increases the quality of our offerings in philosophy in the face of decreasing resources.* We are able to reach more students more effectively in terms of developing the general skills of productive, self-paced learning. From our experience thus far, we believe our courses have direct payoffs in reasoning ability, reading and writing competence, and the ability to analyze new situations.

- *breaks the common pattern of student passivity engendered by the traditional lecture course* which papers over mismatches between teaching and learning styles. Students are forced to be actively involved in and responsible for their own learning. In our courses, passive lecture attendance is not possible; students must log on and work. New technology will be used in support of an old educational goal: keeping the learning process in motion as much as possible for each individual student.

At its heart, philosophy is a dialectic among groups of people over eons. With CSC, our students can be true participants in this tradition, learning philosophy by doing philosophy. And this is just what every philosophy class aims to achieve.[3]

Notes

1. Two years later, Tech's computing facilities for undergraduates and faculty exceed those of most other colleges or universities. This puts us in an interesting position with respect to advising other philosophy teachers, for what we have done is at the moment technologically feasible for only a minority of teachers. Our response is to speak to the results of CSC use; the pitfalls of first-time CSC use in the philosophy classroom; and the problems that remain when hardware, software, and expertise are locally abundant.

2. Our implementation employs the Mac-specific acgi application NetForms, commercially available from Maxum Development at http://www.maxum.com. Our pages are served from two 7500/100 PCI PowerMacs with 16 MB RAM running WebStar 1.3.1, mirrored by our department's 8500 PowerMac Server with 16 MB RAM. All HTML was composed by Gary and Valerie Hardcastle using BBEdit Lite 3.5.1, though in some cases we took advantage of the excellent examples offered by Maxum. Adobe Acrobat 3.0b1 was used to create the PDF files for the lecture notes. DropStuff 4.01 compressed handouts for student downloading. GIFs and backgrounds were created using Canvas 3.5, PowerPoint 4.0, Adobe Photoshop 3.0, GIF Converter 2.3.7, ColorMeister 1.3.5, and Transparency. Students at Virginia Tech generally use Netscape 2.0 as a browser.

3. This work has been supported by generous grants from the Funds for the Improvement for Post-Secondary Education and the Center for Excellence in Undergraduate Teaching at Virginia Tech.

Web Resources

"Epistemology Homepage." http://truth.phil.vt.edu/4224/4224.html (November 1995).

"Homework Assignments for Knowledge and Reality." http://mind.phil.vt.edu/www/1204hw.html or http://WWW.phil.vt.edu/Valerie/1204/1204hw.html (mirror site)(October 1997).

"Introduction to Humanities, Science, and Technology Homepage." http://truth.phil.vt.edu/1504/1504.html (November 1995).

"Knowledge and Reality Homepage." http://mind.phil.vt/www/1204.html or http://www.phil.vt.edu/Valerie/1204/1204.html (mirror site)

"Mind/Brain Resources Homepage." http://mind.phil.vt/www/mind.html

"Virginia Tech's Philosophy of Biology Seminar Homepage." http://mind.phil.vt.edu/biology/philbio.html

"Philosophy of Mind Homepage." http://mind.phil.vt.edu/www/4204.html

"Pragmatism and Logical Positivism Homepage." http://truth.phil.vt.edu/3024/3024.html

"Running Commentary Web Site for Knowledge and Reality Course." http://mind.phil.vt.edu/1204Comment/1204Comment.html or http://www.phil.vt.edu/Valerie/1204/1204Comment/1204Comment.html (mirror site)

"Running Commentary Web Site for Pragmatism and Logical Positivism." http://truth.phil.vt.edu/3024/commentaries/commentarymenu.html

Other Related Sites

"Creating Electronic Discussions in Philosophy." http://mind.phil.vt.edu/WAC/TP.html

"Teaching and Learning with Computers Discussion Group." TLC@VTVM1.CC.VT.EDU

"Virginia Tech Courses on the World Wide Web." http://truth.phil.vt.edu/wwwcourses.html

"World Wide Lecture Hall." http://World Wide Web.utexas.edu/world/lecture/index.html

"Writing Across the Curriculum Discussion Group." WRITE-L@VTVM1.CC.VT.EDU

24 Electronic Conferencing in an Interdisciplinary Humanities Course

MaryAnn Krajnik Crawford
Michigan State University

Kathleen Geissler
Michigan State University

M. Rini Hughes
Michigan State University

Jeffrey Miller
Augustana College

Debbie: Hey guys! How was your day off? I hope you stayed warm. I hate this weather. . . .

John: Hi group. I hope this alias thing works because I don't want to have to do it again. By the way this is John writing to you. . . .

Anne: Hi everyone, I guess if you get this message, it means our alias worked. This whole thing would be more fun if we could write to each other about anything, instead of having to write about this class. So, what are you doing this weekend? . . .

—First e-mail entries, 21 January 1994, IAH 201[1]

In *Communication as Culture: Essays on Media and Society*, James Carey maintains that "the study of culture can also be called the study of communication, for what we are studying in this context are the ways in which experience is worked into understanding and then disseminated and celebrated" (1989, 44). In this chapter, we share a discussion about the use of asynchronous, small-group e-mail assigned in an undergraduate humanities course. Focusing on communicative strategies used by one six-student group, we suggest that this e-mail, by encouraging the students to participate in an intellectual conversation of their own making, helped them create a culture of learning that blurs traditional boundaries between private and public, personal and intellectual areas of thinking and writing.

296

"The U.S. and the World" was inaugurated in fall 1992 as part of our new general education program. This required course spans the history and culture of the United States from the 16th century to the 1980s and asks students to place themselves, their culture, and its history in a global context. From the outset the course has been one that invites (and depends on) multiple perspectives as well as multiple media. Taught by graduate teaching assistants guided by faculty mentors from various disciplines in the College of Arts and Letters, the course enrolls some 3,000 students per semester in paired sections of thirty students each. Two or three times per week, students view twenty-five- to thirty-minute videos produced specifically for this course. The videos mix voices, visuals, and formats; some involve panel discussions, others a single scholar. Students encounter not one authoritative voice, but many, and even these voices are mediated by primary readings: letters, diaries, personal narratives, legal documents, fiction.

The class is writing-intensive and includes a variety of formal and informal writing; but, unlike courses that teach writing or that introduce students to disciplinary discourse, this course uses writing as a way of coming to terms with the material. In asking students to engage in a dialogue between past and present, the course draws on WAC insights about the importance of personal connections and the role of utterance and speculation in active thinking and learning (e.g., Fulwiler 1989; Fulwiler and Young 1990). The use of e-mail, an adaptation of "common" or "team" journals (e.g., Graybeal 1987), fits with the active learning pedagogy we wished for this course.

Working in four- to six-person groups, large enough to provide multiple views yet small enough for efficient reading and response time, students are asked to "engage ideas" and "talk" to each other weekly via an alias on their university e-mail accounts.[2] We encourage students to write two or three screens, but instructors do not, generally, participate in the conversations. The e-mail is also worth 15 percent of the grade, which suggests that we're serious about the value of this activity.

JM: I think there are real differences between e-mail and team journals. Besides changing the medium from handwriting to keyboarding, which could disadvantage some students, the biggest difference, and advantage, is the way it changes communication. Pushing "send" distributes their words to everybody in their group and the teacher. In team journals, students still seem to be writing for the next person, in a linear sequence.

MC: And there's the informality—the conversational language but also the "errors" in spelling, punctuation, and typos. They're almost part of the medium. But I think there's more potential for agreement and disagreement on e-mail, too, which means students are faced with considering not only what, but how, they should write. There's a real audience, and there are real risks involved in sharing and responding.

JM: Plus, some of the students have to get used to the technology as well as each other. Those first messages look like so much "blather," but notice that the class becomes a topic very quickly, too, although in resistance: Anne would rather write about "anything, instead of having to write about this class." They're beginning to build a context for themselves that includes both personal and academic areas.

KG: Then there is that moment where they realize they're no longer supposed to be just getting acquainted and deciding about their semester project [to write editorials] but are supposed to be discussing the content of the class. Suddenly the whole thing takes on a different frame, a different tone:

> *John* (2/9): Hey guys . . . Did all of you read the book? I'm just asking because we have to write things about class to one another on e-mail as part of our grade. Is it just me or was it hard to keep track of who was who in the book. It seemed like they were switching characters every line or so. Otherwise I don't really have too much to say.

> KG: I wonder if the teacher didn't say, "You know, it's time now to start talking about the books."

> JM: Whether she did or not, what's significant is that you get this *group* concern with it.

> RH: And John suggests, "I don't write about books very much!" But his question is to the group here, not the teacher.

MC: To me, John seems uncertain about what's appropriate for this medium, in this context. Maybe it's as much an issue of how as what, an I-don't-know-how-to-start-talking-about-this-intellectual-kind-of-stuff, because later on he does introduce topics and share opinions. Anne's the one who's shown the most resistance: the videos and readings are "boring" (2/2); she can't find topics for her editorials (1/27, 2/2); she doesn't know where the museum is (2/3); she misses meetings (2/9). Yet she's the one who introduces gender as the first "academic" topic, and she does so before Antonio reports checking with the teacher:

> *Anne* (2/9, 17:54 EST): Hi Everyone. . . . Anyway, I read Charlotte Temple and I really liked it. . . . This period of history is usually not very interesting to me, so I was kind of surprised at how much I enjoyed the story. Maybe I will choose an editorial topic somewhere along the lines of women's lives in the Revolutionary War era. This is really the first idea I've had so far, but knowing me, I could change my mind. . . .

> *Antonio* (2/9, 19:30 EST): Hey what's up . . . I talked to Mrs. N, John, and she sayd that all we have to write about is what we either do in class, like watching videos, or talk about our group projects.

KG: Anne's always surprising herself—or us. She worries about topics, yet she always comes up with quite interesting comments. Maybe she doesn't expect that what interests her will be in the frame of the class.

MC: Or the group. "I could change my mind" suggests that she's testing how the others might respond. And notice that Anne really expands gender as a topic after Debbie's support.

RH: Debbie and her capital-letter messages—are these part of the role she takes on as the group-facilitator? She's always telling others about meeting times and deadlines:

> *Debbie* (2/11): HEY GUYS! SO WHAT DID YOU THINK ABOUT CHARLOTTE? PRETTY INTERESTING WOMAN. IT SEEMS THAT WOMEN'S ROLE IN SOCIETY HAS ALWAYS BEEN PRETTY PITI-FUL. I CAN NOT BELIEVE THAT IT DATES BACK TO THAT TIME THAT WOMEN WERE TREATED INFERIOR TO MEN. (EXCUSE ME FOR BEING A WOMAN, GUYS). . . . GRANTED, SOME CHANGES HAVE DEVELOPED BUT GUYS HAVE SOME MERCY ON US! !@#$%&* I DON'T REALLY THINK WE NEED TO MEET THIS WEEK
> . . .

> *Anne* (2/14): . . . I read Debbie's message about Charlotte Temple and I agree with what she said. . . . Lots of times young girls age 15 or 16 are forced to marry old men in their 40's or 50's. . . . The subject of how women are treated carries over from Charlotte Temple to the reading for today about Lucretia Mott and Elizabeth Cady Stanton. . . . For men who liked to control their women, these advocates were a big threat to them. . . . I'd be interested to hear what you guys think of all this, especially what Tony and John think. . . .

JM: What struck me is how much this goes along with what Bakhtin (1981) defines as dialogue. There are utterances, and you never know how they're going to shape what follows. Anne pops up with this stuff that's clearly a concern of hers that's not articulated anywhere previously. All of a sudden here it is, and all of a sudden the other people in the dialogue have to address it and move what they're dealing with into what she's defined:

> *Antonio* (2/15): . . . I think Anne mentioned the idea that women back then were sometimes married with men who were at least three or four times their age. That's still true Anne. How about India. Women in India, don't get to choose. . . . I'm not a sovanistic pig, so don't even think about saying that ok, guys. I think John understands at what I am trying to say. I hope I didn't bore you guys with what I wrote.

> *John* (2/15): . . . I have been reading what you guys have had to say, and I think all of you really know what you are talking about. My opinion about Charlotte Temple is that she was very opressed. . . . Sorry Charlotte, but back then it was pretty impossible to live out those hopes. Not that I agree with that, but that is the truth about how things were. . . . I probably sound chauvanistic, but I'm not. That is just the way I saw the story. . . .

JM: So what interests Anne becomes a part of the cultural frame of the group. As soon as she shares her comments on gender, the two guys in the group say that they're not chauvinistic.

MC: They begin building on each others' views, but it's risky. They invite, even plead, for support. Especially Denise, but I also think about Antonio's "sovanistic." He doesn't know how it's spelled, but that doesn't stop him from trying to communicate. They're taking risks and sharing views that I don't think they would, or could, in class.

JM: And something else this speaks to: providing a vector to move the dialogue and shape it into something else entirely. We don't know if the teacher here has asked anything or not to prompt this response. What's remarkable is that, if indeed that push did occur, there's been a similar push from Anne, from her experience outside of class, to refocus the field of discussion.

KG: Right. What seems to happen is that they have to develop each other's views not a teacher's question. Questions can set a certain frame out of which students tend not to wander.

JM: Questions become almost coercive—you *will* respond.

RH: But they can also be invitations, and then there's another aspect to this— the differential of power, and gender. It's different if students or teachers do the asking.

MC: And not-responding gets noticed, too, which may be related to the hedging in here. Hedging allows room for change and adjustments, creates a safe "out" while maintaining the relationship. In that first gender message, Anne creates a safe place by stating that she might change her mind about gender as a topic worth writing about. It's similar, I suppose, to Brown and Levinson's (1987) notion of "face" in politeness strategies, but there's an intellectual dimension here. By inviting the others to respond, she seems to be negotiating the way topics will be developed as well as her own interest in them. She wants to hear what the others will say. In contrast, Debbie's, "guys, have mercy on us" is a plea to Antonio and John.

RH: Debbie's message also closes off the conversation: too bad our society hasn't changed; that's the way it is. There's nothing to discuss. She tells us what we already know.

KG: It seems to me that there's this other frame operating in this piece, this kind of "male-female" understanding, which is partly Anne's assumption that Antonio and John are going to think differently from the women. But then, when she's invoked with their "not chauvinistic," they're working, all of them, to signal their openness to discussion on a polarizing topic.

MC: Thinking about Bakhtin and dialogue: Antonio's partially agreeing with Anne but also shifting and expanding her views when he mentions "India." He shares his own knowledge about gender, but moves the ideas across geographic and cultural space.

JM: These four here, from Debbie through John, you can really see the development of a culture, if you take that as a culture defined by the process of communication. Anne agrees with Debbie, but Debbie has put the topic forward in such a way that it's difficult for anyone to respond. Anne then makes this invitation to dialogue to Antonio and John, both of whom take her up on it, particularly when Antonio pushes John to join. The dialogue is going, and it's expanding, it's moving outward.

MC: In information and in time, which is an interesting development, because one of the safe places here is to leave gender conflicts as "back then," as John does.

KG: Yes, and "India" works in the same way—"out there."

MC: Right, a different cultural space but in current time. They're building connections. Anne presents gender issues as having a history, including specific references to readings—Lucretia Mott and Elizabeth Cady Stanton. But Antonio states that the problems are "still true." That's an important cultural move. By shifting the topic away from a static "back then," he's positioning their lives in that history: *We* are a part of that.

RH: It's also interesting that the other two women in the group didn't participate in that gender discussion, but they do explain: Tasha's been busy (2/16) and Jane's had a problem with her alias (2/16). And, after that, both of them write consistently and actively, starting with the following week's discussion about slavery. And it's John who introduces the topic. He's catching on to this:

> *John* (2/21): . . . Mrs. N proposed what I thought was a very interesting wuestion today when she asked us wether we aould allow ourselves to become slaves. . . . I came to the conclusion that I would rather run away
> . . . .

KG: And they all begin to agree and disagree more strongly. Look at the way Anne and Tasha actively oppose Jane's suggestion that slavery helped create "character":

> *Anne* (2/23): Hi Guys, It seems like we all have pretty strong opinions. . . . Jane was saying that there were some good things to come out of slavery. I really disagree with that and I disagree with her reasoning. . . . minorities encounter prejudiced people often, just in terms of everyday experiences. This is my opinion on the matter, so anyone can respond with their views.
>
> *Jane* (2/25): I'm glad everyone has something to say about slavery, but no one seems to be getting very deep into the issue. You all seemed to misunderstand what I was trying to say. . . . Slavery DID happen and nothing can change that. In no way do I mean. . . . Write more. . . .
>
> *Tasha* (2/25): Hey guys, . . . At this point I would like to agree with Antonio. . . . I hope we are not just talking about the wrongs of today and spreading peace and respect to all races. It starts with us and an individual examining our situations. . . .

MC: Their messages also became longer over the semester. Anne's first messages are five and ten lines long, her gender discussion is twenty, and her last message is thirty lines. She notices that the others' are writing more, too, but what's important is the way she addresses these "academic" topics now. She adds specific content information, and with no hint of resistance:

> *Anne* (4/22): Since Jim and Fred both decided to write a book this week, I have a lot to respond to. First about Martin Luther King Jr. and the Civil Rights movement. . . . Now, about the Cuban Missile Crisis. . . .

MC: This reminds me of Kurt Spellmeyer's (1993) notion of common ground. By sharing views and negotiating positions, these students seemed to reach some common ground of communication and trust—that their views would be respected, at least as worthy of discussion. And the hedging and the "chit-chat," which seemed so non-intellectual, actually allowed them to develop that ground.

JM: Victor Turner (1977) calls that a "liminal space." It's that risky "in-between" area where communication, and so culture, and learning, can develop. E-mail can provide that.

RH: I agree, but I don't want to lose sight of the teacher's investment in that culture either. As with any assignment, students can choose to cooperate or not regardless of the direction, or freedom, a teacher gives, and there are issues to consider. On a practical level, using e-mail groups requires advance planning. How easy will it be for students to access and use e-mail? If it's too difficult, valuable time will be lost. Another consideration is the teacher's time. Keeping track of the messages doesn't take long, but teachers also have to decide whether or how much they will be involved in the e-mail groups. Maintaining "screen silence," as the teacher did with this group, can make us question what we're doing and why. Then, there's evaluation, which is always thorny but becomes even more so if students seem to be engaging in so much "chit-chat." Clearly, traditional criteria that work for a final draft in hard copy have to be modified if we want to support an intellectual conversation that involves the give-and-take of communication.

MC: That reminds me of another benefit, or maybe mixed blessing, of this e-mail. It helps me reflect on my own practices and expectations. That's the benefit of discussions like this one, but using e-mail provides ongoing feedback. As I read the students' weekly messages, I can't help but think about what's working or not working in the class, where disagreements or problems are occurring. I can see my values reflected as well as my failings. That's positive, but not always comfortable.

John Fiske suggests that the "art of being in-between" requires appropriation (1994, 36), and part of the development of a culture of learning is the appropriation of the discourse of the educational community by the learners who use it. Not all groups function as smoothly or engage discussion as regularly as these students did. However, students who actively engage in e-mail discussions can be expected to turn the experience to their own ends, and not necessarily in ways that coincide with what the teacher had in mind. E-mail seems to facilitate such appropriation since it is done outside the teacher's direct control, but, in turn, it challenges us to understand the way communicative strategies, as well as our own practices, can make such appropriation possible.

Notes

1. Student excerpts are presented verbatim, edited only to conserve space; ellipsis dots represent omitted materials. Student names have been changed to preserve confidentiality.

2. All MSU students have Internet e-mail accounts provided through their technology fee. Computers connected to the Internet are also quite readily available on campus. For this class, we have each student create an "alias" in his or her e-mail program comprised of the addresses of other group members and the teacher so that everyone simultaneously receives a copy of each message. A listserv—e.g., Schwartz (1995)—or a locally networked system with communication software could also allow student e-mail discussions. However, the number we would need makes listservs impractical. In addition, we believe that the size of the e-mail group is important. Larger groups would make the amount of time spent reading and responding prohibitive, or at least discouraging, and provide fewer "safe places" for students, especially younger undergraduates, to become comfortable with each other while writing about academic, intellectual, and often socially sensitive issues.

Works Cited

Bakhtin, Mikhail M. 1981. *The Dialogic Imagination: Four Essays.* Edited by Michael Holquist, translated by Caryl Emerson and Michael Holquist. Austin: University of Texas Press.

Brown, Penelope, and Charles C. Levinson. 1987. *Politeness: Some Universals in Language Usage.* Cambridge: Cambridge University Press.

Carey, James. 1989. *Communication as Culture: Essays on Media and Society.* Boston, MA: Unwin Hyman.

Fiske, John. 1994. *Understanding Popular Culture.* London: Routledge.

Fulwiler, Toby. 1989. "Responding to Student Journals." In *Writing and Response: Theory, Practice, and Research,* edited by Chris M. Anson, 149–73. Urbana, IL: National Council of Teachers of English.

Fulwiler, Toby, and Art Young, eds. 1990. *Programs That Work: Models and Methods for WAC.* Upper Montclair, NJ: Heinemann Boynton/Cook.

Graybeal, Jean. 1987. "The Team Journal." In *The Journal Book,* edited by Toby Fulwiler, 306–11. Portsmouth, NH: Boynton/Cook.

Schwartz, Helen J. 1995. "New Technologies for New Majority Students of Literature." In *When Writing Teachers Teach Literature*, edited by Art Young and Toby Fulwiler, 246–57. Portsmouth, NH: Heinemann Boynton/Cook.

Spellmeyer, Kurt. 1993. *Common Ground: Dialogue, Understanding, and the Teaching of Composition.* Englewood Cliffs, NJ: Prentice Hall.

Turner, Victor. 1977. "Process, System, and Symbol: Toward a New Anthropological Synthesis." *Daedalus* 106: 61–80.

Glossary

ALN Asynchronous Learning Network. Interactive projects that connect students and teachers with software that allows them to write, read, and respond to each other even when they are not online at the same time. Primarily for distance learning, ALNs are sometimes used within a classroom to engage students in highly interactive communication. Pacerforum and FirstClass, used by Gail Hawisher and Michael Pemberton at the University of Illinois at Urbana-Champaign, are examples of software that supports ALNs.

ASC Academic Skills Center. A Guilford College center that helps students develop the various skills needed to be successful in the academy. The URL for ASC's Web page is http://www.guilford.edu/ASC/AcademicSkillsCenter.html.

C&C *Computers and Composition: An International Journal for Teachers of Writing.* An influential journal which has shaped the field of computers and composition. Begun as a newsletter in November 1983 by Kathleen Kiefer and Cynthia Selfe, it is now a tri-annual journal edited by Gail Hawisher and Cynthia Selfe. Its primary focus is on the intersections between communication technologies, composition pedagogy, and theory.

CAC Communication Across the Curriculum. An expansion of the writing-across-the-curriculum movement that broadens the focus from written communication to all other forms of communication, including oral and visual. Although writing continues to be viewed as central to teaching and learning, it is joined in an interactive social process with other forms of communication to promote critical thinking, collaboration, and problem-solving within and across disciplines.

CAISE Center for Advancement in Instruction for Science and Engineering. Center located at Clarkson University which assists the development of technology projects that enhance the science and engineering curriculum. The article by Selber and Karis in this collection describes one such project—a CD-ROM engineering textbook.

CCE Center for Continuing Education. A Guilford College center that assists faculty and staff with projects (computer-mediated and otherwise) and enhances continuing education across the campus. In their article, Strickland and Whitnell describe one project developed through the CCE. The URL for the CCE's Web page is http://www.guilford.edu/CCE/main.html.

CIT Office of Computing and Information Technology. A Spelman College office which provides technical support for computer-mediated projects across the campus (including the project Hocks and Bascelli describe in their article).

CMC Computer-Mediated Communication. Widely used phrase introduced by Lee Sproull and Sara Kiesler (*Connections: New Ways of Working in the Networked Organization* 1991). Stressing the use of technologies to facilitate communication, CMC refers to both the variety of networking technologies that allow users to converse online—listservs, e-mail, Internet relay chat, newsgroups, and MOOs—*and* the kinds of interactions that occur within those online spaces. Many theorists have argued that CMC will help build new communities online that will enhance real-life communities (e.g., Jones's

Cybersociety: Computer-Mediated Communication and Community 1995) while some have argued that CMC decreases community participation (e.g., Doheny-Farina's *The Wired Neighborhood* 1996).

CSC Computer-Supported Communication. Communication (traditionally writing) that is aided by the use of computer technologies. This term is commonly used to refer to the theory of computer usage that Cynthia Selfe offers in *Creating a Computer-Supported Writing Facility: A Blueprint for Action* (1989), in which she emphasizes that students' and instructors' needs must be foregrounded and that computer technologies should be used to meet those needs, not determine them. The focus, then, is on using computers in context to assist teaching and learning writing, rather than teaching computer skills.

CWP Comprehensive Writing Program. A WAC program located at Spelman College. Begun in 1979, it serves to help faculty members across the disciplines include writing into their courses. CWP is one of many such WAC programs located at universities and colleges across the country.

CWS Center for Writing Studies. A cross-disciplinary unit (directed by Gail Hawisher) located at the University of Illinois at Urbana-Champaign. According to its brochure, the Center's "mission is to sustain a community of scholars in writing studies and to provide graduate students with opportunities to study the various practices and discourses related to written communication." Other such units have been established in universities across the country, distinguishing themselves from traditional rhetoric and composition programs by their emphasis on interdisciplinary concerns and a broader definition.

ECAC Electronic Communication Across the Curriculum. A term created by the editors (Donna Reiss, Dickie Selfe, and Art Young) to highlight the evolving intersections between the communication-across-the-curriculum movement and new information technologies. ECAC recognizes that e-mail, synchronous and asynchronous conferencing, multimedia, and the World Wide Web offer new modes of communication to construct and enhance learning within and across disciplines.

HTML Hypertext Markup Language. HTML codes tell an Internet browser (such as Netscape Navigator or Microsoft Explorer) how to display a Web document, but each browser will interpret the HTML commands in different ways and will thus display the document in slightly different formats.

IT Information Technology. Computer technologies designed to facilitate the production and distribution of information across time and distance. These technologies include word processing and e-mail programs, synchronous and asynchronous networks, World Wide Web publishing tools and browsers. Serving to connect people and information, ITs can be used to promote interactions and provide the technological structure for people to share information and ideas.

MOO Multi-user dimension, Object Oriented Environment. Interactive, synchronous virtual environment that allows users to move around virtual rooms/spaces and converse with other users who are virtual inhabitants of the rooms. Unlike MUDs (multi-user dimensions), which were games that dictate participants' paths and usages, MOOs are constantly changing arenas that allow users to create their own virtual spaces and to decide what will happen in those spaces. MOOs encourage users to be creators of the environment, not simply participants in it.

OWL Online Writing Lab. Writing assistance that is mediated by computer technologies. Information technologies are used in various ways to help tutor writing: tutor and learner can meet face-to-face but use the technology to help them search for sources and revise text; students can e-mail writing-related questions to the writing lab tutors and receive a response via e-mail; listservs can be set up to facilitate real-time conferencing about a writing project, and writing labs can establish a database of handouts and suggestions that can be posted online for users to draw upon when they have questions. OWLs do not necessarily imply that tutor and learner never meet face-to-face; instead they highlight the usage of technologies to assist the work of the writing lab.

SGML Standard General Markup Language. A standard computer language that can be translated by all Internet browsers. Because it allows all users to access material posted on the Web (no matter what formatting system used), SGML makes the Web possible. Before SGML, individual computer systems had a difficult time "talking" with one another because they spoke different computer languages. Similar to ASCII (a universal computer language), SGML allows cross-platform computer communication, but unlike ASCII, SGML is hypertextual.

TLTR Teaching, Learning, Technology Roundtable. A project initiated by Steve Gilbert and funded through the American Association of Higher Education (AAHE). At the heart of the project are seminars and workshops led by Gilbert that help participants learn to use information technologies across the disciplines. The project stresses a learner-centered focus which builds a collaborative atmosphere between teacher and learner, an atmosphere that is then enhanced by computer technologies.

URL Uniform Resource Locator. Formally called Universal Resource Locator, a URL is the Internet address of a Web page or file. When using Netscape (a popular Internet browser), the URL is listed in the box labeled "Location" and begins with "http://" and is followed by the address. URLs can be used to locate specific files on the Internet and are used in the citation of those files in articles.

WAC Writing Across the Curriculum. A recent educational movement that views writing at the center of the academic experience in all disciplines. Writing is used as a tool for learning as well as for communication. Two basic arguments sustain WAC programs: (1) writing helps students learn disciplinary content, and (2) writing is integrally linked to the field in which one writes. Therefore, writing should be a component of all college classes, rather than being isolated to composition courses in English departments.

WOW Writers' Online Workshop. An online assistance service offered by the Writers' Workshop at the University of Illinois at Urbana-Champaign. Users can e-mail short, writing-related questions to WOW, and they will receive responses from consultants at the Workshop in a short period of time. The address is wow@uiuc.edu.

WWW World Wide Web. A hypertext-based communication system which connects individual Web pages and maps out the pathways for browsers so that they can find the information they need, information that is located on various computers and servers around the world.

Index

Accounting classes, 242–53
  topics for team-taught writing, 244–46,
    249–51, 252–53
Agent of change, 58
American Association of Higher Education
  (AAHE), xix
Anatomy, 132
Annotated Example Texts and Speeches,
  61–62
Applebee, Arthur, 139
Aristotle, 143
Art, 132
  creative process and, 170–77
Art history, 48, 51–52
Assignments. *See* Online assignments
"As We May Think" (Vannevar), 192
"As We Will Think" (Nelson), 192
Asynchronous learning, 17–39, 125, 187, 265,
  296
  Engineering, 26–28
  English, 23–26
  Writers' Online Workshop, 33–36
Audience, 139–50
  accommodation to, 139, 140, 142
  authority of, 142–43
  collaborating, 141
  entire class as, 209, 211, 215
  imaginary, 139
  resistance to, 139, 142, 143
  rhetorical, 141
  target, 142–43

Bartholomae, David, 77
Bascelli, Daniele, 40, 319
Basseches, Michael, 210
Batson, Trent W., xviii, 244
Baxter, Geneva, 48
Bazerman, Charles, 170
Beaver College, xi
Being Digital (Negroponte), 192
Berthoff, Ann, 175
Bertsch, Michael, 180, 319
Bialostosky, Don H., 159

Biology classes, 162–63, 231–40
Birkerts, Sven, 194
Bishop Museum, 182
Bitzer, Lloyd, 141
Boiarsky, Cynthia, 244
Bradley University, 273–80
Brand, Stewart, 194
Brannon, Lil, 256
Browell, J., 255
Bush, Vannevar, 192
Business classes, 86–101. *See also* Account-
  ing classes; Marketing classes
  international e-mail debate project, 151–61
  MBA curriculum and communication, 97–98
  virtual case, 87–96

CalcQuest, 118
Carey, James, 296
"Case of the Unhappy Client," 87–89
Cayuga Community College, 263–72
Central College, 17
Chadwick, Scott A., 117, 319
Change, xix
Chappell, Virginia, 223
Chavez, Carmen, xviii
Clark, Irene, 5
Clarke College, 6, 207–19
Clarkson University, 102–16
Classrooms
  electronic equipment, 199–201
  layout, 78
  newsroom environment, 251
Clearinghouse function, 26
Clemson University, xvii
Cold Region Technologies, 106
Collaboration
  among WAC faculty, 130, 131
  black writers and white artists, 139–50
  in classroom, 77, 263
  COllaboratory, 180–89
  computer-supported, 242–253
  creative process and, 170–77
  in groups, 26

Guilford students and administration, 195–99
learning and, 120
team writing, 244–46, 264, 265, 267
COllaboratory, 180–89
Generation X project, 182–84
writing requirements, 184–85
Colorado State University, 12
Communication Across the Curriculum
(CAC) and, 57–72
online writing center, 58–66
Common ground, 302
Communication Across the Curriculum
(CAC), xvii–xx
bottom up approach, 58
connecting with computers, xxi–xxii
direct support for students and, 58, 60
institutional culture and, 57–72
instructional software, 59–66
potential of Internet and, 191
World Wide Web and, 129–35
*Communication as Culture: Essays on Media
and Society* (Carey), 296
Communication skills, 255–56
Community
creating, 73–85, 184–85, 186–88
at Guilford College, 191–92
virtual, 191–92, 198, 282–94
of writers, 215, 217, 218
Community college issues, 263–72
drop-out rates, 270, 271
inflexible structures, 263
technological access and, 263–64, 268–69
Computer-mediated communication (CMC),
123
Computers. *See also specific topics*
history of use in universities, x–xi
human interface and, 102–16
humanistic perspectives on, 112–13
impact on culture, xix–xx
institutional logistics, 133–34
mainframes, x
as support to process writing, xi. *See also*
Writing
as support to teaching writing, xii. *See also*
Writing
in writing centers, 3–16
Computers and Composition (C&C), xv, xix,
xxi–xxii
Computer-supported collaboration, 242–53
Computer-supported communication (CSC),
123, 192–93, 283
Cooper, Marilyn, 172
Core course, 79–80
Corliss, George, 223, 229
Cornett, Mark, 105–6
Course on creating Web sites, 192–99

readings, 192–94
sites created, 194–99
Crawford, MaryAnn Krajnik, 296, 319
*Creating a Computer-Supported Writing
Facility: A Blueprint for Action* (Selfe),
129
Creative process
affective side of, 174
creativity partnering, 171–76
definitions, 173
process and, 173, 174
questioning and, 171
Critical thinking, 118, 168, 171, 182, 186,
233, 249, 256
Cummins, Gail Summerskill, 170, 171, 174,
176, 319
Cyberpunk, 214
Cyganowski, Carol Klimick, 244

Della Bitta, Albert, 152–53
Design of Everyday Things, The (Norman),
193
DeSousa, Dalila, 48
Deuel, Peter, 114
Digital composition project, 105–6
Dingle, Doris D., 255
Distance collaboration, 5–8
Distance education. *See* Interactive distance
education
Dorbolo, Jon, 117, 320
Downshifting, 273
Drill-and-practice tutorials, xii

Economics, 89–90
EDGAR, 243
E-journals, 207–19, 221–30. *See also* E-mail
accounting system, 229
classroom carryover, 228
interacting with text, 218
math, 273–80
oral mode of communication, 218
paper topics and, 227
versus paper writing, 208–9, 275, 297–98
posing questions in, 275, 277
role of teacher, 218, 302
role playing in, 212–14
textual evidence and, 226
Elbow, Peter, 215
Electronic Communication Across the
Curriculum (ECAC), ix, 47–50. *See also*
E-mail
assignments, 258–59
Clarkson University and, 103–14
delivery of information to business, 257

within disciplines, xxvii–xxix
evaluation of, 259–61
features of, xxi–xxiii
forum for feedback, 257
interdisciplinary communities, xxvi–xxvii, 140–50
origins of, xv–xvii
programs, xxiii–xxvi
reading suggestions, xxx–xxxi
speed, 257
tenure projects in, xx
Electronic portfolios, 113–14
E-mail, xiii, xvi, xxii. *See also* E-journals
in an interdisciplinary context, 162–68, 296–303
biology and, 231–40
class discussion, 22–23, 296–303
as communication for Web-based course, 117–28
on creative process, 170–77
as epistolary pedagogy, xviii, 296–303
evaluation of, 259–61, 269
e-vision, 144–45
exchanges with scholars, 77
feedback and, 302
medium of, 296–99
relationship building, 105, 124–25
response time, 239
student communication and, 105, 296–303
technical problems, 237–38
time management and, 239, 302
in writing centers, 6–7
as writing tool, 125–26
E-mail debate, 144, 151–61
amount of writing, 154
applicability to universities, 157–58
refutation, 154–57, 158
results, 152–57
style of writing, 154
topics, 151–52, 153, 158
Empowering Education (Shor), 168
Engineering classes, 20, 26–28, 62, 63, 68, 140
human-computer interface and, 102–16
interface design practices, 106–8
usability testing methods, 108–10
English classes, 23–26, 48. *See also* Literature classes
English lab layout, 78
ESL issues, 11, 60, 80, 83, 94, 96
Essid, Joe, 73, 320
Evaluation issues, 29, 73–74, 77, 80, 126, 269–71
electronic communication, 259–60
grading collaborative writing, 246
student evaluations, 165–68

Evergreen State College, 180
Experiential learning, 86–101

Faculty issues
creating community, 73–85
human-computer interface, 110–12
involvement in Writing Across the Curriculum (WAC), 75–76, 129–132
learning curves, 133
modifying teaching, 48–49
networking worldwide, 158
promotion, xx
resistance and, 58, 129–30
student accessibility to faculty, 232–33, 296–303
support for faculty, 65
teaching methods, 95, 215
technical training, 42–44, 129–35
tenure, xx
time constraints of, 131
workshops, 44–47
Faigley, Lester, 172
Feedback, 123, 143, 228–29, 257, 302
real versus imagined, 145
Felter, Maryanne, 263, 320
FirstClass, 19–20, 23, 33–34
Fischer, Katherine M., 207, 320
Flames, 124, 157
Framework-group to framework-group exchange, 120
Freedman, Aviva, 244
Freire's methodology, 214, 217
banking model, 18, 111
Frey, Olivia, 157
Fulwiler, Toby, xi, 33, 129, 130, 215
Fund for the Improvement of Postsecondary Education, 152

Geissler, Kathleen, 296, 320
Gender discussions, 299–301
Generation X project, 182–84
Gilbert, Steve, xix, xxi
Gillespie, Paula, 221, 312
Goldsmith-Conley, Elizabeth, 171
Gophers, 8, 193
Graphics, 140–50
Green, Kenneth C., xix, xxi
Greer, Michael, xxiii
Guilford College
Academic Skills Center, 196
Admission Office, 195
Center for Continuing Education, 195–96
College Woods, 195
Hege Library, 196

logo, 196–97
Quakerism at, 195
Web site, 190–201
women's studies, 198
Gutenberg Elegies, The (Birkerts), 194

Haas, Christina, 94, 177
Hairston, Elaine, 97
Hairston, Maxine, 244
Hall, James Baker, 172
Handa, Carolyn, 244
Hansen, Randall, 255, 321
Harbor House, 181–82
Hardcastle, Gary L., 282, 321
Hardcastle, Valerie Gray, 282, 321
Harris, Muriel, 3, 321
Hawisher, Gail, xxiii, 17, 20, 22, 29, 77, 157, 321
Hewett, Beth, 146
Hickey, Dona J., 73, 321
History classes, 48, 263–72
Hocks, Mary E., 40, 322
Hoover's On-Line, 243
Howard University, writing collaboration, 139–50
Hughes, M. Rini, 296, 322
Human-computer interface, 102–16
interface design practices, 106–8
pedagogical issues, 110–12
usability testing methods, 108–10
Humanities classes, 162, 296–303
"Hyperpersonal" communication, 126
Hypertext markup language, 133, 190, 191–93
footnotes as, 193

Icon placement, 34, 35
Institutional culture, 57–72, 133–34, 263
change, 69–70
faculty resistance and, 58
Interactive distance education, xvii-xviii, 13, 117–28
intellectual community and, 120
student autonomy of, 119
student participation in, 119
Interdisciplinary projects, 140–50, 162–68, 263, 296–303
Interior design, creative process and, 170–77
International projects, 151–61, 181–89
Internet, xiii. *See also* World Wide Web
project at Howard, 140–42
Time magazine article, 290
Internet etiquette, 124
Internet World, 192
Interpersonal sensitivity, 124
InterQuest, 117–28

Concept Analysis, 122–23
Dear Author activity, 122
learning styles and, 122–23
objectives and requirement page, 120
orientation, 120
pedagogy and, 118–21
Virtual Conversations, 122
Interviewing skills, 251
Irmscher, William, 186

Karis, Bill, 102, 322
Kelly, Kevin, 194
Kiefer, Kate, 57, 322
Kim, Chai, 153, 158, 160
Klein, Julie, 167
Klein, Rosemary, 172, 175
Knadler, Steven, 48
Knoblauch, C. H., 256
Kolb, David A., 122

Lakota Sioux Stepping Stone Calendar, 172
Landmark Essays on Writing Across the Curriculum (Bazerman), 170
Landow, George, 191
Langhorst, Rick, 48
Langsam, Deborah M., 231, 322
Langston, M. Diane, 244
Language Connections (Fulwiler), xi
Learning
interactive, 209–14
multiple thinking strategies, 279
as place independent, 120
processes, 279
styles of, 122–23
as time independent, 120
Learning curves, 133
Learning platforms, 93–98
Lecture classes, 282–94
Lehigh University, 86–101
Lexis/Nexis, 243
"Liminal space," 302
Lindsay, Arturo, 48
Listserves, xiii
Literacy, 131, 263
Literature classes, 132–33, 207–19, 221–30.
See also E-journals
"A&P" (Updike), 213
Cat's Eye (Atwood), 227–28
cyberpunk, 214
ethics of characters, 210
"Greasy Lake" (Boyle), 210
Handmaid's Tale (Atwood), 219
"Harrison Bergeron" (Vonnegut), 214–15
imitation of text, 209–11
interactive learning, 209–14

"The Marilyn Monroe Poem" (Grahn), 217
A Midsummer Night's Dream
    (Shakespeare), 212, 213
The Picture of Dorian Gray (Wilde), 225–26
A Portrait of the Artist as a Young Man
    (Joyce), 226–27
Pride and Prejudice (Austen), 224–25
Sandbox (Albee), 212, 213
science fiction, 214–16
Slaughterhouse Five (Vonnegut), 216–17
Snow Crash (Stephenson), 194, 217
Lloyd-Jones, Richard, 139
Lynch, Dennis A., 162, 323

Maimon, Elaine, xi
*Making of Meaning: Metaphors, Models, and
    Maxims for Writing Teachers, The*
    (Berthoff), 175
"Map, The," 93
Marketing classes, 255–61
    redesigning course, 257–59
Marquette University, 221
    writing sequence at, 222
Math anxiety, 274
Math classes, 273–80
Mayadas, Frank, 18–19
McLuhan, Marshall, 193–94
Media Lab, The (Brand), 194
Mellon Multimedia Curriculum Development
    Project, 40–42
Mentors, 46–47, 181
Metapositions, 210
Michigan State University, 296–303
Michigan Technological University, ix, xi, 17
    e-mail project, 162–68
Miller, Jeffrey, 296, 323
Moffett, James, 174
Montana State University, art collaboration,
    140–50
MOOs, xvi, 7, 84, 160, 183–87
    privacy and, 187
Moran, Charles, 157
Morgan, Dan, 207
Multimedia curriculum
    computer and, 53, 111
    consultants, 53
    course projects, 50–52
    expectations, 54
    planning, 52
Multimedia Production Workshop, 44
Mundorf, Norbert, 160
Museum projects, 181–84

Negroponte, Nicholas, 192
Nelson, Theodor H., 190, 192, 194

Netscape, 268–69
Networks, xi, 47–50, 263–72
    communication tools, 59–66
    goals of instruction, 121
    grassroots versus top-down, 134–35
Newman-James, Stephanie, 140, 141
Newsgroups, xvi, 78–79
Norman, Donald, 193
Northern Illinois University, 135

Oakley, Burks, 20, 26–28
Odell, Lee, 139
O'Keeffe, Georgia, 172–75
Ong, Walter, 199
Online assignments, 28–33, 62–64, 163–67,
    215–16, 233–34, 258–59
    accounting, 245–46, 249–51
    biochallenges, 234–39
    guidelines, 33
    incorporating communicating, 118
    incorporating thinking, 118, 168
    incorporating writing, 118
    technical language and, 95
    western civilization, 265–67
Online discussion groups, 10, 24–25, 27, 185,
    209–19, 299–303
    between classes, 216
    international, 151–61
    western civilization, 263–72
Online posts, 210, 216, 225, 226, 227, 228,
    235, 236, 247–49, 280, 288–89, 292–93
Online seminar, 246–49
Online Writing Center (Colorado State
    University), 58, 59–66
    impact of program, 66–69
    instructional uses, 65–66
Online Writing Lab. *See* OWLs
*On (the Color) Line: Networking to End
    Racism*, 140
Oregon State University
    InterQuest program, 117–28
Out of Control (Kelly), 194
OWLs, 3–5, 104
    funding, 11–12
    instructional handouts online, 9
    possibilities of, 12–13
    resources for teachers, 10–11
    resources for writers, 8–10
    staffing, 11–12

PacerForum, 19–21, 27, 33–34
Paik, Nam June, 172
Palmquist, Mike, 57, 323
Pattison, Felicia Squires, 146
Peer-peer exchange, 120, 155–56

Peer tutoring, 223
Pemberton, Michael A., 17, 23–26, 323
Perelman, Chaim, 143
Philosophy classes, 282–94
    InterQuest course in, 117–28
    "running commentary," 285
Plater, William, 8
Portfolios, 126
Portillo, Margaret, 170, 171, 323
Postman, Neil, 181, 194
Process writing, xi, 244
Programs That Work (Fulwiler), 129
Publishing issues, xxiii, 193
Purdue, OWLs and, 6, 8, 10, 11, 12, 13–15
Putnam, Linda, 93

Race issues, 139–50
Radford University, xvii
Rainbow Advantage Program (RAP), 180–82
Redd, Teresa M., 139, 324
Reference Materials, 60–61. *See also* World
    Wide Web, research and
Reiss, Donna, xvi, xviii, 317
Relationship building, 124–25
Rheingold, Howard, 198
Rhetoric goals, 143
Risk-takers, 277
Roane State Community College, 7
Russell, David, 57, 170

San Diego State University, 242–53
    communication course at, 242
Saunders, Peter M., 86, 324
Schrage, Michael, 8
Schultz, Daniel F., 263, 324
Schuster, Charles, 263
Securities and Exchange Commission
    database, 243
Selber, Stuart A., 102, 324
Selfe, Cynthia L., ix, xix, 77, 129, 172, 218,
    324
Selfe, Dickie, xv, 218, 317
Self-image, 277–78
"Send a Paper" program, 64, 65, 67, 68
Service learning, 181–82
Shamoon, Linda K., 151, 325
Shor, Ira, 168, 214
Shulman, Lee, 231
Simulation methods, 87–89, 90–95
Sloan grant, 18–20
Small-group conferences, 26, 47–50, 120,
    163–67, 209, 211, 264–65, 297–303
Snow Crash (Stephenson), 194, 217
Social constructivist theory, 74, 87, 92

Sommers, Nancy, 77
Spanish classes, 48, 50–51
"Sparks," 124
Spellmeyer, Kurt, 302
Spelman College
    Comprehensive Writing Program, 41
    multimedia curriculum, 40–56
Spooner, Michael, xxii
Stephen F. Austin State University, 10
Stephenson, Neal, 194
Sternberg, Robert, 173
Stetson University, 255–61
Straub, Richard, 77
Strickland, Michael B., 190, 325
Students
    autonomy, 119
    empowerment, 190–91
    learning styles, 122–23
    participation, 119
    preferences to teaching methods, 95
    reluctant, 274
    responsibility of, 190–91
    technical training for, 121, 237–38, 263
    use of learning platforms, 96
Summaries, 247, 249, 275, 277
SUNY–Albany, 6
SUNY–Plattsburgh College, 6
Synchronous conferencing, 7–8, 47–50, 80–
    81, 183, 187, 215
"Syntactic maturity," 186

Taylor, Calvin, 175, 317
Taylor, Todd, 129, 325
Teacher-centered model of learning, 77
Teaching, Learning, Technology Roundtable
    (TLTR), xix
Technical communication, 111–12
Technical training, 42–44, 121, 237–38
Technological problems, 237–38, 263
Technopoly (Postman), 194
Tests. *See* Evaluation issues
Text immersion, 185–86, 188
Time magazine, 290
Trust, 123–24
Turner, Victor, 302
Tutorials, 62, 63
Tutors
    creating community, 73–85
    evaluation discussion, 73–74
    OWLs and, 3–5, 67

Understanding Media (McLuhan), 193–94
University of Arkansas–Little Rock, 7
University of Hawaii at Manoa

COllaboratory, 180–89
  Rainbow Advantage Program (RAP), 180–81
University of Illinois at Urbana-Champaign, 6
  asynchronous learning, 17–39
  Sloan grant, 18–20
University of Missouri–Columbia, 6
University of North Carolina at Charlotte,
  biology classes at, 231–40
University of North Carolina–Chapel Hill,
  teacher training and, 129–35
University of Rhode Island, e-mail debate
  project, 151–61
University of Richmond, 73–85
  resources, 85
University of Texas at Austin, 10, 11
University of Wyoming, 6, 11

Vaxnotes conference, 194
Venable, Carol F., 242, 325
Vik, Gretchen N., 242, 325
Virginia Polytechnic Institute and State
  University, 282–94
Virtual distance education. *See* Interactive
  distance education
Virtual voice, 170–71
Virtual Voice of Network Culture, The
  (Zamierowski), 170

Walden3, 180, 183, 186
Wallace-Sanders, Kimberly, 52
Walvoord, Barbara, xx, 17
Watts, Margit Misangyi, 180, 325
Western Civilization classes, 263–72
Whitnell, Robert M., 190, 326
Wildstrom, Stephen, 245
Williams, Terry Tempest, 207
Willis, Meredith Sue, 213
Wired, 29–32, 192
Wolffe, Robert, 273, 326
Women's Studies, 52
Word processing, xvi
Workshops
  incremental, 44–47
  intensive project-oriented program, 44, 47
  mentoring, 46–47
  Multimedia Production Workshop, 44
  scheduling, 46
World Wide Web, xiii, xvi, 104. *See also* E-
  mail; Internet; *specific topics*
  creating sites, 190–201
  discussion threads, 284
  doublespeak on, 217–18
  InterQuest and, 117–28
  intstitutional logistics, 133–34

links, 9–10, 132
relationship building, 124–25
research and, xi, 8–10, 233, 243, 244–46,
  268
"running commentary," 283–94
search engines, 9–10
support for CAC and, 129–35
teacher training and, 129–35
Writers' Online Workshop, 33–36
Writing. *See also* Audience; E-journals;
  E-mail
  about racism, 139–50
  audience, 139–50
  to communicate, xvii
  computer-aided writing, 244
  creative process and, 170–77
  documentation of personal history, 249–50
  e-vision, 144–45
  industry reports, 250
  to learn, xvii, 17, 87, 221–30, 256, 263, 274
  lessons in strategies, 266
  with multimedia curriculm, 40–56
  overgeneralizing, 139
  person, product, and place, 174
  as political act, 218
  process, xi, 244
  purpose, 211, 215
  revision, 144–45
  summaries of published articles, 249
  systems documentation, 251
  team, 244–46, 264, 265, 267
  textual evidence, 211, 226
  as thinking, xii, xiv, 256
  topics for team-taught writing, 244–46
Writing Across the Curriculum (WAC), ix
  asynchronous learning and, 17–39, 33–36
  Clarkson University and, 102–3
  computer connections, xvi–xix
  Core and, 79–80
  creativity project, 170–77
  early studies, xi
  e-mail debate and, 159, 160
  at Lehigh University, 89–90
  literature classes and, 207
  at Marquette, 221, 229
  math and, 274
  personal connection and, 297
  pioneering work in England, xvii
  publishing and, 193
  technological tools and, 263–64
  as technology, xi
  at University of Richmond, 75–76
  World Wide Web and, 129–35
Writing centers
  computers in, 3–16
  distance collaboration, 5–8

Writing Fellows, 76–78
Writing in the Arts and Sciences (Maimon), xi
*Writing Technology: Studies on the Material-
    ity of Literacy* (Haas), 177
Writing to Learn (Zinsser), 90

Xanadu project, 194

Yancey, Kathleen Blake, xxii, 231, 326
Young, Art, x, xv, 129, 130, 318
Young, Richard, 58

Zamierowski, Mark, 170
Zimmerman, Donald E., 57, 326
Zinsser, William, 90

Editors

Donna Reiss (tcreisd@vb.tc.cc.va.us), Associate Professor of English and Humanities at Tidewater Community College–Virginia Beach (TCC), directed the Writing Center from 1980 through 1994 and originated the Grammar Hotline Directory. She teaches writing, literature, and humanities courses, all either computer-enhanced or delivered online. Recent presentations and workshops focus on electronic communication for learning across the curriculum and include TYCA, NCTE, CCCC, Computers and Writing, Writing Across the Curriculum, MLA, and the Epiphany Project. She has developed World Wide Web resources for TCC, the Virginia Community College System, and the Epiphany Project.

Print publications include articles in *Scotia: Interdisciplinary Journal of Scottish Studies, College English, Washington Post Weekend,* and *When Writing Teachers Teach Literature: Bringing Writing to Reading.* Forthcoming are "WAC Wired," with Art Young, a chapter in Sue McLeod and Eric Miraglia's collection on the future of writing across the curriculum, and *Learning Literature in an Era of Change: Innovations in Teaching,* a collection edited with Dona Hickey. She has edited more than fifty regional books and written features for regional publications, including Norfolk's *Virginian-Pilot,* where she was restaurant critic for fifteen years.

Dickie Selfe (rselfe@mtu.edu) is Technical Communication Specialist and Instructor in the Scientific and Technical Communication program at Michigan Technological University (MTU). For the last eight years, he has directed the Center for Computer-Assisted Language Instruction and is currently working on his Ph.D. in Rhetoric and Technical Communication at MTU. His interests are in communication pedagogy and the social and institutional influences of electronic media on that pedagogy.

Presentations at the Conference on College Composition and Communication and the Computers and Writing Conference include "Introduction to Electronic Mail and Global Networks for Teaching and Scholarship"

317

(1994), "Implications of Internet Communication Systems for Professional Technical Communicators and Educators" (1995), and "Surviving the Journey: Practical Strategies for Computers and Writing Program Development" (1995). Recent publications include "The Politics of the Interface: Power and Its Exercise in Electronic Contact Zones" in *College Composition and Communication* (December 1994); "Surfing the Tsunami: Electronic Environments in the Writing Center," *Computers & Composition* (December 1995); and a chapter in Ann Hill Duin's forthcoming collection, *Nonacademic Writing: Social Theory and Technology.*

Art Young (apyoung@clemson.edu) is Campbell Chair in Technical Communication, Professor of English, and Professor of Engineering at Clemson University. In addition to coordinating Clemson's communication-across-the-curriculum program, he serves on the College of Engineering's Effective Technical Communication Committee and collaborates with faculty and students to develop curricula and pedagogical strategies for integrating written, oral, visual, and electronic communications into courses throughout the engineering curriculum.

He has co-edited several books on writing across the curriculum, including *Language Connections: Writing and Reading Across the Curriculum* (1982); *Writing Across the Disciplines: Research into Practice* (1986); *Programs That Work: Models and Methods for Writing Across the Curriculum* (1990); and *Programs and Practices: Writing Across the Secondary Curriculum* (1995). He is also the co-editor of *When Writing Teachers Teach Literature: Bringing Writing to Reading* (1995) and *Critical Theory and the Teaching of Literature* (1996). He has served as a consultant to more than fifty colleges and universities in the United States and Europe.

Contributors

Daniele Bascelli is the Mellon Multimedia Project Coordinator at Spelman College. He develops training programs for faculty and students in the use of computer hardware and software, administers the Macintosh computer classroom and labs, and acts as the LAN administrator and Web manager for this area. He is currently ABD in Comparative Literature at SUNY– Binghamton, and his research includes European Romanticism and Nationalism. He has previously taught English at Algonquin College in Nepean, Ontario, and the Istituto Brittanica in Perugia, Italy.

Michael Bertsch teaches composition at Butte College and at Shasta College, both in northern California where he lives with his wife, son, and dog. He has taught combinations of distance education classes which include the use of MOO platforms. He has also taught distance education classes using two-way video, and phones, and combinations of e-mail and snail mail. In addition, he has for three years brought the Chico Upward Bound classes to the Internet, resulting in two sets of collaborative documents to be found at http://csucub.csuchico.edu/.

Scott A. Chadwick (chadwics@iastate.edu) is Assistant Professor in the Department of Journalism and Mass Communication at Iowa State University. He teaches organizational communication, quantitative research methods, and communication theory. His research focuses on the use of computer-supported communication to solve organizational problems. His recent work has been published in *Technology Studies*.

MaryAnn Krajnik Crawford (mary.ann.crawford@cmich.edu) is Assistant Professor of English at Central Michigan University. She teaches courses in composition, the nature of language, and applied linguistics. Her research and writing focus on issues in oral, written, and electronic text analysis, particularly the intertextual and functional uses of discourse and power. Recent work and publications include *Other Voices, Other Worlds: Reported Speech and Quotations as Social Interaction,* "The Portfolio Project: Sharing Stories," and "Constructing Identities, Implementing Change: A Study of Stories, Texts, and Learning in an Interdisciplinary Arts and Humanities Course."

Gail Summerskill Cummins is Director of the Writing Center and Director of Writing Across the Curriculum at the University of Kentucky. An assistant professor in English, she teaches courses on writing, tutoring, and teaching composition and writes about these topics. An advocate of service learning, she is involved in a variety of technological literacy exchanges between the University of Kentucky and the Kentucky public schools. She is also President of the East Central Writing Center Association, co-founder of the Kentucky Writing Center Association, and founder of the Appalachian Partnership of Peer Tutors.

Jon Dorbolo (dorboloj@ucs.orst.edu) is Distributed Learning Developer for the Communication Media Center at Oregon State University. His academic specialties are in ethics, epistemology, and educational philosophy. He has developed online courses and resources since 1993 and managed several grant projects, including InterQuest SUITE from which the QuestWriter™ distributed course management system was produced. Jon teaches "EdWeb" seminars to faculty on the pedagogy of online teaching. He is the editor of the *American Philosophical Association Philosophy and Computers Newsletter* and was 1996 Oregon Multimedia Educator of the Year.

Joe Essid (jessid@richmond.edu) directs the Writing Center at the University of Richmond, where he also teaches composition, composition theory, and the first-year interdisciplinary Core course. He has published in *Research and Teaching in Developmental Education* and *Kairos* and has presented papers at CCCC, Computers and Writing, and the national WAC conference. In 1995 he joined the Epiphany Project and taught one of the initial six Epiphany courses. His research and teaching interests focus on the networked writing classroom, the role of technology in training peer tutors, and the history of technology.

Maryanne Felter taught at Temple University and the American School of The Hague, the Netherlands, and she is now Associate Professor of English at Cayuga Community College. She has published a textbook on composition, *Reason to Write,* as well as articles in *Eire-Ireland, The Journal of Irish Literature, The Dictionary of Irish Literature,* and *A Casebook of Irish Studies.* She has also given workshops in the use of computer technology in composition and the liberal arts.

Katherine M. Fischer (kfischer@keller.clarke.edu) teaches courses in creative writing, science fiction, poetry, introduction to literature, essay writing, and nature writing at Clarke College in Dubuque, Iowa; she also serves as the director of the writing lab. She has published articles about teaching writing and literature, most recently, using computer technology. She also has had poetry published in various small presses and journals. Currently, she is enrolled in MFA studies at Goddard College in Vermont. As often as possible, however, she escapes to go creek-stomping or sloughing along the backwaters of the Mississippi.

Kathleen Geissler, Associate Professor of English and American Thought and Language at Michigan State University, is Associate Director of the Center for Integrative Studies in the Arts and Humanities, where she is a director of the interdisciplinary undergraduate course that focuses on the diversities of American experience. For that course, she has recently co-authored a CD-ROM titled *Immigration and Migration.* She is co-editor of two forthcoming anthologies, *Doing Feminisms: Teaching and Research in the Academy* and *Valuing Diversity: Race, Class, and Gender in Composition Research,* and is currently revising a book on women's literacy in nineteenth-century America.

Paula Gillespie directs the Ott Memorial Writing Center and teaches in the English Department of Marquette University. She publishes in James Joyce studies, writing centers, and pedagogy. She has been active in Marquette's Writing-Across-the-Curriculum program and has sponsored and led workshops for faculty and teaching assistants. Currently she is co-editing a collection on writing center research and co-authoring a book on criticism of James Joyce's *Ulysses.*

Randall S. Hansen (rhansen@stetson.edu) of the Stetson University Marketing Department has been published in several journals and is co-author of two books, *Dynamic Cover Letters* and *Write Your Way to a Higher GPA,* both published by Ten Speed Press. Besides being an innovator with his varied marketing courses, he is dedicated to communications (verbal and written) and technology and is currently in the process of putting all his course material onto the Internet.

Since 1992, **Gary L. Hardcastle** (garyh@vt.edu) has been Assistant Professor at Virginia Polytechnic Institute and State University, jointly appointed in the Department of Philosophy and the Center for the Study of Science in Society. His research interests are in contemporary theory of knowledge, especially reliabilism, and in the history of the philosophy of science, particularly the history of the philosophy of science in America in the 1930s and 1940s. His publications include "S.S. Stevens and the Origins of Operationism" (*Philosophy of Science,* 1994) and "What Horwich's Minimal Theory of Truth Does Not Explain" (*Southern Journal of Philosophy,* 1996).

Valerie Gray Hardcastle is currently Assistant Professor at Virginia Polytechnic Institute and State University in the Department of Philosophy. Her research and teaching interests are in philosophy of mind, philosophy of psychology, neurophilosophy, and cognitive science. Recent publications include *Locating Consciousness* (1995) and *How to Build a Theory in Cognitive Science* (1996).

Muriel Harris (harrism@omni.cc.purdue.edu), Professor of English and Director of the Writing Lab at Purdue University, founded and continues to edit the *Writing Lab Newsletter.* She authored *Teaching One-to-One: The Writing Conference* and *The Prentice Hall Reference Guide to Grammar and Usage* (3rd edition), and her published articles, book chapters, and conference presentations focus on writing center theory and practice, conferencing one-to-one with students, collaboration, OWLs (Online Writing Labs), and individualized instruction in writing.

Gail E. Hawisher (hawisher@uiuc.edu) is Professor of English and Director of the Center for Writing Studies at the University of Illinois, Urbana-Champaign. With Cynthia L. Selfe, she is also editor of *Computers and Composition: An International Journal for Teachers of Writing, Critical Perspectives on Computers and Composition Instruction* (1989), *Evolving Perspectives on Computers and Composition Studies: Questions for the 1990s* (1991), and *Literacy, Technology, and Society: Confronting the Issues* (1997). Her current research with Patricia Sullivan explores the many online lives of academic women. In addition, she is co-author (with Paul LeBlanc, Charles Moran, and Selfe) of *Computers and the Teaching of Writing in American Higher Education, 1979–1994: A History* (1995).

Dona J. Hickey (dhickey@richmond.edu) is Associate Professor of English at the University of Richmond, where she is Director of Composition and WAC and teaches rhetoric/composition and American Literature. Her publications include *Developing a Written Voice* (1993) and *Figures of Thought* (forthcoming). She is a member of the national Epiphany Project leaders' team and has assisted in the development of Epiphany faculty seminars and materials. Her research and teaching interests are in rhetoric/composition, American literature, and the use of technology.

Mary E. Hocks directs the Comprehensive Writing Program at Spelman College, where she advises faculty on writing across the curriculum. She also teaches professional writing courses in the English department. She is the co-director, with Anne Balsamo, of *Women of the World Talk Back,* a multimedia exhibit that they originally designed for the Fourth World Conference on Women in Beijing, China, in 1995. Her research is on hypertext theory, multimedia development, and writing in multimedia environments. As principal investigator of a Mellon Foundation Grant, her work now involves developing training programs for faculty in writing across the curriculum using multimedia and writing technologies.

M. Rini Hughes (hughesm2@pilot.msu.edu) is a Ph.D. student in the Department of American Studies at Michigan State University. Her research interests center on popular culture representations of family life in the United States from the Civil War era to the present. She teaches humanities and writing courses and recently completed a project with public school teachers developing materials for writing across the curriculum.

Bill Karis (karis@heron.tc.clarkson.edu) is Associate Professor and Chair of the Department of Technical Communications at Clarkson University. He has published articles in *Rhetoric Review, the Journal of Business and Technical Communication, Technical Communication, IEEE Transactions on Professional Communication,* and *Technical Communication Quarterly* (*TCQ*). He is co-editor of *Collaborative Writing in Industry: Investigations in Theory and Practice,* which won an NCTE Award for Excellence in Scientific and Technical Writing in 1993. He is co-editor, with M. Jimmie Killingsworth, of the winter 1997 special issue of *TCQ* focusing on environmental discourse.

Kate Kiefer (kkiefer@vines.colostate.edu) is Professor of English at Colorado State University. Her research interests include writing across the curriculum, computers and composition, and applications of chaos theory to composition studies. Her work has appeared in various NCTE compilations and journals, including *Research in the Teaching of English,* and Kate was a founding co-editor of *Computers and Composition.* In addition to writing three composition textbooks, Kate is completing *Transitions: Teaching Writing in Computer-Supported and Traditional Classrooms* with Mike Palmquist, Jake Hartvigsen, and Barbara Godlew.

Deborah M. Langsam is Associate Professor of Biology at the University of North Carolina at Charlotte. A winner of the NCNB Award for Teaching Excellence, she teaches introductory biology for non-science majors as well as courses in mycology and botany. She is currently working on the development of computer-based interactive lab manuals and CD-ROM study guides for introductory and plant biology courses. She has been an active participant in the American Association of Higher Education's Peer Review of Teaching Project and is interested in the use of portfolios for faculty development and the documentation of teaching effectiveness. She speaks nationally on these topics and facilitates workshops for faculty interested in peer review of teaching.

Dennis A. Lynch is Assistant Professor of Rhetoric and Director of the Writing Programs in the Humanities Department at Michigan Technological University. He has published in *College Composition and Communication, Rhetoric Review,* and *Issues in Applied Linguistics.* His research interests include the teaching of argumentative writing, issues of power and pedagogy, and postmodern challenges to modern rhetorical theory.

Jeffrey Miller is Assistant Professor in the Department of English and Journalism at Augustana College (South Dakota). His dissertation, *Something Completely Different: British Television and American Culture, 1960–1980,* addresses the clash between paradigms of direct effects (transmission) and active audience (ritual-reception) and concomitant issues of hegemony by examining the ways in which domestic American audiences made sense of imported British television texts during the years in question. Formerly a lecturer at the University of Gothenburg in Sweden, he has also presented and published essays on music videos, action-adventure series, the novels of HD, and European reception of the work of Emily Dickinson.

Mike Palmquist (mpalmquist@vines.colostate.edu) is Associate Professor of English at Colorado State University, where he directs the Composition Program and co-directs the Center for Research on Writing and Communication Technologies. His research interests include writing across the curriculum, the effects of computer and network technologies on writing instruction, and the use of hypertext/hypermedia in instructional settings. His work has appeared in *Computers and Composition, Written Communication, IEEE Transactions on Professional Communication, Journal of Engineering Education, Kairos, Council of College Teachers of English Studies,* and *Social Forces,* as well as in edited collections. He is co-author, with Kate Kiefer, Jake Hartvigsen, and Barbara Godlew, of *Transitions: Teaching Writing in Computer-Supported and Traditional Classrooms,* forthcoming from Ablex.

Michael A. Pemberton (michaelp@uiuc.edu) is Assistant Professor of English and Associate Director of the Center for Writing Studies at the University of Illinois, Urbana-Champaign, where he also serves as Director of the campus writing center and Director of Outreach Programs. He has published articles in *College Composition and Communication, The Writing Instructor, Research and Teaching in Developmental Education, Writing Lab Newsletter, Computers and Composition,* and the *Writing Center Journal.* A founding co-editor of the journal *Language and Learning Across the Disciplines,* he is also editor of the *IATE Bulletin* and Vice President of the National Writing Centers Association. His regular column on "Writing Center Ethics" in the *Writing Lab Newsletter* was awarded the Outstanding Scholarship Award from the National Writing Center Association in 1994.

Margaret Portillo is Associate Professor of Interior Design at the University of Kentucky. She teaches courses in color theory, and design communications, and a graduate seminar on creativity. She has authored articles on pedagogy, color, and design and has presented papers on this topic nationally and internationally. She has been recognized for her involvement in the Interior Design Educators Council and serves on the editorial review board of the *Journal of Interior Design.*

Teresa M. Redd, a former writer-editor for Time-Life Books, is Associate Professor of English and Director of Writing Across the Curriculum at Howard University. She has published articles about audience, stylistics, readability, and African American rhetoric in *CEA-MAG Journal, Research in the Teaching of English,* and *Written Communication.* In addition, she has contributed a chapter on African American stylistics to *Composing Social Identity in Written Communication* and edited *Revelations: An Anthology of Expository Essays by and about Blacks.* Currently, she serves on the editorial board of *Written Communication* and the Executive Committee of the Conference on College Composition and Communication (CCCC).

Peter M. Saunders is Associate Professor of Business at Lehigh University and a consultant and trainer for corporations and institutions in the United States and Canada. He also is Director of the Philip Rauch Center for Business Communications and oversees the College's Writing Requirement Program and Writing Clinic. He specializes in written communication, case and simulation development, and usability testing and document design. His publications include *Strategy: Writing at Work* (1992) and he co-authored *A Catalogue of Resource Materials for Teaching Accounting Students Communication Skills* (1995), prepared for the Federation of Schools of Accountancy.

Daniel F. Schultz has been Professor of Behavioral Sciences at Cayuga Community College since 1965. He has taught in Tanzania, East Africa, as well as having served as resident and member of the Skaneateles School Board from 1978 to 1993, President of Associated Community College Faculties from 1969 to 1973, and a member of New York State School Boards Association from 1986 to 1993. He is the author of several articles on community college funding, collective bargaining, and legislation. Currently, he is giving workshops on Computers and Classroom Applications, and Technology in Education. His current interests are in curricular revision in the social sciences and the use of computers both as a research tool and as a teaching strategy.

Stuart A. Selber (selber@ttu.edu) is Assistant Professor in the Technical Communication and Rhetoric program at Texas Tech University, where he works among an active group of computers and writing scholars and teachers in the Department of English. His work has appeared in *Nonacademic Writing: Social Theory and Technology, Electronic Literacies in the Workplace: Technologies of Writing, The Computer Science and Engineering Handbook, the Journal of Computer Documentation, Technical Communication Quarterly,* and numerous other books and journals, including his edited collection *Computers and Technical Communication: Pedagogical and Programmatic Perspectives* (1997). Selber has received publication awards from the National Council of Teachers of English and Computers and Composition.

Cynthia L. Selfe is Professor of Composition and Communication and Chair of the Humanities Department at Michigan Technological University. She is also Associate Chair of the Conference on College Composition and Communication. She is the founder and co-editor of *Computers and Composition: An International Journal for Teachers of Writing* with Gail Hawisher. The author of numerous books, journal articles, and book chapters on computer use in composition classrooms, she is the first woman and the first teacher of English composition to have won the EDUCOM Medal for innovation in teaching with technology in higher education.

Linda K. Shamoon (shamoon@uriacc.uri.edu) is Professor of English, Director of the College Writing Program, and Director of the Faculty Institute on Writing at the University of Rhode Island. She has published articles on the research paper, writing across the curriculum, the place of rhetoric in composition programs, and writing-center practices. In addition to supporting the International E-mail Debate project at the University of Rhode Island, she is a Teaching and Technology Fellow at the University of Rhode Island and is a founding member of the Electronic Democracy Project, a national intercollegiate initiative on preparing students for citizenship in an electronic democracy.

Michael B. Strickland came to Guilford College in 1992. As Assistant Professor of English with a background in rhetoric and composition, he teaches many writing courses, from Basic Writing to Technical and Professional Communications, as well as courses in modern and contemporary American literature. He also teaches courses that cross many traditional disciplinary boundaries, such as a course on the works of paleontologist and science writer Stephen Jay Gould and a first-year seminar course called The Environmental Effects of Development. He uses computers and the Internet in all his courses.

Todd Taylor served as the Coordinator of Computers and Writing at the University of South Florida in Tampa from 1993 to 1996. He is currently Assistant Professor of English at the University of North Carolina at Chapel Hill. He recently co-edited, with Gary A. Olson, *Publishing in Rhetoric and Composition* (1997). He has just completed work, with Janice Walker, on *The Columbia Guide to Online Style*.

Carol F. Venable (carol.venable@sdsu.edu) is Associate Professor in the School of Accountancy at San Diego State University. In 1997, The Center for Educational Technology in Accounting presented her with its Annual Educational Technology Award for her design and implementation of a collaborative learning technology classroom. She has taught auditing, accounting systems, taxation, professional ethics, and communication for accountants. She also has developed self-paced laboratory courses and online computer tutorials. She has published in the areas of accounting, taxation, and accounting pedagogy, and she has given presentations on critical thinking. Current interests include collaborative learning, the use of technology to enhance the learning process, and interdisciplinary applications.

Gretchen N. Vik (gretchen.vik@sdsu.edu), Professor in the Information and Decision Systems Department, has taught business communication at San Diego State University since 1975. An active member of the Association for Business Communication (and President in 1990), she has written three business communication texts for Richard D. Irwin. Since 1980, she has worked with the accounting reports class she developed within the College of Business Administration at SDSU as part of the California State University systemwide graduation writing proficiency requirement. Her current interests include e-mail format, company policies, and legal issues; application of plain English laws for consumers; and effective communication of technical and financial information.

Margit Misangyi Watts (watts@hawaii.edu) has spent the last six years exploring educational philosophy, restructuring undergraduate education at the University of Hawaii at Manoa, learning about the possibilities afforded by new technologies, and speaking about her findings around the country. She directs First Year Experience programs at UH, is an administrator of one virtual community, Walden 3 (a MOO-MUD), works closely with the Hawaii Department of Education in trying to blend K–16 education into a seamless entity, and is editing both a book and a series on education and technology. She describes herself as "continually tweaking the traditional modes until the fields shift," a change architect.

Robert M. Whitnell (whitnellrm@rascal.guilford.edu) has been in the Chemistry Department at Guilford College since 1994. From 1988 to 1994, he was a research associate with Professor Kent Wilson in the Department of Chemistry at the University of California, San Diego, where he discovered the power of computer visualization both in understanding the results of his computer simulations of chemical reactions and in educating his colleagues and students. Toward the end of 1993, he happened upon the Web and quickly saw the importance of this medium for scientific communication. This discovery led to the construction of the Wilson group Web site, (http://www-wilson.ucsd.edu), one of the first by any research group in chemistry, and eventually to the construction of the Guilford College Web site (http://www.guilford.edu). He teaches general and physical chemistry and chairs the college's Computer Advisory Committee.

Robert Wolffe taught elementary school grades 2–5 for fourteen years in the Cincinnati area, where he was also a department chair for Math, Science, and Social Studies. For the past seven years, first at Hanover College and now at Bradley University in Peoria, Illinois, he has worked in teacher preparation with a focus on Math and Science Education and the use of technologies. Areas of scholarly interest include constructivist theory, implications of brain-based research to learning and teaching, and instructional approaches affecting student attitudes.

Kathleen Blake Yancey is Associate Professor of English at University of North Carolina at Charlotte, where she teaches undergraduate and graduate courses in writing, in methods of teaching and tutoring, and in writing assessment and rhetorical theory. She edited *Portfolios in the Writing Classroom* (1992) and co-edited *Situating Portfolios* (1997) and *Assessing Writing Across the Curriculum* (1997), and she co-founded and co-edits the journal *Assessing Writing*. She also guest edited the 1996 special issue of *Computers and Composition* focused on the electronic portfolio. Yancey's current book-length project is tentatively titled *A Rhetoric of Reflection*, due to be published in 1998.

Donald E. Zimmerman, Professor in the Technical Journalism Department at Colorado State University, co-directs the Center for Research on Writing and Communication Technologies. His research focuses on information design, Web page design, hypertext design, professional communication, professional communication instruction, and usability testing.

*This book was typeset in Times Roman by Electronic Imaging.
Typefaces used on the cover were Friz Quadrata BT and Garamond.
The book was printed on 50-lb. Offset by Versa Press.*